THE TWENTIETH CENTURY

OTHER BOOKS BY HOWARD ZINN

La Guardia in Congress   1959

The Southern Mystique   1964

SNCC: The New Abolitionists   1964

New Deal Thought (editor)   1965

Vietnam: The Logic of Withdrawal   1967

Disobedience and Democracy   1968

The Politics of History   1970

The Pentagon Papers: Critical Essays (editor, with Noam Chomsky)   1972

Postwar America   1973

Justice in Everyday Life (editor)   1974

Declarations of Independence: Cross-Examining American Ideology   1991

Failure to Quit: Reflections of an Optimistic Historian   1993

You Can't Be Neutral on a Moving Train   1994

The Zinn Reader   1997

THE TWENTIETH CENTURY

A PEOPLE'S HISTORY

REVISED AND UPDATED EDITION

FROM THE AUTHOR'S
A PEOPLE'S HISTORY OF THE UNITED STATES,
WITH NEW CHAPTERS
ON THE BUSH AND CLINTON PRESIDENCIES

HOWARD ZINN

HarperPerennial
A Division of HarperCollins*Publishers*

ACKNOWLEDGMENTS

To Akwesasne Notes, Mohawk Nation, for the passage from Ila Abernathy's poem.

To Dodd, Mead & Company, for the passage from "We Wear the Mask" from *The Complete Poems of Paul Laurence Dunbar.*

To Harper & Row, for "Incident" from *On These I Stand* by Countee Cullen. Copyright 1925 by Harper & Row, Publishers, Inc.; renewed 1953 by Ida M. Cullen. Reprinted by permission of the publisher.

To *The New Trail*, 1953 School Yearbook of the Phoenix Indian School, Phoenix, Arizona, for the poem "It Is Not!"

To Random House, Inc., for the passage from "I, Too," copyright 1926 by Alfred A. Knopf, Inc., and renewed 1954 by Langston Hughes; and for the "Dream Deferred" passage from "Lenox Avenue Mural," copyright 1951 by Langston Hughes. Reprinted from *Selected Poems of Langston Hughes*, by permission of the publisher.

To Esta Seaton, for her poem "Her Life," which first appeared in *The Ethnic American Woman* by Edith Blicksilver, Kendall/Hunt Publishing Company, 1978. By permission of *Minnesota Review.*

To Warner Bros., for the excerpt from "Brother, Can You Spare a Dime?" Lyric by Jay Gorney, Music by E. Y. Harburg. © 1932 Warner Bros. Inc. Copyright Renewed. All Rights Reserved. Used By Permission.

To Hugh Van Dusen and Kate Ekrem of HarperCollins.

To Rick Balkin, my literary agent.

This work is an abridgement of *A People's History of the United States.*

First HarperPerennial edition published 1998.

Library of Congress Cataloging-in-Publication Data

Zinn, Howard, 1922–
    The twentieth century, a people's history / Howard Zinn. — Rev. and updated ed.
      p. cm.
    Includes bibliographical references (p.   ) and index.
    ISBN 0-06-095198-2
    1. United States—History—20th century.   I. Title.
  E741.Z55   1998
  973.9—dc21   97-34309

98 99 00 01 02 ❖/RRD 10 9 8 7 6 5 4 3 2

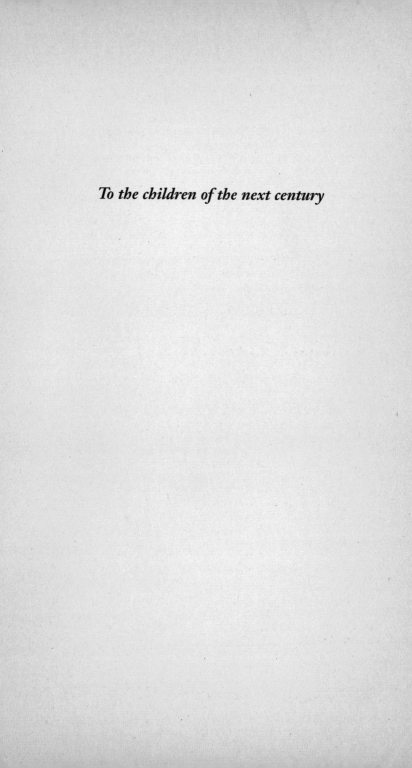

To the children of the next century

CONTENTS

PREFACE

My book *A People's History of the United States* started with Christopher Columbus and ended in the mid-1970s. This volume, drawn from the latter half of that book, is intended for the reader who wants to concentrate on this century. It is also an opportunity for me to carry the story further, into the 1990s, with several new chapters, including one on the first term of the Clinton presidency.

But I must explain my point of view. It is obvious in the very first pages of the larger *People's History*, when I tell about Columbus and emphasize not his navigational skill and fortitude in making his way to the Western Hemisphere, but his cruel treatment of the Indians he found here, torturing them, exterminating them in his greed for gold, his desperation to bring riches to his patrons back in Spain. In other words, my focus is not on the achievements of the heroes of traditional history, but on all those people who were the victims of those achievements, who suffered silently or fought back magnificently.

The rest of what I have to say about my view of history is reprinted from the first chapter of *A People's History of the United States*.

To emphasize the heroism of Columbus and his successors as navigators and discoverers, and to deemphasize their genocide, is not a technical necessity but an ideological choice. It serves—unwittingly—to justify what was done.

My point is not that we must, in telling history, accuse, judge, condemn Columbus *in absentia*. It is too late for that; it would be a useless scholarly exercise in morality. But the easy acceptance of atrocities as a deplorable but necessary price to pay for progress (Hiroshima and Vietnam to save Western civilization; Kronstadt and Hungary to save socialism; nuclear proliferation to save us all)—that is still with us. One reason these atrocities are still with us is that we have learned to bury them in a mass of other facts, as radioactive wastes are buried in containers in the earth. We have learned to give them exactly the same proportion of attention that teachers and writers often give them in the most respectable of classrooms and textbooks. This learned sense of moral proportion, coming from the apparent objectivity of the scholar, is accepted more easily than when it comes from politicians at press conferences. It is therefore more deadly.

The treatment of heroes (Columbus) and their victims (the Arawaks)—the quiet acceptance of conquest and murder in the name of progress—is only one aspect of a certain approach to history, in which the past is told from the point of view of governments, conquerors, diplomats, leaders. It is as if they, like Columbus, deserve universal acceptance, as if they—the Founding Fathers, Jackson, Lincoln, Wilson, Roosevelt, Kennedy, the leading members of Congress, the famous Justices of the Supreme Court—represent the nation as a whole. The pretense is that there really is such a thing as "the United States," subject to occasional conflicts and quarrels, but fundamentally a community of people with common interests. It is as if there really is a "national interest," represented in the Constitution, in territorial expansion, in the laws passed by Congress, the decisions of the courts, the development of capitalism, the culture of education and the mass media.

"History is the memory of states," wrote Henry Kissinger in his first book, *A World Restored*, in which he proceeded to tell the history of nineteenth-century Europe from the viewpoint of the leaders of Austria and England, ignoring the millions who suffered from those statesmen's policies. From his standpoint, the "peace" that Europe had before the French Revolution was "restored" by the diplomacy of a few national leaders. But for factory workers in England, farmers in France, colored people in

Asia and Africa, women and children everywhere except in the upper classes, it was a world of conquest, violence, hunger, exploitation—a world not restored but disintegrated.

My viewpoint, in telling the history of the United States, is different: that we must not accept the memory of states as our own. Nations are not communities and never have been. The history of any country, presented as the history of a family, conceals fierce conflicts of interest (sometimes exploding, most often repressed) between conquerors and conquered, masters and slaves, capitalists and workers, dominators and dominated in race and sex. And in such a world of conflict, a world of victims and executioners, it is the job of thinking people, as Albert Camus suggested, not to be on the side of the executioners.

Thus, in that inevitable taking of sides which comes from selection and emphasis in history, I prefer to try to tell the story of the discovery of America from the viewpoint of the Arawaks, of the Constitution from the standpoint of the slaves, of Andrew Jackson as seen by the Cherokees, of the Civil War as seen by the New York Irish, of the Mexican War as seen by the deserting soldiers of Scott's army, of the rise of industrialism as seen by the young women in the Lowell textile mills, of the Spanish-American War as seen by the Cubans, the conquest of the Philippines as seen by black soldiers on Luzon, the Gilded Age as seen by southern farmers, the First World War as seen by socialists, the Second World War as seen by pacifists, the New Deal as seen by blacks in Harlem, the postwar American empire as seen by peons in Latin America. And so on, to the limited extent that any one person, however he or she strains, can "see" history from the standpoint of others.

My point is not to grieve for the victims and denounce the executioners. Those tears, that anger, cast into the past, deplete our moral energy for the present. And the lines are not always clear. In the long run, the oppressor is also a victim. In the short run (and so far, human history has consisted only of short runs), the victims, themselves desperate and tainted with the culture that oppresses them, turn on other victims.

Still, understanding the complexities, this book will be skeptical of governments and their attempts, through politics and culture, to ensnare ordinary people in a giant web of nationhood pretending to a common interest. I will try not to overlook the cruelties that victims inflict on one another as they are jammed together in the boxcars of the system. I don't want to romanticize them. But I do remember (in rough paraphrase) a statement I once read: "The cry of the poor is not always just, but if you don't listen to it, you will never know what justice is."

I don't want to invent victories for people's movements. But to think that history-writing must aim simply to recapitulate the failures that dominate the past is to make historians collaborators in an endless cycle of defeat. If history is to be creative, to anticipate a possible future without denying the past, it should, I believe, emphasize new possibilities by disclosing those hidden episodes of the past when, even if in brief flashes, people showed their ability to resist, to join together, occasionally to win. I am supposing, or perhaps only hoping, that our future may be found in the past's fugitive moments of compassion rather than in its solid centuries of warfare.

That, being as blunt as I can, is my approach to the history of the United States. The reader may as well know that before going on.

Boston, 1980, 1984, 1997

THE EMPIRE AND THE PEOPLE

Theodore Roosevelt wrote to a friend in the year 1897: "In strict confidence . . . I should welcome almost any war, for I think this country needs one."

The year of the massacre at Wounded Knee, 1890, it was officially declared by the Bureau of the Census that the internal frontier was closed. The profit system, with its natural tendency for expansion, had already begun to look overseas. The severe depression that began in 1893 strengthened an idea developing within the political and financial elite of the country: that overseas markets for American goods might relieve the problem of underconsumption at home and prevent the economic crises that in the 1890s brought class war.

And would not a foreign adventure deflect some of the rebellious energy that went into strikes and protest movements toward an external enemy? Would it not unite people with government, with the armed forces, instead of against them? This was probably not a conscious plan among most of the elite—but a natural development from the twin drives of capitalism and nationalism.

Expansion overseas was not a new idea. Even before the war

against Mexico carried the United States to the Pacific, the Monroe Doctrine looked southward into and beyond the Caribbean. Issued in 1823 when the countries of Latin America were winning independence from Spanish control, it made plain to European nations that the United States considered Latin America its sphere of influence. Not long after, some Americans began thinking into the Pacific: of Hawaii, Japan, and the great markets of China.

There was more than thinking; the American armed forces had made forays overseas. A State Department list, "Instances of the Use of United States Armed Forces Abroad 1798–1945" (presented by Secretary of State Dean Rusk to a Senate committee in 1962 to cite precedents for the use of armed force against Cuba), shows 103 interventions in the affairs of other countries between 1798 and 1895. A sampling from the list, with the exact description given by the State Department:

1852–53—Argentina. Marines were landed and maintained in Buenos Aires to protect American interests during a revolution.

1853—Nicaragua—to protect American lives and interests during political disturbances.

1853–54—Japan—The "Opening of Japan" and the Perry Expedition. [The State Department does not give more details, but this involved the use of warships to force Japan to open its ports to the United States.]

1853–54—Ryukyu and Bonin Islands—Commodore Perry on three visits before going to Japan and while waiting for a reply from Japan made a naval demonstration, landing marines twice, and secured a coaling concession from the ruler of Naha on Okinawa. He also demonstrated in the Bonin Islands. All to secure facilities for commerce.

1854—Nicaragua—San Juan del Norte [Greytown was destroyed to avenge an insult to the American Minister to Nicaragua.]

1855—Uruguay—U.S. and European naval forces landed to protect American interests during an attempted revolution in Montevideo.

1859—China—For the protection of American interests in Shanghai.

1860—Angola, Portuguese West Africa—To protect American lives and property at Kissembo when the natives became troublesome.

1893—Hawaii—Ostensibly to protect American lives and property; actually to promote a provisional government under Sanford B. Dole. This action was disavowed by the United States.

1894—Nicaragua—To protect American interests at Bluefields following a revolution.

Thus, by the 1890s, there had been much experience in overseas probes and interventions. The ideology of expansion was widespread in the upper circles of military men, politicians, businessmen—and even among some of the leaders of farmers' movements who thought foreign markets would help them.

Captain A. T. Mahan of the U.S. navy, a popular propagandist for expansion, greatly influenced Theodore Roosevelt and other American leaders. The countries with the biggest navies would inherit the earth, he said. "Americans must now begin to look outward." Senator Henry Cabot Lodge of Massachusetts wrote in a magazine article:

In the interests of our commerce . . . we should build the Nicaragua canal, and for the protection of that canal and for the sake of our commercial supremacy in the Pacific we should control the Hawaiian islands and maintain our influence in Samoa. . . . and when the Nicaraguan canal is built, the island of Cuba . . . will become a necessity. . . . The great nations are rapidly absorbing for their future expansion and their present defense all the waste places of the earth. It is a movement which makes for civilization and the advancement of the race. As one of the great nations of the world the United States must not fall out of the line of march.

A Washington *Post* editorial on the eve of the Spanish-American war:

A new consciousness seems to have come upon us—the consciousness of strength—and with it a new appetite, the yearning to show our strength. . . . Ambition, interest, land hunger, pride, the mere joy of fighting, whatever it may be, we are animated by a new sensation. We are face to face with a strange destiny. The taste of Empire is in the mouth of the people even as the taste of blood in the jungle. . . .

Was that taste in the mouth of the people through some instinctive lust for aggression or some urgent self-interest? Or was it a taste (if indeed it existed) created, encouraged, advertised, and exaggerated by the millionaire press, the military, the government, the eager-to-please scholars of the time? Political scientist John Burgess of Columbia University said the Teutonic and Anglo-Saxon races were "particularly endowed with the capacity for establishing national states . . . they are entrusted . . . with the mission of conducting the political civilization of the modern world."

Several years before his election to the presidency, William McKinley said: "We want a foreign market for our surplus products." Senator Albert Beveridge of Indiana in early 1897 declared: "American factories are making more than the American people can use; American soil is producing more than they can consume. Fate has written our policy for us; the trade of the world must and shall be ours." The Department of State explained in 1898:

It seems to be conceded that every year we shall be confronted with an increasing surplus of manufactured goods for sale in foreign markets if American operatives and artisans are to be kept employed the year around. The enlargement of foreign consumption of the products of our mills and workshops has, therefore, become a serious problem of statesmanship as well as of commerce.

These expansionist military men and politicians were in touch with one another. One of Theodore Roosevelt's biographers tells us: "By 1890, Lodge, Roosevelt, and Mahan had begun exchanging views," and that they tried to get Mahan off sea duty "so that he could continue full-time his propaganda for expansion." Roosevelt once sent Henry Cabot Lodge a copy of a poem by Rudyard Kipling, saying it was "poor poetry, but good sense from the expansionist standpoint."

When the United States did not annex Hawaii in 1893 after some Americans (the combined missionary and pineapple interests of the Dole family) set up their own government, Roosevelt called this hesitancy "a crime against white civilization." And he told the Naval War College: "All the great masterful races have been fighting races. . . . No triumph of peace is quite so great as the supreme triumph of war."

Roosevelt was contemptuous of races and nations he considered inferior. When a mob in New Orleans lynched a number of Italian immigrants, Roosevelt thought the United States should offer the Italian government some remuneration, but privately he wrote his sister that he thought the lynching was "rather a good thing" and told her he had said as much at a dinner with "various dago diplomats . . . all wrought up by the lynching."

William James, the philosopher, who became one of the leading anti-imperialists of his time, wrote about Roosevelt that he "gushes over war as the ideal condition of human society, for the manly strenuousness which it involves, and treats peace as a condition of blubberlike and swollen ignobility, fit only for huckstering weaklings, dwelling in gray twilight and heedless of the higher life. . . ."

Roosevelt's talk of expansionism was not just a matter of manliness and heroism; he was conscious of "our trade relations with China." Lodge was aware of the textile interests in Massachusetts that looked to Asian markets. Historian Marilyn Young has written of the work of the American China Development Company to expand American influence in China for commercial reasons, and of State Department instructions to the American emissary in China to "employ all proper methods for the extension of American interests in China." She says (The Rhetoric of Empire) that the talk about markets in China was far greater than the actual amount of dollars involved at the time, but this talk was important in shaping American policy toward Hawaii, the Philippines, and all of Asia.

While it was true that in 1898, 90 percent of American products were sold at home, the 10 percent sold abroad amounted to a billion dollars. Walter Lafeber writes (*The New Empire*): "By 1893, American trade exceeded that of every country in the world except England. Farm products, of course, especially in the key tobacco, cotton, and wheat areas, had long depended heavily on international markets for their prosperity." And in the twenty years up to 1895, new investments by American capitalists overseas reached a billion dollars. In 1885, the steel industry's publication *Age of Steel* wrote that the internal markets were insufficient and the overproduction of industrial products "should be relieved and prevented in the future by increased foreign trade."

Oil became a big export in the 1880s and 1890s: by 1891, the Rockefeller family's Standard Oil Company accounted for 90 percent of American exports of kerosene and controlled 70 percent of the world market. Oil was now second to cotton as the leading product sent overseas.

There were demands for expansion by large commercial farmers, including some of the Populist leaders, as William Appleman Williams has shown in *The Roots of the Modern American Empire*. Populist Congressman Jerry Simpson of Kansas told Congress in 1892 that with a huge agricultural surplus, farmers "must of necessity seek a foreign market." True, he was not calling for aggression or conquest—but once foreign markets were seen as important to prosperity, expansionist policies, even war, might have wide appeal.

Such an appeal would be especially strong if the expansion looked like an act of generosity—helping a rebellious group overthrow foreign rule—as in Cuba. By 1898, Cuban rebels had been fighting their Spanish conquerors for three years in an attempt to win independence. By that time, it was possible to create a national mood for intervention.

It seems that the business interests of the nation did not at first want military intervention in Cuba. American merchants did not need colonies or wars of conquest if they could just have free access to markets. This idea of an "open door" became the dominant theme of American foreign policy in the twentieth century. It was a more sophisticated approach to imperialism than the traditional empire-building of Europe. William Appleman Williams, in *The Tragedy of American Diplomacy*, says:

> This national argument is usually interpreted as a battle between imperialists led by Roosevelt and Lodge and anti-imperialists led by William Jennings Bryan and Carl Schurz. It is far more accurate and illuminating, however, to view it as a three-cornered fight. The third group was a coalition of businessmen, intellectuals, and politicians who opposed traditional colonialism and advocated instead a policy of an open door through which America's preponderant economic strength would enter and dominate all underdeveloped areas of the world.

However, this preference on the part of some business groups and politicians for what Williams calls the idea of "informal empire," without war, was always subject to change. If peaceful imperialism turned out to be impossible, military action might be needed.

For instance, in late 1897 and early 1898, with China weakened by a recent war with Japan, German military forces occupied the Chinese port of Tsingtao at the mouth of Kiaochow Bay and demanded a naval station there, with rights to railways and coal mines on the nearby peninsula of Shantung. Within the next few months, other European powers moved in on China, and the partition of China by the major imperialist powers was under way, with the United States left behind.

At this point, the New York *Journal of Commerce*, which had advocated peaceful development of free trade, now urged old-fashioned military colonialism. Julius Pratt, a historian of U.S. expansionism, describes the turnabout:

> This paper, which has been heretofore characterized as pacifist, anti-imperialist, and devoted to the development of commerce in a free-trade world, saw the foundation of its faith crumbling as a result of

the threatened partition of China. Declaring that free access to the markets of China, with its 400,000,000 people, would largely solve the problem of the disposal of our surplus manufactures, the *Journal* came out not only for a stern insistence upon complete equality of rights in China but unreservedly also for an isthmian canal, the acquisition of Hawaii, and a material increase in the navy—three measures which it had hitherto strenuously opposed. Nothing could be more significant than the manner in which this paper was converted in a few weeks. . . .

There was a similar turnabout in U.S. business attitudes on Cuba in 1898. Businessmen had been interested, from the start of the Cuban revolt against Spain, in the effect on commercial possibilities there. There already was a substantial economic interest in the island, which President Grover Cleveland summarized in 1896:

It is reasonably estimated that at least from $30,000,000 to $50,000,000 of American capital are invested in the plantations and in railroad, mining, and other business enterprises on the island. The volume of trade between the United States and Cuba, which in 1889 amounted to about $64,000,000, rose in 1893 to about $103,000,000.

Popular support of the Cuban revolution was based on the thought that they, like the Americans of 1776, were fighting a war for their own liberation. The United States government, however, the conservative product of another revolutionary war, had power and profit in mind as it observed the events in Cuba. Neither Cleveland, President during the first years of the Cuban revolt, nor McKinley, who followed, recognized the insurgents officially as belligerents; such legal recognition would have enabled the United States to give aid to the rebels without sending an army. But there may have been fear that the rebels would win on their own and keep the United States out.

There seems also to have been another kind of fear. The Cleveland administration said a Cuban victory might lead to "the establishment of a white and a black republic," since Cuba had a mixture of the two races. And the black republic might be dominant. This idea was expressed in 1896 in an article in *The Saturday Review* by a young and eloquent imperialist, whose mother was American and whose father was English—Winston Churchill. He wrote that while Spanish rule was bad and the rebels had the support of the people, it would be better for Spain to keep control:

> A grave danger represents itself. Two-fifths of the insurgents in the field are negroes. These men . . . would, in the event of success, demand a predominant share in the government of the country . . . the result being, after years of fighting, another black republic.

The reference to "another" black republic meant Haiti, whose revolution against France in 1803 had led to the first nation run by blacks in the New World. The Spanish minister to the United States wrote to the U.S. Secretary of State:

> In this revolution, the negro element has the most important part. Not only the principal leaders are colored men, but at least eight-tenths of their supporters. . . . and the result of the war, if the Island can be declared independent, will be a secession of the black element and a black Republic.

As Philip Foner says in his two-volume study *The Spanish-Cuban-American War*, "The McKinley Administration had plans for dealing with the Cuban situation, but these did not include independence for the island." He points to the administration's instructions to its minister to Spain, Stewart Woodford, asking him to try to settle the war because it "injuriously affects the normal function of business, and tends to delay the condition of prosperity," but not mentioning freedom and justice for the Cubans. Foner explains the rush of the McKinley administration into war (its ultimatum gave Spain little time to negotiate) by the fact that "if the United States waited too long, the Cuban revolutionary forces would emerge victorious, replacing the collapsing Spanish regime."

In February 1898, the U.S. battleship *Maine*, in Havana harbor as a symbol of American interest in the Cuban events, was destroyed by a mysterious explosion and sank, with the loss of 268 men. There was no evidence ever produced on the cause of the explosion, but excitement grew swiftly in the United States, and McKinley began to move in the direction of war. Walter Lafeber says:

> The President did not want war; he had been sincere and tireless in his efforts to maintain the peace. By mid-March, however, he was beginning to discover that, although he did not want war, he did want what only a war could provide; the disappearance of the terrible uncertainty in American political and economic life, and a solid basis from which to resume the building of the new American commercial empire.

At a certain point in that spring, both McKinley and the business community began to see that their object, to get Spain out of Cuba, could not be accomplished without war, and that their accompanying object, the securing of American military and economic influence in Cuba, could not be left to the Cuban rebels, but could be ensured only by U.S. intervention. The New York *Commercial Advertiser*, at first against war, by March 10 asked intervention in Cuba for "humanity and love of freedom, and above all, the desire that the commerce and industry of every part of the world shall have full freedom of development in the whole world's interest."

Before this, Congress had passed the Teller Amendment, pledging the United States not to annex Cuba. It was initiated and supported by those people who were interested in Cuban independence and opposed to American imperialism, and also by business people who saw the "open door" as sufficient and military intervention unnecessary. But by the spring of 1898, the business community had developed a hunger for action. The

Journal of Commerce said: "The Teller amendment . . . must be interpreted in a sense somewhat different from that which its author intended it to bear."

There were special interests who would benefit directly from war. In Pittsburgh, center of the iron industry, the Chamber of Commerce advocated force, and the *Chattanooga Tradesman* said that the possibility of war "has decidedly stimulated the iron trade." It also noted that "actual war would very decidedly enlarge the business of transportation." In Washington, it was reported that a "belligerent spirit" had infected the Navy Department, encouraged "by the contractors for projectiles, ordnance, ammunition and other supplies, who have thronged the department since the destruction of the Maine."

Russell Sage, the banker, said that if war came, "There is no question as to where the rich men stand." A survey of businessmen said that John Jacob Astor, William Rockefeller, and Thomas Fortune Ryan were "feeling militant." And J. P. Morgan believed further talk with Spain would accomplish nothing.

On March 21, 1898, Henry Cabot Lodge wrote McKinley a long letter, saying he had talked with "bankers, brokers, businessmen, editors, clergymen and others" in Boston, Lynn, and Nahant, and "everybody," including "the most conservative classes," wanted the Cuban question "solved." Lodge reported: "They said for business one shock and then an end was better than a succession of spasms such as we must have if this war in Cuba went on." On March 25, a telegram arrived at the White House from an adviser to McKinley, saying: "Big corporations here now believe we will have war. Believe all would welcome it as relief to suspense."

Two days after getting this telegram, McKinley presented an ultimatum to Spain, demanding an armistice. He said nothing about independence for Cuba. A spokesman for the Cuban rebels, part of a group of Cubans in New York, interpreted this to mean the U.S. simply wanted to replace Spain. He responded:

In the face of the present proposal of intervention without previous recognition of independence, it is necessary for us to go a step farther and say that we must and will regard such intervention as nothing less than a declaration of war by the United States against the Cuban revolutionists. . . .

Indeed, when McKinley asked Congress for war on April 11, he did not recognize the rebels as belligerents or ask for Cuban independence. Nine days later, Congress, by joint resolution, gave McKinley the power to intervene. When American forces moved into Cuba, the rebels welcomed them, hoping the Teller Amendment would guarantee Cuban independence.

Many histories of the Spanish-American war have said that "public opinion" in the United States led McKinley to declare war on Spain and send forces to Cuba. True, certain influential newspapers had been pushing hard, even hysterically. And many Americans, seeing the aim of intervention as Cuban independence—and with the Teller Amendment as guarantee of this intention—supported the idea. But would McKinley have gone to war because of the press and some portion of the public (we had no public opinion surveys at that time) without the urging of the business community? Several years after the Cuban war, the chief of the Bureau of Foreign Commerce of the Department of Commerce wrote about that period:

> Underlying the popular sentiment, which might have evaporated in time, which forced the United States to take up arms against Spanish rule in Cuba, were our economic relations with the West Indies and the South American republics. . . . The Spanish-American War was but an incident of a general movement of expansion which had its roots in the changed environment of an industrial capacity far beyond our domestic powers of consumption. It was seen to be necessary for us not only to find foreign purchasers for our goods, but to provide the means of making access to foreign markets easy, economical and safe.

American labor unions had sympathy for the Cuban rebels as soon as the insurrection against Spain began in 1895. But they opposed American expansionism. Both the Knights of Labor and the American Federation of Labor spoke against the idea of annexing Hawaii, which McKinley proposed in 1897. Despite the feeling for the Cuban rebels, a resolution calling for U.S. intervention was defeated at the 1897 convention of the AFL. Samuel Gompers of the AFL wrote to a friend: "The sympathy of our movement with Cuba is genuine, earnest, and sincere, but this does not for a moment imply that we are committed to certain adventurers who are apparently suffering from Hysteria. . . ."

When the explosion of the *Maine* in February led to excited calls for war in the press, the monthly journal of the International Association of Machinists agreed it was a terrible disaster, but it noted that the deaths of workers in industrial accidents drew no such national clamor. It pointed to the Lattimer Massacre of September 10, 1897, during a coal strike in Pennsylvania. Miners marching on a highway to the Lattimer mine—Austrians, Hungarians, Italians, Germans—who had originally been imported as strikebreakers but then organized themselves, refused to disperse, whereupon the sheriff and his deputies opened fire, killing nineteen of them, most shot in the back, with no outcry in the press. The labor journal said that the

> . . . carnival of carnage that takes place every day, month and year in the realm of industry, the thousands of useful lives that are annually sacrificed to the Moloch of greed, the blood tribute paid by labor to capitalism, brings forth no shout for vengeance and reparation. . . . Death comes in thousands of instances in mill and mine, claims his victims, and no popular uproar is heard.

The official organ of the Connecticut AFL, *The Craftsman*, also warned about the hysteria worked up by the sinking of the *Maine*:

> A gigantic . . . and cunningly-devised scheme is being worked ostensibly to place the United States in the front rank as a naval and military power. The real reason is that the capitalists will have the whole

thing and, when any workingmen dare to ask for the living wage . . . they will be shot down like dogs in the streets.

Some unions, like the United Mine Workers, called for U.S. intervention after the sinking of the *Maine*. But most were against war. The treasurer of the American Longshoremen's Union, Bolton Hall, wrote "A Peace Appeal to Labor," which was widely circulated:

If there is a war, you will furnish the corpses and the taxes, and others will get the glory. Speculators will make money out of it—that is, out of you. Men will get high prices for inferior supplies, leaky boats, for shoddy clothes and pasteboard shoes, and you will have to pay the bill, and the only satisfaction you will get is the privilege of hating your Spanish fellow-workmen, who are really your brothers and who have had as little to do with the wrongs of Cuba as you have.

Socialists opposed the war. One exception was the Jewish *Daily Forward. The People*, newspaper of the Socialist Labor party, called the issue of Cuban freedom "a pretext" and said the government wanted war to "distract the attention of the workers from their real interests." The *Appeal to Reason*, another Socialist newspaper, said the movement for war was "a favorite method of rulers for keeping the people from redressing domestic wrongs." In the San Francisco *Voice of Labor* a Socialist wrote: "It is a terrible thing to think that the poor workers of this country should be sent to kill and wound the poor workers of Spain merely because a few leaders may incite them to do so."

But after war was declared, Foner says, "the majority of the trade unions succumbed to the war fever." Samuel Gompers called the war "glorious and righteous" and claimed that 250,000 trade unionists had volunteered for military service. The United Mine Workers pointed to higher coal prices as a result of the war and said: "The coal and iron trades have not been so healthy for some years past as at present."

The war brought more employment and higher wages, but

also higher prices. Foner says: "Not only was there a startling increase in the cost of living, but, in the absence of an income tax, the poor found themselves paying almost entirely for the staggering costs of the war through increased levies on sugar, molasses, tobacco, and other taxes. . . ." Gompers, publicly for the war, privately pointed out that the war had led to a 20 percent reduction of the purchasing power of workers' wages.

On May Day, 1898, the Socialist Labor party organized an antiwar parade in New York City, but the authorities would not allow it to take place, while a May Day parade called by the Jewish *Daily Forward*, urging Jewish workers to support the war, was permitted. The Chicago *Labor World* said: "This has been a poor man's war—paid for by the poor man. The rich have profited by it, as they always do. . . ."

The Western Labor Union was founded at Salt Lake City on May 10, 1898, because the AFL had not organized unskilled workers. It wanted to bring together all workers "irrespective of occupation, nationality, creed or color" and "sound the death knell of every corporation and trust that has robbed the American laborer of the fruits of his toil. . . ." The union's publication, noting the annexation of Hawaii during the war, said this proved that "the war which started as one of relief for the starving Cubans has suddenly changed to one of conquest."

The prediction made by longshoreman Bolton Hall, of wartime corruption and profiteering, turned out to be remarkably accurate. Richard Morris's *Encyclopedia of American History* gives startling figures:

> Of the more than 274,000 officers and men who served in the army during the Spanish-American War and the period of demobilization, 5,462 died in the various theaters of operation and in camps in the U.S. Only 379 of the deaths were battle casualties, the remainder being attributed to disease and other causes.

The same figures are given by Walter Millis in his book *The Martial Spirit*. In the *Encyclopedia* they are given tersely, and without mention of the "embalmed beef" (an army general's term) sold to the army by the meatpackers—meat preserved with boric acid, nitrate of potash, and artificial coloring matter.

In May of 1898, Armour and Company, the big meatpacking company of Chicago, sold the army 500,000 pounds of beef which had been sent to Liverpool a year earlier and had been returned. Two months later, an army inspector tested the Armour meat, which had been stamped and approved by an inspector of the Bureau of Animal Industry, and found 751 cases containing rotten meat. In the first sixty cases he opened, he found fourteen tins already burst, "the effervescent putrid contents of which were distributed all over the cases." (The description comes from the *Report of the Commission to Investigate the Conduct of the War Department in the War with Spain*, made to the Senate in 1900.) Thousands of soldiers got food poisoning. There are no figures on how many of the five thousand noncombat deaths were caused by that.

The Spanish forces were defeated in three months, in what John Hay, the American Secretary of State, later called a "splendid little war." The American military pretended that the Cuban rebel army did not exist. When the Spanish surrendered, no Cuban was allowed to confer on the surrender, or to sign it. General William Shafter said no armed rebels could enter the capital city of Santiago, and told the Cuban rebel leader, General Calixto García, that not Cubans, but the old Spanish civil authorities, would remain in charge of the municipal offices in Santiago.

American historians have generally ignored the role of the Cuban rebels in the war; Philip Foner, in his history, was the first to print García's letter of protest to General Shafter:

I have not been honored with a single word from yourself informing me about the negotiations for peace or the terms of the capitulation by the Spaniards.

. . . when the question arises of appointing authorities in Santiago de Cuba . . . I cannot see but with the deepest regret that such authorities are not elected by the Cuban people, but are the same ones selected by the Queen of Spain. . . .

A rumor too absurd to be believed, General, describes the reason of your measures and of the orders forbidding my army to enter Santiago for fear of massacres and revenge against the Spaniards. Allow me, sir, to protest against even the shadow of such an idea. We are not savages ignoring the rules of civilized warfare. We are a poor, ragged army, as ragged and poor as was the army of your forefathers in their noble war for independence. . . .

Along with the American army in Cuba came American capital. Foner writes:

Even before the Spanish flag was down in Cuba, U.S. business interests set out to make their influence felt. Merchants, real estate agents, stock speculators, reckless adventurers, and promoters of all kinds of get-rich schemes flocked to Cuba by the thousands. Seven syndicates battled each other for control of the franchises for the Havana Street Railway, which were finally won by Percival Farquhar, representing the Wall Street interests of New York. Thus, simultaneously with the military occupation began . . . commercial occupation.

The *Lumbermen's Review*, spokesman for the lumber industry, said in the midst of the war: "The moment Spain drops the reigns of government in Cuba . . . the moment will arrive for American lumber interests to move into the island for the products of Cuban forests. Cuba still possesses 10,000,000 acres of virgin forest abounding in valuable timber . . . nearly every foot of which would be saleable in the United States and bring high prices."

Americans began taking over railroad, mine, and sugar properties when the war ended. In a few years, $30 million of American capital was invested. United Fruit moved into the Cuban sugar industry. It bought 1,900,000 acres of land for about twenty cents an acre. The American Tobacco Company arrived. By the end of the occupation, in 1901, Foner estimates that at least 80 percent of the export of Cuba's minerals were in American hands, mostly Bethlehem Steel.

During the military occupation a series of strikes took place.

In September 1899, a gathering of thousands of workers in Havana launched a general strike for the eight-hour day, saying, ". . . we have determined to promote the struggle between the worker and the capitalist. For the workers of Cuba will no longer tolerate remaining in total subjection." The American General William Ludlow ordered the mayor of Havana to arrest eleven strike leaders, and U.S. troops occupied railroad stations and docks. Police moved through the city breaking up meetings. But the economic activity of the city had come to a halt. Tobacco workers struck. Printers struck. Bakers went on strike. Hundreds of strikers were arrested, and some of the imprisoned leaders were intimidated into calling for an end to the strike.

The United States did not annex Cuba. But a Cuban Constitutional Convention was told that the United States army would not leave Cuba until the Platt Amendment, passed by Congress in February 1901, was incorporated into the new Cuban Constitution. This Amendment gave the United States "the right to intervene for the preservation of Cuban independence, the maintenance of a government adequate for the protection of life, property, and individual liberty. . . ." It also provided for the United States to get coaling or naval stations at certain specified points.

The Teller Amendment and the talk of Cuban freedom before and during the war had led many Americans—and Cubans—to expect genuine independence. The Platt Amendment was now seen, not only by the radical and labor press, but by newspapers and groups all over the United States, as a betrayal. A mass meeting of the American Anti-Imperialist League at Faneuil Hall in Boston denounced it, ex-governor George Boutwell saying: "In disregard of our pledge of freedom and sovereignty to Cuba we are imposing on that island conditions of colonial vassalage."

In Havana, a torchlight procession of fifteen thousand Cubans marched on the Constitutional Convention, urging them to reject the Amendment. But General Leonard Wood, head of the occupation forces, assured McKinley: "The people of Cuba lend themselves readily to all sorts of demonstrations and parades, and little significance should be attached to them."

A committee was delegated by the Constitutional Convention to reply to the United States' insistence that the Platt Amendment be included in the Constitution. The committee report, *Penencia a la Convención*, was written by a black delegate from Santiago. It said:

> For the United States to reserve to itself the power to determine when this independence was threatened, and when, therefore, it should intervene to preserve it, is equivalent to handing over the keys to our house so that they can enter it at any time, whenever the desire seizes them, day or night, whether with good or evil design.

And:

> The only Cuban governments that would live would be those which count on the support and benevolence of the United States, and the clearest result of this situation would be that we would only have feeble and miserable governments . . . condemned to live more attentive to obtaining the blessings of the United States than to serving and defending the interests of Cuba. . . .

The report termed the request for coaling or naval stations "a mutilation of the fatherland." It concluded:

> A people occupied militarily is being told that before consulting their own government, before being free in their own territory, they should grant the military occupants who came as friends and allies, rights and powers which would annul the sovereignty of these very people. That is the situation created for us by the method which the United States has just adopted. It could not be more obnoxious and inadmissible.

With this report, the Convention overwhelmingly rejected the Platt Amendment.

Within the next three months, however, the pressure from the United States, the military occupation, the refusal to allow the

Cubans to set up their own government until they acquiesced, had its effect; the Convention, after several refusals, adopted the Platt Amendment. General Leonard Wood wrote in 1901 to Theodore Roosevelt: "There is, of course, little or no independence left Cuba under the Platt Amendment."

Cuba was thus brought into the American sphere, but not as an outright colony. However, the Spanish-American war did lead to a number of direct annexations by the United States. Puerto Rico, a neighbor of Cuba in the Caribbean, belonging to Spain, was taken over by U.S. military forces. The Hawaiian Islands, one-third of the way across the Pacific, which had already been penetrated by American missionaries and pineapple plantation owners, and had been described by American officials as "a ripe pear ready to be plucked," was annexed by joint resolution of Congress in July of 1898. Around the same time, Wake Island, 2,300 miles west of Hawaii, on the route to Japan, was occupied. And Guam, the Spanish possession in the Pacific, almost all the way to the Philippines, was taken. In December of 1898, the peace treaty was signed with Spain, officially turning over to the United States Guam, Puerto Rico, and the Philippines, for a payment of $20 million.

There was heated argument in the United States about whether or not to take the Philippines. As one story has it, President McKinley told a group of ministers visiting the White House how he came to his decision:

> Before you go I would like to say just a word about the Philippine business. . . . The truth is I didn't want the Philippines, and when they came to us as a gift from the gods, I did not know what to do with them. . . . I sought counsel from all sides—Democrats as well as Republicans—but got little help.
>
> I thought first we would only take Manila; then Luzon, then other islands, perhaps, also.
>
> I walked the floor of the White House night after night until midnight; and I am not ashamed to tell you, gentlemen, that I went down on my knees and prayed Almighty God for light and guidance

more than one night. And one night late it came to me this way—I don't know how it was, but it came:

1. That we could not give them back to Spain—that would be cowardly and dishonorable.
2. That we could not turn them over to France or Germany, our commercial rivals in the Orient—that would be bad business and discreditable.
3. That we could not leave them to themselves—they were unfit for self-government—and they would soon have anarchy and misrule over there worse than Spain's was; and
4. That there was nothing left for us to do but to take them all and to educate the Filipinos, and uplift and civilize and Christianize them, and by God's grace do the very best we could by them, as our fellow men for whom Christ also died. And then I went to bed and went to sleep and slept soundly.

The Filipinos did not get the same message from God. In February 1899, they rose in revolt against American rule, as they had rebelled several times against the Spanish. Emilio Aguinaldo, a Filipino leader, who had earlier been brought back from China by U.S. warships to lead soldiers against Spain, now became leader of the *insurrectos* fighting the United States. He proposed Filipino independence within a U.S. protectorate, but this was rejected.

It took the United States three years to crush the rebellion, using seventy thousand troops—four times as many as were landed in Cuba—and thousands of battle casualties, many times more than in Cuba. It was a harsh war. For the Filipinos the death rate was enormous from battle casualties and from disease.

The taste of empire was on the lips of politicians and business interests throughout the country now. Racism, paternalism, and talk of money mingled with talk of destiny and civilization. In the Senate, Albert Beveridge spoke, January 9, 1900, for the dominant economic and political interests of the country:

Mr. President, the times call for candor. The Philippines are ours forever. . . . And just beyond the Philippines are China's illimitable markets. We will not retreat from either. . . . We will not renounce our part in the mission of our race, trustee, under God, of the civilization of the world. . . .

The Pacific is our ocean. . . . Where shall we turn for consumers of our surplus? Geography answers the question. China is our natural customer. . . . The Philippines give us a base at the door of all the East. . . .

No land in America surpasses in fertility the plains and valleys of Luzon. Rice and coffee, sugar and cocoanuts, hemp and tobacco. . . . The wood of the Philippines can supply the furniture of the world for a century to come. At Cebu the best informed man on the island told me that 40 miles of Cebu's mountain chain are practically mountains of coal. . . .

I have a nugget of pure gold picked up in its present form on the banks of a Philippine creek. . . .

My own belief is that there are not 100 men among them who comprehend what Anglo-Saxon self-government even means, and there are over 5,000,000 people to be governed.

It has been charged that our conduct of the war has been cruel. Senators, it has been the reverse. . . . Senators must remember that we are not dealing with Americans or Europeans. We are dealing with Orientals.

The fighting with the rebels began, McKinley said, when the insurgents attacked American forces. But later, American soldiers testified that the United States had fired the first shot. After the war, an army officer speaking in Boston's Faneuil Hall said his colonel had given him orders to provoke a conflict with the insurgents.

In February 1899, a banquet took place in Boston to celebrate the Senate's ratification of the peace treaty with Spain. President McKinley himself had been invited by the wealthy textile manufacturer W. B. Plunkett to speak. It was the biggest banquet in the nation's history: two thousand diners, four hundred waiters. McKinley said that "no imperial designs lurk in the American mind," and at the same banquet, to the same diners, his Postmaster General, Charles Emory Smith, said that "what we want is a market for our surplus."

William James, the Harvard philosopher, wrote a letter to the Boston *Transcript* about "the cold pot grease of McKinley's cant at the recent Boston banquet" and said the Philippine operation "reeked of the infernal adroitness of the great department store, which has reached perfect expertness in the art of killing silently, and with no public squalling or commotion, the neighboring small concerns."

James was part of a movement of prominent American businessmen, politicians, and intellectuals who formed the Anti-Imperialist League in 1898 and carried on a long campaign to educate the American public about the horrors of the Philippine war and the evils of imperialism. It was an odd group (Andrew Carnegie belonged), including antilabor aristocrats and scholars, united in a common moral outrage at what was being done to the Filipinos in the name of freedom. Whatever their differences on other matters, they would all agree with William James's angry statement: "God damn the U.S. for its vile conduct in the Philippine Isles."

The Anti-Imperialist League published the letters of soldiers doing duty in the Philippines. A captain from Kansas wrote: "Caloocan was supposed to contain 17,000 inhabitants. The Twentieth Kansas swept through it, and now Caloocan contains not one living native." A private from the same outfit said he had "with my own hand set fire to over fifty houses of Filipinos after the victory at Caloocan. Women and children were wounded by our fire."

A volunteer from the state of Washington wrote: "Our fighting blood was up, and we all wanted to kill 'niggers.' . . . This shooting human beings beats rabbit hunting all to pieces."

It was a time of intense racism in the United States. In the years between 1889 and 1903, on the average, every week, two Negroes were lynched by mobs—hanged, burned, mutilated. The Filipinos were brown-skinned, physically identifiable, strange-speaking and strange-looking to Americans. To the usual indiscriminate brutality of war was thus added the factor of racial hostility.

In November 1901, the Manila correspondent of the Philadelphia *Ledger* reported:

> The present war is no bloodless, opera bouffe engagement; our men have been relentless, have killed to exterminate men, women, children, prisoners and captives, active insurgents and suspected people from lads of ten up, the idea prevailing that the Filipino as such was little better than a dog. . . . Our soldiers have pumped salt water into men to make them talk, and have taken prisoners people who held up their hands and peacefully surrendered, and an hour later, without an atom of evidence to show that they were even *insurrectos*, stood them on a bridge and shot them down one by one, to drop into the water below and float down, as examples to those who found their bullet-loaded corpses.

Early in 1901 an American general returning to the United States from southern Luzon said:

> One-sixth of the natives of Luzon have either been killed or have died of the dengue fever in the last few years. The loss of life by killing alone has been very great, but I think not one man has been slain except where his death has served the legitimate purposes of war. It has been necessary to adopt what in other countries would probably be thought harsh measures.

Secretary of War Elihu Root responded to the charges of brutality: "The war in the Philippines has been conducted by the American army with scrupulous regard for the rules of civilized warfare. . . . with self-restraint and with humanity never surpassed."

In Manila, a Marine named Littletown Waller, a major, was accused of shooting eleven defenseless Filipinos, without trial, on the island of Samar. Other marine officers described his testimony:

The major said that General Smith instructed him to kill and burn, and said that the more he killed and burned the better pleased he would be; that it was no time to take prisoners, and that he was to make Samar a howling wilderness. Major Waller asked General Smith to define the age limit for killing, and he replied "Everything over ten."

In the province of Batangas, the secretary of the province estimated that of the population of 300,000, one-third had been killed by combat, famine, or disease.

Mark Twain commented on the Philippine war:

We have pacified some thousands of the islanders and buried them; destroyed their fields; burned their villages, and turned their widows and orphans out-of-doors; furnished heartbreak by exile to some dozens of disagreeable patriots; subjugated the remaining ten millions by Benevolent Assimilation, which is the pious new name of the musket; we have acquired property in the three hundred concubines and other slaves of our business partner, the Sultan of Sulu, and hoisted our protecting flag over that swag.

And so, by these Providences of God—and the phrase is the government's, not mine—we are a World Power.

American firepower was overwhelmingly superior to anything the Filipino rebels could put together. In the very first battle, Admiral Dewey steamed up the Pasig River and fired 500-pound shells into the Filipino trenches. Dead Filipinos were piled so high that the Americans used their bodies for breastworks. A British witness said: "This is not war; it is simply massacre and murderous butchery." He was wrong; it was war.

For the rebels to hold out against such odds for years meant that they had the support of the population. General Arthur MacArthur, commander of the Filipino war, said: ". . . I believed that Aguinaldo's troops represented only a faction. I did not like to believe that the whole population of Luzon—the native population, that is—was opposed to us." But he said he was "reluctantly compelled" to believe this because the guerrilla tactics of the Filipino army "depended upon almost complete unity of action of the entire native population."

Despite the growing evidence of brutality and the work of the Anti-Imperialist League, some of the trade unions in the United States supported the action in the Philippines. The Typographical Union said it liked the idea of annexing more territory because English-language schools in those areas would help the printing trade. The publication of the glassmakers saw value in new territories that would buy glass. The railroad brotherhoods saw shipment of U.S. goods to the new territories meaning more work for railroad workers. Some unions repeated what big business was saying, that territorial expansion, by creating a market for surplus goods, would prevent another depression.

On the other hand, when the *Leather Workers' Journal* wrote that an increase in wages at home would solve the problem of surplus by creating more purchasing power inside the country, the *Carpenters' Journal* asked: "How much better off are the workingmen of England through all its colonial possessions?" The *National Labor Tribune*, publication of the Iron, Steel, and Tin Workers, agreed that the Philippines were rich with resources, but added:

> The same can be said of this country, but if anybody were to ask you if you owned a coal mine, a sugar plantation, or railroad you would have to say no . . . all those things are in the hands of the trusts controlled by a few. . . .

When the treaty for annexation of the Philippines was up for debate in Congress in early 1899, the Central Labor Unions of Boston and New York opposed it. There was a mass meeting in New York against annexation. The Anti-Imperialist League circulated more than a million pieces of literature against taking the Philippines. (Foner says that while the League was organized and dominated by intellectuals and business people, a large part of its half-million members were working-class people, including women and blacks.) Locals of the League held meetings all over the country. The campaign against the Treaty was a powerful one, and when the Senate did ratify it, it was by one vote.

The mixed reactions of labor to the war—lured by economic advantage, yet repelled by capitalist expansion and violence—ensured that labor could not unite either to stop the war or to conduct class war against the system at home. The reactions of black soldiers to the war were also mixed: there was the simple need to get ahead in a society where opportunities for success were denied the black man, and the military life gave such possibilities. There was race pride, the need to show that blacks were as courageous, as patriotic, as anyone else. And yet, there was with all this the consciousness of a brutal war, fought against colored people, a counterpart of the violence committed against black people in the United States.

Willard Gatewood, in his book *Smoked Yankees and the Struggle for Empire*, reproduces and analyzes 114 letters to Negro newspapers written by black soldiers in the period 1898–1902. The letters show all those conflicting emotions. Black soldiers encamped in Tampa, Florida, ran into bitter race hatred by white inhabitants there. And then, after they fought with distinction in Cuba, Negroes were not rewarded with officers' commissions; white officers commanded black regiments.

Negro soldiers in Lakeland, Florida, pistol-whipped a drug-store owner when he refused to serve one of them, and then, in a confrontation with a white crowd, killed a civilian. In Tampa, a race riot began when drunken white soldiers used a Negro child as a target to show their marksmanship; Negro soldiers retaliated, and then the streets "ran red with negro blood," according to press dispatches. Twenty-seven Negro soldiers and three whites were severely wounded. The chaplain of a black regiment in Tampa wrote to the Cleveland *Gazette:*

Is America any better than Spain? Has she not subjects in her very midst who are murdered daily without a trial of judge or jury? Has she not subjects in her own borders whose children are half-fed and half-clothed, because their father's skin is black. . . . Yet the Negro is loyal to his country's flag.

The same chaplain, George Prioleau, talks of black veterans of the Cuban war "unkindly and sneeringly received" in Kansas City, Missouri. He says that "these black boys, heroes of our country, were not allowed to stand at the counters of restaurants and eat a sandwich and drink a cup of coffee, while the white soldiers were welcomed and invited to sit down at the tables and eat free of cost."

But it was the Filipino situation that aroused many blacks in the United States to militant opposition to the war. The senior bishop of the African Methodist Episcopal Church, Henry M. Turner, called the campaign in the Philippines "an unholy war of conquest" and referred to the Filipinos as "sable patriots."

There were four black regiments on duty in the Philippines. Many of the black soldiers established rapport with the brown-skinned natives on the islands, and were angered by the term "nigger" used by white troops to describe the Filipinos. An "unusually large number" of black troops deserted during the Philippines campaign, Gatewood says. The Filipino rebels often addressed themselves to "The Colored American Soldier" in posters, reminding them of lynchings back home, asking them not to serve the white imperialist against other colored people.

Some deserters joined the Filipino rebels. The most famous of these was David Fagan of the 24th Infantry. According to Gatewood: "He accepted a commission in the insurgent army and for two years wreaked havoc upon the American forces."

From the Philippines, William Simms wrote:

I was struck by a question a little Filipino boy asked me, which ran about this way: "Why does the American Negro come . . . to fight us where we are much a friend to him and have not done anything to him. He is all the same as me and me all the same as you. Why don't you fight those people in America who burn Negroes, that make a beast of you . . . ?"

Another soldier's letter of 1899:

Our racial sympathies would naturally be with the Filipinos. They are fighting manfully for what they conceive to be their best interests. But we cannot for the sake of sentiment turn our back upon our own country.

Patrick Mason, a sergeant in the 24th Infantry, wrote to the Cleveland *Gazette*, which had taken a strong stand against annexation of the Philippines:

Dear Sir: I have not had any fighting to do since I have been here and don't care to do any. I feel sorry for these people and all that have come under the control of the United States. I don't believe they will be justly dealt by. The first thing in the morning is the "Nigger" and the last thing at night is the "Nigger." ... You are right in your opinions. I must not say much as I am a soldier. ...

A black infantryman named William Fulbright wrote from Manila in June 1901 to the editor of a paper in Indianapolis: "This struggle on the islands has been naught but a gigantic scheme of robbery and oppression."

Back home, while the war against the Filipinos was going on, a group of Massachusetts Negroes addressed a message to President McKinley:

We the colored people of Massachusetts in mass meeting assembled ... have resolved to address ourselves to you in an open letter, notwithstanding your extraordinary, your incomprehensible silence on the subject of our wrongs. ...

... you have seen our sufferings, witnessed from your high place our awful wrongs and miseries, and yet you have at no time and on no occasion opened your lips on our behalf. ...

With one accord, with an anxiety that wrenched our hearts with cruel hopes and fears, the Colored people of the United States turned to you when Wilmington, North Carolina was held for two dreadful days and nights in the clutch of a bloody revolution; when Negroes, guilty of no crime except the color of their skin and a desire to exercise the rights of their American citizenship, were butchered like dogs in the streets of that ill-fated town . . . for want of federal aid, which you would not and did not furnish. . . .

It was the same thing with that terrible ebullition of mob spirit at Phoenix, South Carolina, when black men were hunted and murdered, and white men [these were white radicals in Phoenix] shot and driven out of that place by a set of white savages. . . . We looked in vain for some word or some act from you. . . .

And when you made your Southern tour a little later, and we saw how cunningly you catered to Southern race prejudice. . . . How you preached patience, industry, moderation to your long-suffering black fellow citizens, and patriotism, jingoism and imperialism to your white ones. . . .

The "patience, industry, and moderation" preached to blacks, the "patriotism" preached to whites, did not fully sink in. In the first years of the twentieth century, despite all the demonstrated power of the state, large numbers of blacks, whites, men, women became impatient, immoderate, unpatriotic.

2

THE SOCIALIST CHALLENGE

War and jingoism might postpone, but could not fully suppress, the class anger that came from the realities of ordinary life. As the twentieth century opened, that anger reemerged. Emma Goldman, the anarchist and feminist, whose political consciousness was shaped by factory work, the Haymarket executions, the Homestead strike, the long prison term of her lover and comrade, Alexander Berkman, the depression of the 1890s, the strike struggles of New York, her own imprisonment on Blackwell's Island, spoke at a meeting some years after the Spanish-American war:

> How our hearts burned with indignation against the atrocious Spaniards! ... But when the smoke was over, the dead buried, and the cost of the war came back to the people in an increase in the price of commodities and rent—that is, when we sobered up from our patriotic spree—it suddenly dawned on us that the cause of the Spanish-American war was the price of sugar.... that the lives, blood, and money of the American people were used to protect the interests of the American capitalists.

Mark Twain was neither an anarchist nor a radical. By 1900, at sixty-five, he was a world-acclaimed writer of funny-serious-American-to-the-bone stories. He watched the United States and other Western countries go about the world and wrote in the New York *Herald* as the century began: "I bring you the stately matron named Christendom, returning bedraggled, besmirched, and dishonored from pirate raids in Kiao-Chou, Manchuria, South Africa, and the Philippines, with her soul full of meanness, her pocket full of boodle, and her mouth full of pious hypocrisies."

There were writers of the early twentieth century who spoke for socialism or criticized the capitalist system harshly—not obscure pamphleteers, but among the most famous of American literary figures, whose books were read by millions: Upton Sinclair, Jack London, Theodore Dreiser, Frank Norris.

Upton Sinclair's novel *The Jungle*, published in 1906, brought the conditions in the meatpacking plants of Chicago to the shocked attention of the whole country, and stimulated demand for laws regulating the meat industry. But also, through the story of an immigrant laborer, Jurgis Rudkus, it spoke of socialism, of how beautiful life might be if people cooperatively owned and worked and shared the riches of the earth. *The Jungle* was first published in the Socialist newspaper *Appeal to Reason*; it was then read by millions as a book, and was translated into seventeen languages.

One of the influences on Upton Sinclair's thinking was a book, *People of the Abyss*, by Jack London. London was a member of the Socialist party. He had come out of the slums of San Francisco, the child of an unwed mother. He had been a newsboy, a cannery worker, a sailor, a fisherman, had worked in a jute mill and a laundry, hoboed the railroads to the East Coast, been clubbed by a policeman on the streets of New York and arrested for vagrancy in Niagara Falls, watched men beaten and tortured in jail, pirated oysters in San Francisco Bay, read Flaubert, Tolstoy, Melville, and the *Communist Manifesto*, preached socialism in the Alaskan gold camps in the winter of 1896, sailed 2,000 miles back through the Bering Sea, and became a world-famous writer of adventure books. In 1906, he wrote his novel *The Iron Heel*, with its warning of a fascist America, its ideal of a socialist brotherhood of man. In the course of it, through his characters, he indicts the system.

> In the face of the facts that modern man lives more wretchedly than the cave-man, and that his producing power is a thousand times greater than that of the cave-man, no other conclusion is possible than that the capitalist class has mismanaged . . . criminally and selfishly mismanaged.

And with this attack, the vision:

> Let us not destroy those wonderful machines that produce efficiently and cheaply. Let us control them. Let us profit by their efficiency and cheapness. Let us run them for ourselves. That, gentlemen, is socialism. . . .

It was a time when even a self-exiled literary figure living in Europe and not prone to political statements—the novelist Henry James—could tour the United States in 1904 and see the country as a "huge Rappacini garden, rank with each variety of the poison-plant of the money passion."

"Muckrakers," who raked up the mud and the muck, contributed to the atmosphere of dissent by simply telling what they saw. Some of the new mass-circulation magazines, ironically enough in the interest of profit, printed their articles: Ida Tarbell's exposure of the Standard Oil Company; Lincoln Steffens's stories of corruption in the major American cities.

By 1900, neither the patriotism of the war nor the absorption of energy in elections could disguise the troubles of the system. The process of business concentration had gone forward; the control by bankers had become more clear. As technology developed and corporations became larger, they needed more capital, and it was the bankers who had this capital. By 1904, more than a thousand railroad lines had been consolidated into six great combinations, each allied with either Morgan or Rockefeller interests. As Cochran and Miller say:

> The imperial leader of the new oligarchy was the House of Morgan. In its operations it was ably assisted by the First National Bank of New York (directed by George F. Baker) and the National City Bank of New York (presided over by James Stillman, agent of the Rockefeller interests). Among them, these three men and their financial associates occupied 341 directorships in 112 great corporations. The total resources of these corporations in 1912 was $22,245,000,000, more than the assessed value of all property in the twenty-two states and territories west of the Mississippi River. . . .

Morgan had always wanted regularity, stability, predictability. An associate of his said in 1901:

> With a man like Mr. Morgan at the head of a great industry, as against the old plan of many diverse interests in it, production would become more regular, labor would be more steadily employed at better wages, and panics caused by over-production would become a thing of the past.

But even Morgan and his associates were not in complete control of such a system. In 1907, there was a panic, financial collapse, and crisis. True, the very big businesses were not hurt, but profits after 1907 were not as high as capitalists wanted, industry was not expanding as fast as it might, and industrialists began to look for ways to cut costs.

One way was Taylorism. Frederick W. Taylor had been a steel company foreman who closely analyzed every job in the mill, and worked out a system of finely detailed division of labor, increased mechanization, and piecework wage systems, to increase production and profits. In 1911, he published a book on "scientific management" that became powerfully influential in the business world. Now management could control every detail of the worker's energy and time in the factory. As Harry Braverman said (*Labor and Monopoly Capital*), the purpose of Taylorism was to make workers interchangeable, able to do the simple tasks that the new division of labor required—like standard parts divested of individuality and humanity, bought and sold as commodities.

It was a system well fitted for the new auto industry. In 1909, Ford sold 10,607 autos; in 1913, 168,000; in 1914, 248,000 (45 percent of all autos produced). The profit: $30 million.

With immigrants a larger proportion of the labor force (in the Carnegie plants of Allegheny County in 1907, of the 14,359 common laborers, 11,694 were Eastern Europeans), Taylorism, with its simplified unskilled jobs, became more feasible.

In New York City, the new immigrants went to work in the sweatshops. The poet Edwin Markham wrote in *Cosmopolitan* magazine, January 1907:

In unaired rooms, mothers and fathers sew by day and by night. Those in the home sweatshop must work cheaper than those in the factory sweatshops. . . . And the children are called in from play to drive and drudge beside their elders. . . .

All the year in New York and in other cities you may watch children radiating to and from such pitiful homes. Nearly any hour on the East Side of New York City you can see them—pallid boy or spindling girl—their faces dulled, their backs bent under a heavy load of garments piled on head and shoulders, the muscles of the whole frame in a long strain. . . .

Is it not a cruel civilization that allows little hearts and little shoulders to strain under these grown-up responsibilities, while in the same city, a pet cur is jeweled and pampered and aired on a fine lady's velvet lap on the beautiful boulevards?

The city became a battlefield. On August 10, 1905, the New York *Tribune* reported that a strike at Federman's bakery on the Lower East Side led to violence when Federman used scab labor to continue producing:

Strikers or their sympathizers wrecked the bake shop of Philip Federman at No. 183 Orchard Street early last night amid scenes of the most tumultuous excitement. Policemen smashed heads right and left with their nightsticks after two of their number had been roughly dealt with by the mob. . . .

There were five hundred garment factories in New York. A woman later recalled the conditions of work:

. . . dangerously broken stairways . . . windows few and so dirty. . . . The wooden floors that were swept once a year. . . . Hardly any other light but the gas jets burning by day and by night . . . the filthy, malodorous lavatory in the dark hall. No fresh drinking water. . . . mice and roaches. . . .

During the winter months . . . how we suffered from the cold. In the summer we suffered from the heat. . . .

In these disease-breeding holes we, the youngsters together with the men and women toiled from seventy and eighty hours a week! Saturdays and Sundays included! . . . A sign would go up on Saturday afternoon: "If you don't come in on Sunday, you need not come in on Monday." . . . Children's dreams of a day off shattered. We wept, for after all, we were only children. . . .

At the Triangle Shirtwaist Company, in the winter of 1909, women organized and decided to strike. Soon they were walking the picket line in the cold, knowing they could not win while the other factories were operating. A mass meeting was called of workers in the other shops, and Clara Lemlich, in her teens, an eloquent speaker, still bearing the signs of her recent beating on the picket line, stood up: "I offer a resolution that a general strike be declared now!" The meeting went wild; they voted to strike.

Pauline Newman, one of the strikers, recalled years later the beginning of the general strike:

Thousands upon thousands left the factories from every side, all of them walking down toward Union Square. It was November, the cold winter was just around the corner, we had no fur coats to keep warm, and yet there was the spirit that led us on and on until we got to some hall. . . .

I can see the young people, mostly women, walking down and not caring what might happen . . . the hunger, cold, loneliness. . . . They just didn't care on that particular day; that was their day.

The union had hoped three thousand would join the strike. Twenty thousand walked out. Every day a thousand new members joined the union, the International Ladies Garment Workers Union, which before this had few women. Colored women were active in the strike, which went on through the winter, against police, against scabs, against arrests and prison. In more than three hundred shops, workers won their demands. Women now became officials in the union. Pauline Newman again:

We tried to educate ourselves. I would invite the girls to my rooms, and we took turns reading poetry in English to improve our understanding of the language. One of our favorites was Thomas Hood's "Song of the Shirt," and another . . . Percy Bysshe Shelley's "Mask of Anarchy." . . .

"Rise like lions after slumber
In unvanquishable number!
Shake your chains to earth, like dew
Which in sleep had fallen on you—
Ye are many, they are few!"

The conditions in the factories did not change much. On the afternoon of March 25, 1911, a fire at the Triangle Shirtwaist Company that began in a rag bin swept through the eighth, ninth, and tenth floors, too high for fire ladders to reach. The fire chief of New York had said that his ladders could reach only to the seventh floor. But half of New York's 500,000 workers spent all day, perhaps twelve hours, above the seventh floor. The laws said factory doors had to open outward. But at the Triangle Company the doors opened in. The law said the doors could not be locked during working hours, but at the Triangle Company doors were usually locked so the company could keep track of the employees. And so, trapped, the young women were burned to death at their worktables, or jammed against the locked exit door, or leaped to their deaths down the elevator shafts. The New York *World* reported:

> . . . screaming men and women and boys and girls crowded out on the many window ledges and threw themselves into the streets far below. They jumped with their clothing ablaze. The hair of some of the girls streamed up aflame as they leaped. Thud after thud sounded on the pavements. It is a ghastly fact that on both the Greene Street and Washington Place sides of the building there grew mounds of the dead and dying. . . .
>
> From opposite windows spectators saw again and again pitiable companionships formed in the instant of death—girls who placed their arms around each other as they leaped.

When it was over, 146 Triangle workers, mostly women, were burned or crushed to death. There was a memorial parade down Broadway, and 100,000 marched.

There were more fires. And accidents. And sickness. In the year 1904, 27,000 workers were killed on the job, in manufacturing, transport, and agriculture. In one year, 50,000 accidents took place in New York factories alone. Hat and cap makers were getting respiratory diseases, quarrymen were inhaling deadly chemicals, lithographic printers were getting arsenic poisoning. A New York State Factory Investigation Commission reported in 1912:

> Sadie is an intelligent, neat, clean girl, who has worked from the time she got her working papers in embroidery factories. . . . In her work she was accustomed to use a white powder (chalk or talcum was usual) which was brushed over the perforated designs and thus transferred to the cloth. The design was easily brushed off when made of chalk or of talcum. . . . Her last employer therefore commenced using white lead powder, mixed with rosin, which cheapened the work as the

powder could not be rubbed off and necessitate restamping.

None of the girls knew of the change in powder, nor of the danger in its use. . . .

Sadie had been a very strong, healthy girl, good appetite and color; she began to be unable to eat. . . . Her hands and feet swelled, she lost the use of one hand, her teeth and gums were blue. When she finally had to stop work, after being treated for months for stomach trouble, her physician advised her to go to a hospital. There the examination revealed the fact that she had lead poisoning. . . .

According to a report of the Commission on Industrial Relations, in 1914, 35,000 workers were killed in industrial accidents and 700,000 injured. That year the income of forty-four families making $1 million or more equaled the total income of 100,000 families earning $500 a year. The record shows an exchange between Commissioner Harris Weinstock of the Commission on Industrial Relations and President John Osgood, head of a Colorado coal company controlled by the Rockefellers:

WEINSTOCK: If a worker loses his life, are his dependents compensated in any way?

OSGOOD: Not necessarily. In some cases they are and in some cases not.

WEINSTOCK: If he is crippled for life is there any compensation?

OSGOOD: No sir, there is none. . . .

WEINSTOCK: Then the whole burden is thrown directly upon their shoulders.

OSGOOD: Yes, sir.

WEINSTOCK: The industry bears none of it?

OSGOOD: No, the industry bears none of it.

Unionization was growing. Shortly after the turn of the century there were 2 million members of labor unions (one in fourteen workers), 80 percent of them in the American Federation of Labor. The AFL was an exclusive union—almost all male, almost all white, almost all skilled workers. Although the number of women workers kept growing—it doubled from 4 million in 1890 to 8 million in 1910, and women were one-fifth of the labor force—only one in a hundred belonged to a union.

Black workers in 1910 made one-third of the earnings of white workers. Although Samuel Gompers, head of the AFL, would make speeches about its belief in equal opportunity, the Negro was excluded from most AFL unions. Gompers kept saying he did not want to interfere with the "internal affairs" of the South: "I regard the race problem as one with which you people of the Southland will have to deal; without the interference, too, of meddlers from the outside."

In the reality of struggle, rank-and-file workers overcame these separations from time to time. Foner quotes Mary McDowell's account of the formation of a women's union in the Chicago stockyards:

It was a dramatic occasion on that evening, when an Irish girl at the door called out—"A Colored sister asks admission. What shall I do with her?" And the answer came from the Irish young woman in the chair—"Admit her, of course, and let all of you give her a hearty welcome!"

In New Orleans in 1907 a general strike on the levees, involving ten thousand workers (longshoremen, teamsters, freight handlers), black and white, lasted twenty days. The head of the Negro longshoremen, E. S. Swan, said:

The whites and Negroes were never before so strongly cemented in a common bond and in my 39 years of experience of the levee, I never saw such solidarity. In all the previous strikes the Negro was used against the white man but that condition is now past and both races are standing together for their common interests. . . .

These were exceptions. In general, the Negro was kept out of the trade union movement. W. E. B. Du Bois wrote in 1913: "The net result of all this has been to convince the American

Negro that his greatest enemy is not the employer who robs him, but his fellow white workingman."

Racism was practical for the AFL. The exclusion of women and foreigners was also practical. These were mostly unskilled workers, and the AFL, confined mostly to skilled workers, was based on the philosophy of "business unionism" (in fact, the chief official of each AFL union was called the "business agent"), trying to match the monopoly of production by the employer with a monopoly of workers by the union. In this way it won better conditions for some workers, and left most workers out.

AFL officials drew large salaries, hobnobbed with employers, even moved in high society. A press dispatch from Atlantic City, New Jersey, the fashionable seaside resort, in the summer of 1910:

> Engaged in a game of bathing suit baseball with President Sam Gompers, Secretary Frank Morrison and other leaders of the A.F. of L. on the beach this morning, John Mitchell, former head of the mine workers' union, lost a $1000 diamond ring presented to him by his admirers after the settlement of the big Pennsylvania coal strike. Capt. George Berke, a veteran life guard, found the ring, whereupon Mitchell peeled a hundred dollar bill from a roll he carried in his pocket and handed it to the captain as a reward for his find.

The well-paid leaders of the AFL were protected from criticism by tightly controlled meetings and by "goon" squads—hired toughs originally used against strikebreakers but after a while used to intimidate and beat up opponents inside the union.

In this situation—terrible conditions of labor, exclusivity in union organization—working people wanting radical change, seeing the root of misery in the capitalist system, moved toward a new kind of labor union. One morning in June 1905, there met in a hall in Chicago a convention of two hundred socialists, anarchists, and radical trade unionists from all over the United States. They were forming the I. W. W.—the Industrial Workers of the World. Big Bill Haywood, a leader of the Western Federation of

Miners, recalled in his autobiography that he picked up a piece of board that lay on the platform and used it for a gavel to open the convention:

> Fellow workers. . . . This is the Continental Congress of the working-class. We are here to confederate the workers of this country into a working-class movement that shall have for its purpose the emancipation of the working-class from the slave bondage of capitalism. . . . The aims and objects of this organization shall be to put the working-class in possession of the economic power, the means of life, in control of the machinery of production and distribution, without regard to the capitalist masters.

On the speakers' platform with Haywood were Eugene Debs, leader of the Socialist party, and Mother Mary Jones, a seventy-five-year-old white-haired woman who was an organizer for the United Mine Workers of America. The convention drew up a constitution, whose preamble said:

> The working class and the employing class have nothing in common. There can be no peace so long as hunger and want are found among millions of working people and the few, who make up the employing class, have all the good things of life.
>
> Between these two classes a struggle must go on until all the toilers come together on the political as well as on the industrial field, and take and hold that which they produce by their labor, through an economic organization of the working class without affiliation with any political party. . . .

One of the IWW pamphlets explained why it broke with the AFL idea of craft unions:

> The directory of unions of Chicago shows in 1903 a total of 56 different unions in the packing houses, divided up still more in 14 different national trades unions of the American Federation of Labor.

What a horrible example of an army divided against itself in the face of a strong combination of employers. . . .

The IWW (or "Wobblies," as they came to be called, for reasons not really clear) aimed at organizing all workers in any industry into "One Big Union," undivided by sex, race, or skills. They argued against making contracts with the employer, because this had so often prevented workers from striking on their own, or in sympathy with other strikers, and thus turned union people into strikebreakers. Negotiations by leaders for contracts replaced continuous struggle by the rank and file, the Wobblies believed.

They spoke of "direct action":

Direct action means industrial action directly by, for, and of the workers themselves, without the treacherous aid of labor misleaders or scheming politicians. A strike that is initiated, controlled, and settled by the workers directly affected is direct action. . . . Direct action is industrial democracy.

One IWW pamphlet said: "Shall I tell you what direct action means? The worker on the job shall tell the boss when and where he shall work, how long and for what wages and under what conditions."

The IWW people were militant, courageous. Despite a reputation given them by the press, they did not believe in initiating violence, but did fight back when attacked. In McKees Rocks, Pennsylvania, they led a strike of six thousand workers in 1909 against an affiliate of the U.S. Steel Company, defied the state troopers, and battled with them. They promised to take a trooper's life for every worker killed (in one gun battle four strikers and three troopers were killed), and managed to keep picketing the factories until the strike was won.

The IWW saw beyond strikes:

Strikes are mere incidents in the class war; they are tests of strength, periodical drills in the course of which the workers train themselves for concerted action. This training is most necessary to prepare the masses for the final "catastrophe," the general strike which will complete the expropriation of the employers.

The idea of anarcho-syndicalism was developing strongly in Spain and Italy and France at this time—that the workers would take power, not by seizing the state machinery in an armed rebellion, but by bringing the economic system to a halt in a general strike, then taking it over to use for the good of all. IWW organizer Joseph Ettor said:

> If the workers of the world want to win, all they have to do is recognize their own solidarity. They have nothing to do but fold their arms and the world will stop. The workers are more powerful with their hands in their pockets than all the property of the capitalists. . . .

It was an immensely powerful idea. In the ten exciting years after its birth, the IWW became a threat to the capitalist class, exactly when capitalist growth was enormous and profits huge. The IWW never had more than five to ten thousand enrolled members at any one time; people came and went, and perhaps a hundred thousand were members at one time or another. But their energy, their persistence, their inspiration to others, their ability to mobilize thousands at one place, one time, made them an influence on the country far beyond their numbers. They traveled everywhere (many were unemployed or migrant workers); they organized, wrote, spoke, sang, spread their message and their spirit.

They were attacked with all the weapons the system could put together: the newspapers, the courts, the police, the army, mob violence. Local authorities passed laws to stop them from speaking; the IWW defied these laws. In Missoula, Montana, a lumber and mining area, hundreds of Wobblies arrived by boxcar after some had been prevented from speaking. They were arrested one after another until they clogged the jails and the courts, and finally forced the town to repeal its antispeech ordinance.

In Spokane, Washington, in 1909, an ordinance was passed to stop street meetings, and an IWW organizer who insisted on speaking was arrested. Thousands of Wobblies marched into the center of town to speak. One by one they spoke and were arrested, until six hundred were in jail. Jail conditions were brutal, and several men died in their cells, but the IWW won the right to speak.

In Fresno, California, in 1911, there was another free speech fight. The San Francisco *Call* commented:

> It is one of those strange situations which crop up suddenly and are hard to understand. Some thousands of men, whose business it is to work with their hands, tramping and stealing rides, suffering hardships and facing dangers—to get into jail. . . .

In jail they sang, they shouted, they made speeches through the bars to groups that gathered outside the prison. As Joyce Kornbluh reports in her remarkable collection of IWW documents, *Rebel Voices*:

> They took turns lecturing about the class struggle and leading the singing of Wobbly songs. When they refused to stop, the jailor sent for fire department trucks and ordered the fire hoses turned full force on the prisoners. The men used their mattresses as shields, and quiet was only restored when the icy water reached knee-high in the cells.

When city officials heard that thousands more were planning to come into town, they lifted the ban on street speaking and released the prisoners in small groups.

That same year in Aberdeen, Washington, once again laws against free speech, arrests, prison, and, unexpectedly, victory. One of the men arrested, "Stumpy" Payne, a carpenter, farm hand, editor of an IWW newspaper, wrote about the experience:

Here they were, eighteen men in the vigor of life, most of whom came long distances through snow and hostile towns by beating their way, penniless and hungry, into a place where a jail sentence was the gentlest treatment that could be expected, and where many had already been driven into the swamps and beaten nearly to death. . . . Yet here they were, laughing with boyish glee at tragic things that to them were jokes. . . .

But what was the motive behind the actions of these men? . . . Why were they here? Is the call of Brotherhood in the human race greater than any fear or discomfort, despite the efforts of the masters of life for six thousand years to root out that call of Brotherhood from our minds?

In San Diego, Jack White, a Wobbly arrested in a free-speech fight in 1912, sentenced to six months in the county jail on a bread and water diet, was asked if he had anything to say to the court. A stenographer recorded what he said:

The prosecuting attorney, in his plea to the jury, accused me of saying on a public platform at a public meeting, "To hell with the courts, we know what justice is." He told a great truth when he lied, for if he had searched the innermost recesses of my mind he could have found that thought, never expressed by me before, but which I express now, "To hell with your courts, I know what justice is," for I have sat in your court room day after day and have seen members of my class pass before this, the so-called bar of justice. I have seen you, Judge Sloane, and others of your kind, send them to prison because they dared to infringe upon the sacred rights of property. You have become blind and deaf to the rights of man to pursue life and happiness, and you have crushed those rights so that the sacred right of property shall be preserved. Then you tell me to respect the law. I do not. I did violate the law, as I will violate every one of your laws and still come before you and say "To hell with the courts." . . .

The prosecutor lied, but I will accept his lie as a truth and say again so that you, Judge Sloane, may not be mistaken as to my attitude, "To hell with your courts, I know what justice is."

There were also beatings, tarrings and featherings, defeats. One IWW member, John Stone, tells of being released from the jail at San Diego at midnight with another IWW man and forced into an automobile:

We were taken out of the city, about twenty miles, where the machine stopped. . . . a man in the rear struck me with a blackjack several times on the head and shoulders; the other man then struck me on the mouth with his fist. The men in the rear then sprang around and kicked me in the stomach. I then started to run away; and heard a bullet go past me. I stopped. . . . In the morning I examined Joe Marko's condition and found that the back of his head had been split open.

In 1916, in Everett, Washington, a boatload of Wobblies was fired on by two hundred armed vigilantes gathered by the sheriff, and five Wobblies were shot to death, thirty-one wounded. Two of the vigilantes were killed, nineteen wounded. The following year—the year the United States entered World War I—vigilantes in Montana seized IWW organizer Frank Little, tortured him, and hanged him, leaving his body dangling from a railroad trestle.

Joe Hill, an IWW organizer, wrote dozens of songs—biting, funny, class-conscious, inspiring—that appeared in IWW publications and in its *Little Red Song Book*. He became a legend in his time and after. His song "The Preacher and the Slave" had a favorite IWW target, the church:

Long-haired preachers come out every night,
Try to tell you what's wrong and what's right;
But when asked how 'bout something to eat
They will answer with voices so sweet:

You will eat, bye and bye,
In that glorious land above the sky;
Work and pray, live on hay,
You'll get pie in the sky when you die.

His song "Rebel Girl" was inspired by the strike of women at the textile mills in Lawrence, Massachusetts, and especially by the IWW leader of that strike, Elizabeth Gurley Flynn:

> *There are women of many descriptions*
> *In this queer world, as everyone knows,*
> *Some are living in beautiful mansions,*
> *And are wearing the finest of clothes.*
> *There are blue-blooded queens and princesses,*
> *Who have charms made of diamonds and pearl,*
> *But the only and Thoroughbred Lady*
> *Is the Rebel Girl.*

In November 1915, Joe Hill was accused of killing a grocer in Salt Lake City, Utah, in a robbery. There was no direct evidence presented to the court that he had committed the murder, but there were enough pieces of evidence to persuade a jury to find him guilty. The case became known throughout the world, and ten thousand letters went to the governor in protest, but with machine guns guarding the entrance to the prison, Joe Hill was executed by a firing squad. He had written Bill Haywood just before this: "Don't waste any time in mourning. Organize."

The IWW became involved in a set of dramatic events in Lawrence, Massachusetts, in the year 1912, where the American Woolen Company owned four mills. The work force were immigrant families—Portuguese, French-Canadian, English, Irish, Russian, Italian, Syrian, Lithuanian, German, Polish, Belgian—who lived in crowded, flammable wooden tenements. The average wage was $8.76 a week. A woman physician in Lawrence, Dr. Elizabeth Shapleigh, wrote:

> A considerable number of the boys and girls die within the first two or three years after beginning work . . . thirty-six out of every 100 of all the men and women who work in the mill die before or by the time they are twenty-five years of age.

It was in January, midwinter, when pay envelopes distributed to weavers at one of the mills—Polish women—showed that their wages, already too low to feed their families, had been reduced. They stopped their looms and walked out of the mill. The next day, five thousand workers at another mill quit work, marched to still another mill, rushed the gates, shut off the power to the looms, and called on the other workers to leave. Soon ten thousand workers were on strike.

A telegram went to Joseph Ettor, a twenty-six-year-old Italian, an IWW leader in New York, to come to Lawrence to help conduct the strike. He came. A committee of fifty was set up, representing every nationality among the workers, to make the important decisions. Less than a thousand millworkers belonged to the IWW, but the AFL had ignored the unskilled workers, and so they turned to the IWW leadership in the strike.

The IWW organized mass meetings and parades. The strikers had to supply food and fuel for 50,000 people (the entire population of Lawrence was 86,000); soup kitchens were set up, and money began arriving from all over the country—from trade unions, IWW locals, socialist groups, individuals.

The mayor called out the local militia; the governor ordered out the state police. A parade of strikers was attacked by police a few weeks after the strike began. This led to rioting all that day. In the evening, a striker, Anna LoPizzo, was shot and killed. Witnesses said a policeman did it, but the authorities arrested Joseph Ettor and another IWW organizer who had come to Lawrence, a poet named Arturo Giovanitti. Neither was at the scene of the shooting, but the charge was that "Joseph Ettor and Arturo Giovanitti did incite, procure, and counsel or command the said person whose name is not known to commit the said murder. . . ."

With Ettor, head of the strike committee, in jail, Big Bill Haywood was called in to replace him; other IWW organizers, including Elizabeth Gurley Flynn, came into Lawrence. Now there were twenty-two companies of militia and two troops of cavalry in the city. Martial law was declared, and citizens were forbidden to talk on the street. Thirty-six strikers were arrested, many sentenced to a year in prison. On Tuesday, January 30, a young Syrian striker, John Ramy, was bayoneted to death. But the strikers were still out, and the mills were not working. Ettor said: "Bayonets cannot weave cloth."

In February, the strikers began mass picketing, seven thousand to ten thousand pickets in an endless chain, marching through the mill districts, with white armbands: "Don't be a scab." But their food was running out and the children were hungry. It was proposed by the New York *Call*, a Socialist newspaper, that the children of strikers be sent to sympathetic families in other cities to take care of them while the strike lasted. This had been done by strikers in Europe, never in the United States—but in three days, the *Call* got four hundred letters offering to take children. The IWW and the Socialist party began to organize the children's exodus, taking applications from families who wanted them, arranging medical exams for the youngsters.

On February 10, over a hundred children, aged four to fourteen, left Lawrence for New York City. They were greeted at Grand Central Station by five thousand Italian Socialists singing the "Marseillaise" and the "Internationale." The following week, another hundred children came to New York, and thirty-five to Barre, Vermont. It was becoming clear: if the children were taken care of, the strikers could stay out, for their spirit was high. The city officials in Lawrence, citing a statute on child neglect, said no more children would be permitted to leave Lawrence.

Despite the city edict, a group of forty children assembled on February 24 to go to Philadelphia. The railroad station was filled with police, and the scene that followed was described to Congressmen by a member of the Women's Committee of Philadelphia:

When the time approached to depart, the children arranged in a long line, two by two, in orderly procession, with their parents near at hand, were about to make their way to the train when the police closed in on us with their clubs, beating right and left, with no thought of children, who were in the most desperate danger of being trampled to death. The mothers and children were thus hurled in a mass and bodily dragged to a military truck, and even then clubbed, irrespective of the cries of the panic-stricken women and children. . . .

A week after that, women returning from a meeting were surrounded by police and clubbed; one pregnant woman was carried unconscious to a hospital and gave birth to a dead child.

Still, the strikers held out. "They are always marching and singing," reporter Mary Heaton Vorse wrote. "The tired, gray crowds ebbing and flowing perpetually into the mills had waked and opened their mouths to sing."

The American Woolen Company decided to give in. It offered raises of 5 to 11 percent (the strikers insisted that the largest increases go to the lowest-paid), time and a quarter for overtime, and no discrimination against those who had struck. On March 14, 1912, ten thousand strikers gathered on the Lawrence Common and, with Bill Haywood presiding, voted to end the strike.

Ettor and Giovanitti went on trial. Support for them had been mounting all over the country. There were parades in New York and Boston; on September 30, fifteen thousand Lawrence workers struck for twenty-four hours to show their support for the two men. After that, two thousand of the most active strikers were fired, but the IWW threatened to call another strike, and they were put back. A jury found Ettor and Giovanitti not guilty, and that afternoon, ten thousand people assembled in Lawrence to celebrate.

The IWW took its slogan "One Big Union" seriously. Women, foreigners, black workers, the lowliest and most unskilled of workers, were included when a factory or mine was organized. When the Brotherhood of Timber Workers organized in Louisiana and invited Bill Haywood to speak to them in 1912 (shortly after the Lawrence victory), he expressed surprise that no Negroes were at the meeting. He was told it was against the law to have interracial meetings in Louisiana. Haywood told the convention:

> You work in the same mills together. Sometimes a black man and a white man chop down the same tree together. You are meeting in convention now to discuss the conditions under which you labor. . . . Why not be sensible about this and call the Negroes into the Convention? If it is against the law, this is one time when the law should be broken.

Negroes were invited into the convention, which then voted to affiliate with the IWW.

In 1900 there were 500,000 women office workers—in 1870 there had been 19,000. Women were switchboard operators, store workers, nurses. Half a million were teachers. The teachers formed a Teachers League that fought against the automatic firing of women who became pregnant. The following "Rules for Female Teachers" were posted by the school board of one town in Massachusetts:

1. Do not get married.
2. Do not leave town at any time without permission of the school board.
3. Do not keep company with men.
4. Be home between the hours of 8 P.M. and 6 A.M.
5. Do not loiter downtown in ice cream stores.
6. Do not smoke.
7. Do not get into a carriage with any man except your father or brother.
8. Do not dress in bright colors.
9. Do not dye your hair.
10. Do not wear any dress more than two inches above the ankle.

The conditions of women working in a Milwaukee brewery were described by Mother Mary Jones, who worked there briefly in 1910 (she was close to eighty at this time):

Condemned to slave daily in the wash-room in wet shoes and wet clothes, surrounded with foul-mouthed, brutal foremen . . . the poor girls work in the vile smell of sour beer, lifting cases of empty and full bottles weighing from 100 to 150 pounds. . . . Rheumatism is one of the chronic ailments and is closely followed by consumption. . . . The foreman even regulates the time the girls may stay in the toilet room. . . . Many of the girls have no home nor parents and are forced to feed and clothe and shelter themselves . . . on $3.00 a week. . . .

In the laundries, women organized. In 1909, the *Handbook* of the Women's Trade Union Industrial League wrote about women in steam laundries:

How would you like to iron a shirt a minute? Think of standing at a mangle just above the washroom with the hot steam pouring up through the floor for 10, 12, 14 and sometimes 17 hours a day! Sometimes the floors are made of cement and then it seems as though one were standing on hot coals, and the workers are dripping with perspiration. . . . They are . . . breathing air laden with particles of soda, ammonia, and other chemicals! The Laundry Workers Union . . . in one city reduced this long day to 9 hours, and has increased the wages 50 percent. . . .

Labor struggles could make things better, but the country's resources remained in the hands of powerful corporations whose motive was profit, whose power commanded the government of the United States. There was an idea in the air, becoming clearer and stronger, an idea not just in the theories of Karl Marx but in the dreams of writers and artists through the ages: that people might cooperatively use the treasures of the earth to make life better for everyone, not just a few.

Around the turn of the century, strike struggles were multiplying—in the 1890s there had been about a thousand strikes a year; by 1904 there were four thousand strikes a year. Law and military force again and again took the side of the rich. It was a time when hundreds of thousands of Americans began to think of socialism.

Debs wrote in 1904, three years after the formation of the Socialist party:

> The "pure and simple" trades union of the past does not answer the requirements of today. . . .
>
> The attempt of each trade to maintain its own independence separately and apart from others results in increasing jurisdictional entanglements, fruitful of dissension, strife and ultimate disruption. . . .
>
> The members of a trades union should be taught . . . that the labor movement means more, infinitely more, than a paltry increase in wages and the strike necessary to secure it; that while it engages to do all that possibly can be done to better the working conditions of its members, its higher object is to overthrow the capitalist system of private ownership of the tools of labor, abolish wage-slavery and achieve the freedom of the whole working class and, in fact, of all mankind. . . .

What Debs accomplished was not in theory, or analysis, but in expressing eloquently, passionately, what people were feeling. The writer Heywood Broun once quoted a fellow Socialist speaking of Debs: "That old man with the burning eyes actually believes that there can be such a thing as the brotherhood of man. And that's not the funniest part of it. As long as he's around I believe it myself."

Eugene Debs had become a Socialist while in jail in the Pullman strike. Now he was the spokesman of a party that made him its presidential candidate five times. The party at one time had 100,000 members, and 1,200 office holders in 340 municipalities. Its main newspaper, *Appeal to Reason*, for which Debs wrote, had half a million subscribers, and there were many other Socialist newspapers around the country, so that, all together, perhaps a million people read the Socialist press.

Socialism moved out of the small circles of city immigrants—Jewish and German socialists speaking their own languages—and became American. The strongest Socialist state organization was in Oklahoma, which in 1914 had twelve thousand dues-paying members (more than New York State), and elected over a hundred Socialists to local office, including six to the Oklahoma state legislature. There were fifty-five weekly Socialist newspapers in Oklahoma, Texas, Louisiana, Arkansas, and summer encampments that drew thousands of people.

James Green describes these Southwest radicals, in his book *Grass-Roots Socialism*, as "indebted homesteaders, migratory tenant farmers, coal miners and railroad workers, 'redbone' lumberjacks from the piney woods, preachers and schoolteachers from the sunbaked prairies . . . village artisans and atheists . . . the unknown people who created the strongest regional Socialist movement in United States history." Green continues:

> The Socialist movement . . . was painstakingly organized by scores of former Populists, militant miners, and blacklisted railroad workers, who were assisted by a remarkable cadre of professional agitators and educators and inspired by occasional visits from national figures like Eugene V. Debs and Mother Jones. . . . This core of organizers grew to include indigenous dissenters. . . . a much larger group of amateur agitators who canvassed the region selling newspapers, forming reading groups, organizing locals, and making soapbox speeches.

There was almost a religious fervor to the movement, as in the eloquence of Debs. In 1906, after the imprisonment in Idaho of Bill Haywood and two other officers of the Western Federation of Miners on an apparently faked murder charge, Debs wrote a flaming article in the *Appeal to Reason:*

> Murder has been plotted and is about to be executed in the name and under the forms of law. . . .
> It is a foul plot; a damnable conspiracy; a hellish outrage. . . .
> If they attempt to murder Moyer, Haywood and their brothers, a million revolutionists, at least, will meet them with guns. . . .
> Capitalist courts never have done, and never will do, anything for the working class. . . .

> A special revolutionary convention of the proletariat . . . would be in order, and, if extreme measures are required, a general strike could be ordered and industry paralyzed as a preliminary to a general uprising.
>
> If the plutocrats begin the program, we will end it.

Theodore Roosevelt, after reading this, sent a copy to his Attorney General, W. H. Moody, with a note: "Is it possible to proceed against Debs and the proprietor of this paper criminally?"

As the Socialists became more successful at the polls (Debs got 900,000 votes in 1912, double what he had in 1908), and more concerned with increasing that appeal, they became more critical of IWW tactics of "sabotage" and "violence," and in 1913 removed Bill Haywood from the Socialist Party Executive Committee, claiming he advocated violence (although some of Debs's writings were far more inflammatory).

Women were active in the socialist movement, more as rank-and-file workers than as leaders—and, sometimes, as sharp critics of socialist policy. Helen Keller, for instance, the gifted blind-mute-deaf woman with her extraordinary social vision, commented on the expulsion of Bill Haywood in a letter to the New York *Call*:

> It is with the deepest regret that I have read the attacks upon Comrade Haywood . . . such an ignoble strife between two factions which should be one, and that, too, at a most critical period in the struggle of the proletariat. . . .
>
> What? Are we to put difference of party tactics before the desperate needs of the workers? . . . While countless women and children are breaking their hearts and ruining their bodies in long days of toil, we are fighting one another. Shame upon us!

Only 3 percent of the Socialist party's members were women in 1904. At the national convention that year, there were only eight women delegates. But in a few years, local socialist women's organizations, and a national magazine, *Socialist Woman*, began bringing more women into the party, so that by 1913, 15 percent of the membership was women. The editor of *Socialist Woman*, Josephine Conger-Kaneko, insisted on the importance of separate groups for women:

> In the separate organization the most unsophisticated little woman may soon learn to preside over a meeting, to make motions, and to defend her stand with a little "speech". After a year or two of this sort of practice she is ready to work with the men. And there is a mighty difference between working *with* the men, and simply sitting in obedient reverence under the shadow of their aggressive power.

Socialist women were active in the feminist movement of the early 1990s. According to Kate Richards O'Hare, the Socialist leader from Oklahoma, New York women socialists were superbly organized. During the 1915 campaign in New York for a referendum on women's suffrage, in one day at the climax of the campaign, they distributed 60,000 English leaflets, 50,000 Yiddish leaflets, sold 2,500 one-cent books and 1,500 five-cent books, put up 40,000 stickers, and held 100 meetings.

But were there problems of women that went beyond politics and economics, that would not be solved automatically by a socialist system? Once the economic base of sexual oppression was corrected, would equality follow? Battling for the vote, or for anything less than revolutionary change—was that pointless? The argument became sharper as the women's movement of the early twentieth century grew, as women spoke out more, organized, protested, paraded—for the vote, and for recognition as equals in every sphere, including sexual relations and marriage.

Charlotte Perkins Gilman, whose writing emphasized the crucial question of economic equality between the sexes, wrote a poem called "The Socialist and the Suffragist," ending with:

> "A lifted world lifts women up,"
> The Socialist explained.

"You cannot lift the world at all
While half of it is kept so small,"
the Suffragist maintained.
The world awoke, and tartly spoke:
"Your work is all the same;
Work together or work apart,
Work, each of you, with all your heart—
Just get into the game!"

When Susan Anthony, at eighty, went to hear Eugene Debs speak (twenty-five years before, he had gone to hear her speak, and they had not met since then), they clasped hands warmly, then had a brief exchange. She said, laughing: "Give us suffrage, and we'll give you socialism." Debs replied: "Give us socialism and we'll give you suffrage."

There were women who insisted on uniting the two aims of socialism and feminism, like Crystal Eastman, who imagined new ways of men and women living together and retaining their independence, different from traditional marriage. She was a socialist, but wrote once that a woman "knows that the whole of woman's slavery is not summed up in the profit system, nor her complete emancipation assured by the downfall of capitalism."

In the first fifteen years of the twentieth century, there were more women in the labor force, more with experience in labor struggles. Some middle-class women, conscious of women's oppression and wanting to do something, were going to college and becoming aware of themselves as not just housewives. The historian William Chafe writes (*Women and Equality*):

Female college students were infused with a self-conscious sense of mission and a passionate commitment to improve the world. They became doctors, college professors, settlement house workers, business women, lawyers, and architects. Spirited by an intense sense of purpose as well as camaraderie, they set a remarkable record of accomplishment in the face of overwhelming odds. Jane Addams, Grace and Edith Abbott, Alice Hamilton, Julia Lathrop, Florence

Kelley—all came out of this pioneering generation and set the agenda of social reform for the first two decades of the 20th century.

They were defying the culture of mass magazines, which were spreading the message of woman as companion, wife, home-maker. Some of these feminists married; some did not. All struggled with the problem of relations with men, like Margaret Sanger, pioneer of birth control education, who suffered a nervous breakdown inside an apparently happy but confining marriage; she had to leave husband and children to make a career for herself and feel whole again. Sanger had written in *Woman and the New Race*: "No woman can call herself free who does not own and control her own body. No woman can call herself free until she can choose conscientiously whether she will or will not be a mother."

It was a complicated problem. Kate Richards O'Hare, for example, believed in the home, but thought socialism would make that better. When she ran for Congress in 1910 in Kansas City she said: "I long for domestic life, home and children with every fiber of my being. . . . Socialism is needed to restore the home."

On the other hand, Elizabeth Gurley Flynn wrote in her auto-biography, *Rebel Girl*:

A domestic life and possibly a large family had no attraction for me. . . . I wanted to speak and write, to travel, to meet people, to see places, to organize for the I.W.W. I saw no reason why I, as a woman, should give up my work for this. . . .

While many women in this time were radicals, socialists, anarchists, an even larger number were involved in the campaign for suffrage, and the mass support for feminism came from them. Veterans of trade union struggles joined the suffrage movement, like Rose Schneiderman of the Garment Workers. At a Cooper Union meeting in New York, she replied to a politician who said that women, given the vote, would lose their femininity:

Women in the laundries . . . stand for thirteen or fourteen hours in the terrible steam and heat with their hands in hot starch. Surely these women won't lose any more of their beauty and charm by putting a ballot in a ballot box once a year than they are likely to lose standing in foundries or laundries all year round.

Every spring in New York, the parades for women's suffrage kept growing. In 1912, a news report:

All along Fifth Avenue from Washington Square, where the parade formed, to 57th Street, where it disbanded, were gathered thousands of men and women of New York. They blocked every cross street on the line of march. Many were inclined to laugh and jeer, but none did. The sight of the impressive column of women striding five abreast up the middle of the street stifled all thought of ridicule. . . . women doctors, women lawyers . . . women architects, women artists, actresses and sculptors; women waitresses, domestics; a huge division of industrial workers . . . all marched with an intensity and purpose that astonished the crowds that lined the streets.

From Washington, in the spring of 1913, came a *New York Times* report:

In a woman's suffrage demonstration to-day the capital saw the greatest parade of women in its history. . . . In the parade over 5000 women passed down Pennsylvania Avenue. . . . It was an astonishing demonstration. It was estimated . . . that 500,000 persons watched the women march for their cause.

Some women radicals were skeptical. Emma Goldman, the anarchist and feminist, spoke her mind forcefully, as always, on the subject of women's suffrage:

Our modern fetish is universal suffrage. . . . The women of Australia and New Zealand can vote, and help make the laws. Are the labor conditions better there? . . .

The history of the political activities of man proves that they have given him absolutely nothing that he could not have achieved in a more direct, less costly, and more lasting manner. As a matter of fact, every inch of ground he has gained has been through a constant fight, a ceaseless struggle for self-assertion, and not through suffrage. There is no reason whatever to assume that woman, in her climb to emancipation, has been, or will be, helped by the ballot. . . .

Her development, her freedom, her independence, must come from and through herself. First, by asserting herself as a personality. Second, by refusing the right to anyone over her body; by refusing to bear children, unless she wants them; by refusing to be a servant to God, the State, society, the husband, the family, etc. by making her life simpler, but deeper and richer. . . . Only that, and not the ballot, will set woman free. . . .

And Helen Keller, writing in 1911 to a suffragist in England:

Our democracy is but a name. We vote? What does that mean? It means that we choose between two bodies of real, though not avowed, autocrats. We choose between Tweedledum and Tweedledee. . . .

You ask for votes for women. What good can votes do when ten-elevenths of the land of Great Britain belongs to 200,000 and only one-eleventh to the rest of the 40,000,000? Have your men with their millions of votes freed themselves from this injustice?

Emma Goldman was not postponing the changing of woman's condition to some future socialist era—she wanted action more direct, more immediate, than the vote. Helen Keller, while not an anarchist, also believed in continuous struggle outside the ballot box. Blind, deaf, she fought with her spirit, her pen. When she became active and openly socialist, the Brooklyn *Eagle*, which had previously treated her as a heroine, wrote that "her mistakes spring out of the manifest limitations of her development." Her response was not accepted by the *Eagle*, but printed in the New York *Call*. She wrote that when once she met the editor of the

Brooklyn *Eagle* he complimented her lavishly. "But now that I have come out for socialism he reminds me and the public that I am blind and deaf and especially liable to error. . . ." She added:

> Oh, ridiculous Brooklyn *Eagle*! What an ungallant bird it is! Socially blind and deaf, it defends an intolerable system, a system that is the cause of much of the physical blindness and deafness which we are trying to prevent. . . . The *Eagle* and I are at war. I hate the system which it represents. . . . When it fights back, let it fight fair. . . . It is not fair fighting or good argument to remind me and others that I cannot see or hear. I can read. I can read all the socialist books I have time for in English, German and French. If the editor of the Brooklyn *Eagle* should read some of them, he might be a wiser man, and make a better newspaper. If I ever contribute to the Socialist movement the book that I sometimes dream of, I know what I shall name it: Industrial Blindness and Social Deafness.

Mother Jones did not seem especially interested in the feminist movement. She was busy organizing textile workers and miners, and organizing their wives and children. One of her many feats was the organization of a children's march to Washington to demand the end of child labor (as the twentieth century opened, 284,000 children between the ages of ten and fifteen worked in mines, mills, factories). She described this:

> In the spring of 1903, I went to Kensington, Pennsylvania, where seventy-five thousand textile workers were on strike. Of this number at least ten thousand were little children. The workers were striking for more pay and shorter hours. Every day little children came into Union Headquarters, some with their hands off, some with the thumb missing, some with their fingers off at the knuckle. They were stooped little things, round shouldered and skinny. . . .
>
>   I asked some of the parents if they would let me have their little boys and girls for a week or ten days, promising to bring them back safe and sound. . . . A man named Sweeny was marshall. . . . A few men and women went with me. . . . The children carried knapsacks

on their backs in which was a knife and fork, a tin cup and plate. . . . One little fellow had a drum and another had a fife. . . . We carried banners that said: . . . "We want time to play. . . .

The children marched through New Jersey and New York and down to Oyster Bay to try to see President Theodore Roosevelt, but he refused to see them. "But our march had done its work. We had drawn the attention of the nation to the crime of child labor."

That same year, children working sixty hours a week in textile mills in Philadelphia went on strike, carrying signs: "WE WANT TO GO TO SCHOOL!" "55 HOURS OR NOTHING!"

One gets a sense of the energy and fire of some of those turn-of-the-century radicals by looking at the police record of Elizabeth Gurley Flynn:

1906–16, Organizer, lecturer for I.W.W.
   1918–24, Organizer, Workers Defense Union
   Arrested in New York, 1906, free-speech case, dismissed; active in Spokane, Washington, free-speech fight, 1909; arrested, Missoula, Montana, 1909, in free-speech fight of I.W.W., Spokane, Washington, free-speech fight of I.W.W., hundreds arrested; in Philadelphia arrested three times, 1911, at strike meetings of Baldwin Locomotive Works; active in Lawrence textile strike, 1912; hotel-workers strike, 1912, New York; Paterson textile strike, 1913; defense work for Ettor-Giovanitti case, 1912; Mesaba Range strike, Minnesota, 1916; Everett IWW case, Spokane, Washington, 1916; Joe Hill defense, 1914. Arrested Duluth, Minnesota, 1917, charged with vagrancy under law passed to stop I.W.W. and pacifist speakers, case dismissed. Indicted in Chicago IWW case, 1917. . . .

Black women faced double oppression. A Negro nurse wrote to a newspaper in 1912:

We poor colored women wage-earners in the South are fighting a terrible battle. . . . On the one hand, we are assailed by black men, who should be our natural protectors; and, whether in the cook kitchen, at the washtub, over the sewing machine, behind the baby carriage, or at the ironing board, we are but little more than pack horses, beasts of burden, slaves! . . .

In this early part of the twentieth century, labeled by generations of white scholars as "the Progressive period," lynchings were reported every week; it was the low point for Negroes, North and South, "the nadir," as Rayford Logan, a black historian, put it. In 1910 there were 10 million Negroes in the United States, and 9 million of them were in the South.

The government of the United States (between 1901 and 1921, the Presidents were Theodore Roosevelt, William Howard Taft, Woodrow Wilson)—whether Republican or Democrat—watched Negroes being lynched, observed murderous riots against blacks in Statesboro, Georgia, Brownsville, Texas, and Atlanta, Georgia, and did nothing.

There were Negroes in the Socialist party, but the Socialist party did not go much out of its way to act on the race question. As Ray Ginger writes of Debs: "When race prejudice was thrust at Debs, he always publicly repudiated it. He always insisted on absolute equality. But he failed to accept the view that special measures were sometimes needed to achieve this equality."

Blacks began to organize: a National Afro-American Council formed in 1903 to protest against lynching, peonage, discrimination, disfranchisement; the National Association of Colored Women, formed around the same time, condemned segregation and lynchings. In Georgia in 1906 there was an Equal Rights Convention, which pointed to 260 Georgia Negroes lynched since 1885. It asked the right to vote, the right to enter the militia, to be on juries. It agreed blacks should work hard. "And at the same time we must agitate, complain, protest and keep protesting against the invasion of our manhood rights. . . ."

W. E. B. Du Bois, teaching in Atlanta, Georgia, in 1905, sent out a letter to Negro leaders throughout the country, calling them to a conference just across the Canadian border from Buffalo, near Niagara Falls. It was the start of the "Niagara Movement."

Du Bois, born in Massachusetts, the first black to receive a Ph.D. degree from Harvard University (1895), had just written and published his poetic, powerful book *The Souls of Black Folk*. Du Bois was a Socialist sympathizer, although only briefly a party member.

One of his associates in calling the Niagara meeting was William Monroe Trotter, a young black man in Boston, of militant views, who edited a weekly newspaper, the *Guardian*. In it he attacked the moderate ideas of Booker T. Washington. When, in the summer of 1903, Washington spoke to an audience of two thousand at a Boston church, Trotter and his supporters prepared nine provocative questions, which caused a commotion and led to fistfights. Trotter and a friend were arrested. This may have added to the spirit of indignation which led Du Bois to spearhead the Niagara meeting. The tone of the Niagara group was strong:

> We refuse to allow the impression to remain that the Negro-American assents to inferiority, is submissive under oppression and apologetic before insults. Through helplessness we may submit, but the voice of protest of ten million Americans must never cease to assail the ears of their fellows so long as America is unjust.

A race riot in Springfield, Illinois, prompted the formation of the National Association for the Advancement of Colored People in 1910. Whites dominated the leadership of the new organization; Du Bois was the only black officer. He was also the first editor of the NAACP periodical *The Crisis*. The NAACP concentrated on legal action and education, but Du Bois represented in it that spirit which was embodied in the Niagara movement's declaration: "Persistent manly agitation is the way to liberty."

What was clear in this period to blacks, to feminists, to labor organizers and socialists, was that they could not count on the national government. True, this was the "Progressive Period," the start of the Age of Reform; but it was a reluctant reform, aimed at quieting the popular risings, not making fundamental changes.

What gave it the name "Progressive" was that new laws were passed. Under Theodore Roosevelt, there was the Meat Inspection Act, the Hepburn Act to regulate railroads and pipelines, a Pure Food and Drug Act. Under Taft, the Mann-Elkins Act put telephone and telegraph systems under the regulation of the Interstate Commerce Commission. In Woodrow Wilson's presidency, the Federal Trade Commission was introduced to control the growth of monopolies, and the Federal Reserve Act to regulate the country's money and banking system. Under Taft were proposed the Sixteenth Amendment to the Constitution, allowing a graduated income tax, and the Seventeenth Amendment, providing for the election of Senators directly by popular vote instead of by the state legislatures, as the original Constitution provided. Also at this time, a number of states passed laws regulating wages and hours, providing for safety inspection of factories and compensation for injured workmen.

It was a time of public investigations aimed at soothing protest. In 1913 the Pujo Committee of Congress studied the concentration of power in the banking industry, and the Commission on Industrial Relations of the Senate held hearings on labor-management conflict.

Undoubtedly, ordinary people benefited to some extent from these changes. The system was rich, productive, complex; it could give enough of a share of its riches to enough of the working class to create a protective shield between the bottom and the top of the society. A study of immigrants in New York between 1905 and 1915 finds that 32 percent of Italians and Jews rose out of the manual class to higher levels (although not to *much* higher levels). But it was also true that many Italian immigrants did not find the opportunities inviting enough for them to stay. In one four-year period, seventy-three Italians left New York for every one hundred that arrived. Still, enough Italians became construction workers, enough Jews became businessmen and professionals, to create a middle-class cushion for class conflict.

Fundamental conditions did not change, however, for the vast majority of tenant farmers, factory workers, slum dwellers, miners, farm laborers, working men and women, black and white. Robert Wiebe sees in the Progressive movement an attempt by the system to adjust to changing conditions in order to achieve more stability. "Through rules with impersonal sanctions, it sought continuity and predictability in a world of endless change. It assigned far greater power to government . . . and it encouraged the centralization of authority." Harold Faulkner concluded that this new emphasis on strong government was for the benefit of "the most powerful economic groups."

Gabriel Kolko calls it the emergence of "political capitalism," where the businessmen took firmer control of the political system because the private economy was not efficient enough to forestall protest from below. The businessmen, Kolko says, were not opposed to the new reforms; they initiated them, pushed them, to stabilize the capitalist system in a time of uncertainty and trouble.

For instance, Theodore Roosevelt made a reputation for himself as a "trust-buster" (although his successor, Taft, a "conservative," while Roosevelt was a "Progressive," launched more antitrust suits than did Roosevelt). In fact, as Wiebe points out, two of J. P. Morgan's men—Elbert Gary, chairman of U.S. Steel, and George Perkins, who would later become a campaigner for Roosevelt—"arranged a general understanding with Roosevelt by which . . . they would cooperate in any investigation by the Bureau of Corporations in return for a guarantee of their companies' legality." They would do this through private negotiations with the President. "A gentleman's agreement between reasonable people," Wiebe says, with a bit of sarcasm.

The panic of 1907, as well as the growing strength of the Socialists, Wobblies, and trade unions, speeded the process of reform. According to Wiebe: "Around 1908 a qualitative shift in outlook occurred among large numbers of these men of authority. . . ." The emphasis was now on "enticements and compromises." It continued with Wilson, and "a great many reform-minded citizens indulged the illusion of a progressive fulfillment."

What radical critics now say of those reforms was said at the time (1901) by the *Bankers' Magazine*: "As the business of the country has learned the secret of combination, it is gradually subverting the power of the politician and rendering him subservient to its purposes. . . ."

There was much to stabilize, much to protect. By 1904, 318 trusts, with capital of more than seven billion dollars, controlled 40% of the U.S. manufacturing.

In 1909, a manifesto of the new Progressivism appeared—a book called *The Promise of American Life* by Herbert Croly, editor of the *New Republic* and an admirer of Theodore Roosevelt. He saw the need for discipline and regulation if the American system were to continue. Government should do more, he said, and he hoped to see the "sincere and enthusiastic imitation of heroes and saints"—by whom he may have meant Theodore Roosevelt.

Richard Hofstadter, in his biting chapter on the man the public saw as the great lover of nature and physical fitness, the war hero, the Boy Scout in the White House, says: "The advisers to whom Roosevelt listened were almost exclusively representatives of industrial and finance capital—men like Hanna, Robert Bacon, and George W. Perkins of the House of Morgan, Elihu Root, Senator Nelson W. Aldrich . . . and James Stillman of the Rockefeller interests." Responding to his worried brother-in-law writing from Wall Street, Roosevelt replied: "I intend to be most conservative, but in the interests of the corporations themselves and above all in the interests of the country."

Roosevelt supported the regulatory Hepburn Act because he feared something worse. He wrote to Henry Cabot Lodge that the railroad lobbyists who opposed the bill were wrong: "I think they are very short-sighted not to understand that to beat it means to increase the movement for government ownership of the railroads." His action against the trusts was to induce them to accept government regulation, in order to prevent destruction. He prosecuted the Morgan railroad monopoly in the Northern Securities Case, considering it an antitrust victory, but it hardly changed anything, and, although the Sherman Act provided for criminal penalties, there was no prosecution of the men who had planned the monopoly—Morgan, Harriman, Hill.

As for Woodrow Wilson, Hofstadter points out he was a conservative from the start. As a historian and political scientist, Wilson wrote *(The State):* "In politics nothing radically novel may safely be attempted." He urged "slow and gradual" change. His attitude toward labor, Hofstadter says, was "generally hostile," and he spoke of the "crude and ignorant minds" of the Populists.

James Weinstein *(The Corporate Ideal in the Liberal State)* has studied the reforms of the Progressive period, especially the process by which business and government, sometimes with the aid of labor leaders, worked out the legislative changes they thought necessary. Weinstein sees "a conscious and successful effort to guide and control the economic and social policies of federal, state, and municipal governments by various business groupings in their own long-range interest. . . ." While the "original impetus" for reform came from protesters and radicals, "in the current century, particularly on the federal level, few reforms were enacted without the tacit approval, if not the guidance, of the large corporate interests." These interests assembled liberal reformers and intellectuals to aid them in such matters.

Weinstein's definition of liberalism—as a means of stabilizing the system in the interests of big business—is different from that of the liberals themselves. Arthur Schlesinger writes: "Liberalism in America has been ordinarily the movement on the part of the other sections of society to restrain the power of the business community." If Schlesinger is describing the hope or intent of these other sections, he may be right. If he is describing the actual effect of these liberal reforms, that restraint has not happened.

The controls were constucted skillfully. In 1900, a man named Ralph Easley, a Republican and conservative, a schoolteacher and journalist, organized the National Civic Federation. Its aim was to get better relations between capital and labor. Its officers were mostly big businessmen, and important national politicians, but its first vice-president, for a long time, was Samuel Gompers of the AFL. Not all big businesses liked what the National Civic

Federation was doing. Easley called these critics anarchists, opposed to the rational organization of the system. "In fact," Easley wrote, "our enemies are the Socialists among the labor people and the anarchists among the capitalists."

The NCF wanted a more sophisticated approach to trade unions, seeing them as an inevitable reality, therefore wanting to come to agreements with them rather than fight with them: better to deal with a conservative union than face a militant one. After the Lawrence textile strike of 1912, John Golden, head of the conservative AFL Textile Union Workers, wrote Easley that the strike had given manufacturers "a very rapid education" and "some of them are falling all over themselves now to do business with our organization."

The National Civic Federation did not represent all opinions in the business world; the National Association of Manufacturers didn't want to recognize organized labor in any way. Many businessmen did not want even the puny reforms proposed by the Civic Federation—but the Federation's approach represented the sophistication and authority of the modern state, determined to do what was best for the capitalist class as a whole, even if this irritated some capitalists. The new approach was concerned with the long-range stability of the system, even at the cost, sometimes, of short-term profits.

Thus, the Federation drew up a model workmen's compensation bill in 1910, and the following year twelve states passed laws for compensation or accident insurance. When the Supreme Court said that year that New York's workmen's compensation law was unconstitutional because it deprived corporations of property without due process of law, Theodore Roosevelt was angry. Such decisions, he said, added "immensely to the strength of the Socialist Party." By 1920, forty-two states had workmen's compensation laws. As Weinstein says: "It represented a growing maturity and sophistication on the part of many large corporation leaders who had come to understand, as Theodore Roosevelt often told them, that social reform was truly conservative."

As for the Federal Trade Commission, established by Congress in 1914 presumably to regulate trusts, a leader of the Civic Federation reported after several years of experience with it that it "has apparently been carrying on its work with the purpose of securing the confidence of well-intentioned business men, members of the great corporations as well as others."

In this period, cities also put through reforms, many of them giving power to city councils instead of mayors, or hiring city managers. The idea was more efficiency, more stability. "The end result of the movements was to place city government firmly in the hands of the business class," Weinstein says. What reformers saw as more democracy in city government, urban historian Samuel Hays sees as the centralization of power in fewer hands, giving business and professional men more direct control over city government.

The Progressive movement, whether led by honest reformers like Senator Robert La Follette of Wisconsin or disguised conservatives like Roosevelt (who was the Progressive party candidate for President in 1912), seemed to understand it was fending off socialism. The Milwaukee *Journal*, a Progressive organ, said the conservatives "fight socialism blindly . . . while the Progressives fight it intelligently and seek to remedy the abuses and conditions upon which it thrives."

Frank Munsey, a director of U.S. Steel, writing to Roosevelt, seeing him as the best candidate for 1912, confided in him that the United States must move toward a more "parental guardianship of the people" who needed "the sustaining and guiding hand of the State." It was "the work of the state to think for the people and plan for the people," the steel executive said.

It seems quite clear that much of this intense activity for Progressive reform was intended to head off socialism. Easley talked of "the menace of Socialism as evidenced by its growth in the colleges, churches, newspapers." In 1910, Victor Berger became the first member of the Socialist party elected to Congress; in 1911, seventy-three Socialist mayors were elected, and twelve hundred lesser officials in 340 cities and towns. The press spoke of "The Rising Tide of Socialism."

A privately circulated memorandum suggested to one of the departments of the National Civic Federation: "In view of the rapid spread in the United States of socialistic doctrines," what was needed was "a carefully planned and wisely directed effort to instruct public opinion as to the real meaning of socialism." The memorandum suggested that the campaign "must be very skill-fully and tactfully carried out," that it "should not violently attack socialism and anarchism as such" but should be "patient and per-suasive" and defend three ideas: "individual liberty; private prop-erty; and inviolability of contract."

It is hard to say how many Socialists saw clearly how useful reform was to capitalism, but in 1912, a left-wing Socialist from Connecticut, Robert LaMonte, wrote: "Old age pensions and insurance against sickness, accident and unemployment are cheaper, are better business than jails, poor houses, asylums, hos-pitals." He suggested that progressives would work for reforms, but Socialists must make only "impossible demands," which would reveal the limitations of the reformers.

Did the Progressive reforms succeed in doing what they intended—stabilize the capitalist system by repairing its worst defects, blunt the edge of the Socialist movement, restore some measure of class peace in a time of increasingly bitter clashes between capital and labor? To some extent, perhaps. But the Socialist party continued to grow. The IWW continued to agi-tate. And shortly after Woodrow Wilson took office there began in Colorado one of the most bitter and violent struggles between workers and corporate capital in the history of the country.

This was the Colorado coal strike that began in September 1913 and culminated in the "Ludlow Massacre" of April 1914. Eleven thousand miners in southern Colorado, mostly foreign-born—Greeks, Italians, Serbs—worked for the Colorado Fuel & Iron Corporation, which was owned by the Rockefeller family. Aroused by the murder of one of their organizers, they went on strike against low pay, dangerous conditions, and feudal domina-tion of their lives in towns completely controlled by the mining companies. Mother Jones, at this time an organizer for the

United Mine Workers, came into the area, fired up the miners with her oratory, and helped them in those critical first months of the strike, until she was arrested, kept in a dungeonlike cell, and then forcibly expelled from the state.

When the strike began, the miners were immediately evicted from their shacks in the mining towns. Aided by the United Mine Workers Union, they set up tents in the nearby hills and carried on the strike, the picketing, from these tent colonies. The gunmen hired by the Rockefeller interests—the Baldwin-Felts Detective Agency—using Gatling guns and rifles, raided the tent colonies. The death list of miners grew, but they hung on, drove back an armored train in a gun battle, fought to keep out strikebreakers. With the miners resisting, refusing to give in, the mines not able to operate, the Colorado governor (referred to by a Rockefeller mine manager as "our little cowboy governor") called out the National Guard, with the Rockefellers supplying the Guard's wages.

The miners at first thought the Guard was sent to protect them, and greeted its arrivals with flags and cheers. They soon found out the Guard was there to destroy the strike. The Guard brought strike-breakers in under cover of night, not telling them there was a strike. Guardsmen beat miners, arrested them by the hundreds, rode down with their horses parades of women in the streets of Trinidad, the central town in the area. And still the miners refused to give in. When they lasted through the cold winter of 1913–1914, it became clear that extraordinary measures would be needed to break the strike.

In April 1914, two National Guard companies were stationed in the hills overlooking the largest tent colony of strikers, the one at Ludlow, housing a thousand men, women, children. On the morning of April 20, a machine gun attack began on the tents. The miners fired back. Their leader, a Greek named Lou Tikas, was lured up into the hills to discuss a truce, then shot to death by a company of National Guardsmen. The women and children dug pits beneath the tents to escape the gunfire. At dusk, the Guard moved down from the hills with torches, set fire to the tents, and the families fled into the hills; thirteen people were killed by gunfire.

The following day, a telephone linesman going through the ruins of the Ludlow tent colony lifted an iron cot covering a pit in one of the tents and found the charred, twisted bodies of eleven children and two women. This became known as the Ludlow Massacre.

The news spread quickly over the country. In Denver, the United Mine Workers issued a "Call to Arms"—"Gather together for defensive purposes all arms and ammunition legally available." Three hundred armed strikers marched from other tent colonies into the Ludlow area, cut telephone and telegraph wires, and prepared for battle. Railroad workers refused to take soldiers from Trinidad to Ludlow. At Colorado Springs, three hundred union miners walked off their jobs and headed for the Trinidad district, carrying revolvers, rifles, shotguns.

In Trinidad itself, miners attended a funeral service for the twenty-six dead at Ludlow, then walked from the funeral to a nearby building, where arms were stacked for them. They picked up rifles and moved into the hills, destroying mines, killing mine guards, exploding mine shafts. The press reported that "the hills in every direction seem suddenly to be alive with men."

In Denver, eighty-two soldiers in a company on a troop train headed for Trinidad refused to go. The press reported: "The men declared they would not engage in the shooting of women and children. They hissed the 350 men who did start and shouted imprecations at them."

Five thousand people demonstrated in the rain on the lawn in front of the state capital at Denver asking that the National Guard officers at Ludlow be tried for murder, denouncing the governor as an accessory. The Denver Cigar Makers Union voted to send five hundred armed men to Ludlow and Trinidad. Women in the United Garment Workers Union in Denver announced four hundred of their members had volunteered as nurses to help the strikers.

All over the country there were meetings, demonstrations.

Pickets marched in front of the Rockefeller office at 26 Broadway, New York City. A minister protested in front of the church where Rockefeller sometimes gave sermons, and was clubbed by the police.

The *New York Times* carried an editorial on the events in Colorado, which were now attracting international attention. The *Times* emphasis was not on the atrocity that had occurred, but on the mistake in tactics that had been made. Its editorial on the Ludlow Massacre began: "Somebody blundered. . . ." Two days later, with the miners armed and in the hills of the mine district, the *Times* wrote: "With the deadliest weapons of civilization in the hands of savage-minded men, there can be no telling to what lengths the war in Colorado will go unless it is quelled by force. . . . The President should turn his attention from Mexico long enough to take stern measures in Colorado."

The governor of Colorado asked for federal troops to restore order, and Woodrow Wilson complied. This accomplished, the strike petered out. Congressional committees came in and took thousands of pages of testimony. The union had not won recognition. Sixty-six men, women, and children had been killed. Not one militiaman or mine guard had been indicted for crime.

Still, Colorado had been a scene of ferocious class conflict, whose emotional repercussions had rolled through the entire country. The threat of class rebellion was clearly still there in the industrial conditions of the United States, in the undeterred spirit of rebellion among working people—whatever legislation had been passed, whatever liberal reforms were on the books, whatever investigations were undertaken and words of regret and conciliation uttered.

The *Times* had referred to Mexico. On the morning that the bodies were discovered in the tent pit at Ludlow, American warships were attacking Vera Cruz, a city on the coast of Mexico—bombarding it, occupying it, leaving a hundred Mexicans dead—because Mexico had arrested American sailors and refused to apologize to the United States with a twenty-one-gun salute. Could patriotic fervor and the military spirit cover up class struggle? Unemployment, hard times, were growing in 1914. Could guns divert attention and create some national consensus against an external enemy? It surely was a coincidence—the bombardment of Vera Cruz, the attack on the Ludlow colony. Or perhaps it was, as someone once described human history, "the natural selection of accidents." Perhaps the affair in Mexico was an instinctual response of the system for its own survival, to create a unity of fighting purpose among a people torn by internal conflict.

The bombardment of Vera Cruz was a small incident. But in four months the First World War would begin in Europe.

3

WAR IS THE HEALTH
OF THE STATE

"War is the health of the state," the radical writer Randolph Bourne said, in the midst of the First World War. Indeed, as the nations of Europe went to war in 1914, the governments flourished, patriotism bloomed, class struggle was stilled, and young men died in frightful numbers on the battlefields—often for a hundred yards of land, a line of trenches.

In the United States, not yet in the war, there was worry about the health of the state. Socialism was growing. The IWW seemed to be everywhere. Class conflict was intense. In the summer of 1916, during a Preparedness Day parade in San Francisco, a bomb exploded, killing nine people; two local radicals, Tom Mooney and Warren Billings, were arrested and would spend twenty years in prison. Shortly after that Senator James Wadsworth of New York suggested compulsory military training for all males to avert the danger that "these people of ours shall be divided into classes." Rather: "We must let our young men know that they owe some responsibility to this country."

The supreme fulfillment of that responsibility was taking place in Europe. Ten million were to die on the battlefield; 20

million were to die of hunger and disease related to the war. And no one since that day has been able to show that the war brought any gain for humanity that would be worth one human life. The rhetoric of the socialists, that it was an "imperialist war," now seems moderate and hardly arguable. The advanced capitalist countries of Europe were fighting over boundaries, colonies, spheres of influence; they were competing for Alsace-Lorraine, the Balkans, Africa, the Middle East.

The war came shortly after the opening of the twentieth century, in the midst of exultation (perhaps only among the elite in the Western world) about progress and modernization. One day after the English declared war, Henry James wrote to a friend: "The plunge of civilization into this abyss of blood and darkness . . . is a thing that so gives away the whole long age during which we have supposed the world to be . . . gradually bettering." In the first Battle of the Marne, the British and French succeeded in blocking the German advance on Paris. Each side had 500,000 casualties.

The killing started very fast, and on a large scale. In August 1914, a volunteer for the British army had to be 5 feet 8 inches to enlist. By October, the requirement was lowered to 5 feet 5 inches. That month there were thirty thousand casualties, and then one could be 5 feet 3. In the first three months of war, almost the entire original British army was wiped out.

For three years the battle lines remained virtually stationary in France. Each side would push forward, then back, then forward again—for a few yards, a few miles, while the corpses piled up. In 1916 the Germans tried to break through at Verdun; the British and French counterattacked along the Seine, moved forward a few miles, and lost 600,000 men. One day, the 9th Battalion of the King's Own Yorkshire Light Infantry launched an attack with eight hundred men. Twenty-four hours later, there were eighty-four left.

Back home, the British were not told of the slaughter. One English writer recalled: "The most bloody defeat in the history of Britain . . . might occur . . . and our Press come out bland and copious and graphic with nothing to show that we had not had quite a good day—a victory really. . . ." The same thing was happening on the German side; as Erich Maria Remarque wrote in his great novel, on days when men by the thousands were being blown apart by machine guns and shells, the official dispatches announced "All Quiet on the Western Front."

In July 1916, British General Douglas Haig ordered eleven divisions of English soldiers to climb out of their trenches and move toward the German lines. The six German divisions opened up with their machine guns. Of the 110,000 who attacked, 20,000 were killed, 40,000 more wounded—all those bodies strewn on no man's land, the ghostly territory between the contending trenches. On January 1, 1917, Haig was promoted to field marshal. What happened that summer is described tersely in William Langer's *An Encyclopedia of World History*:

> Despite the opposition of Lloyd George and the skepticism of some of his subordinates, Haig proceeded hopefully to the main offensive. The third battle of Ypres was a series of 8 heavy attacks, carried through in driving rain and fought over ground water-logged and muddy. No break-through was effected, and the total gain was about 5 miles of territory, which made the Ypres salient more inconvenient than ever and cost the British about 400,000 men.

The people of France and Britain were not told the extent of the casualties. When, in the last year of the war, the Germans attacked ferociously on the Somme, and left 300,000 British soldiers dead or wounded, London newspapers printed the following, we learn from Paul Fussell's *The Great War and Modern Memory*:

WHAT CAN I DO?

How the Civilian May Help in this Crisis.

Be cheerful. . . .

Write encouragingly to friends at the front. . . .

Don't repeat foolish gossip.

Don't listen to idle rumors.

Don't think you know better than Haig.

Into this pit of death and deception came the United States, in the spring of 1917. Mutinies were beginning to occur in the French army. Soon, out of 112 divisions, 68 would have mutinies; 629 men would be tried and condemned, 50 shot by firing squads. American troops were badly needed.

President Woodrow Wilson had promised that the United States would stay neutral in the war: "There is such a thing as a nation being too proud to fight." But in April of 1917, the Germans had announced they would have their submarines sink any ship bringing supplies to their enemies; and they had sunk a number of merchant vessels. Wilson now said he must stand by the right of Americans to travel on merchant ships in the war zone. "I cannot consent to any abridgement of the rights of American citizens in any respect. . . ."

As Richard Hofstadter points out *(The American Political Tradition):* "This was rationalization of the flimsiest sort. . . ." The British had also been intruding on the rights of American citizens on the high seas, but Wilson was not suggesting we go to war with them. Hofstadter says Wilson "was forced to find legal reasons for policies that were based not upon law but upon the balance of power and economic necessities."

It was unrealistic to expect that the Germans should treat the United States as neutral in the war when the U.S. had been shipping great amounts of war materials to Germany's enemies. In early 1915, the British liner *Lusitania* was torpedoed and sunk by a German submarine. She sank in eighteen minutes, and 1,198 people died, including 124 Americans. The United States claimed the *Lusitania* carried an innocent cargo, and therefore the torpedoing was a monstrous German atrocity. Actually, the *Lusitania* was heavily armed: it carried 1,248 cases of 3-inch shells, 4,927 boxes of cartridges (1,000 rounds in each box), and 2,000 more cases of small-arms ammunition. Her manifests were falsified to hide this fact, and the British and American governments lied about the cargo.

Hofstadter wrote of "economic necessities" behind Wilson's war policy. In 1914 a serious recession had begun in the United

States. J. P. Morgan later testified: "The war opened during a period of hard times. . . . Business throughout the country was depressed, farm prices were deflated, unemployment was serious, the heavy industries were working far below capacity and bank clearings were off." But by 1915, war orders for the Allies (mostly England) had stimulated the economy, and by April 1917 more than $2 billion worth of goods had been sold to the Allies. As Hofstadter says: "America became bound up with the Allies in a fateful union of war and prosperity."

Prosperity depended much on foreign markets, it was believed by the leaders of the country. In 1897, the private foreign investments of the United States amounted to $700 million dollars. By 1914 they were $3½ billion. Wilson's Secretary of State, William Jennings Bryan, while a believer in neutrality in the war, also believed that the United States needed overseas markets; in May of 1914 he praised the President as one who had "opened the doors of all the weaker countries to an invasion of American capital and American enterprise."

Back in 1907, Woodrow Wilson had said in a lecture at Columbia University: "Concessions obtained by financiers must be safeguarded by ministers of state, even if the sovereignty of unwilling nations be outraged in the process. . . . the doors of the nations which are closed must be battered down." In his 1912 campaign he said: "Our domestic markets no longer suffice, we need foreign markets." In a memo to Bryan he described his aim as "an open door to the world," and in 1914 he said he supported "the righteous conquest of foreign markets."

With World War I, England became more and more a market for American goods and for loans at interest. J. P. Morgan and Company acted as agents for the Allies, and when, in 1915, Wilson lifted the ban on private bank loans to the Allies, Morgan could now begin lending money in such great amounts as to both make great profit and tie American finance closely to the interest of a British victory in the war against Germany.

The industrialists and the political leaders talked of prosperity as if it were classless, as if everyone gained from Morgan's loans.

True, the war meant more production, more employment, but did the workers in the steel plants gain as much as U.S. Steel, which made $348 million in profit in 1916 alone? When the United States entered the war, it was the rich who took even more direct charge of the economy. Financier Bernard Baruch headed the War Industries Board, the most powerful of the wartime government agencies. Bankers, railroad men, and industrialists dominated these agencies.

A remarkably perceptive article on the nature of the First World War appeared in May 1915 in the *Atlantic Monthly*. Written by W. E. B. Du Bois, it was titled "The African Roots of War." It was a war for empire, of which the struggle between Germany and the Allies over Africa was both symbol and reality: ". . . in a very real sense Africa is a prime cause of this terrible overturning of civilization which we have lived to see." Africa, Du Bois said, is "the Land of the Twentieth Century," because of the gold and diamonds of South Africa, the cocoa of Angola and Nigeria, the rubber and ivory of the Congo, the palm oil of the West Coast.

Du Bois saw more than that. He was writing several years before Lenin's *Imperialism*, which noted the new possibility of giving the working class of the imperial country a share of the loot. He pointed to the paradox of greater "democracy" in America alongside "increased aristocracy and hatred toward darker races." He explained the paradox by the fact that "the white workingman has been asked to share the spoil of exploiting 'chinks and niggers.'" Yes, the average citizen of England, France, Germany, the United States, had a higher standard of living than before. But: "Whence comes this new wealth? . . . It comes primarily from the darker nations of the world—Asia and Africa, South and Central America, the West Indies, and the islands of the South Seas."

Du Bois saw the ingenuity of capitalism in uniting exploiter and exploited—creating a safety valve for explosive class conflict. "It is no longer simply the merchant prince, or the aristocratic monopoly, or even the employing class, that is exploiting the world: it is the nation, a new democratic nation composed of united capital and labor."

The United States fitted that idea of Du Bois. American capitalism needed international rivalry—and periodic war—to create an artificial community of interest between rich and poor, supplanting the genuine community of interest among the poor that showed itself in sporadic movements. How conscious of this were individual entrepreneurs and statesmen? That is hard to know. But their actions, even if half-conscious, instinctive drives to survive, matched such a scheme. And in 1917 this demanded a national consensus for war.

The government quickly succeeded in creating such a consensus, according to the traditional histories. Woodrow Wilson's biographer Arthur Link wrote: "In the final analysis American policy was determined by the President and public opinion." In fact, there is no way of measuring public opinion at that time, and there is no persuasive evidence that the public wanted war. The government had to work hard to create its consensus. That there was no spontaneous urge to fight is suggested by the strong measures taken: a draft of young men, an elaborate propaganda campaign throughout the country, and harsh punishment for those who refused to get in line.

Despite the rousing words of Wilson about a war "to end all wars" and "to make the world safe for democracy," Americans did not rush to enlist. A million men were needed, but in the first six weeks after the declaration of war only 73,000 volunteered. Congress voted overwhelmingly for a draft.

George Creel, a veteran newspaperman, became the government's official propagandist for the war; he set up a Committee on Public Information to persuade Americans the war was right. It sponsored 75,000 speakers, who gave 750,000 four-minute speeches in five thousand American cities and towns. It was a massive effort to excite a reluctant public. At the beginning of 1917, a member of the National Civic Federation had complained that "neither workingmen nor farmers" were taking "any part or interest in the efforts of the security or defense leagues or other movements for national preparedness."

The day after Congress declared war, the Socialist party met in emergency convention in St. Louis and called the declaration "a crime against the people of the United States." In the summer of 1917, Socialist antiwar meetings in Minnesota drew large crowds—five thousand, ten thousand, twenty thousand farmers—protesting the war, the draft, profiteering. A local newspaper in Wisconsin, the Plymouth *Review*, said that probably no party ever gained more rapidly in strength than the Socialist party just at the present time." It reported that "thousands assemble to hear Socialist speakers in places where ordinarily a few hundred are considered large assemblages." The Akron *Beacon-Journal*, a conservative newspaper in Ohio, said there was "scarcely a political observer . . . but what will admit that were an election to come now a mighty tide of socialism would inundate the Middle West." It said the country had "never embarked upon a more unpopular war."

In the municipal elections of 1917, against the tide of propaganda and patriotism, the Socialists made remarkable gains. Their candidate for mayor of New York, Morris Hillquit, got 22 percent of the vote, five times the normal Socialist vote there. Ten Socialists were elected to the New York State legislature. In Chicago, the party vote went from 3.6 percent in 1915 to 34.7 percent in 1917. In Buffalo, it went from 2.6 percent to 30.2 percent.

George Creel and the government were behind the formation of an American Alliance for Labor and Democracy, whose president was Samuel Gompers and whose aim was to "unify sentiment in the nation" for the war. There were branches in 164 cities; many labor leaders went along. According to James Weinstein, however, the Alliance did not work: "Rank-and-file working class support for the war remained lukewarm. . . ." And although some prominent Socialists—Jack London, Upton Sinclair, Clarence Darrow—became prowar after the U.S. entered, most Socialists continued their opposition.

Congress passed, and Wilson signed, in June of 1917, the Espionage Act. From its title one would suppose it was an act against spying. However, it had a clause that provided penalties up to twenty years in prison for "Whoever, when the United States is at war, shall wilfully cause or attempt to cause insubordination, disloyalty, mutiny, or refusal of duty in the military or naval forces of the United States, or shall wilfully obstruct the recruiting or enlistment service of the U.S. . . ." Unless one had a theory about the nature of governments, it was not clear how the Espionage Act would be used. It even had a clause that said "nothing in this section shall be construed to limit or restrict . . . any discussion, comment, or criticism of the acts or policies of the Government. . . ." But its double-talk concealed a singleness of purpose. The Espionage Act was used to imprison Americans who spoke or wrote against the war.

Two months after the law passed, a Socialist named Charles Schenck was arrested in Philadelphia for printing and distributing fifteen thousand leaflets that denounced the draft law and the war. The leaflet recited the Thirteenth Amendment provision against "involuntary servitude" and said the Conscription Act violated this. Conscription, it said, was "a monstrous deed against humanity in the interests of the financiers of Wall Street." And: "Do not submit to intimidation."

Schenck was indicted, tried, found guilty, and sentenced to six months in jail for violating the Espionage Act. (It turned out to be one of the shortest sentences given in such cases.) Schenck appealed, arguing that the Act, by prosecuting speech and writing, violated the First Amendment: "Congress shall make no law . . . abridging the freedom of speech, or of the press. . . ."

The Supreme Court's decision was unanimous and was written by its most famous liberal, Oliver Wendell Holmes. He summarized the contents of the leaflet and said it was undoubtedly intended to "obstruct" the carrying out of the draft law. Was Schenck protected by the First Amendment? Holmes said:

The most stringent protection of free speech would not protect a man in falsely shouting fire in a theatre and causing a panic. . . . The question in every case is whether the words used are used in such circumstances and are of such a nature as to create a clear and present danger that they will bring about the substantive evils that Congress has a right to prevent.

Holmes's analogy was clever and attractive. Few people would think free speech should be conferred on someone shouting fire in a theater and causing a panic. But did that example fit criticism of the war? Zechariah Chafee, a Harvard law school professor, wrote later *(Free Speech in the United States)* that a more apt analogy for Schenck was someone getting up between the acts at a theater and declaring that there were not enough fire exits. To play further with the example: was not Schenck's act more like someone shouting, not falsely, but truly, to people about to buy tickets and enter a theater, that there was a fire raging inside?

Perhaps free speech could not be tolerated by any reasonable person if it constituted a "clear and present danger" to life and liberty; after all, free speech must compete with other vital rights. But was not the war itself a "clear and present danger," indeed, more clear and more present and more dangerous to life than any argument against it? Did citizens not have a right to object to war, a right to be a danger to dangerous policies?

(The Espionage Act, thus approved by the Supreme Court, has remained on the books all these years since World War I, and although it is supposed to apply only in wartime, it has been constantly in force since 1950, because the United States has legally been in a "state of emergency" since the Korean war. In 1963, the Kennedy administration pushed a bill [unsuccessfully] to apply the Espionage Act to statements uttered by Americans abroad; it was concerned, in the words of a cable from Secretary of State Rusk to Ambassador Lodge in Vietnam, about journalists in Vietnam writing "critical articles . . . on Diem and his government" that were "likely to impede the war effort.")

The case of Eugene Debs soon came before the Supreme Court. In June of 1918, Debs visited three Socialists who were in prison for opposing the draft, and then spoke, across the street from the jail, to an audience he kept enthralled for two hours. He was one of the country's great orators, and was interrupted again and again by laughter and applause. "Why, the other day, by a vote of five-to-four—a kind of craps game, come seven, come eleven—they declared the child labor law unconstitutional." He spoke of his comrades in jail. He dealt with the charges that Socialists were pro-German. "I hate, I loathe, I despise Junkers and Junkerdom. I have no earthly use for the Junkers of Germany, and not one particle more use for the Junkers in the United States." (Thunderous applause and cheers.)

> They tell us that we live in a great free republic; that our institutions are democratic; that we are a free and self-governing people. That is too much, even for a joke. . . .
>
> Wars throughout history have been waged for conquest and plunder. . . . And that is war in a nutshell. The master class has always declared the wars; the subject class has always fought the battles. . . .

Debs was arrested for violating the Espionage Act. There were draft-age youths in his audience, and his words would "obstruct the recruiting or enlistment service."

His words were intended to do much more than that:

> Yes, in good time we are going to sweep into power in this nation and throughout the world. We are going to destroy all enslaving and degrading capitalist institutions and re-create them as free and humanizing institutions. The world is daily changing before our eyes. The sun of capitalism is setting; the sun of Socialism is rising. . . . In due time the hour will strike and this great cause triumphant . . . will proclaim the emancipation of the working class and the brotherhood of all mankind. (Thunderous and prolonged applause.)

Debs refused at his trial to take the stand in his defense, or to call a witness on his behalf. He denied nothing about what he said. But before the jury began its deliberations, he spoke to them:

> I have been accused of obstructing the war. I admit it. Gentlemen, I abhor war. I would oppose war if I stood alone. . . . I have sympathy

with the suffering, struggling people everywhere. It does not make any difference under what flag they were born, or where they live. . . .

The jury found him guilty of violating the Espionage Act. Debs addressed the judge before sentencing:

Your honor, years ago I recognized my kinship with all living beings, and I made up my mind that I was not one bit better than the meanest on earth. I said then, and I say now, that while there is a lower class, I am in it; while there is a criminal element, I am of it; while there is a soul in prison, I am not free.

The judge denounced those "who would strike the sword from the hand of this nation while she is engaged in defending herself against a foreign and brutal power." He sentenced Debs to ten years in prison.

Debs's appeal was not heard by the Supreme Court until 1919. The war was over. Oliver Wendell Holmes, for a unanimous court, affirmed Debs's guilt. Holmes discussed Debs's speech: "He then expressed opposition to Prussian militarism in a way that naturally might have been thought to be intended to include the mode of proceeding in the United States." Holmes said Debs made "the usual contrasts between capitalists and laboring men . . . with the implication running through it all that the working men are not concerned in the war." Thus, Holmes said, the "natural and intended effect" of Debs's speech would be to obstruct recruiting.

Debs was locked up in the West Virginia state penitentiary, and then in the Atlanta federal penitentiary, where he spent thirty-two months until, at the age of sixty-six, he was released by President Harding in 1921.

About nine hundred people went to prison under the Espionage Act. This substantial opposition was put out of sight, while the visible national mood was represented by military bands, flag waving, the mass buying of war bonds, the majority's acquiescence to the draft and the war. This acquiescence was achieved by shrewd public relations and by intimidation—an effort organized with all the power of the federal government and the money of big business behind it. The magnitude of that campaign to discourage opposition says something about the spontaneous feelings of the population toward the war.

The newspapers helped create an atmosphere of fear for possible opponents of the war. In April of 1917, the *New York Times* quoted Elihu Root (former Secretary of War, a corporation lawyer) as saying: "We must have no criticism now." A few months later it quoted him again that "there are men walking about the streets of this city tonight who ought to be taken out at sunrise tomorrow and shot for treason." At the same time, Theodore Roosevelt was talking to the Harvard Club about Socialists, IWWs, and others who wanted peace as "a whole raft of sexless creatures."

In the summer of 1917, the American Defense Society was formed. The New York *Herald* reported: "More than one hundred men enrolled yesterday in the American Vigilante Patrol at the offices of the American Defense Society. . . . The Patrol was formed to put an end to seditious street oratory."

The Department of Justice sponsored an American Protective League, which by June of 1917 had units in six hundred cities and towns, a membership of nearly 100,000. The press reported that their members were "the leading men in their communities . . . bankers . . . railroad men . . . hotel men." One study of the League describes their methods:

> The mails are supposed to be sacred. . . . But let us call the American Protective League sometimes almost clairvoyant as to letters done by suspects. . . . It is supposed that breaking and entering a man's home or office place without warrant is burglary. Granted. But the League has done that thousands of times and has never been detected!

The League claimed to have found 3 million cases of disloyalty. Even if these figures are exaggerated, the very size and scope of the League gives a clue to the amount of "disloyalty."

The states organized vigilante groups. The Minnesota Commission of Public Safety, set up by state law, closed saloons and moving picture theaters, took count of land owned by aliens, boosted Liberty bonds, tested people for loyalty. The Minneapolis *Journal* carried an appeal by the Commission "for all patriots to join in the suppression of antidraft and seditious acts and sentiment."

The national press cooperated with the government. The *New York Times* in the summer of 1917 carried an editorial: "It is the duty of every good citizen to communicate to proper authorities any evidence of sedition that comes to his notice." And the *Literary Digest* asked its readers "to clip and send to us any editorial utterances they encounter which seem to them seditious or treasonable." Creel's Committee on Public Information advertised that people should "report the man who spreads pessimistic stories. Report him to the Department of Justice." In 1918, the Attorney General said: "It is safe to say that never in its history has this country been so thoroughly policed."

Why these huge efforts? On August 1, 1917, the New York *Herald* reported that in New York City ninety of the first hundred draftees claimed exemption. In Minnesota, headlines in the Minneapolis *Journal* of August 6 and 7 read: "DRAFT OPPOSITION FAST SPREADING IN STATE," and "CONSCRIPTS GIVE FALSE ADDRESSES." In Florida, two Negro farm hands went into the woods with a shotgun and mutilated themselves to avoid the draft: one blew off four fingers of his hand; the other shot off his arm below the elbow. Senator Thomas Hardwick of Georgia said "there was undoubtedly general and widespread opposition on the part of many thousands . . . to the enactment of the draft law. Numerous and largely attended mass meetings held in every part of the State protested against it. . . ." Ultimately, over 330,000 men were classified as draft evaders.

In Oklahoma, the Socialist party and the IWW had been active among tenant farmers and sharecroppers who formed a "Working Class Union." At a mass meeting of the Union, plans were made to destroy a railroad bridge and cut telegraph wires in order to block military enlistments. A march on Washington was planned for draft objectors throughout the country. (This was called the Green Corn Rebellion because they planned to eat green corn on their march.) Before the Union could carry out its plans, its members were rounded up and arrested, and soon 450 individuals accused of rebellion were in the state penitentiary. Leaders were given three to ten years in jail, others sixty days to two years.

On July 1, 1917, radicals organized a parade in Boston against the war, with banners:

IS THIS A POPULAR WAR, WHY CONSCRIPTION?
WHO STOLE PANAMA? WHO CRUSHED HAITI?
WE DEMAND PEACE.

The New York *Call* said eight thousand people marched, including "4000 members of the Central Labor Union, 2000 members of the Lettish Socialist Organizations, 1500 Lithuanians, Jewish members of cloak trades, and other branches of the party." The parade was attacked by soldiers and sailors, on orders from their officers.

The Post Office Department began taking away the mailing privileges of newspapers and magazines that printed antiwar articles. *The Masses*, a socialist magazine of politics, literature, and art, was banned from the mails. It had carried an editorial by Max Eastman in the summer of 1917, saying, among other things: "For what specific purposes are you shipping our bodies, and the bodies of our sons, to Europe? For my part, I do not recognize the right of a government to draft me to a war whose purposes I do not believe in."

In Los Angeles, a film was shown that dealt with the American Revolution and depicted British atrocities against the colonists. It was called *The Spirit of '76*. The man who made the film was prosecuted under the Espionage Act because, the judge said, the film tended "to question the good faith of our ally, Great Britain." He was sentenced to ten years in prison. The case was officially listed as *U.S. v. Spirit of '76.*

In a small town in South Dakota, a farmer and socialist named Fred Fairchild, during an argument about the war, said, according to his accusers: "If I were of conscription age and had no dependents and were drafted, I would refuse to serve. They could shoot me, but they could not make me fight." He was tried under the Espionage Act, sentenced to a year and a day at Leavenworth penitentiary. And so it went, multiplied two thousand times (the number of prosecutions under the Espionage Act).

About 65,000 men declared themselves conscientious objectors and asked for noncombatant service. At the army bases where they worked, they were often treated with sadistic brutality. Three men who were jailed at Fort Riley, Kansas, for refusing to perform any military duties, combatant or noncombatant, were taken one by one into the corridor and:

> . . . a hemp rope slung over the railing of the upper tier was put about their necks, hoisting them off their feet until they were at the point of collapse. Meanwhile the officers punched them on their ankles and shins. They were then lowered and the rope was tied to their arms, and again they were hoisted off their feet. This time a garden hose was played on their faces with a nozzle about six inches from them, until they collapsed completely. . . .

Schools and universities discouraged opposition to the war. At Columbia University, J. McKeen Cattell, a psychologist, a long-time critic of the Board of Trustees' control of the university, and an opponent of the war, was fired. A week later, in protest, the famous historian Charles Beard resigned from the Columbia faculty, charging the trustees with being "reactionary and visionless in politics, narrow and medieval in religion. . . ."

In Congress, a few voices spoke out against the war. The first woman in the House of Representatives, Jeannette Rankin, did not respond when her name was called in the roll call on the declaration of war. One of the veteran politicians of the House, a supporter of the war, went to her and whispered, "Little woman, you cannot afford not to vote. You represent the womanhood of the country. . . ." On the next roll call she stood up: "I want to stand by my country, but I cannot vote for war. I vote No." A popular song of the time was: "I Didn't Raise My Boy to Be a Soldier." It was overwhelmed, however, by songs like "Over There," "It's a Grand Old Flag," and "Johnny Get Your Gun."

Socialist Kate Richards O'Hare, speaking in North Dakota in July of 1917, said, it was reported, that "the women of the United States were nothing more nor less than brood sows, to raise children to get into the army and be made into fertilizer." She was arrested, tried, found guilty, and sentenced to five years in the Missouri state penitentiary. In prison she continued to fight. When she and fellow prisoners protested the lack of air, because the window above the cell block was kept shut, she was pulled out in the corridor by guards for punishment. In her hand she was carrying a book of poems, and as she was dragged out she flung the book up at the window and broke it, the fresh air streaming in, her fellow prisoners cheering.

Emma Goldman and her fellow anarchist, Alexander Berkman (he had already been locked up fourteen years in Pennsylvania; she had served a year on Blackwell's Island), were sentenced to prison for opposing the draft. She spoke to the jury:

> Verily, poor as we are in democracy how can we give of it to the world? . . . a democracy conceived in the military servitude of the masses, in their economic enslavement, and nurtured in their tears and blood, is not democracy at all. It is despotism—the cumulative result of a chain of abuses which, according to that dangerous document, the Declaration of Independence, the people have the right to overthrow. . . .

The war gave the government its opportunity to destroy the IWW. The IWW newspaper, the *Industrial Worker*, just before the declaration of war, wrote: "Capitalists of America, we will fight against you, not for you! Conscription! There is not a power

in the world that can make the working class fight if they refuse."
Philip Foner, in his history of the IWW, says that the Wobblies
were not as active against the war as the Socialists, perhaps
because they were fatalistic, saw the war as inevitable, and
thought that only victory in class struggle, only revolutionary
change, could end war.

In early September 1917, Department of Justice agents made
simultaneous raids on forty-eight IWW meeting halls across the
country, seizing correspondence and literature that would become
courtroom evidence. Later that month, 165 IWW leaders were
arrested for conspiring to hinder the draft, encourage desertion,
and intimidate others in connection with labor disputes. One
hundred and one went on trial in April 1918; it lasted five months,
the longest criminal trial in American history up to that time.
John Reed, the Socialist writer just back from reporting on the
Bolshevik Revolution in Russia *(Ten Days That Shook the World)*,
covered the IWW trial for *The Masses* magazine and described the
defendants:

> I doubt if ever in history there has been a sight just like them. One
> hundred and one lumberjacks, harvest hands, miners, editors . . .
> who believe the wealth of the world belongs to him who creates it
> . . . the outdoor men, hard-rock blasters, tree-fellers, wheat-binders,
> longshoremen, the boys who do the strongwork of the world. . . .

The IWW people used the trial to tell about their activities,
their ideas. Sixty-one of them took the stand, including Big Bill
Haywood, who testified for three days. One IWW man told the
court:

> You ask me why the I.W.W. is not patriotic to the United States. If
> you were a bum without a blanket; if you had left your wife and kids
> when you went west for a job, and had never located them since; if
> your job had never kept you long enough in a place to qualify you to
> vote; if you slept in a lousy, sour bunkhouse, and ate food just as rot-
> ten as they could give you and get by with it; if deputy sheriffs shot

your cooking cans full of holes and spilled your grub on the ground; if your wages were lowered on you when the bosses thought they had you down; if there was one law for Ford, Suhr, and Mooney, and another for Harry Thaw; if every person who represented law and order and the nation beat you up, railroaded you to jail, and the good Christian people cheered and told them to go to it, how in hell do you expect a man to be patriotic? This war is a business man's war and we don't see why we should go out and get shot in order to save the lovely state of affairs that we now enjoy.

The jury found them all guilty. The judge sentenced Haywood and fourteen others to twenty years in prison; thirty-three were given ten years, the rest shorter sentences. They were fined a total of $2,500,000. The IWW was shattered. Haywood jumped bail and fled to revolutionary Russia, where he remained until his death ten years later.

The war ended in November 1918. Fifty thousand American soldiers had died, and it did not take long, even in the case of patriots, for bitterness and disillusionment to spread through the country. This was reflected in the literature of the postwar decade. John Dos Passos, in his novel *1919*, wrote of the death of John Doe:

In the tarpaper morgue at Chalons-sur-Marne in the reek of chloride of lime and the dead, they picked out the pine box that held all that was left of . . . John Doe. . . .

   . . . the scraps of dried viscera and skin bundled in khaki
   they took to Chalons-sur-Marne
   and laid it out neat in a pine coffin
   and took it home to God's Country on a battleship
   and buried it in a sarcophagus in the Memorial Amphitheatre in
   the Arlington National Cemetery
   and draped the Old Glory over it
   and the bugler played taps
   and Mr. Harding prayed to God and the diplomats and the generals and the admirals and the brass hats and the politicians and the

handsomely dressed ladies out of the society column of the Washington Post stood up solemn

and thought how beautiful sad Old Glory God's Country it was to have the bugler play taps and the three volleys made their ears ring.

Where his chest ought to have been they pinned the Congressional Medal. . . .

Ernest Hemingway would write *A Farewell to Arms*. Years later a college student named Irwin Shaw would write a play, *Bury the Dead*. And a Hollywood screenwriter named Dalton Trumbo would write a powerful and chilling antiwar novel about a torso and brain left alive on the battlefield of World War I, *Johnny Got His Gun*. Ford Madox Ford wrote *No More Parades*.

With all the wartime jailings, the intimidation, the drive for national unity, when the war was over, the Establishment still feared socialism. There seemed to be a need again for the twin tactics of control in the face of revolutionary challenge: reform and repression.

The first was suggested by George L. Record, one of Wilson's friends, who wrote to him in early 1919 that something would have to be done for economic democracy, "to meet this menace of socialism." He said: "You should become the real leader of the radical forces in America, and present to the country a constructive program of fundamental reform, which shall be an alternative to the program presented by the socialists, and the Bolsheviki. . . ."

That summer of 1919, Wilson's adviser Joseph Tumulty reminded him that the conflict between the Republicans and Democrats was unimportant compared with that which threatened them both:

What happened in Washington last night in the attempt upon the Attorney General's life is but a symptom of the terrible unrest that is stalking about the country. . . . As a Democrat I would be disappointed to see the Republican Party regain power. That is not what depresses one so much as to see growing steadily from day to day, under our very eyes, a movement that, if it is not checked, is bound to express itself in attack upon everything we hold dear. In this era of industrial and social unrest both parties are in disrepute with the average man. . . .

"What happened in Washington last night" was the explosion of a bomb in front of the home of Wilson's Attorney General A. Mitchell Palmer. Six months after that bomb exploded, Palmer carried out the first of his mass raids on aliens—immigrants who were not citizens. A law passed by Congress near the end of the war provided for the deportation of aliens who opposed organized government or advocated the destruction of property. Palmer's men, on December 21, 1919, picked up 249 aliens of Russian birth (including Emma Goldman and Alexander Berkman), put them on a transport, and deported them to what had become Soviet Russia. The Constitution gave no right to Congress to deport aliens, but the Supreme Court had said, back in 1892, in affirming the right of Congress to exclude Chinese, that as a matter of self-preservation, this was a natural right of the government.

In January 1920, four thousand persons were rounded up all over the country, held in seclusion for long periods of time, brought into secret hearings, and ordered deported. In Boston, Department of Justice agents, aided by local police, arrested six hundred people by raiding meeting halls or by invading their homes in the early morning. A troubled federal judge described the process:

> Pains were taken to give spectacular publicity to the raid, and to make it appear that there was great and imminent public danger. . . . The arrested aliens, in most instances perfectly quiet and harmless working people, many of them not long ago Russian peasants, were handcuffed in pairs, and then, for the purposes of transfer on trains and through the streets of Boston, chained together. . . .

In the spring of 1920, a typesetter and anarchist named Andrea Salsedo was arrested in New York by FBI agents and held for eight weeks in the FBI offices on the fourteenth floor of the Park Row Building, not allowed to contact family or friends or lawyers. Then his crushed body was found on the pavement below the building and the FBI said he had committed suicide by jumping from the fourteenth floor window.

Two friends of Salsedo, anarchists and workingmen in the Boston area, having just learned of his death, began carrying guns. They were arrested on a streetcar in Brockton, Massachusetts, and charged with a holdup and murder that had taken place two weeks before at a shoe factory. These were Nicola Sacco and Bartolomeo Vanzetti. They went on trial, were found guilty, and spent seven years in jail while appeals went on, and while all over the country and the world, people became involved in their case. The trial record and the surrounding circumstances suggested that Sacco and Vanzetti were sentenced to death because they were anarchists and foreigners. In August 1927, as police broke up marches and picket lines with arrests and beatings, and troops surrounded the prison, they were electrocuted.

Sacco's last message to his son Dante, in his painfully learned English, was a message to millions of others in the years to come:

> So, Son, instead of crying, be strong, so as to be able to comfort your mother . . . take her for a long walk in the quiet country, gathering wild flowers here and there. . . . But remember always, Dante, in the play of happiness, don't you use all for yourself only. . . . help the persecuted and the victim because they are your better friends. . . . In this struggle of life you will find more and love and you will be loved.

There had been reforms. The patriotic fervor of war had been invoked. The courts and jails had been used to reinforce the idea that certain ideas, certain kinds of resistance, could not be tolerated. And still, even from the cells of the condemned, the message was going out: the class war was still on in that supposedly classless society, the United States. Through the twenties and the thirties, it was still on.

4

SELF-HELP IN HARD TIMES

The war was hardly over, it was February 1919, the IWW leadership was in jail, but the IWW idea of the general strike became reality for five days in Seattle, Washington, when a walkout of 100,000 working people brought the city to a halt.

It began with 35,000 shipyard workers striking for a wage increase. They appealed for support to the Seattle Central Labor Council, which recommended a city-wide strike, and in two weeks 110 locals—mostly American Federation of Labor, only a few IWW—voted to strike. The rank and file of each striking local elected three members to a General Strike Committee, and on February 6, 1919, at 10:00 A.M., the strike began.

Unity was not easy to achieve. The IWW locals were in tension with the AFL locals. Japanese locals were admitted to the General Strike Committee but were not given a vote. Still, sixty thousand union members were out, and forty thousand other workers joined in sympathy.

Seattle workers had a radical tradition. During the war, the president of the Seattle AFL, a socialist, was imprisoned for opposing the draft, was tortured, and there were great labor rallies in the streets to protest.

The city now stopped functioning, except for activities organized by the strikers to provide essential needs. Firemen agreed to stay on the job. Laundry workers handled only hospital laundry. Vehicles authorized to move carried signs "Exempted by the General Strike Committee." Thirty-five neighborhood milk stations were set up. Every day thirty thousand meals were prepared in large kitchens, then transported to halls all over the city and served cafeteria style, with strikers paying twenty-five cents a meal, the general public thirty-five cents. People were allowed to eat as much as they wanted of the beef stew, spaghetti, bread, and coffee.

A Labor War Veteran's Guard was organized to keep the peace. On the blackboard at one of its headquarters was written: "The purpose of this organization is to preserve law and order without the use of force. No volunteer will have any police power or be allowed to carry weapons of any sort, but to use persuasion only." During the strike, crime in the city decreased. The commander of the U.S. army detachment sent into the area told the strikers' committee that in forty years of military experience he hadn't seen so quiet and orderly a city. A poem printed in the Seattle *Union Record* (a daily newspaper put out by labor people) by someone named Anise:

What scares them most is
That NOTHING HAPPENS!
They are ready
For DISTURBANCES.
They have machine guns
And soldiers,
But this SMILING SILENCE
   Is uncanny.
The business men
Don't understand
That sort of weapon . . .
It is your SMILE

That is UPSETTING
Their reliance
  On Artillery, brother!
It is the garbage wagons
That go along the street
Marked "EXEMPT
by STRIKE COMMITTEE."
It is the milk stations
That are getting better daily,
And the three hundred
WAR Veterans of Labor
Handling the crowds
WITHOUT GUNS,
For these things speak
Of a NEW POWER
And a NEW WORLD
That they do not feel
At HOME in.

The mayor swore in 2,400 special deputies, many of them students at the University of Washington. Almost a thousand sailors and marines were brought into the city by the U.S. government. The general strike ended after five days, according to the General Strike Committee because of pressure from the international officers of the various unions, as well as the difficulties of living in a shut-down city.

The strike had been peaceful. But when it was over, there were raids and arrests: on the Socialist party headquarters, on a printing plant. Thirty-nine members of the IWW were jailed as "ring-leaders of anarchy."

In Centralia, Washington, where the IWW had been organizing lumber workers, the lumber interests made plans to get rid of the IWW. On November 11, 1919, Armistice Day, the Legion paraded through town with rubber hoses and gas pipes, and the IWW prepared for an attack. When the Legion passed the IWW hall, shots were fired—it is unclear who fired first. They stormed the hall, there was more firing, and three Legion men were killed.

Inside the headquarters was an IWW member, a lumberjack named Frank Everett, who had been in France as a soldier while the IWW national leaders were on trial for obstructing the war effort. Everett was in army uniform and carrying a rifle. He emptied it into the crowd, dropped it, and ran for the woods, followed by a mob. He started to wade across the river, found the current too strong, turned, shot the leading man dead, threw his gun into the river, and fought the mob with his fists. They dragged him back to town behind an automobile, suspended him from a telegraph pole, took him down, locked him in jail. That night, his jailhouse door was broken down, he was dragged out, put on the floor of a car, his genitals were cut off, and then he was taken to a bridge, hanged, and his body riddled with bullets.

No one was ever arrested for Everett's murder, but eleven Wobblies were put on trial for killing an American Legion leader during the parade, and six of them spent fifteen years in prison.

Why such a reaction to the general strike, to the organizing of the Wobblies? A statement by the mayor of Seattle suggests that the Establishment feared not just the strike itself but what it symbolized. He said:

> The so-called sympathetic Seattle strike was an attempted revolution. That there was no violence does not alter the fact. . . . The intent, openly and covertly announced, was for the overthrow of the industrial system; here first, then everywhere. . . . True, there were no flashing guns, no bombs, no killings. Revolution, I repeat, doesn't need violence. The general strike, as practiced in Seattle, is of itself the weapon of revolution, all the more dangerous because quiet. To succeed, it must suspend everything; stop the entire life stream of a community. . . . That is to say, it puts the government out of operation. And that is all there is to revolt—no matter how achieved.

Furthermore, the Seattle general strike took place in the midst of a wave of postwar rebellions all over the world. A writer in *The Nation* commented that year:

The most extraordinary phenomenon of the present time . . . is the unprecedented revolt of the rank and file. . . .

In Russia it has dethroned the Czar. . . . In Korea and India and Egypt and Ireland it keeps up an unyielding resistance to political tyranny. In England it brought about the railway strike, against the judgement of the men's own executives. In Seattle and San Francisco it has resulted in the stevedores' recent refusal to handle arms or supplies destined for the overthrow of the Soviet Government. In one district of Illinois it manifested itself in a resolution of striking miners, unanimously requesting their state executive "to go to Hell". In Pittsburgh, according to Mr. Gompers, it compelled the reluctant American Federation officers to call the steel strike, lest the control pass into the hands of the I.W.W.'s and other "radicals". In New York, it brought about the longshoremen's strike and kept the men out in defiance of union officials, and caused the upheaval in the printing trade, which the international officers, even though the employers worked hand in glove with them, were completely unable to control.

The common man . . . losing faith in the old leadership, has experienced a new access of self-confidence, or at least a new reck- lessness, a readiness to take chances on his own account . . . authority cannot any longer be imposed from above; it comes automatically from below.

In the steel mills of western Pennsylvania later in 1919, where men worked twelve hours a day, six days a week, doing exhaust- ing work under intense heat, 100,000 steelworkers were signed up in twenty different AFL craft unions. A National Committee attempting to tie them together in their organizing drive found in the summer of 1919 "the men are letting it be known that if we do not do something for them they will take the matter into their own hands."

The National Council was getting telegrams like the one from the Johnstown Steel Workers Council: "Unless the National Committee authorizes a national strike vote to be taken this week we will be compelled to go on strike here alone." William Z. Foster (later a Communist leader, at this time secretary-treasurer to the National Committee in charge of organizing) received a telegram from organizers in the Youngstown district: "We cannot be expected to meet the enraged workers, who will consider us traitors if strike is postponed."

There was pressure from President Woodrow Wilson and Samuel Gompers, AFL president, to postpone the strike. But the steelworkers were too insistent, and in September 1919, not only the 100,000 union men but 250,000 others went out on strike.

The sheriff of Allegheny County swore in as deputies five thousand employees of U.S. Steel who had not gone on strike, and announced that outdoor meetings would be forbidden. A report of the Interchurch World Movement made at the time said:

> In Monessen . . . the policy of the State Police was simply to club men off the streets and drive them into their homes. . . . In Braddock . . . when a striker was clubbed in the street he would be taken to jail, kept there over night. . . . Many of those arrested in Newcastle . . . were ordered not to be released until the strike was over.

The Department of Justice moved in, carrying out raids on workers who were aliens, holding them for deportation. At Gary, Indiana, federal troops were sent in.

Other factors operated against the strikers. Most were recent immigrants, of many nationalities, many languages. Sherman Service, Inc., hired by the steel corporations to break the strike, instructed its men in South Chicago: "We want you to stir up as much bad feeling as you possibly can between the Serbians and the Italians. Spread data among the Serbians that the Italians are going back to work. . . . Urge them to go back to work or the Italians will get their jobs." More than thirty thousand black workers were brought into the area as strikebreakers—they had been excluded from AFL unions and so felt no loyalty to unionism.

As the strike dragged on, the mood of defeat spread, and workers began to drift back to work. After ten weeks, the number

of strikers was down to 110,000, and then the National Committee called the strike off.

In the year following the war, 120,000 textile workers struck
in New England and New Jersey, and 30,000 silk workers struck
in Paterson, New Jersey. In Boston the police went out on strike,
and in New York City cigarmakers, shirtmakers, carpenters, bakers, teamsters, and barbers were out on strike. In Chicago, the
press reported, "More strikes and lockouts accompany the mid-
summer heat than ever known before at any one time." Five
thousand workers at International Harvester and five thousand
city workers were in the streets.

When the twenties began, however, the situation seemed
under control. The IWW was destroyed, the Socialist party
falling apart. The strikes were beaten down by force, and the
economy was doing just well enough for just enough people to
prevent mass rebellion.

Congress, in the twenties, put an end to the dangerous, turbulent flood of immigrants (14 million between 1900 and 1920) by
passing laws setting immigration quotas: the quotas favored
Anglo-Saxons, kept out black and yellow people, limited severely
the coming of Latins, Slavs, Jews. No African country could send
more than 100 people; 100 was the limit for China, for Bulgaria,
for Palestine; 34,007 could come from England or Northern Ireland, but only 3,845 from Italy; 51,227 from Germany, but only
124 from Lithuania; 28,567 from the Irish Free State, but only
2,248 from Russia.

The Ku Klux Klan was revived in the 1920s, and it spread into
the North. By 1924 it had 4½ million members. The NAACP
seemed helpless in the face of mob violence and race hatred everywhere. The impossibility of the black person's ever being considered equal in white America was the theme of the nationalist movement led in the 1920s by Marcus Garvey. He preached black pride,
racial separation, and a return to Africa, which to him held the only
hope for black unity and survival. But Garvey's movement, inspiring as it was to some blacks, could not make much headway against
the powerful white supremacy currents of the postwar decade.

There was some truth to the standard picture of the twenties as a time of prosperity and fun—the Jazz Age, the Roaring Twenties. Unemployment was down, from 4,270,000 in 1921 to a little over 2 million in 1927. The general level of wages for workers rose. Some farmers made a lot of money. The 40 percent of all families who made over $2,000 a year could buy new gadgets: autos, radios, refrigerators. Millions of people were not doing badly—and they could shut out of the picture the others—the tenant farmers, black and white, the immigrant families in the big cities either without work or not making enough to get the basic necessities.

But prosperity was concentrated at the top. While from 1922 to 1929 real wages in manufacturing went up per capita 1.4 percent a year, the holders of common stocks gained 16.4 percent a year. Six million families (42 percent of the total) made less than $1,000 a year. One-tenth of 1 percent of the families at the top received as much income as 42 percent of the families at the bottom, according to a report of the Brookings Institution. Every year in the 1920s, about 25,000 workers were killed on the job and 100,000 permanently disabled. Two million people in New York City lived in tenements condemned as firetraps.

The country was full of little industrial towns like Muncie, Indiana, where, according to Robert and Helen Lynd (*Middletown*), the class system was revealed by the time people got up in the morning: for two-thirds of the city's families, "the father gets up in the dark in winter, eats hastily in the kitchen in the gray dawn, and is at work from an hour to two and a quarter hours before his children have to be at school."

There were enough well-off people to push the others into the background. And with the rich controlling the means of dispensing information, who would tell? Historian Merle Curti observed about the twenties:

It was, in fact, only the upper ten percent of the population that enjoyed a marked increase in real income. But the protests which such facts normally have evoked could not make themselves widely or effectively felt. This was in part the result of the grand strategy of the major political parties. In part it was the result of the fact that almost all the chief avenues to mass opinion were now controlled by large-scale publishing industries.

Some writers tried to break through: Theodore Dreiser, Sinclair Lewis, Lewis Mumford. F. Scott Fitzgerald, in an article, "Echoes of the Jazz Age," said: "It was borrowed time anyway— the whole upper tenth of a nation living with the insouciance of a grand duc and the casualness of chorus girls." He saw ominous signs amid that prosperity: drunkenness, unhappiness, violence:

A classmate killed his wife and himself on Long Island, another tumbled "accidentally" from a skyscraper in Philadelphia, another purposely from a skyscraper in New York. One was killed in a speakeasy in Chicago; another was beaten to death in a speak-easy in New York and crawled home to the Princeton Club to die; still another had his skull crushed by a maniac's axe in an insane asylum where he was confined.

Sinclair Lewis captured the false sense of prosperity, the shallow pleasure of the new gadgets for the middle classes, in his novel *Babbitt*:

It was the best of nationally advertised and quantitatively produced alarm-clocks, with all modern attachments, including cathedral chime, intermittent alarm, and a phosphorescent dial. Babbitt was proud of being awakened by such a rich device. Socially it was almost as creditable as buying expensive cord tires.

He sulkily admitted now that there was no more escape, but he lay and detested the grind of the real-estate business, and disliked his family, and disliked himself for disliking them.

Women had finally, after long agitation, won the right to vote in 1920 with the passage of the Nineteenth Amendment, but voting was still a middle-class and upper-class activity. Eleanor

Flexner, recounting the history of the movement, says the effect of female suffrage was that "women have shown the same tendency to divide along orthodox party lines as male voters."

Few political figures spoke out for the poor of the twenties. One was Fiorello La Guardia, a Congressman from a district of poor immigrants in East Harlem (who ran, oddly, on both Socialist and Republican tickets). In the mid-twenties he was made aware by people in his district of the high price of meat. When La Guardia asked Secretary of Agriculture William Jardine to investigate the high price of meat, the Secretary sent him a pamphlet on how to use meat economically. La Guardia wrote back:

> I asked for help and you send me a bulletin. The people of New York City cannot feed their children on Department bulletins.... Your bulletins ... are of no use to the tenement dwellers of this great city. The housewives of New York have been trained by hard experience on the economical use of meat. What we want is the help of your department on the meat profiteers who are keeping the hard-working people of this city from obtaining proper nourishment.

During the presidencies of Harding and Coolidge in the twenties, the Secretary of the Treasury was Andrew Mellon, one of the richest men in America. In 1923, Congress was presented with the "Mellon Plan," calling for what looked like a general reduction of income taxes, except that the top income brackets would have their tax rates lowered from 50 percent to 25 percent, while the lowest-income group would have theirs lowered from 4 percent to 3 percent. A few Congressmen from working-class districts spoke against the bill, like William P. Connery of Massachusetts:

> I am not going to have my people who work in the shoe factories of Lynn and in the mills in Lawrence and the leather industry of Peabody, in these days of so-called Republican prosperity when they are working but three days in the week think that I am in accord with the provisions of this bill.... When I see a provision in this

Mellon tax bill which is going to save Mr. Mellon himself $800,000 on his income tax and his brother $600,000 on his, I cannot give it my support.

The Mellon Plan passed. In 1928, La Guardia toured the poorer districts of New York and said: "I confess I was not prepared for what I actually saw. It seemed almost incredible that such conditions of poverty could really exist."

Buried in the general news of prosperity in the twenties were, from time to time, stories of bitter labor struggles. In 1922, coal miners and railroad men went on strike, and Senator Burton Wheeler of Montana, a Progressive elected with labor votes, visited the strike area and reported:

All day long I have listened to heartrending stories of women evicted from their homes by the coal companies. I heard pitiful pleas of little children crying for bread. I stood aghast as I heard most amazing stories from men brutally beaten by private policemen. It has been a shocking and nerve-racking experience.

A textile strike in Rhode Island in 1922 among Italian and Portuguese workers failed, but class feelings were awakened and some of the strikers joined radical movements. Luigi Nardella recalled:

. . . my oldest brother, Guido, he started the strike. Guido pulled the handles on the looms in the Royal Mills, going from one section to the next shouting, "Strike! Strike!" . . . When the strike started we didn't have any union organizers. . . . We got together a group of girls and went from mill to mill, and that morning we got five mills out. We'd motion to the girls in the mills, "Come out! Come out!" Then we'd go on to the next. . . .

Somebody from the Young Workers' League came out to bring a check, and invited me to a meeting, and I went. Then I joined, and in a few years I was in the Risorgimento Club in Providence. We were anti-Fascists. I spoke on street corners, bring a stand, jump up and talk to good crowds. And we led the support for Sacco and Vanzetti. . . .

After the war, with the Socialist party weakened, a Communist party was organized, and Communists were involved in the organization of the Trade Union Education League, which tried to build a militant spirit inside the AFL. When a Communist named Ben Gold, of the furriers' section of the TUEL, challenged the AFL union leadership at a meeting, he was knifed and beaten. But in 1926, he and other Communists organized a strike of furriers who formed mass picket lines, battled the police to hold their lines, were arrested and beaten, but kept striking, until they won a forty-hour week and a wage increase.

Communists again played a leading part in the great textile strike that spread through the Carolinas and Tennessee in the spring of 1929. The mill owners had moved to the South to escape unions, to find more subservient workers among the poor whites. But these workers rebelled against the long hours, the low pay. They particularly resented the "stretch-out"—an intensification of work. For instance, a weaver who had operated twenty-four looms and got $18.91 a week would be raised to $23, but he would be "stretched out" to a hundred looms and had to work at a punishing pace.

The first of the textile strikes was in Tennessee, where five hundred women in one mill walked out in protest against wages of $9 to $10 a week. Then at Gastonia, North Carolina, workers joined a new union, the National Textile Workers Union, led by Communists, which admitted both blacks and whites to membership. When some of them were fired, half of the two thousand workers went out on strike. An atmosphere of anti-Communism and racism built up and violence began. Textile strikes began to spread across South Carolina.

One by one the various strikes were settled, with some gains, but not at Gastonia. There, with the textile workers living in a tent colony, and refusing to renounce the Communists in their leadership, the strike went on. But strikebreakers were brought in and the mills kept operating. Desperation grew; there were violent clashes with the police. One dark night, the chief of police was killed in a gun battle and sixteen strikers and sympathizers were indicted for murder, including Fred Beal, a Communist party organizer. Ultimately seven were tried and given sentences of from five to twenty years. They were released on bail, and left the state; the Communists escaped to Soviet Russia. Through all the defeats, the beatings, the murders, however, it was the beginning of textile mill unionism in the South.

The stock market crash of 1929, which marked the beginning of the Great Depression of the United States, came directly from wild speculation which collapsed and brought the whole economy down with it. But, as John Galbraith says in his study of that event (*The Great Crash*), behind that speculation was the fact that "the economy was fundamentally unsound." He points to very unhealthy corporate and banking structures, an unsound foreign trade, much economic misinformation, and the "bad distribution of income" (the highest 5 percent of the population received about one-third of all personal income).

A socialist critic would go further and say that the capitalist system was by its nature unsound: a system driven by the one overriding motive of corporate profit and therefore unstable, unpredictable, and blind to human needs. The result of all that: permanent depression for many of its people, and periodic crises for almost everybody. Capitalism, despite its attempts at self-reform, its organization for better control, was still in 1929 a sick and underpendable system.

After the crash, the economy was stunned, barely moving. Over five thousand banks closed and huge numbers of businesses, unable to get money, closed too. Those that continued laid off employees and cut the wages of those who remained, again and again. Industrial production fell by 50 percent, and by 1933 perhaps 15 million (no one knew exactly)—one-fourth or one-third of the labor force—were out of work. The Ford Motor Company, which in the spring of 1929 had employed 128,000 workers, was down to 37,000 by August of 1931. By the end of 1930, almost half the 280,000 textile mill workers in New England were out of work. Former President Calvin Coolidge commented with his customary wisdom: "When more and more people are thrown out of work, unemployment results." He spoke again in early 1931, "This country is not in good condition."

Clearly, those responsible for organizing the economy did not know what had happened, were baffled by it, refused to recognize it, and found reasons other than the failure of the system. Herbert Hoover had said, not long before the crash: "We in America today are nearer to the final triumph over poverty than ever before in the history of any land." Henry Ford, in March 1931, said the crisis was here because "the average man won't really do a day's work unless he is caught and cannot get out of it. There is plenty of work to do if people would do it." A few weeks later he laid off 75,000 workers.

There were millions of tons of food around, but it was not profitable to transport it, to sell it. Warehouses were full of clothing, but people could not afford it. There were lots of houses, but they stayed empty because people couldn't pay the rent, had been evicted, and now lived in shacks in quickly formed "Hoovervilles" built on garbage dumps.

Brief glimpses of reality in the newspapers could have been multiplied by the millions: A *New York Times* story in early 1932:

After vainly trying to get a stay of dispossession until January 15 from his apartment at 46 Hancock Street in Brooklyn, yesterday, Peter J. Cornell, 48 years old, a former roofing contractor out of work and penniless, fell dead in the arms of his wife.

A doctor gave the cause of his death as heart disease, and the police said it had at least partly been caused by the bitter disappointment of a long day's fruitless attempt to prevent himself and his family being put out on the street. . . .

Cornell owed $5 in rent in arrears and $39 for January which his landlord required in advance. Failure to produce the money resulted in a dispossess order being served on the family yesterday and to take effect at the end of the week.

After vainly seeking assistance elsewhere, he was told during the day by the Home Relief Bureau that it would have no funds with which to help him until January 15.

A dispatch from Wisconsin to *The Nation*, in late 1932:

Throughout the middle west the tension between the farmers and authorities has been growing . . . as a result of tax and foreclosure sales. In many cases evictions have been prevented only by mass action on the part of the farmers. However, until the Cichon homestead near Elkhorn, Wisconsin, was besieged on December 6 by a host of deputy sheriffs armed with machine-guns, rifles, shotguns, and tear-gas bombs, there had been no actual violence. Max Cichon's property was auctioned off at a foreclosure sale last August, but he refused to allow either the buyer or the authorities to approach his home. He held off unwelcome visitors with a shotgun. The sheriff called upon Cichon to submit peacefully. When he refused to do so, the sheriff ordered deputies to lay down a barrage of machine-gun and rifle fire . . . Cichon is now in jail in Elkhorn, and his wife and two children, who were with him in the house, are being cared for in the county hospital. Cichon is not a trouble-maker. He enjoys the confidence of his neighbors, who only recently elected him justice of the peace of the town of Sugar Creek. That a man of his standing and disposition should go to such lengths in defying the authorities is a clear warning that we may expect further trouble in the agricultural districts unless the farmers are soon helped.

A tenement dweller on 113th Street in East Harlem wrote to Congressman Fiorello La Guardia in Washington:

You know my condition is bad. I used to get pension from the government and they stopped. It is now nearly seven months I am out of work. I hope you will try to do something for me. . . . I have four children who are in need of clothes and food. . . . My daughter who is eight is very ill and not recovering. My rent is due two months and I am afraid of being put out.

In Oklahoma, the farmers found their farms sold under the auctioneer's hammer, their farms turning to dust, the tractors coming in and taking over. John Steinbeck, in his novel of the depression, *The Grapes of Wrath*, describes what happened:

And the dispossessed, the migrants, flowed into California, two hundred and fifty thousand, and three hundred thousand. Behind them new tractors were going on the land and the tenants were being forced off. And new waves were on the way, new waves of the dispossessed and the homeless, hard, intent, and dangerous. . . .

And a homeless hungry man, driving the road with his wife beside him and his thin children in the back seat, could look at the fallow fields which might produce food but not profit, and that man could know how a fallow field is a sin and the unused land a crime against the thin children. . . .

And in the south he saw the golden oranges hanging on the trees, the little golden oranges on the dark green trees; and guards with shotguns patrolling the lines so a man might not pick an orange for a thin child, oranges to be dumped if the price was low. . . .

These people were becoming "dangerous," as Steinbeck said. The spirit of rebellion was growing. Mauritz Hallgren, in a 1933 book, *Seeds of Revolt*, compiled newspaper reports of things happening around the country:

England, Arkansas, January 3, 1931. The long drought that ruined hundreds of Arkansas farms last summer had a dramatic sequel late today when some 500 farmers, most of them white men and many of them armed, marched on the business section of this town. . . . Shouting that they must have food for themselves and their families, the invaders announced their intention to take it from the stores unless it were provided from some other source without cost.

Detroit, July 9, 1931. An incipient riot by 500 unemployed men turned out of the city lodging house for lack of funds was quelled by police reserves in Cadillac Square tonight. . . .

Indiana Harbor, Indiana, August 5, 1931. Fifteen hundred jobless men stormed the plant of the Fruit Growers Express Company here, demanding that they be given jobs to keep from starving. The company's answer was to call the city police, who routed the jobless with menacing clubs.

Boston, November 10, 1931. Twenty persons were treated for injuries, three were hurt so seriously that they may die, and dozens of others were nursing wounds from flying bottles, lead pipe, and stones after clashes between striking longshoremen and Negro strikebreakers along the Charlestown-East Boston waterfront.

Detroit, November 28, 1931. A mounted patrolman was hit on the head with a stone and unhorsed and one demonstrator was arrested during a disturbance in Grand Circus Park this morning when 2000 men and women met there in defiance of police orders.

Chicago, April 1, 1932. Five hundred school children, most with haggard faces and in tattered clothes, paraded through Chicago's downtown section to the Board of Education offices to demand that the school system provide them with food.

Boston, June 3, 1932. Twenty-five hungry children raided a buffet lunch set up for Spanish War veterans during a Boston parade. Two automobile-loads of police were called to drive them away.

New York, January 21, 1933. Several hundred jobless surrounded a restaurant just off Union Square today demanding they be fed without charge. . . .

Seattle, February 16, 1933. A two-day siege of the County-City Building, occupied by an army of about 5,000 unemployed, was ended early tonight, deputy sheriffs and police evicting the demonstrators after nearly two hours of efforts.

Yip Harburg, the songwriter, told Studs Terkel about the year 1932: "I was walking along the street at that time, and you'd see the bread lines. The biggest one in New York City was owned by William Randolph Hearst. He had a big truck with several people on it, and big cauldrons of hot soup, bread. Fellows with burlap on their feet were lined up all around Columbus Circle, and went for blocks and blocks around the park, waiting." Harburg had to write a song for the show *Americana*. He wrote "Brother, Can You Spare a Dime?"

Once in khaki suits,
Gee, we looked swell,
Full of that Yankee Doodle-de-dum.
Half a million boots went sloggin' through Hell,
I was the kid with the drum.
Say, don't you remember, they called me Al—
It was Al all the time.
Say, don't you remember I'm your pal—
Brother, can you spare a dime?

It was not just a song of despair. As Yip Harburg told Terkel:

In the song the man is really saying: I made an investment in this country. Where the hell are my dividends? . . . It's more than just a bit of pathos. It doesn't reduce him to a beggar. It makes him a dignified human, asking questions—and a bit outraged, too, as he should be.

The anger of the veteran of the First World War, now without work, his family hungry, led to the march of the Bonus Army to Washington in the spring and summer of 1932. War veterans, holding government bonus certificates which were due years in the future, demanded that Congress pay off on them now, when the money was desperately needed. And so they began to move to Washington from all over the country, with wives and children or alone. They came in broken-down old autos, stealing rides on freight trains, or hitchhiking. They were miners from West Virginia, sheet metal workers from Columbus, Georgia, and unemployed Polish veterans from Chicago. One family—husband, wife, three-year-old boy—spent three months on freight trains coming from California. Chief Running Wolf, a jobless Mescalero Indian from New Mexico, showed up in full Indian dress, with bow and arrow.

More than twenty thousand came. Most camped across the Potomac River from the Capitol on Anacostia Flats where, as John Dos Passos wrote, "the men are sleeping in little lean-tos built out of old newspapers, cardboard boxes, packing crates, bits of tin or tarpaper roofing, every kind of cockeyed makeshift shelter from the rain scraped together out of the city dump." The bill to pay off on the bonus passed the House, but was defeated in the Senate, and some veterans, discouraged, left. Most stayed—some encamped in government buildings near the Capitol, the rest on Anacostia Flats, and President Hoover ordered the army to evict them.

Four troops of cavalry, four companies of infantry, a machine gun squadron, and six tanks assembled near the White House. General Douglas MacArthur was in charge of the operation, Major Dwight Eisenhower his aide. George S. Patton was one of the officers. MacArthur led his troops down Pennsylvania Avenue, used tear gas to clear veterans out of the old buildings, and set the buildings on fire. Then the army moved across the bridge to Anacostia. Thousands of veterans, wives, children, began to run as the tear gas spread. The soldiers set fire to some of the huts, and soon the whole encampment was ablaze. When it was all over, two veterans had been shot to death, an eleven-week-old baby had died, an eight-year-old boy was partially blinded by gas, two police had fractured skulls, and a thousand veterans were injured by gas.

The hard, hard times, the inaction of the government in helping, the action of the government in dispersing war veterans—all had their effect on the election of November 1932. Democratic party candidate Franklin D. Roosevelt defeated Herbert Hoover overwhelmingly, took office in the spring of 1933, and began a program of reform legislation which became famous as the "New Deal." When a small veterans' march on Washington took place early in his administration, he greeted them and provided coffee; they met with one of his aides and went home. It was a sign of Roosevelt's approach.

The Roosevelt reforms went far beyond previous legislation. They had to meet two pressing needs: to reorganize capitalism in such a way to overcome the crisis and stabilize the system; also, to head off the alarming growth of spontaneous rebellion in the early years of the Roosevelt administration—organization of tenants and the unemployed, movements of self-help, general strikes in several cities.

That first objective—to stabilize the system for its own protection—was most obvious in the major law of Roosevelt's first months in office, the National Recovery Act (NRA). It was designed to take control of the economy through a series of codes agreed on by management, labor, and the government, fixing prices and wages, limiting competition. From the first, the NRA was dominated by big businesses and served their interests. As Bernard Bellush says (*The Failure of the N.R.A.*), its Title I "turned much of the nation's power over to highly organized, well-financed trade associations and industrial combines. The unorganized public, otherwise known as the consumer, along with the members of the fledgling trade-union movement, had virtually nothing to say about the initial organization of the National Recovery Administration, or the formulation of basic policy."

Where organized labor was strong, Roosevelt moved to make some concessions to working people. But: "Where organized labor was weak, Roosevelt was unprepared to withstand the pressures of industrial spokesmen to control the . . . NRA codes." Barton Bernstein (*Towards a New Past*) confirms this: "Despite the annoyance of some big businessmen with Section 7a, the NRA reaffirmed and consolidated their power. . . ." Bellush sums up his view of the NRA:

The White House permitted the National Association of Manufacturers, the Chamber of Commerce, and allied business and trade
associations to assume overriding authority.... Indeed, private
administration became public administration, and private government became public government, insuring the marriage of capitalism
with statism.

When the Supreme Court in 1935 declared the NRA unconstitutional, it claimed it gave too much power to the President,
but, according to Bellush, "... FDR surrendered an inordinate
share of the power of government, through the NRA, to industrial spokesmen throughout the country."

Also passed in the first months of the new administration, the
AAA (Agricultural Adjustment Administration) was an attempt to
organize agriculture. It favored the larger farmers as the NRA
favored big business. The TVA (Tennessee Valley Authority) was
an unusual entrance of government into business—a government-
owned network of dams and hydroelectric plants to control floods
and produce electric power in the Tennessee Valley. It gave jobs
to the unemployed, helped the consumer with lower electric
rates, and in some respect deserved the accusation that it was
"socialistic." But the New Deal's organization of the economy
was aimed mainly at stabilizing the economy, and secondly at giving enough help to the lower classes to keep them from turning a
rebellion into a real revolution.

That rebellion was real when Roosevelt took office. Desperate
people were not waiting for the government to help them; they
were helping themselves, acting directly. Aunt Molly Jackson, a
woman who later became active in labor struggles in Appalachia,
recalled how she walked into the local store, asked for a 24-pound
sack of flour, gave it to her little boy to take it outside, then filled
a sack of sugar and said to the storekeeper, "Well, I'll see you in
ninety days. I have to feed some children ... I'll pay you, don't
worry." And when he objected, she pulled out her pistol (which,
as a midwife traveling alone through the hills, she had a permit to
carry) and said: "Martin, if you try to take this grub away from

me, God knows that if they electrocute me for it tomorrow, I'll shoot you six times in a minute." Then, as she recalls, "I walked out, I got home, and these seven children was so hungry that they was a-grabbin the raw dough off-a their mother's hands and crammin it into their mouths and swallowing it whole."

All over the country, people organized spontaneously to stop evictions. In New York, in Chicago, in other cities—when word spread that someone was being evicted, a crowd would gather; the police would remove the furniture from the house, put it out in the street, and the crowd would bring the furniture back. The Communist party was active in organizing Workers Alliance groups in the cities. Mrs. Willye Jeffries, a black woman, told Studs Terkel about evictions:

A lot of 'em was put out. They'd call and have the bailiffs come and sit them out, and as soon as they'd leave, we would put 'em back where they came out. All we had to do was call Brother Hilton. . . . Look, such and such a place, there's a family sittin' out there. Everybody passed through the neighborhood, was a member of the Workers Alliance, had one person they would call. When that one person came, he'd have about fifty people with him. . . . Take that stuff right on back up there. The men would connect those lights and go to the hardware and get gas pipe, and connect that stove back. Put the furniture back just like you had it, so it don't look like you been out the door.

Unemployed Councils were formed all over the country. They were described by Charles R. Walker, writing in *The Forum* in 1932:

I find it is no secret that Communists organize Unemployed Councils in most cities and usually lead them, but the councils are organized democratically and the majority rules. In one I visited at Lincoln Park, Michigan, there were three hundred members of which eleven were Communists. . . . The Council had a right wing, a left wing, and a center. The chairman of the Council . . . was also the local commander of the American Legion. In Chicago there are 45 branches of the Unemployed Council, with a total membership of 22,000.

The Council's weapon is democratic force of numbers, and their function is to prevent evictions of the destitute, or if evicted to bring pressure to bear on the Relief Commission to find a new home; if an unemployed worker has his gas or his water turned off because he can't pay for it, to see the proper authorities; to see that the unemployed who are shoeless and clothesless get both; to eliminate through publicity and pressure discriminations between Negroes and white persons, or against the foreign born, in matters of relief . . . to march people down to relief headquarters and demand they be fed and clothed. Finally to provide legal defense for all unemployed arrested for joining parades, hunger marches, or attending union meetings.

People organized to help themselves, since business and government were not helping them in 1931 and 1932. In Seattle, the fishermen's union caught fish and exchanged them with people who picked fruit and vegetables, and those who cut wood exchanged that. There were twenty-two locals, each with a commissary where food and firewood were exchanged for other goods and services: barbers, seamstresses, and doctors gave of their skills in return for other things. By the end of 1932, there were 330 self-help organizations in thirty-seven states, with over 300,000 members. By early 1933, they seem to have collapsed; they were attempting too big a job in an economy that was more and more a shambles.

Perhaps the most remarkable example of self-help took place in the coal district of Pennsylvania, where teams of unemployed miners dug small mines on company property, mined coal, trucked it to cities, and sold it below the commercial rate. By 1934, 5 million tons of this "bootleg" coal were produced by twenty thousand men using four thousand vehicles. When attempts were made to prosecute, local juries would not convict, local jailers would not imprison.

These were simple actions, taken out of practical need, but they had revolutionary possibilities. Paul Mattick, a Marxist writer, commented:

> All that is really necessary for the workers to do in order to end their miseries is to perform such simple things as to take from where there is, without regard to established property principles or social philosophies, and to start to produce for themselves. Done on a broad social scale, it will lead to lasting results; on a local, isolated plane it will be . . . defeated. . . . The bootleg miners have shown in a rather clear and impressive way, that the so-much bewailed absence of a socialist ideology on the part of the workers really does not prevent workers from acting quite anticapitalistically, quite in accordance with their own needs. Breaking through the confines of private property in order to live up to their own necessities, the miners' action is, at the same time a manifestation of the most important part of class consciousness—namely, that the problems of the workers can be solved only by themselves.

Were the New Dealers—Roosevelt and his advisers, the businessmen who supported him—also class-conscious? Did they understand that measures must be quickly taken, in 1933 and 1934, to give jobs, food baskets, relief, to wipe out the idea "that the problems of the workers can be solved only by themselves"? Perhaps, like the workers' class consciousness, it was a set of actions arising not from held theory, but from instinctive practical necessity.

Perhaps it was such a consciousness that led to the Wagner-Connery Bill, introduced in Congress in early 1934, to regulate labor disputes. The bill provided elections for union representation, a board to settle problems and handle grievances. Was this not exactly the kind of legislation to do away with the idea that "the problems of the workers can be solved only by themselves"? Big business thought it was too helpful to labor and opposed it. Roosevelt was cool to it. But in the year 1934 a series of labor outbursts suggested the need for legislative action.

A million and a half workers in different industries went on strike in 1934. That spring and summer, longshoremen on the West Coast, in a rank-and-file insurrection against their own union leadership as well as against the shippers, held a conven-

[text obscured] d the abolition of the shape-up (a kind of early-

[text obscured] market where work gangs were chosen for the

[text obscured] out on strike.

[text obscured] and miles of Pacific coastline were quickly tied up.

[text obscured] cooperated, refusing to truck cargo to the piers,

[text obscured] workers joined the strike. When the police moved

[text obscured] piers, the strikers resisted en masse, and two were

[text obscured] gunfire. A mass funeral procession for the strikers

[text obscured] er tens of thousands of supporters. And then a

[text obscured] vas called in San Francisco, with 130,000 workers

[text obscured] mobilized.

[text obscured] d special police were sworn in and 4,500 National

[text obscured] sembled, with infantry, machine gun, tank and

[text obscured] The Los Angeles *Times* wrote:

[text obscured] n in San Francisco is not correctly described by the phrase general strike." What is actually in progress there is an insurrection, a Communist-inspired and -led revolt against organized government. There is but one thing to be done—put down the revolt with any force necessary.

The pressure became too strong. There were the troops. There was the AFL pushing to end the strike. The longshoremen accepted a compromise settlement. But they had shown the potential of a general strike.

That same summer of 1934, a strike of teamsters in Minneapolis was supported by other working people, and soon nothing was moving in the city except milk, ice, and coal trucks given exemptions by the strikers. Farmers drove their products into town and sold them directly to the people in the city. The police attacked and two strikers were killed. Fifty thousand people attended a mass funeral. There was an enormous protest meeting

and a march on City Hall. After a month, the employers gave in
to the teamsters' demands.

In the fall of that same year, 1934, came the largest strike of
all—325,000 textile workers in the South. They left the mills and
set up flying squadrons in trucks and autos to move through the
strike areas, picketing, battling guards, entering the mills, unbelt-
ing machinery. Here too, as in the other cases, the strike impetus
came from the rank and file, against a reluctant union leadership
at the top. The *New York Times* said: "The grave danger of the situation is that it will get completely out of the hands of the leaders."

Again, the machinery of the state was set in motion. Deputies
and armed strikebreakers in South Carolina fired on pickets,
killing seven, wounding twenty others. But the strike was spreading to New England. In Lowell, Massachusetts, 2,500 textile
workers rioted; in Saylesville, Rhode Island, a crowd of five thousand people defied state troopers who were armed with machine
guns, and shut down the textile mill. In Woonsocket, Rhode
Island, two thousand people, aroused because someone had been
shot and killed by the National Guard, stormed through the town
and closed the mill.

By September 18, 421,000 textile workers were on strike
throughout the country. There were mass arrests, organizers
were beaten, and the death toll rose to thirteen. Roosevelt now
stepped in and set up a board of mediation, and the union called
off the strike.

In the rural South, too, organizing took place, often stimulated by Communists, but nourished by the grievances of poor
whites and blacks who were tenant farmers or farm laborers,
always in economic difficulties but hit even harder by the Depression. The Southern Tenant Farmers Union started in Arkansas,
with black and white sharecroppers, and spread to other areas.
Roosevelt's AAA was not helping the poorest of farmers; in fact
by encouraging farmers to plant less, it forced tenants and sharecroppers to leave the land. By 1935, of 6,800,000 farmers,
2,800,000 were tenants. The average income of a sharecropper

was $312 a year. Farm laborers, moving from farm to farm, area to area, no land of their own, in 1933 were earning about $300 a year.

Black farmers were the worst off, and some were attracted to the strangers who began appearing in their area during the Depression, suggesting they organize. Nate Shaw recalls, in Theodore Rosengarten's remarkable interview (*All God's Dangers*):

> And durin of the pressure years, a union begin to operate in this country, called it the Sharecroppers Union—that was a nice name, I thought . . . and I knowed what was goin on was a turnabout on the southern man, white and colored; it was somethin unusual. And I heard about it bein a organization for the poor class of people— that's just what I wanted to get into, too. I wanted to know the secrets of it enough that I could become in the knowledge of it. . . .
>
> Mac Sloane, white man, said "You stay out of it. These niggers runnin around here carryin on some kind of meetin—you better stay out of it."
>
> I said to myself, "You a fool if you think you can keep me from joinin". I went right on and joined it, just as quick as the next meetin come. . . . And he done just the thing to push me into it—gived me orders not to join.
>
> The teachers of this organization begin to drive through this country—they couldn't let what they was doin be known. One of em was a colored fella; I disremember his name but he did a whole lot of time, holdin meetins with us—that was part of this job. . . .
>
> Had the meetins at our houses or anywhere we could keep a look and a watch-out that nobody was comin in on us. Small meetins, sometimes there'd be a dozen . . . niggers was scared, niggers was scared, that's tellin the truth.

Nate Shaw told of what happened when a black farmer who hadn't paid his debts was about to be dispossessed:

> The deputy said, "I'm goin to take all old Virgil Jones got this mornin." . . .

> I begged him not to do it, begged him. "You'll dispossess him of bein able to feed his family."

Nate Shaw then told the deputy he was not going to allow it. The deputy came back with more men, and one of them shot and wounded Shaw, who then got his gun and fired back. He was arrested in late 1932, and served twelve years in an Alabama prison. His story is a tiny piece of the great unrecorded drama of the southern poor in those years of the Sharecroppers Union. Years after his release from prison, Nate Shaw spoke his mind on color and class:

> O, it's plain as your hand. The poor white man and the poor black man is sittin in the same saddle today—big dudes done branched em off that way. The control of a man, the controllin power, is in the hands of the rich man. . . . That class is standin together and the poor white man is out there on the colored list—I've caught that: ways and actions a heap of times speaks louder than words. . . .

Hosea Hudson, a black man from rural Georgia, at the age of ten a plowhand, later an iron worker in Birmingham, was aroused by the case of the Scottsboro Boys in 1931 (nine black youths accused of raping two white girls and convicted on flimsy evidence by all-white juries). That year he joined the Communist party. In 1932 and 1933, he organized unemployed blacks in Birmingham. He recalls:

> Deep in the winter of 1932 we Party members organized a unemployed mass meeting to be held on the old courthouse steps, on 3rd Avenue, North Birmingham. . . . It was about 7000 or more people turned out . . . Negroes and whites. . . .
>
>   In 1932 and '33 we began to organize these unemployed block committees in the various communities of Birmingham. . . . If someone get out of food. . . . We wouldn't go around and just say, "That's too bad". We make it our business to go see this person. . . . And if the person was willing . . . we'd work with them. . . .

Block committees would meet every week, had a regular meeting. We talked about the welfare question, what was happening, we read the *Daily Worker* and the *Southern Worker* to see what was going on about unemployed relief, what people doing in Cleveland ... struggles in Chicago ... or we talk about the latest developments in the Scottsboro case. We kept up, we was on top, so people always wanted to come cause we had something different to tell them every time.

In 1934 and 1935 hundreds of thousands of workers, left out of the tightly controlled, exclusive unions of the American Federation of Labor, began organizing in the new mass production industries—auto, rubber, packinghouse. The AFL could not ignore them; it set up a Committee for Industrial Organization to organize these workers outside of craft lines, by industry, all workers in a plant belonging to one union. This Committee, headed by John Lewis, then broke away and became the CIO—the Congress of Industrial Organizations.

But it was rank-and-file strikes and insurgencies that pushed the union leadership, AFL and CIO, into action. Jeremy Brecher tells the story in his book *Strike!* A new kind of tactic began among rubber workers in Akron, Ohio, in the early thirties—the sit-down strike. The workers stayed in the plant instead of walking out, and this had clear advantages: they were directly blocking the use of strikebreakers; they did not have to act through union officials but were in direct control of the situation themselves; they did not have to walk outside in the cold and rain, but had shelter; they were not isolated, as in their work, or on the picket line; they were thousands under one roof, free to talk to one another, to form a community of struggle. Louis Adamic, a labor writer, describes one of the early sit-downs:

Sitting by their machines, cauldrons, boilers and work benches, they talked. Some realized for the first time how important they were in the process of rubber production. Twelve men had practically stopped the works! ... Superintendents, foremen, and straw bosses were dashing about. . . . In less than an hour the dispute was settled, full victory for the men.

In early 1936, at the Firestone rubber plant in Akron, makers of truck tires, their wages already too low to pay for food and rent, were faced with a wage cut. When several union men were fired, others began to stop work, to sit down on the job. In one day the whole of plant #1 was sitting down. In two days, plant #2 was sitting down, and management gave in. In the next ten days there was a sit-down at Goodyear. A court issued an injunction against mass picketing. It was ignored, and 150 deputies were sworn in. But they soon faced ten thousand workers from all over Akron. In a month the strike was won.

The idea spread through 1936. In December of that year began the longest sit-down strike of all, at Fisher Body plant #1 in Flint, Michigan. It started when two brothers were fired, and it lasted until February 1937. For forty days there was a community of two thousand strikers. "It was like war," one said. "The guys with me became my buddies." Sidney Fine in *Sit-Down* describes what happened. Committees organized recreation, information, classes, a postal service, sanitation. Courts were set up to deal with those who didn't take their turn washing dishes or who threw rubbish or smoked where it was prohibited or brought in liquor. The "punishment" consisted of extra duties; the ultimate punishment was expulsion from the plant. A restaurant owner across the street prepared three meals a day for two thousand strikers. There were classes in parliamentary procedure, public speaking, history of the labor movement. Graduate students at the University of Michigan gave courses in journalism and creative writing.

There were injunctions, but a procession of five thousand armed workers encircled the plant and there was no attempt to enforce the injunction. Police attacked with tear gas and the workers fought back with firehoses. Thirteen strikers were wounded by gunfire, but the police were driven back. The governor called out the National Guard. By this time the strike had spread to other General Motors plants. Finally there was a settlement, a six-month contract, leaving many questions unsettled but recognizing that from now on, the company would have to deal not with individuals but with a union.

In 1936 there were forty-eight sitdown strikes. In 1937 there were 477: electrical workers in St. Louis; shirt workers in Pulaski, Tennessee; broom workers in Pueblo, Colorado; trash collectors in Bridgeport, Connecticut; gravediggers in New Jersey; seventeen blind workers at the New York Guild for the Jewish Blind; prisoners in an Illinois penitentiary; and even thirty members of a National Guard Company who had served in the Fisher Body sitdown, and now sat down themselves because they had not been paid.

The sit-downs were especially dangerous to the system because they were not controlled by the regular union leadership. An AFL business agent for the Hotel and Restaurant Employees said:

> You'd be sitting in the office any March day of 1937, and the phone would ring and the voice at the other end would say: "My name is Mary Jones; I'm a soda clerk at Liggett's; we've thrown the manager out and we've got the keys. What do we do now?" And you'd hurry over to the company to negotiate and over there they'd say, "I think it's the height of irresponsibility to call a strike before you've ever asked for a contract" and all you could answer was, "You're so right."

It was to stabilize the system in the face of labor unrest that the Wagner Act of 1935, setting up a National Labor Relations Board, had been passed. The wave of strikes in 1936, 1937, 1938, made the need even more pressing. In Chicago, on Memorial Day, 1937, a strike at Republic Steel brought the police out, firing at a mass picket line of strikers, killing ten of them. Autopsies showed the bullets had hit the workers in the back as they were running away: this was the Memorial Day Massacre. But Republic Steel was organized, and so was Ford Motor Company, and the other huge plants in steel, auto, rubber, meatpacking, the electrical industry.

The Wagner Act was challenged by a steel corporation in the courts, but the Supreme Court found it constitutional—that the government could regulate interstate commerce, and that strikes hurt interstate commerce. From the trade unions' point of view, the new law was an aid to union organizing. From the government's point of view it was an aid to the stability of commerce.

Unions were not wanted by employers, but they were more controllable—more stabilizing for the system than the wildcat strikes, the factory occupations of the rank and file. In the spring of 1937, a *New York Times* article carried the headline "Unauthorized Sit-Downs Fought by CIO Unions." The story read: "Strict orders have been issued to all organizers and representatives that they will be dismissed if they authorize any stoppages of work without the consent of the international officers. . . ." The *Times* quoted John L. Lewis, dynamic leader of the CIO: "A CIO contract is adequate protection against sit-downs, lie-downs, or any other kind of strike."

The Communist party, some of whose members played critical roles in organizing CIO unions, seemed to take the same position. One Communist leader in Akron was reported to have said at a party strategy meeting after the sit-downs: "Now we must work for regular relations between the union and the employers—and strict observance of union procedure on the part of the workers."

Thus, two sophisticated ways of controlling direct labor action developed in the mid-thirties. First, the National Labor Relations Board would give unions legal status, listen to them, settling certain of their grievances. Thus it could moderate labor rebellion by channeling energy into elections—just as the constitutional system channeled possibly troublesome energy into voting. The NLRB would set limits in economic conflict as voting did in political conflict. And second, the workers' organization itself, the union, even a militant and aggressive union like the CIO, would channel the workers' insurrectionary energy into contracts, negotiations, union meetings, and try to minimize strikes, in order to build large, influential, even respectable organizations.

The history of those years seems to support the argument of Richard Cloward and Frances Piven, in their book *Poor People's Movements*, that labor won most during its spontaneous uprisings, before the unions were recognized or well organized: "Factory workers had their greatest influence, and were able to exact their most substantial concessions from government, during the Great Depression, in the years before they were organized into unions. Their power during the Depression was not rooted in organization, but in disruption."

Piven and Cloward point out that union membership rose enormously in the forties, during the Second World War (the CIO and AFL had over 6 million members each by 1945), but its power was less than before—its gains from the use of strikes kept getting whittled down. The members appointed to the NLRB were less sympathetic to labor, the Supreme Court declared sit-downs to be illegal, and state governments were passing laws to hamper strikes, picketing, boycotts.

The coming of World War II weakened the old labor militancy of the thirties because the war economy created millions of new jobs at higher wages. The New Deal had succeeded only in reducing unemployment from 13 million to 9 million. It was the war that put almost everyone to work, and the war did something else: patriotism, the push for unity of all classes against enemies overseas, made it harder to mobilize anger against the corporations. During the war, the CIO and AFL pledged to call no strikes.

Still, the grievances of workers were such—wartime "controls" meant their wages were being controlled better than prices—that they felt impelled to engage in many wildcat strikes: there were more strikes in 1944 than in any previous year in American history, says Jeremy Brecher.

The thirties and forties showed more clearly than before the dilemma of working people in the United States. The system responded to workers' rebellions by finding new forms of control—internal control by their own organizations as well as outside control by law and force. But along with the new controls came new concessions. These concessions didn't solve basic problems; for many people they solved nothing. But they helped enough people to create an atmosphere of progress and improvement, to restore some faith in the system.

The minimum wage of 1938, which established the forty-hour week and outlawed child labor, left many people out of its provisions and set very low minimum wages (twenty-five cents an hour the first year). But it was enough to dull the edge of resentment. Housing was built for only a small percentage of the people who needed it. "A modest, even parsimonious, beginning," Paul Conkin says (*F.D.R. and the Origins of the Welfare State*), but the sight of federally subsidized housing projects, playgrounds, vermin-free apartments, replacing dilapidated tenements, was refreshing. The TVA suggested exciting possibilities for regional planning to give jobs, improve areas, and provide cheap power, with local instead of national control. The Social Security Act gave retirement benefits and unemployment insurance, and matched state funds for mothers and dependent children—but it excluded farmers, domestic workers, and old people, and offered no health insurance. As Conkin says: "The meager benefits of Social Security were insignificant in comparison to the building of security for large, established businesses."

The New Deal gave federal money to put thousands of writers, artists, actors, and musicians to work—in a Federal Theatre Project, a Federal Writers Project, a Federal Art Project: murals were painted on public buildings; plays were put on for working-class audiences who had never seen a play; hundreds of books and pamphlets were written and published. People heard a symphony for the first time. It was an exciting flowering of arts for the people, such as had never happened before in American history, and which has not been duplicated since. But in 1939, with the country more stable and the New Deal reform impulse weakened, programs to subsidize the arts were eliminated.

When the New Deal was over, capitalism remained intact. The rich still controlled the nation's wealth, as well as its laws, courts, police, newspapers, churches, colleges. Enough help had been given to enough people to make Roosevelt a hero to millions, but the same system that had brought depression and crisis—the system of waste, of inequality, of concern for profit over human need—remained.

For black people, the New Deal was psychologically encouraging (Mrs. Roosevelt was sympathetic; some blacks got posts in the administration), but most blacks were ignored by the New Deal programs. As tenant farmers, as farm laborers, as migrants, as domestic workers, they didn't qualify for unemployment insurance, minimum wages, social security, or farm subsidies. Roosevelt, careful not to offend southern white politicians whose political support he needed, did not push a bill against lynching. Blacks and whites were segregated in the armed forces. And black workers were discriminated against in getting jobs. They were the last hired, the first fired. Only when A. Philip Randolph, head of the Sleeping-Car Porters Union, threatened a massive march on Washington in 1941 would Roosevelt agree to sign an executive order establishing a Fair Employment Practices Committee. But the FEPC had no enforcement powers and changed little.

Black Harlem, with all the New Deal reforms, remained as it was. There 350,000 people lived, 233 persons per acre compared with 133 for the rest of Manhattan. In twenty-five years, its population had multiplied six times. Ten thousand families lived in rat-infested cellars and basements. Tuberculosis was common. Perhaps half of the married women worked as domestics. They traveled to the Bronx and gathered on street corners—"slave markets," they were called—to be hired. Prostitution crept in. Two young black women, Ella Baker and Marvel Cooke, wrote about this in *The Crisis* in 1935:

> Not only is human labor bartered and sold for the slave wage, but human love is also a marketable commodity. Whether it is labor or love, the women arrive as early as eight a.m. and remain as late as one p.m. or until they are hired. In rain or shine, hot or cold, they wait to work for ten, fifteen, and twenty cents per hour.

In Harlem Hospital in 1932, proportionately twice as many people died as in Bellevue Hospital, which was in the white area downtown. Harlem was a place that bred crime—"the bitter blossom of poverty," as Roi Ottley and William Weatherby say in their essay "The Negro in New York."

On March 19, 1935, even as the New Deal reforms were being passed, Harlem exploded. Ten thousand Negroes swept through the streets, destroying the property of white merchants. Seven hundred policemen moved in and brought order. Two blacks were killed.

In the mid-thirties, a young black poet named Langston Hughes wrote a poem, "Let America Be America Again":

> . . . I am the poor white, fooled and pushed apart,
> I am the Negro bearing slavery's scars.
> I am the red man driven from the land,
> I am the immigrant clutching the hope I seek—
> And finding only the same old stupid plan.
> Of dog eat dog, of mighty crush the weak. . . .
>
> O, let America be America again—
> The land that never has been yet—
> And yet must be—the land where every man is free.
> The land that's mine—the poor man's, Indian's, Negro's
>   ME—
> Who made America,
> Whose sweat and blood, whose faith and pain,
> Whose hand at the foundry, whose plow in the rain,
> Must bring back our mighty dream again.
>
> Sure, call me any ugly name you choose—
> The steel of freedom does not stain.
> From those who live like leeches on the people's lives,
> We must take back our land again,
> America! . . .

To white Americans of the thirties, however, North and South, blacks were invisible. Only the radicals made an attempt to break the racial barriers: Socialists, Trotskyists, Communists most of all. The CIO, influenced by the Communists, was organizing blacks in the mass production industries. Blacks were still being used as strikebreakers, but now there were also attempts to bring blacks and whites together against their common enemy. A woman named Mollie Lewis, writing in *The Crisis*, in 1938, told of her experience in a steel strike in Gary, Indiana:

> While the municipal government of Gary continues to keep the children apart in a system of separate schools, their parents are getting together in the union and in the auxiliary. . . . The only public eating place in Gary where both races may be freely served is a cooperative restaurant largely patronized by members of the union and auxiliary. . . .
>
> When the black and white workers and members of their families are convinced that their basic economic interests are the same, they may be expected to make common cause for the advancement of these interests. . . .

There was no great feminist movement in the thirties. But many women became involved in the labor organizing of those years. A Minnesota poet, Meridel LeSeuer, was thirty-four when the great teamsters' strike tied up Minneapolis in 1934. She became active in it, and later described her experiences:

> I have never been in a strike before. . . . The truth is I was afraid. . . . "Do you need any help?" I said eagerly. . . . We kept on pouring thousands of cups of coffee, feeding thousands of men. . . . The cars were coming back. The announcer cried, "This is murder." . . . I saw them taking men out of cars and putting them on the hospital cots, on the floor. . . . The picket cars keep coming in. Some men have walked back from the market, holding their own blood in. . . . Men, women and children are massing outside, a living circle close packed

for protection. . . . We have living blood on our skirts. . . .

Tuesday, the day of the funeral, one thousand more militia were massed downtown.

It was over ninety in the shade. I went to the funeral parlors and thousands of men and women were massed there waiting in the terrific sun. One block of women and children were standing two hours waiting. I went over and stood near them. I didn't know whether I could march. I didn't like marching in parades. . . . Three women drew me in. "We want all to march," they said gently. "Come with us.". . .

Sylvia Woods spoke to Alice and Staughton Lynd years later about her experiences in the thirties as a laundry worker and union organizer:

You have to tell people things they can see. Then they'll say, "Oh, I never thought of that" or "I have never seen it like that." . . . Like Tennessee. He hated black people. A poor sharecropper. . . . He danced with a black woman. . . . So I have seen people change. This is the faith you've got to have in people.

Many Americans began to change their thinking in those days of crisis and rebellion. In Europe, Hitler was on the march. Across the Pacific, Japan was invading China. The Western empires were being threatened by new ones. For the United States, war was not far off.

5

A People's War?

"We, the governments of Great Britain and the United States, in the name of India, Burma, Malaya, Australia, British East Africa, British Guiana, Hongkong, Siam, Singapore, Egypt, Palestine, Canada, New Zealand, Northern Ireland, Scotland, Wales, as well as Puerto Rico, Guam, the Philippines, Hawaii, Alaska, and the Virgin Islands, hereby declare most emphatically, that this is not an imperialist war." Thus went a skit put on in the United States in the year 1939 by the Communist party.

Two years later, Germany invaded Soviet Russia, and the American Communist party, which had repeatedly described the war between the Axis Powers and the Allied Powers as an imperialist war, now called it a "people's war" against Fascism. Indeed almost all Americans were now in agreement—capitalists, Communists, Democrats, Republicans, poor, rich, and middle class—that this was indeed a people's war.

Was it?

By certain evidence, it was the most popular war the United States had ever fought. Never had a greater proportion of the country participated in a war: 18 million served in the armed forces, 10 million overseas; 25 million workers gave of their pay envelope regularly for war bonds. But could this be considered a manufactured support, since all the power of the nation—not only of the government, but the press, the church, and even the chief radical organizations—was behind the calls for all-out war? Was there an undercurrent of reluctance; were there unpublicized signs of resistance?

It was a war against an enemy of unspeakable evil. Hitler's Germany was extending totalitarianism, racism, militarism, and overt aggressive warfare beyond what an already cynical world had experienced. And yet, did the governments conducting this war—England, the United States, the Soviet Union—represent something significantly different, so that their victory would be a blow to imperialism, racism, totalitarianism, militarism, in the world?

Would the behavior of the United States during the war—in military action abroad, in treatment of minorities at home—be in keeping with a "people's war"? Would the country's wartime policies respect the rights of ordinary people everywhere to life, liberty, and the pursuit of happiness? And would postwar America, in its policies at home and overseas, exemplify the values for which the war was supposed to have been fought?

These questions deserve thought. At the time of World War II, the atmosphere was too dense with war fervor to permit them to be aired.

For the United States to step forward as a defender of helpless countries matched its image in American high school history textbooks, but not its record in world affairs. It had instigated a war with Mexico and taken half of that country. It had pretended to help Cuba win freedom from Spain, and then planted itself in Cuba with a military base, investments, and rights of intervention. It had seized Hawaii, Puerto Rico, Guam, and fought a brutal war to subjugate the Filipinos. It had "opened" Japan to its trade with gunboats and threats. It had declared an Open Door Policy in China as a means of assuring that the United States would have opportunities equal to other imperial powers in exploiting China. It had sent troops to Peking with other nations, to assert Western supremacy in China, and kept them there for over thirty years.

While demanding an Open Door in China, it had insisted (with the Monroe Doctrine and many military interventions) on a Closed Door in Latin America—that is, closed to everyone but the United States. It had engineered a revolution against Colombia and created the "independent" state of Panama in order to build and control the Canal. It sent five thousand marines to Nicaragua in 1926 to counter a revolution, and kept a force there for seven years. It intervened in the Dominican Republic for the fourth time in 1916 and kept troops there for eight years. It intervened for the second time in Haiti in 1915 and kept troops there for nineteen years. Between 1900 and 1933, the United States intervened in Cuba four times, in Nicaragua twice, in Panama six times, in Guatemala once, in Honduras seven times. By 1924 the finances of half of the twenty Latin American states were being directed to some extent by the United States. By 1935, over half of U.S. steel and cotton exports were being sold in Latin America.

Just before World War I ended, in 1918, an American force of seven thousand landed at Vladivostok as part of an Allied intervention in Russia, and remained until early 1920. Five thousand more troops were landed at Archangel, another Russian port, also as part of an Allied expeditionary force, and stayed for almost a year. The State Department told Congress: "All these operations were to offset effects of the Bolshevik revolution in Russia."

In short, if the entrance of the United States into World War II was (as so many Americans believed at the time, observing the Nazi invasions) to defend the principle of nonintervention in the affairs of other countries, the nation's record cast doubt on its ability to uphold that principle.

What seemed clear at the time was that the United States was a democracy with certain liberties, while Germany was a dictatorship persecuting its Jewish minority, imprisoning dissidents, whatever their religion, while proclaiming the supremacy of the Nordic "race." However, blacks, looking at anti-Semitism in Germany, might not see their own situation in the U.S. as much different. And the United States had done little about Hitler's policies of persecution. Indeed, it had joined England and France in appeasing Hitler throughout the thirties. Roosevelt and his Secretary of State, Cordell Hull, were hesitant to criticize publicly Hitler's anti-Semitic policies; when a resolution was introduced in the Senate in January 1934 asking the Senate and the President to express "surprise and pain" at what the Germans were doing to the Jews, and to ask restoration of Jewish rights, the State Department "caused this resolution to be buried in committee," according to Arnold Offner *(American Appeasement)*.

When Mussolini's Italy invaded Ethiopia in 1935, the U.S. declared an embargo on munitions but let American businesses send oil to Italy in huge quantities, which was essential to Italy's carrying on the war. When a Fascist rebellion took place in Spain in 1936 against the elected socialist-liberal government, the Roosevelt administration sponsored a neutrality act that had the effect of shutting off help to the Spanish government while Hitler and Mussolini gave critical aid to Franco. Offner says:

> . . . the United States went beyond even the legal requirements of its neutrality legislation. Had aid been forthcoming from the United States and from England and France, considering that Hitler's position on aid to Franco was not firm at least until November 1936, the Spanish Republicans could well have triumphed. Instead, Germany gained every advantage from the Spanish civil war.

Was this simply poor judgment, an unfortunate error? Or was it the logical policy of a government whose main interest was not stopping Fascism but advancing the imperial interests of the United States? For those interests, in the thirties, an anti-Soviet policy seemed best. Later, when Japan and Germany threatened U.S. world interests, a pro-Soviet, anti-Nazi policy became preferable. Roosevelt was as much concerned to end the oppression of Jews as Lincoln was to end slavery during the Civil War; their priority in policy (whatever their personal compassion for victims of persecution) was not minority rights, but national power.

It was not Hitler's attacks on the Jews that brought the United States into World War II, any more than the enslavement of 4 million blacks brought Civil War in 1861. Italy's attack on Ethiopia, Hitler's invasion of Austria, his takeover of Czechoslovakia, his attack on Poland—none of those events caused the United States to enter the war, although Roosevelt did begin to give important aid to England. What brought the United States fully into the war was the Japanese attack on the American naval base at Pearl Harbor, Hawaii, on December 7, 1941. Surely it was not the humane concern for Japan's bombing of civilians that led to Roosevelt's outraged call for war—Japan's attack on China in 1937, her bombing of civilians at Nanking, had not provoked the United States to war. It was the Japanese attack on a link in the American Pacific Empire that did it.

So long as Japan remained a well-behaved member of that imperial club of Great Powers who—in keeping with the Open Door Policy—were sharing the exploitation of China, the United States did not object. It had exchanged notes with Japan in 1917 saying "the Government of the United States recognizes that Japan has special interests in China." In 1928, according to Akira Iriye (*After Imperialism*), American consuls in China supported the coming of Japanese troops. It was when Japan threatened potential U.S. markets by its attempted takeover of China, but especially as it moved toward the tin, rubber, and oil of Southeast Asia, that the United States became alarmed and took those measures which led to the Japanese attack: a total embargo on scrap iron, a total embargo on oil in the summer of 1941.

As Bruce Russett says (*No Clear and Present Danger*): "Throughout the 1930s the United States government had done little to resist the Japanese advance on the Asian continent." But: "The Southwest Pacific area was of undeniable economic importance to the United States—at the time most of America's tin and rubber came from there, as did substantial quantities of other raw materials."

Pearl Harbor was presented to the American public as a sudden, shocking, immoral act. Immoral it was, like any bombing—but not really sudden or shocking to the American government. Russett says: "Japan's strike against the American naval base climaxed a long series of mutually antagonistic acts. In initiating economic sanctions against Japan the United States undertook actions that were widely recognized in Washington as carrying grave risks of war."

Putting aside the wild accusations against Roosevelt (that he knew about Pearl Harbor and didn't tell, or that he deliberately provoked the Pearl Harbor raid—these are without evidence), it does seem clear that he did as James Polk had done before him in the Mexican war and Lyndon Johnson after him in the Vietnam war—he lied to the public for what he thought was a right cause. In September and October 1941, he misstated the facts in two incidents involving German submarines and American destroyers. A historian sympathetic to Roosevelt, Thomas A. Bailey, has written:

> Franklin Roosevelt repeatedly deceived the American people during the period before Pearl Harbor. . . . He was like the physician who must tell the patient lies for the patient's own good . . . because the masses are notoriously shortsighted and generally cannot see danger until it is at their throats. . . .

One of the judges in the Tokyo War Crimes Trial after World War II, Radhabinod Pal, dissented from the general verdicts against Japanese officials and argued that the United States had clearly provoked the war with Japan and expected Japan to act. Richard Minear (*Victors' Justice*) sums up Pal's view of the embargoes on scrap iron and oil, that "these measures were a clear and potent threat to Japan's very existence." The records show that a White House conference two weeks before Pearl Harbor anticipated a war and discussed how it should be justified.

A State Department memorandum on Japanese expansion, a year before Pearl Harbor, did not talk of the independence of China or the principle of self-determination. It said:

> . . . our general diplomatic and strategic position would be considerably weakened—by our loss of Chinese, Indian and South Seas

markets (and by our loss of much of the Japanese market for our goods, as Japan would become more and more self-sufficient) as well as by insurmountable restrictions upon our access to the rubber, tin, jute, and other vital materials of the Asian and Oceanic regions.

Once joined with England and Russia in the war (Germany and Italy declared war on the United States right after Pearl Harbor), did the behavior of the United States show that her war aims were humanitarian, or centered on power and profit? Was she fighting the war to end the control by some nations over others or to make sure the controlling nations were friends of the United States? In August 1941, Roosevelt and Churchill met off the coast of Newfoundland and released to the world the Atlantic Charter, setting forth noble goals for the postwar world, saying their countries "seek no aggrandizement, territorial or other," and that they respected "the right of all peoples to choose the form of government under which they will live." The Charter was celebrated as declaring the right of nations to self-determination.

Two weeks before the Atlantic Charter, however, the U.S. Acting Secretary of State, Sumner Welles, had assured the French government that they could keep their empire intact after the end of the war: "This Government, mindful of its traditional friendship for France, has deeply sympathized with the desire of the French people to maintain their territories and to preserve them intact." The Department of Defense history of Vietnam (*The Pentagon Papers*) itself pointed to what it called an "ambivalent" policy toward Indochina, noting that "in the Atlantic Charter and other pronouncements, the U.S. proclaimed support for national self-determination and independence" but also "early in the war repeatedly expressed or implied to the French an intention to restore to France its overseas empire after the war."

In late 1942, Roosevelt's personal representative assured French General Henri Giraud: "It is thoroughly understood that French sovereignty will be re-established as soon as possible throughout all the territory, metropolitan or colonial, over which flew the French flag in 1939." (These pages, like the others in the *Pentagon Papers*, are marked "TOP SECRET—Sensitive.") By 1945 the "ambivalent" attitude was gone. In May, Truman assured the French he did not question her "sovereignty over Indochina." That fall, the United States urged Nationalist China, put temporarily in charge of the northern part of Indochina by the Potsdam Conference, to turn it over to the French, despite the obvious desire of the Vietnamese for independence.

That was a favor for the French government. But what about the United States' own imperial ambitions during the war? What about the "aggrandizement, territorial or other" that Roosevelt had renounced in the Atlantic Charter?

In the headlines were the battles and troop movements: the invasion of North Africa in 1942, Italy in 1943, the massive, dramatic cross-Channel invasion of German-occupied France in 1944, the bitter battles as Germany was pushed back toward and over her frontiers, the increasing bombardment by the British and American air forces. And, at the same time, the Russian victories over the Nazi armies (the Russians, by the time of the cross-Channel invasion, had driven the Germans out of Russia, and were engaging 80 percent of the German troops). In the Pacific, in 1943 and 1944, there was the island-by-island move of American forces toward Japan, finding closer and closer bases for the thunderous bombardment of Japanese cities.

Quietly, behind the headlines in battles and bombings, American diplomats and businessmen worked hard to make sure that when the war ended, American economic power would be second to none in the world. United States business would penetrate areas that up to this time had been dominated by England. The Open Door Policy of equal access would be extended from Asia to Europe, meaning that the United States intended to push England aside and move in.

That is what happened to the Middle East and its oil. In August 1945 a State Department officer said that "a review of the diplomatic history of the past 35 years will show that petroleum has historically played a larger part in the external relations of the United States than any other commodity." Saudi Arabia was the largest oil pool in the Middle East. The ARAMCO oil corporation, through Secretary of the Interior Harold Ickes, got Roosevelt to agree to Lend Lease aid to Saudi Arabia, which would involve the U.S. government there and create a shield for the interests of ARAMCO. In 1944 Britain and the U.S. signed a pact on oil agreeing on "the principle of equal opportunity," and Lloyd Gardner concludes (*Economic Aspects of New Deal Diplomacy*) that "the Open Door Policy was triumphant throughout the Middle East."

Historian Gabriel Kolko, after a close study of American wartime policy (*The Politics of War*), concludes that "the American economic war aim was to save capitalism at home and abroad." In April 1944 a State Department official said: "As you know, we've got to plan on enormously increased production in this country after the war, and the American domestic market can't absorb all that production indefinitely. There won't be any question about our needing greatly increased foreign markets."

Anthony Sampson, in his study of the international oil business (*The Seven Sisters*), says:

> By the end of the war the dominant influence in Saudi Arabia was unquestionably the United States. King Ibn Saud was regarded no longer as a wild desert warrior, but as a key piece in the power-game, to be wooed by the West. Roosevelt, on his way back from Yalta in February 1945, entertained the King on the cruiser *Quincy*, together with his entourage of fifty, including two sons, a prime minister, an astrologer and flocks of sheep for slaughter.

Roosevelt then wrote to Ibn Saud, promising the United States would not change its Palestine policy without consulting the Arabs. In later years, the concern for oil would constantly compete with political concern for the Jewish state in the Middle East, but at this point, oil seemed more important.

With British imperial power collapsing during World War II,

the United States was ready to move in. Hull said early in the war:

> Leadership toward a new system of international relationships in trade and other economic affairs will devolve very largely upon the United States because of our great economic strength. We should assume this leadership, and the responsibility that goes with it, primarily for reasons of pure national self-interest.

Before the war was over, the administration was planning the outlines of the new international economic order, based on partnership between government and big business. Lloyd Gardner says of Roosevelt's chief adviser, Harry Hopkins, who had organized the relief programs of the New Deal: "No conservative outdid Hopkins in championing foreign investment, and its protection."

The poet Archibald MacLeish, then an Assistant Secretary of State, spoke critically of what he saw in the postwar world: "As things are now going, the peace we will make, the peace we seem to be making, will be a peace of oil, a peace of gold, a peace of shipping, a peace, in brief . . . without moral purpose or human interest. . . ."

During the war, England and the United States set up the International Monetary Fund to regulate international exchanges of currency; voting would be proportional to capital contributed, so American dominance would be assured. The International Bank for Reconstruction and Development was set up, supposedly to help reconstruct war-destroyed areas, but one of its first objectives was, in its own words, "to promote foreign investment."

The economic aid countries would need after the war was already seen in political terms: Averell Harriman, ambassador to Russia, said in early 1944: "Economic assistance is one of the most effective weapons at our disposal to influence European political events in the direction we desire. . . ."

The creation of the United Nations during the war was presented to the world as international cooperation to prevent future wars. But the U.N. was dominated by the Western imperial countries—the United States, England, and France—and a new imperial power, with military bases and powerful influence in Eastern Europe—the Soviet Union. An important conservative Republican Senator, Arthur Vandenburg, wrote in his diary about the United Nations Charter:

> ...thing about it is that it is so conservative from a nationalist standpoint. It is based virtually on a four-power alliance. . . . This is anything but a wild-eyed internationalist dream of a world State. . . . I am deeply impressed (and surprised) to find Hull so carefully guarding our American veto in his scheme of things.

The plight of the Jews in German-occupied Europe, which many people thought was at the heart of the war against the Axis, was not a chief concern of Roosevelt. Henry Feingold's research (The Politics of Rescue) shows that, while the Jews were being put in camps and the process of annihilation was beginning that would end in the horrifying extermination of 6 million Jews and millions of non-Jews, Roosevelt failed to take steps that might have saved thousands of lives. He did not see it as a high priority; he left it to the State Department, and in the State Department anti-Semitism and a cold bureaucracy became obstacles to action.

Was the war being fought to establish that Hitler was wrong in his ideas of white Nordic supremacy over "inferior" races? The United States' armed forces were segregated by race. When troops were jammed onto the *Queen Mary* in early 1945 to go to combat duty in the European theater, the blacks were stowed down in the depths of the ship near the engine room, as far as possible from the fresh air of the deck, in a bizarre reminder of the slave voyages of old.

The Red Cross, with government approval, separated the blood donations of black and white. It was, ironically, a black physician named Charles Drew who developed the blood bank system. He was put in charge of the wartime donations, and then fired when he tried to end blood segregation. Despite the urgent need for wartime labor, blacks were still being discriminated against for jobs. A spokesman for a West Coast aviation plant said: "The Negro will be considered only as janitors and in other similar capacities. . . . Regardless of their training as aircraft workers, we will not employ them." Roosevelt never did anything to enforce the orders of the Fair Employment Practices Commission he had set up.

The Fascist nations were notorious in their insistence that the woman's place was in the home. Yet, the war against Fascism, although it utilized women in defense industries where they were desperately needed, took no special steps to change the subordinate role of women. The War Manpower Commission, despite the large numbers of women in war work, kept women off its policymaking bodies. A report of the Women's Bureau of the Department of Labor, by its director, Mary Anderson, said the War Manpower Commission had "doubts and uneasiness" about "what was then regarded as a developing attitude of militancy or a crusading spirit on the part of women leaders. . . ."

In one of its policies, the United States came close to direct duplication of Fascism. This was in its treatment of the Japanese-Americans living on the West Coast. After the Pearl Harbor attack, anti-Japanese hysteria spread in the government. One Congressman said: "I'm for catching every Japanese in America, Alaska and Hawaii now and putting them in concentration camps. . . . Damn them! Let's get rid of them!"

Franklin D. Roosevelt did not share this frenzy, but he calmly signed Executive Order 9066, in February 1942, giving the army the power, without warrants or indictments or hearings, to arrest every Japanese-American on the West Coast—110,000 men, women, and children—to take them from their homes, transport them to camps far into the interior, and keep them there under prison conditions. Three-fourths of these were Nisei—children born in the United States of Japanese parents and therefore American citizens. The other fourth—the Issei, born in Japan— were barred by law from becoming citizens. In 1944 the Supreme Court upheld the forced evacuation on the grounds of military necessity. The Japanese remained in those camps for over three years.

Michi Weglyn was a young girl when her family experienced evacuation and detention. She tells *(Years of Infamy)* of bungling in the evacuation, of misery, confusion, anger, but also of Japanese-American dignity and fighting back. There were strikes, petitions, mass meetings, refusal to sign loyalty oaths, riots against the camp authorities. The Japanese resisted to the end.

Not until after the war did the story of the Japanese-Americans begin to be known to the general public. The month the war ended in Asia, September 1945, an article appeared in *Harper's Magazine* by Yale Law Professor Eugene V. Rostow, calling the Japanese evacuation "our worst wartime mistake." Was it a "mistake"—or was it an action to be expected from a nation with a long history of racism and which was fighting a war, not to end racism, but to retain the fundamental elements of the American system?

It was a war waged by a government whose chief beneficiary— despite volumes of reforms—was a wealthy elite. The alliance between big business and the government went back to the very first proposals of Alexander Hamilton to Congress after the Revolutionary War. By World War II that partnership had developed and intensified. During the Depression, Roosevelt had once denounced the "economic royalists," but he always had the support of certain important business leaders. During the war, as Bruce Catton saw it from his post in the War Production Board: "The economic royalists, denounced and derided . . . had a part to play now. . . ."

Catton *(The War Lords of Washington)* described the process of industrial mobilization to carry on the war, and how in this process wealth became more and more concentrated in fewer and fewer large corporations. In 1940 the United States had begun sending large amounts of war supplies to England and France. By 1941 three-fourths of the value of military contracts were handled by fifty-six large corporations. A Senate report, "Economic Concentration and World War II," noted that the government contracted for scientific research in industry during the war, and although two thousand corporations were involved, of $1 billion spent, $400 million went to ten large corporations.

Management remained firmly in charge of decision making during the war, and although 12 million workers were organized in the CIO and AFL, labor was in a subordinate position. Labor-management committees were set up in five thousand factories, as a gesture toward industrial democracy, but they acted mostly as disciplinary groups for absentee workers, and devices for increasing production. Catton writes: "The big operators who made the working decisions had decided that nothing very substantial was going to be changed."

Despite the overwhelming atmosphere of patriotism and total dedication to winning the war, despite the no-strike pledges of the AFL and CIO, many of the nation's workers, frustrated by the freezing of wages while business profits rocketed skyward, went on strike. During the war, there were fourteen thousand strikes, involving 6,770,000 workers, more than in any comparable period in American history. In 1944 alone, a million workers were on strike, in the mines, in the steel mills, in the auto and transportation equipment industries.

When the war ended, the strikes continued in record numbers—3 million on strike in the first half of 1946. According to Jeremy Brecher (*Strike!*), if not for the disciplinary hand of the unions there might have been "a general confrontation between the workers of a great many industries, and the government, supporting the employers."

In Lowell, Massachusetts, for example, according to an unpublished manuscript by Marc Miller ("The Irony of Victory: Lowell During World War II"), there were as many strikes in 1943 and 1944 as in 1937. It may have been a "people's war," but here was dissatisfaction at the fact that the textile mill profits grew 600 percent from 1940 to 1946, while wage increases in cotton goods industries went up 36 percent. How little the war changed the difficult condition of women workers is shown by the fact that in Lowell, among women war workers with children, only 5 percent could have their children taken care of by nursery schools; the others had to make their own arrangements.

Beneath the noise of enthusiastic patriotism, there were many people who thought war was wrong, even in the circumstances of Fascist aggression. Out of 10 million drafted for the armed forces during World War II, only 43,000 refused to fight. But this was three times the proportion of C.O.'s (conscientious objectors) in World War I. Of these 43,000, about 6,000 went to prison, which was, proportionately, four times the number of C.O.'s who went to prison during World War I. Of every six men in federal prison, one was there as a C.O.

Many more than 43,000 refusers did not show up for the draft at all. The government lists about 350,000 cases of draft evasion, including technical violations as well as actual desertion, so it is hard to tell the true number, but it may be that the number of men who either did not show up or claimed C.O. status was in the hundreds of thousands—not a small number. And this in the face of an American community almost unanimously for the war.

Among those soldiers who were not conscientious objectors, who seemed willing fighters, it is hard to know how much resentment there was against authority, against having to fight in a war whose aims were unclear, inside a military machine whose lack of democracy was very clear. No one recorded the bitterness of enlisted men against the special privileges of officers in the army of a country known as a democracy. To give just one instance: combat crews in the air force in the European theater, going to the base movies between bombing missions, found two lines—an officers' line (short), and an enlisted men's line (very long). There were two mess halls, even as they prepared to go into combat: the enlisted men's food was different—worse—than the officers'.

The literature that followed World War II, James Jones's *From Here to Eternity*, Joseph Heller's *Catch-22*, and Norman Mailer's *The Naked and the Dead*, captured this GI anger against the army "brass." In *The Naked and the Dead*, the soldiers talk in battle, and one of them says: "The only thing wrong with this Army is it never lost a war."

Toglio was shocked. "You think we ought to lose this one?"

Red found himself carried away. "What have I against the goddam Japs? You think I care if they keep this fuggin jungle? What's it to me if Cummings gets another star?"

"General Cummings, he's a good man," Martinez said.

"There ain't a good officer in the world," Red stated.

There seemed to be widespread indifference, even hostility, on the part of the Negro community to the war despite the attempts of Negro newspapers and Negro leaders to mobilize black sentiment. Lawrence Wittner (*Rebels Against War*) quotes a black journalist: "The Negro . . . is angry, resentful, and utterly apathetic about the war. 'Fight for what?' he is asking. 'This war doesn't mean a thing to me. If we win I lose, so what?'" A black army officer, home on furlough, told friends in Harlem he had been in hundreds of bull sessions with Negro soldiers and found no interest in the war.

A student at a Negro college told his teacher: "The Army jimcrows us. The Navy lets us serve only as messmen. The Red Cross refuses our blood. Employers and labor unions shut us out. Lynchings continue. We are disenfranchised, jim-crowed, spat upon. What more could Hitler do than that?" NAACP leader Walter White repeated this to a black audience of several thousand people in the Midwest, thinking they would disapprove, but instead, as he recalled: "To my surprise and dismay the audience burst into such applause that it took me some thirty or forty seconds to quiet it."

In January 1943, there appeared in a Negro newspaper this "Draftee's Prayer":

Dear Lord, today
I go to war:
To fight, to die,
Tell me what for?
Dear Lord, I'll fight,
I do not fear,

Germans or Japs;
My fears are here.
Americal

But there was no organized Negro opposition to the war. In fact, there was little organized opposition from any source. The Communist party was enthusiastically in support. The Socialist party was divided, unable to make a clear statement one way or the other.

A few small anarchist and pacifist groups refused to back the war. The Women's International League for Peace and Freedom said: ". . . war between nations or classes or races cannot permanently settle conflicts or heal the wounds that brought them into being." The *Catholic Worker* wrote: "We are still pacifists. . . ."

The difficulty of merely calling for "peace" in a world of capitalism, Fascism, Communism—dynamic ideologies, aggressive actions—troubled some pacifists. They began to speak of "revolutionary nonviolence." A. J. Muste of the Fellowship of Reconciliation said in later years: "I was not impressed with the sentimental, easygoing pacifism of the earlier part of the century. People then felt that if they sat and talked pleasantly of peace and love, they would solve the problems of the world." The world was in the midst of a revolution, Muste realized, and those against violence must take revolutionary action, but without violence. A movement of revolutionary pacifism would have to "make effective contacts with oppressed and minority groups such as Negroes, share-croppers, industrial workers."

Only one organized socialist group opposed the war unequivocally. This was the Socialist Workers Party. The Espionage Act of 1917, still on the books, applied to wartime statements. But in 1940, with the United States not yet at war, Congress passed the Smith Act. This took Espionage Act prohibitions against talk or writing that would lead to refusal of duty in the armed forces and applied them to peacetime. The Smith Act also made it a crime to advocate the overthrow of the government by force and violence, or to join any group that advocated this, or to publish anything with such ideas. In Minneapolis in 1943, eighteen members of the Socialist Workers party were convicted for belonging to a party whose ideas, expressed in its Declaration of Principles, and in the *Communist Manifesto*, were said to violate the Smith Act. They were sentenced to prison terms, and the Supreme Court refused to review their case.

A few voices continued to insist that the real war was inside each nation: Dwight Macdonald's wartime magazine *Politics* presented, in early 1945, an article by the French worker-philosopher Simone Weil:

> Whether the mask is labelled Fascism, Democracy, or Dictatorship of the Proletariat, our great adversary remains the Apparatus—the bureaucracy, the police, the military. Not the one facing us across the frontier or the battlelines, which is not so much our enemy as our brothers' enemy, but the one that calls itself our protector and makes us its slaves. No matter what the circumstances, the worst betrayal will always be to subordinate ourselves to this Apparatus, and to trample underfoot, in its service, all human values in ourselves and in others.

Still, the vast bulk of the American population was mobilized, in the army, and in civilian life, to fight the war, and the atmosphere of war enveloped more and more Americans. Public opinion polls show large majorities of soldiers favoring the draft for the postwar period. Hatred against the enemy, against the Japanese particularly, became widespread. Racism was clearly at work. *Time* magazine, reporting the battle of Iwo Jima, said: "The ordinary unreasoning Jap is ignorant. Perhaps he is human. Nothing . . . indicates it."

So, there was a mass base of support for what became the heaviest bombardment of civilians ever undertaken in any war: the aerial attacks on German and Japanese cities. One might argue that this popular support made it a "people's war." But if "people's war" means a war of people against attack, a defensive war—if it means a war fought for humane reasons instead of for the privileges of an elite, a war against the few, not the many—then the tactics of all-out aerial assault against the populations of Germany and Japan destroy that notion.

Italy had bombed cities in the Ethiopian war; Italy and Germany had bombed civilians in the Spanish Civil War; at the start of World War II German planes dropped bombs on Rotterdam in Holland, Coventry in England, and elsewhere. Roosevelt had described these as "inhuman barbarism that has profoundly shocked the conscience of humanity."

These German bombings were very small compared with the British and American bombings of German cities. In January 1943 the Allies met at Casablanca and agreed on large-scale air attacks to achieve "the destruction and dislocation of the German military, industrial and economic system and the undermining of the morale of the German people to the point where their capacity for armed resistance is fatally weakened." And so, the saturation bombing of German cities began—with thousand-plane raids on Cologne, Essen, Frankfurt, Hamburg. The English flew at night with no pretense of aiming at "military" targets; the Americans flew in the daytime and pretended precision, but bombing from high altitudes made that impossible. The climax of this terror bombing was the bombing of Dresden in early 1945, in which the tremendous heat generated by the bombs created a vacuum into which fire leaped swiftly in a great firestorm through the city. More than 100,000 died in Dresden. (Winston Churchill, in his wartime memoirs, confined himself to this account of the incident: "We made a heavy raid in the latter month on Dresden, then a centre of communication of Germany's Eastern Front.")

The bombing of Japanese cities continued the strategy of saturation bombing to destroy civilian morale; one nighttime fire-bombing of Tokyo took 80,000 lives. And then, on August 6, 1945, came the lone American plane in the sky over Hiroshima, dropping the first atomic bomb, leaving perhaps 100,000 Japanese dead, and tens of thousands more slowly dying from radiation poisoning. Twelve U.S. navy fliers in the Hiroshima city jail were killed in the bombing, a fact that the U.S. government has never officially acknowledged, according to historian Martin Sherwin (*A World Destroyed*). Three days later, a second atomic bomb was dropped on the city of Nagasaki, with perhaps 50,000 killed.

The justification for these atrocities was that this would end the war quickly, making unnecessary an invasion of Japan. Such an invasion would cost a huge number of lives, the government said—a million, according to Secretary of State Byrnes; half a million, Truman claimed was the figure given him by General George Marshall. (When the papers of the Manhattan Project— the project to build the atom bomb—were released years later, they showed that Marshall urged a warning to the Japanese about the bomb, so people could be removed and only military targets hit.) These estimates of invasion losses were not realistic, and seem to have been pulled out of the air to justify bombings which, as their effects became known, horrified more and more people. Japan, by August 1945, was in desperate shape and ready to surrender. *New York Times* military analyst Hanson Baldwin wrote, shortly after the war:

> The enemy, in a military sense, was in a hopeless strategic position by the time the Potsdam demand for unconditional surrender was made on July 26.
>
> Such then, was the situation when we wiped out Hiroshima and Nagasaki.
>
> Need we have done it? No one can, of course, be positive, but the answer is almost certainly negative.

The United States Strategic Bombing Survey, set up by the War Department in 1944 to study the results of aerial attacks in the war, interviewed hundreds of Japanese civilian and military leaders after Japan surrendered, and reported just after the war:

> Based on a detailed investigation of all the facts and supported by the testimony of the surviving Japanese leaders involved, it is the Survey's opinion that certainly prior to 31 December 1945, and in all probability prior to 1 November 1945, Japan would have surren-

dered even if the atomic bombs had not been dropped, even if Russia had not entered the war, and even if no invasion had been planned or contemplated.

But could American leaders have known this in August 1945? The answer is, clearly, yes. The Japanese code had been broken, and Japan's messages were being intercepted. It was known the Japanese had instructed their ambassador in Moscow to work on peace negotiations with the Allies. Japanese leaders had begun talking of surrender a year before this, and the Emperor himself had begun to suggest, in June 1945, that alternatives to fighting to the end be considered. On July 13, Foreign Minister Shigenori Togo wired his ambassador in Moscow: "Unconditional surrender is the only obstacle to peace. . . ." Martin Sherwin, after an exhaustive study of the relevant historical documents, concludes: "Having broken the Japanese code before the war, American Intelligence was able to—and did—relay this message to the President, but it had no effect whatever on efforts to bring the war to a conclusion."

If only the Americans had not insisted on unconditional surrender—that is, if they were willing to accept one condition to the surrender, that the Emperor, a holy figure to the Japanese, remain in place—the Japanese would have agreed to stop the war.

Why did the United States not take that small step to save both American and Japanese lives? Was it because too much money and effort had been invested in the atomic bomb not to drop it? General Leslie Groves, head of the Manhattan Project, described Truman as a man on a toboggan, the momentum too great to stop it. Or was it, as British scientist P. M. S. Blackett suggested (*Fear, War, and the Bomb*), that the United States was anxious to drop the bomb before the Russians entered the war against Japan?

The Russians had secretly agreed (they were officially not at war with Japan) they would come into the war ninety days after the end of the European war. That turned out to be May 8, and so, on August 8, the Russians were due to declare war on Japan.

But by then the big bomb had been dropped, and the next day a second one would be dropped on Nagasaki; the Japanese would surrender to the United States, not the Russians, and the United States would be the occupier of postwar Japan. In other words, Blackett says, the dropping of the bomb was "the first major operation of the cold diplomatic war with Russia. . . ." Blackett is supported by American historian Gar Alperovitz (*Atomic Diplomacy*), who notes a diary entry for July 28, 1945, by Secretary of the Navy James Forrestal, describing Secretary of State James F. Byrnes as "most anxious to get the Japanese affair over with before the Russians got in."

Truman had said, "The world will note that the first atomic bomb was dropped on Hiroshima, a military base. That was because we wished in this first attack to avoid, insofar as possible, the killing of civilians." It was a preposterous statement. Those 100,000 killed in Hiroshima were almost all civilians. The U.S. Strategic Bombing Survey said in its official report: "Hiroshima and Nagasaki were chosen as targets because of their concentration of activities and population."

The dropping of the second bomb on Nagasaki seems to have been scheduled in advance, and no one has ever been able to explain why it was dropped. Was it because this was a plutonium bomb whereas the Hiroshima bomb was a uranium bomb? Were the dead and irradiated of Nagasaki victims of a scientific experiment? Martin Sherwin says that among the Nagasaki dead were probably American prisoners of war. He notes a message of July 31 from Headquarters, U.S. Army Strategic Air Forces, Guam, to the War Department:

> Reports prisoner of war sources, not verified by photos, give location of Allied prisoner of war camp one mile north of center of city of Nagasaki. Does this influence the choice of this target for initial Centerboard operation? Request immediate reply.

The reply: "Targets previously assigned for Centerboard remain unchanged."

True, the war then ended quickly. Italy had been defeated a year earlier. Germany had recently surrendered, crushed primarily by the armies of the Soviet Union on the Eastern Front, aided by the Allied armies on the West. Now Japan surrendered. The Fascist powers were destroyed.

But what about fascism—as idea, as reality? Were its essential elements—militarism, racism, imperialism—now gone? Or were they absorbed into the already poisoned bones of the victors? A. J. Muste, the revolutionary pacifist, had predicted in 1941: "The problem after a war is with the victor. He thinks he has just proved that war and violence pay. Who will now teach him a lesson?"

The victors were the Soviet Union and the United States (also England, France and Nationalist China, but they were weak). Both these countries now went to work—without swastikas, goose-stepping, or officially declared racism, but under the cover of "socialism" on one side, and "democracy" on the other, to carve out their own empires of influence. They proceeded to share and contest with one another the domination of the world, to build military machines far greater than the Fascist countries had built, to control the destinies of more countries than Hitler, Mussolini, and Japan had been able to do. They also acted to control their own populations, each country with its own techniques—crude in the Soviet Union, sophisticated in the United States—to make their rule secure.

The war not only put the United States in a position to dominate much of the world; it created conditions for effective control at home. The unemployment, the economic distress, and the consequent turmoil that had marked the thirties, only partly relieved by New Deal measures, had been pacified, overcome by the greater turmoil of the war. The war brought higher prices for farmers, higher wages, enough prosperity for enough of the population to assume against the rebellions that so threatened the thirties. As Lawrence Wittner writes, "The war rejuvenated American capitalism." The biggest gains were in corporate profits, which rose from $6.4 billion in 1940 to $10.8 billion in 1944.

But enough went to workers and farmers to make them feel the system was doing well for them.

It was an old lesson learned by governments: that war solves problems of control. Charles E. Wilson, the president of General Electric Corporation, was so happy about the wartime situation that he suggested a continuing alliance between business and the military for "a permanent war economy."

That is what happened. When, right after the war, the American public, war-weary, seemed to favor demobilization and disarmament, the Truman administration (Roosevelt had died in April 1945) worked to create an atmosphere of crisis and cold war. True, the rivalry with the Soviet Union was real—that country had come out of the war with its economy wrecked and 20 million people dead, but was making an astounding comeback, rebuilding its industry, regaining military strength. The Truman administration, however, presented the Soviet Union as not just a rival but an immediate threat.

In a series of moves abroad and at home, it established a climate of fear—a hysteria about Communism—which would steeply escalate the military budget and stimulate the economy with war-related orders. This combination of policies would permit more aggressive actions abroad, more repressive actions at home.

Revolutionary movements in Europe and Asia were described to the American public as examples of Soviet expansionism—thus recalling the indignation against Hitler's aggressions.

In Greece, which had been a right-wing monarchy and dictatorship before the war, a popular left-wing National Liberation Front (the EAM) was put down by a British army of intervention immediately after the war. A right-wing dictatorship was restored. When opponents of the regime were jailed, and trade union leaders removed, a left-wing guerrilla movement began to grow against the regime, soon consisting of 17,000 fighters, 50,000 active supporters, and perhaps 250,000 sympathizers, in a country of 7 million. Great Britain said it could not handle the rebellion, and asked the United States to come in. As a State Department officer said later: "Great Britain had within the hour handed the job of world leadership . . . to the United States."

The United States responded with the Truman Doctrine, the name given to a speech Truman gave to Congress in the spring of 1947, in which he asked for $400 million in military and economic aid to Greece and Turkey. Truman said the U.S. must help "free peoples who are resisting attempted subjugation by armed minorities or by outside pressures."

In fact, the biggest outside pressure was the United States. The Greek rebels were getting some aid from Yugoslavia, but no aid from the Soviet Union, which during the war had promised Churchill a free hand in Greece if he would give the Soviet Union its way in Rumania, Poland, Bulgaria. The Soviet Union, like the United States, did not seem to be willing to help revolutions it could not control.

Truman said the world "must choose between alternative ways of life." One was based on "the will of the majority . . . distinguished by free institutions"; the other was based on "the will of a minority . . . terror and oppression . . . the suppression of personal freedoms." Truman's adviser Clark Clifford had suggested that in his message Truman connect the intervention in Greece to something less rhetorical, more practical—"the great natural resources of the Middle East" (Clifford meant oil), but Truman didn't mention that.

The United States moved into the Greek civil war, not with soldiers, but with weapons and military advisers. In the last five months of 1947, 74,000 tons of military equipment were sent by the United States to the right-wing government in Athens, including artillery, dive bombers, and stocks of napalm. Two hundred and fifty army officers, headed by General James Van Fleet, advised the Greek army in the field. Van Fleet started a policy—standard in dealing with popular insurrections—of forcibly removing thousands of Greeks from their homes in the countryside, to try to isolate the guerrillas, to remove the source of their support.

With that aid, the rebellion was defeated by 1949. United States economic and military aid continued to the Greek government. Investment capital from Esso, Dow Chemical, Chrysler, and other U.S. corporations flowed into Greece. But illiteracy, poverty, and starvation remained widespread there, with the country in the hands of what Richard Barnet (*Intervention and Revolution*) called "a particularly brutal and backward military dictatorship."

In China, a revolution was already under way when World War II ended, led by a Communist movement with enormous mass support. A Red Army, which had fought against the Japanese, now fought to oust the corrupt dictatorship of Chiang Kai-shek, which was supported by the United States. The United States, by 1949, had given $2 billion in aid to Chiang Kai-shek's forces, but, according to the State Department's own White Paper on China, Chiang Kai-shek's government had lost the confidence of its own troops and its own people. In January 1949, Chinese Communist forces moved into Peking, the civil war was over, and China was in the hands of a revolutionary movement, the closest thing, in the long history of that ancient country, to a people's government, independent of outside control.

The United States was trying, in the postwar decade, to create a national consensus—excluding the radicals, who could not support a foreign policy aimed at suppressing revolution—of conservatives and liberals, Republicans and Democrats, around the policies of cold war and anti-Communism. Such a coalition could best be created by a liberal Democratic President, whose aggressive policy abroad would be supported by conservatives, and whose welfare programs at home (Truman's "Fair Deal") would be attractive to liberals. If, in addition, liberals and traditional Democrats could—the memory of the war was still fresh—support a foreign policy against "aggression," the radical-liberal bloc created by World War II would be broken up. And perhaps, if the anti-Communist mood became strong enough, liberals could support repressive moves at home which in ordinary times would be seen as violating the liberal tradition of tolerance. In 1950, there came an event that speeded the formation of the liberal-conservative consensus—Truman's undeclared war in Korea.

Korea, occupied by Japan for thirty-five years, was liberated from Japan after World War II and divided into North Korea, a socialist dictatorship, part of the Soviet sphere of influence, and South Korea, a right-wing dictatorship, in the American sphere. There had been threats back and forth between the two Koreas, and when on June 25, 1950, North Korean armies moved southward across the 38th parallel in an invasion of South Korea, the United Nations, dominated by the United States, asked its members to help "repel the armed attack." Truman ordered the American armed forces to help South Korea, and the American army became the U.N. army. Truman said: "A return to the rule of force in international affairs would have far-reaching effects. The United States will continue to uphold the rule of law."

The United States' response to "the rule of force" was to reduce Korea, North and South, to a shambles, in three years of bombing and shelling. Napalm was dropped, and a BBC journalist described the result:

> In front of us a curious figure was standing, a little crouched, legs straddled, arms held out from his sides. He had no eyes, and the whole of his body, nearly all of which was visible through tatters of burnt rags, was covered with a hard black crust speckled with yellow pus. . . . He had to stand because he was no longer covered with a skin, but with a crust-like crackling which broke easily. . . . I thought of the hundreds of villages reduced to ash which I personally had seen and realized the sort of casualty list which must be mounting up along the Korean front.

Perhaps 2 million Koreans, North and South, were killed in the Korean war, all in the name of opposing "the rule of force."

As for the rule of law Truman spoke about, the American military moves seemed to go beyond that. The U.N. resolution had called for action "to repel the armed attack and to restore peace and security in the area." But the American armies, after pushing the North Koreans back across the 38th parallel, advanced all the way up through North Korea to the Yalu River, on the border of

China—which provoked the Chinese into entering the war. The Chinese then swept southward and the war was stalemated at the 38th parallel until peace negotiations restored, in 1953, the old boundary between North and South.

The Korean war mobilized liberal opinion behind the war and the President. It created the kind of coalition that was needed to, sustain a policy of intervention abroad, militarization of the economy at home. This meant trouble for those who stayed outside the coalition as radical critics. Alonzo Hamby noted (*Beyond the New Deal*) that the Korean war was supported by *The New Republic*, by *The Nation*, and by Henry Wallace (who in 1948 had run against Truman on a left coalition Progressive party ticket). The liberals didn't like Senator Joseph McCarthy (who hunted for Communists everywhere, even among liberals), but the Korean war, as Hamby says, "had given McCarthyism a new lease on life."

The left had become very influential in the hard times of the thirties, and during the war against Fascism. The actual membership of the Communist party was not large—fewer than 100,000 probably—but it was a potent force in trade unions numbering millions of members, in the arts, and among countless Americans who may have been led by the failure of the capitalist system in the thirties to look favorably on Communism and Socialism. Thus, if the Establishment, after World War II, was to make capitalism more secure in the country, and to build a consensus of support for the American Empire, it had to weaken and isolate the left.

Two weeks after presenting to the country the Truman Doctrine for Greece and Turkey, Truman issued, on March 22, 1947, Executive Order 9835, initiating a program to search out any "infiltration of disloyal persons" in the U.S. government. In their book *The Fifties*, Douglas Miller and Marion Nowack comment:

> Though Truman would later complain of the "great wave of hysteria" sweeping the nation, his commitment to victory over communism, to completely safeguarding the United States from external

and internal threats, was in large measure responsible for creating that very hysteria. Between the launching of his security program in March 1947 and December 1952, some 6.6 million persons were investigated. Not a single case of espionage was uncovered, though about 500 persons were dismissed in dubious cases of "questionable loyalty." All of this was conducted with secret evidence, secret and often paid informers, and neither judge nor jury. Despite the failure to find subversion, the broad scope of the official Red hunt gave popular credence to the notion that the government was riddled with spies. A conservative and fearful reaction coursed the country. Americans became convinced of the need for absolute security and the preservation of the established order.

World events right after the war made it easier to build up public support for the anti-Communist crusade at home. In 1948, the Communist party in Czechoslovakia ousted non-Communists from the government and established their own rule. The Soviet Union that year blockaded Berlin, which was a jointly occupied city isolated inside the Soviet sphere of East Germany, forcing the United States to airlift supplies into Berlin. In 1949, there was the Communist victory in China, and in that year also, the Soviet Union exploded its first atomic bomb. In 1950 the Korean war began. These were all portrayed to the public as signs of a world Communist conspiracy.

Not as publicized as the Communist victories, but just as disturbing to the American government, was the upsurge all over the world of colonial peoples demanding independence. Revolutionary movements were growing—in Indochina against the French; in Indonesia against the Dutch; in the Philippines, armed rebellion against the United States.

In Africa there were rumblings of discontent in the form of strikes. Basil Davidson (*Let Freedom Come*) tells of the longest recorded strike (160 days) in African history, of 19,000 railwaymen in French West Africa in 1947, whose message to the governor general showed the new mood of militancy: "Open your prisons, make ready your machine guns and cannon. Nevertheless, at midnight on 10 October, if our demands are not met, we declare the general strike." The year before in South Africa, 100,000 gold mine workers stopped work, demanding ten shillings (about $2.50) a day in wages, the greatest strike in the history of South Africa, and it took a military attack to get them back to work. In 1950, in Kenya, there was a general strike against starvation wages.

So it was not just Soviet expansion that was threatening to the United States government and to American business interests. In fact, China, Korea, Indochina, the Philippines, represented local Communist movements, not Russian fomentation. It was a general wave of anti-imperialist insurrection in the world, which would require gigantic American effort to defeat: national unity for militarization of the budget, for the suppression of domestic opposition to such a foreign policy. Truman and the liberals in Congress proceeded to try to create a new national unity for the postwar years—with the executive order on loyalty oaths, Justice Department prosecutions, and anti-Communist legislation.

In this atmosphere, Senator Joseph McCarthy of Wisconsin could go even further than Truman. Speaking to a Women's Republican Club in Wheeling, West Virginia, in early 1950, he held up some papers and shouted: "I have here in my hand a list of 205—a list of names that were made known to the Secretary of State as being members of the Communist Party and who nevertheless are still working and shaping policy in the State Department." The next day, speaking in Salt Lake City, McCarthy claimed he had a list of fifty-seven (the number kept changing) such Communists in the State Department. Shortly afterward, he appeared on the floor of the Senate with photostatic copies of about a hundred dossiers from State Department loyalty files. The dossiers were three years old, and most of the people were no longer with the State Department, but McCarthy read from them anyway, inventing, adding, and changing as he read. In one case, he changed the dossier's description of "liberal" to "communistically inclined," in another form "active fellow traveler" to "active Communist," and so on.

McCarthy kept on like this for the next few years. As chairman of the Permanent Investigations Sub-Committee of a Senate Committee on Government Operations, he investigated the State Department's information program, its Voice of America, and its overseas libraries, which included books by people McCarthy considered Communists. The State Department reacted in panic, issuing a stream of directives to its library centers across the world. Forty books were removed, including *The Selected Works of Thomas Jefferson*, edited by Philip Foner, and *The Children's Hour* by Lillian Hellman. Some books were burned.

McCarthy became bolder. In the spring of 1954 he began hearings to investigate supposed subversives in the military. When he began attacking generals for not being hard enough on suspected Communists, he antagonized Republicans as well as Democrats, and in December 1954, the Senate voted overwhelmingly to censure him for "conduct . . . unbecoming a Member of the United States Senate." The censure resolution avoided criticizing McCarthy's anti-Communist lies and exaggerations; it concentrated on minor matters—on his refusal to appear before a Senate Subcommittee on Privileges and Elections, and his abuse of an army general at his hearings.

At the very time the Senate was censuring McCarthy, Congress was putting through a whole series of anti-Communist bills. Liberal Hubert Humphrey introduced an amendment to one of them to make the Communist party illegal, saying: "I do not intend to be a half patriot. . . . Either Senators are for recognizing the Communist Party for what it is, or they will continue to trip over the niceties of legal technicalities and details."

The liberals in the government were themselves acting to exclude, persecute, fire, and even imprison Communists. It was just that McCarthy had gone too far, attacking not only Communists but liberals, endangering that broad liberal-conservative coalition which was considered essential. For instance, Lyndon Johnson, as Senate minority leader, worked not only to pass the censure resolution on McCarthy but also to keep it within the narrow bounds of "conduct . . . unbecoming a Member of the

United States Senate" rather than questioning McCarthy's anti-Communism.

John F. Kennedy was cautious on the issue, didn't speak out against McCarthy (he was absent when the censure vote was taken and never said how he would have voted). McCarthy's insistence that Communism had won in China because of softness on Communism in the American government was close to Kennedy's own view, expressed in the House of Representatives, January 1949, when the Chinese Communists took over Peking. Kennedy said:

> Mr. Speaker, over this weekend we have learned the extent of the disaster that has befallen China and the United States. The responsibility for the failure of our foreign policy in the Far East rests squarely with the White House and the Department of State.
>
> The continued insistence that aid would not be forthcoming unless a coalition government with the Communists was formed, was a crippling blow to the National Government.
>
> So concerned were our diplomats and their advisers, the Lattimores and the Fairbanks [both scholars in the field of Chinese history, Owen Lattimore a favorite target of McCarthy, John Fairbank, a Harvard professor], with the imperfection of the democratic system in China after 20 years of war and the tales of corruption in high places that they lost sight of our tremendous stake in a non-Communist China. . . .
>
> This House must now assume the responsibility of preventing the onrushing tide of Communism from engulfing all of Asia.

When, in 1950, Republicans sponsored an Internal Security Act for the registration of organizations found to be "Communist-action" or "Communist-front," liberal Senators did not fight that head-on. Instead, some of them, including Hubert Humphrey and Herbert Lehman, proposed a substitute measure, the setting up of detention centers (really, concentration camps) for suspected subversives, who, when the President declared an "internal security emergency," would be held without trial. The detention-camp bill became not a substitute for, but an addition to, the Internal Security Act, and the proposed camps were set up, ready for use. (In 1968, a time of general disillusionment with anti-Communism, this law was repealed.)

Truman's executive order on loyalty in 1947 required the Department of Justice to draw up a list of organizations it decided were "totalitarian, fascist, communist or subversive . . . or as seeking to alter the form of government of the United States by unconstitutional means." Not only membership in, but also "sympathetic association" with, any organization on the Attorney General's list would be considered in determining disloyalty. By 1954, there were hundreds of groups on this list, including, besides the Communist party and the Ku Klux Klan, the Chopin Cultural Center, the Cervantes Fraternal Society, the Committee for the Negro in the Arts, the Committee for the Protection of the Bill of Rights, the League of American Writers, the Nature Friends of America, People's Drama, the Washington Bookshop Association, and the Yugoslav Seaman's Club.

It was not McCarthy and the Republicans, but the liberal Democratic Truman administration, whose Justice Department initiated a series of prosecutions that intensified the nation's anti-Communist mood. The most important of these was the prosecution of Julius and Ethel Rosenberg in the summer of 1950.

The Rosenbergs were charged with espionage. The major evidence was supplied by a few people who had already confessed to being spies, and were either in prison or under indictment. David Greenglass, the brother of Ethel Rosenberg, was the key witness. He had been a machinist at the Manhattan Project laboratory at Los Alamos, New Mexico, in 1944–1945 when the atomic bomb was being made there and testified that Julius Rosenberg had asked him to get information for the Russians. Greenglass said he had made sketches from memory for his brother-in-law of experiments with lenses to be used to detonate atomic bombs. He said Rosenberg had given him half of the cardboard top to a box of Jell-O, and told him a man would show up in New Mexico with the other half, and that, in June 1945, Harry Gold appeared with the other half of the box top, and Greenglass gave him information he had memorized.

Gold, already serving a thirty-year sentence in another espionage case, came out of jail to corroborate Greenglass's testimony. He had never met the Rosenbergs, but said a Soviet embassy official gave him half of a Jell-O box top and told him to contact Greenglass, saying, "I come from Julius." Gold said he took the sketches Greenglass had drawn from memory and gave them to the Russian official.

There were troubling aspects to all this. Did Gold cooperate in return for early release from prison? After serving fifteen years of his thirty-year sentence, he was paroled. Did Greenglass—under indictment at the time he testified—also know that his life depended on his cooperation? He was given fifteen years, served half of it, and was released. How reliable a memorizer of atomic information was David Greenglass, an ordinary-level machinist, not a scientist, who had taken six courses at Brooklyn Polytechnical Institute and flunked five of them? Gold's and Greenglass's stories had first not been in accord. But they were both placed on the same floor of the Tombs prison in New York before the trial, giving them a chance to coordinate their testimony.

How reliable was Gold's testimony? It turned out that he had been prepared for the Rosenberg case by four hundred hours of interviews with the FBI. It also turned out that Gold was a frequent and highly imaginative liar. He was a witness in a later trial where defense counsel asked Gold about his invention of a fictional wife and fictional children. The attorney asked: ". . . you lied for a period of six years?" Gold responded: "I lied for a period of sixteen years, not alone six years." Gold was the only witness at the trial to connect Julius Rosenberg and David Greenglass to the Russians. The FBI agent who had questioned Gold was interviewed twenty years after the case by a journalist. He was asked about the password Gold was supposed to have used— "Julius sent me." The FBI man said:

Gold couldn't remember the name he had given. He thought he had said: I come from————or something like that. I suggested, "Might it have been Julius?"

That refreshed his memory.

When the Rosenbergs were found guilty, and Judge Irving Kaufman pronounced sentence, he said:

> I believe your conduct in putting into the hands of the Russians the A-bomb years before our best scientists predicted Russia would perfect the bomb has already caused the Communist aggression in Korea with the resultant casualties exceeding 50,000 Americans and who knows but that millions more of innocent people may pay the price of your treason. . . .

He sentenced them both to die in the electric chair.

Morton Sobell was also on trial as a co-conspirator with the Rosenbergs. The chief witness against him was an old friend, the best man at his wedding, a man who was facing possible perjury charges by the federal government for lying about his political past. This was Max Elitcher, who testified that he had once driven Sobell to a Manhattan housing project where the Rosenbergs lived, and that Sobell got out of the car, took from the glove compartment what appeared to be a film can, went off, and then returned without the can. There was no evidence about what was in the film can. The case against Sobell seemed so weak that Sobell's lawyer decided there was no need to present a defense. But the jury found Sobell guilty, and Kaufman sentenced him to thirty years in prison. He was sent to Alcatraz, parole was repeatedly denied, and he spent nineteen years in various prisons before he was released.

FBI documents subpoenaed in the 1970s showed that Judge Kaufman had conferred with the prosecutors secretly about the sentences he would give in the case. Another document shows that after three years of appeal a meeting took place between

Attorney General Herbert Brownell and Chief Justice Fred Vinson of the Supreme Court, and the chief justice assured the Attorney General that if any Supreme Court justice gave a stay of execution, he would immediately call a full court session and override it.

There had been a worldwide campaign of protest. Albert Einstein, whose letter to Roosevelt early in the war had initiated work on the atomic bomb, appealed for the Rosenbergs, as did Jean-Paul Sartre, Pablo Picasso, and the sister of Bartolomeo Vanzetti. There was an appeal to President Truman, just before he left office in the spring of 1953. It was turned down. Then, another appeal to the new President, Dwight Eisenhower, was also turned down.

At the last moment, Justice William O. Douglas granted a stay of execution. Chief Justice Vinson sent out special jets to bring the vacationing justices back to Washington from various parts of the country. They canceled Douglas's stay in time for the Rosenbergs to be executed June 19, 1953. It was a demonstration to the people of the country, though very few could identify with the Rosenbergs, of what lay at the end of the line for those the government decided were traitors.

In that same period of the early fifties, the House Un-American Activities Committee was at its heyday, interrogating Americans about their Communist connections, holding them in contempt if they refused to answer, distributing millions of pamphlets to the American public: "One Hundred Things You Should Know About Communism" ("Where can Communists be found? Everywhere"). Liberals often criticized the Committee, but in Congress, liberals and conservatives alike voted to fund it year after year. By 1958, only one member of the House of Representatives (James Roosevelt) voted against giving it money. Although Truman criticized the Committee, his own Attorney General had expressed, in 1950, the same idea that motivated its investigations: "There are today many Communists in America. They are everywhere—in factories, offices, butcher shops, on street corners, in private business—and each carries in himself the germs of death for society."

Liberal intellectuals rode the anti-Communist bandwagon. *Commentary* magazine denounced the Rosenbergs and their supporters. One of *Commentary*'s writers, Irving Kristol, asked in March 1952: "Do we defend our rights by protecting Communists?" His answer: "No."

It was Truman's Justice Department that prosecuted the leaders of the Communist party under the Smith Act, charging them with conspiring to teach and advocate the overthrow of the government by force and violence. The evidence consisted mostly of the fact that the Communists were distributing Marxist-Leninist literature, which the prosecution contended called for violent revolution. There was certainly not evidence of any immediate danger of violent revolution by the Communist party. The Supreme Court decision was given by Truman's appointee, Chief Justice Vinson. He stretched the old doctrine of the "clear and present danger" by saying there was a clear and present conspiracy to make a revolution at some convenient time. And so, the top leadership of the Communist party was put in prison, and soon after, most of its organizers went underground.

Undoubtedly, there was success in the attempt to make the general public fearful of Communists and ready to take drastic actions against them—imprisonment at home, military action abroad. The whole culture was permeated with anti-Communism. The large-circulation magazines had articles like "How Communists Get That Way" and "Communists Are After Your Child." The *New York Times* in 1956 ran an editorial: "We would not knowingly employ a Communist party member in the news or editorial departments . . . because we would not trust his ability to report the news objectively or to comment on it honestly. . . ." An FBI informer's story about his exploits as a Communist who became an FBI agent—"I Led Three Lives"—was serialized in five hundred newspapers and put on television. Hollywood movies had titles like *I Married a Communist* and *I Was a Communist for the FBI*. Between 1948 and 1954, more than forty anti-Communist films came out of Hollywood.

Even the American Civil Liberties Union, set up specifically to defend the liberties of Communists and all other political groups, began to wilt in the cold war atmosphere. It had already started in this direction back in 1940 when it expelled one of its charter members, Elizabeth Gurley Flynn, because she was a member of the Communist party. In the fifties, the ACLU was hesitant to defend Corliss Lamont, its own board member, and Owen Lattimore, when both were under attack. It was reluctant to defend publicly the Communist leaders during the first Smith Act trial, and kept completely out of the Rosenberg case, saying no civil liberties issues were involved.

Young and old were taught that anti-Communism was heroic. Three million copies were sold of the book by Mickey Spillane published in 1951, *One Lonely Night*, in which the hero, Mike Hammer, says: "I killed more people tonight than I have fingers on my hands. I shot them in cold blood and enjoyed every minute of it. . . . They were Commies . . . red sons-of-bitches who should have died long ago. . . ." A comic strip hero, Captain America, said: "Beware, commies, spies, traitors, and foreign agents! Captain America, with all loyal, free men behind him, is looking for you. . . ." And in the fifties, schoolchildren all over the country participated in air raid drills in which a Soviet attack on America was signaled by sirens: the children had to crouch under their desks until it was "all clear."

It was an atmosphere in which the government could get mass support for a policy of rearmament. The system, so shaken in the thirties, had learned that war production could bring stability and high profits. Truman's anti-Communism was attractive. The business publication *Steel* had said in November 1946—even before the Truman Doctrine—that Truman's policies gave "the firm assurance that maintaining and building our preparations for war will be big business in the United States for at least a considerable period ahead."

That prediction turned out to be accurate. At the start of 1950, the total U.S. budget was about $40 billion, and the military part of it was about $12 billion. But by 1955, the military part alone was $40 billion out of a total of $62 billion.

In 1960, the military budget was $45.8 billion—49.7 percent of the budget. That year John F. Kennedy was elected President, and he immediately moved to increase military spending. In fourteen months, the Kennedy administration added $9 billion to defense funds, according to Edgar Bottome *(The Balance of Terror)*.

By 1962, based on a series of invented scares about Soviet military build-ups, a false "bomber gap" and a false "missile gap," the United States had overwhelming nuclear superiority. It had the equivalent, in nuclear weapons, of 1,500 Hiroshima-size atomic bombs, far more than enough to destroy every major city in the world—the equivalent, in fact, of 10 tons of TNT for every man, woman, and child on earth. To deliver these bombs, the United States had more than 50 intercontinental ballistic missiles, 80 missiles on nuclear submarines, 90 missiles on stations overseas, 1,700 bombers capable of reaching the Soviet Union, 300 fighter-bombers on aircraft carriers, able to carry atomic weapons, and 1,000 land-based supersonic fighters able to carry atomic bombs.

The Soviet Union was obviously behind—it had between fifty and a hundred intercontinental ballistic missiles and fewer than two hundred long-range bombers. But the U.S. budget kept mounting, the hysteria kept growing, the profits of corporations getting defense contracts multiplied, and employment and wages moved ahead just enough to keep a substantial number of Americans dependent on war industries for their living.

By 1970, the U.S. military budget was $80 billion and the corporations involved in military production were making fortunes. Two-thirds of the 40 billion spent on weapons systems was going to twelve or fifteen giant industrial corporations, whose main reason for existence was to fulfill government military contracts. Senator Paul Douglass, an economist and chairman of the Joint Economic Committee of the Senate, noted that "six-sevenths of these contracts are not competitive. . . . In the alleged interest of secrecy, the government picks a company and draws up a contract in more or less secret negotiations."

C. Wright Mills, in his book of the fifties, *The Power Elite*, counted the military as part of the top elite, along with politicians and corporations. These elements were more and more intertwined. A Senate report showed that the one hundred largest defense contractors, who held 67.4 percent of the military contracts, employed more than two thousand former high-ranking officers of the military.

Meanwhile, the United States, giving economic aid to certain countries, was creating a network of American corporate control over the globe, and building its political influence over the countries it aided. The Marshall Plan of 1948, which gave $16 billion in economic aid to Western European countries in four years, had an economic aim: to build up markets for American exports. George Marshall (a general, then Secretary of State) was quoted in an early 1948 State Department bulletin: "It is idle to think that a Europe left to its own efforts . . . would remain open to American business in the same way that we have known it in the past."

The Marshall Plan also had a political motive. The Communist parties of Italy and France were strong, and the United States decided to use pressure and money to keep Communists out of the cabinets of those countries. When the Plan was beginning, Truman's Secretary of State Dean Acheson said: "These measures of relief and reconstruction have been only in part suggested by humanitarianism. Your Congress has authorized and your Government is carrying out, a policy of relief and reconstruction today chiefly as a matter of national self-interest."

From 1952 on, foreign aid was more and more obviously designed to build up military power in non-Communist countries. In the next ten years, of the $50 billion in aid granted by the United States to ninety countries, only $5 billion was for nonmilitary economic development.

When John F. Kennedy took office, he launched the Alliance for Progress, a program of help for Latin America, emphasizing social reform to better the lives of people. But it turned out to be mostly military aid to keep in power right-wing dictatorships and enable them to stave off revolutions.

From military aid, it was a short step to military intervention. What Truman had said at the start of the Korean war about "the rule of force" and the "rule of law" was again and again, under Truman and his successors, contradicted by American action. In Iran, in 1953, the Central Intelligence Agency succeeded in overthrowing a government which nationalized the oil industry. In Guatemala, in 1954, a legally elected government was overthrown by an invasion force of mercenaries trained by the CIA at military bases in Honduras and Nicaragua and supported by four American fighter planes flown by American pilots. The invasion put into power Colonel Carlos Castillo Armas, who had at one time received military training at Fort Leavenworth, Kansas.

The government that the United States overthrew was the most democratic Guatemala had ever had. The President, Jacobo Arbenz, was a left-of-center Socialist; four of the fifty-six seats in the Congress were held by Communists. What was most unsettling to American business interests was that Arbenz had expropriated 234,000 acres of land owned by United Fruit, offering compensation that United Fruit called "unacceptable." Armas, in power, gave the land back to United Fruit, abolished the tax on interest and dividends to foreign investors, eliminated the secret ballot, and jailed thousands of political critics.

In 1958, the Eisenhower government sent thousands of marines to Lebanon to make sure the pro-American government there was not toppled by a revolution, and to keep an armed presence in that oil-rich area.

The Democrat-Republican, liberal-conservative agreement to prevent or overthrow revolutionary governments whenever possible—whether Communist, Socialist, or anti–United Fruit—became most evident in 1961 in Cuba. That little island 90 miles from Florida had gone through a revolution in 1959 by a rebel force led by Fidel Castro, in which the American-backed dictator, Fulgencio Batista, was overthrown. The revolution was a direct threat to American business interests. Franklin D. Roosevelt's Good Neighbor Policy had repealed the Platt Amendment (which permitted American intervention in Cuba), but the United

States still kept a naval base in Cuba at Guantanamo, and U.S. business interests still dominated the Cuban economy. American companies controlled 80 to 100 percent of Cuba's utilities, mines, cattle ranches, and oil refineries, 40 percent of the sugar industry, and 50 percent of the public railways.

Fidel Castro had spent time in prison after he led an unsuccessful attack in 1953 on an army barracks in Santiago. Out of prison, he went to Mexico, met Argentine revolutionary Che Guevara, and returned in 1956 to Cuba. His tiny force fought guerrilla warfare from the jungles and mountains against Batista's army, drawing more and more popular support, then came out of the mountains and marched across the country to Havana. The Batista government fell apart on New Year's Day 1959.

In power, Castro moved to set up a nationwide system of education, of housing, of land distribution to landless peasants. The government confiscated over a million acres of land from three American companies, including United Fruit.

Cuba needed money to finance its programs, and the United States was not eager to lend it. The International Monetary Fund, dominated by the United States, would not loan money to Cuba because Cuba would not accept its "stabilization" conditions, which seemed to undermine the revolutionary program that had begun. When Cuba now signed a trade agreement with the Soviet Union, American-owned oil companies in Cuba refused to refine crude oil that came from the Soviet Union. Castro seized these companies. The United States cut down on its sugar buying from Cuba, on which Cuba's economy depended, and the Soviet Union immediately agreed to buy all the 700,000 tons of sugar that the United States would not buy.

Cuba had changed. The Good Neighbor Policy did not apply. In the spring of 1960, President Eisenhower secretly authorized the Central Intelligence Agency to arm and train anti-Castro Cuban exiles in Guatemala for a future invasion of Cuba. When Kennedy took office in the spring of 1961 the CIA had 1,400 exiles, armed and trained. He moved ahead with the plans, and on April 17, 1961, the CIA-trained force, with some Americans participating, landed at the Bay of Pigs on the south shore of Cuba, 90 miles from Havana. They expected to stimulate a general rising against Castro. But it was a popular regime. There was no rising. In three days, the CIA forces were crushed by Castro's army.

The whole Bay of Pigs affair was accompanied by hypocrisy and lying. The invasion was a violation—recalling Truman's "rule of law"—of a treaty the U.S. had signed, the Charter of the Organization of American States, which reads: "No state or group of states has the right to intervene, directly or indirectly, for any reason whatever, in the internal or external affairs of any other state."

Four days before the invasion—because there had been press reports of secret bases and CIA training for invaders—President Kennedy told a press conference: ". . . there will not be, under any conditions, any intervention in Cuba by United States armed forces." True, the landing force was Cuban, but it was all organized by the United States, and American war planes, including American pilots, were involved; Kennedy had approved the use of unmarked navy jets in the invasion. Four American pilots of those planes were killed, and their families were not told the truth about how those men died.

The success of the liberal-conservative coalition in creating a national anti-Communist consensus was shown by how certain important news publications cooperated with the Kennedy administration in deceiving the American public on the Cuban invasion. *The New Republic* was about to print an article on the CIA training of Cuban exiles, a few weeks before the invasion. Historian Arthur Schlesinger was given copies of the article in advance. He showed them to Kennedy, who asked that the article not be printed, and *The New Republic* went along.

James Reston and Turner Catledge of the *New York Times*, on the government's request, did not run a story about the imminent invasion. Arthur Schlesinger said of the *New York Times* action: "This was another patriotic act, but in retrospect I have wondered whether, if the press had behaved irresponsibly, it would not have spared the country a disaster." What seemed to bother him, and other liberals in the cold war consensus, was not that the United States was interfering in revolutionary movements in other countries, but that it was doing so unsuccessfully.

Around 1960, the fifteen-year effort since the end of World War II to break up the Communist-radical upsurge of the New Deal and wartime years seemed successful. The Communist party was in disarray—its leaders in jail, its membership shrunken, its influence in the trade union movement very small. The trade union movement itself had become more controlled, more conservative. The military budget was taking half of the national budget, but the public was accepting this.

The radiation from the testing of nuclear weapons had dangerous possibilities for human health, but the public was not aware of that. The Atomic Energy Commission insisted that the deadly effects of atomic tests were exaggerated, and an article in 1955 in the *Reader's Digest* (the largest-circulation magazine in the United States) said: "The scare stories about this country's atomic tests are simply not justified."

In the mid-fifties, there was a flurry of enthusiasm for air-raid shelters; the public was being told these would keep them safe from atomic blasts. A government consultant and scientist, Herman Kahn, wrote a book, *On Thermonuclear War*, in which he explained that it was possible to have a nuclear war without total destruction of the world, that people should not be so frightened of it. A political scientist named Henry Kissinger wrote a book published in 1957 in which he said: "With proper tactics, nuclear war need not be as destructive as it appears. . . ."

The country was on a permanent war economy which had big pockets of poverty, but there were enough people at work, making enough money, to keep things quiet. The distribution of wealth was still unequal. From 1944 to 1961, it had not changed much: the lowest fifth of the families received 5 percent of all the income; the highest fifth received 45 percent of all the income. In 1953, 1.6 percent of the adult population owned more than 80 percent of the corporate stock and nearly 90 percent of the corporate bonds. About 200 giant corporations out of 200,000 corporations—one-tenth of 1 percent of all corporations—controlled about 60 percent of the manufacturing wealth of the nation.

When John F. Kennedy presented his budget to the nation after his first year in office, it was clear that, liberal Democrat or not, there would be no major change in the distribution of income or wealth or tax advantages. *New York Times* columnist James Reston summed up Kennedy's budget messages as avoiding any "sudden transformation of the home front" as well as "a more ambitious frontal attack on the unemployment problem." Reston said:

He agreed to a tax break for business investment in plant expansion and modernization. He is not spoiling for a fight with the Southern conservatives over civil rights. He has been urging the unions to keep wage demands down so that prices can be competitive in the world markets and jobs increased. And he has been trying to reassure the business community that he does not want any cold war with them on the home front.

... this week in his news conference he refused to carry out his promise to bar discrimination in Government-insured housing, but talked instead of postponing this until there was a "national consensus" in its favor. . . .

During these twelve months the President has moved over into the decisive middle ground of American politics. . . .

On this middle ground, all seemed secure. Nothing had to be done for blacks. Nothing had to be done to change the economic structure. An aggressive foreign policy could continue. The country seemed under control. And then, in the 1960s, came a series of explosive rebellions in every area of American life, which showed that all the system's estimates of security and success were wrong.

6

"Or Does It Explode?"

The black revolt of the 1950s and 1960s—North and South—came as a surprise. But perhaps it should not have. The memory of oppressed people is one thing that cannot be taken away, and for such people, with such memories, revolt is always an inch below the surface. For blacks in the United States, there was the memory of slavery, and after that of segregation, lynching, humiliation. And it was not just a memory but a living presence—part of the daily lives of blacks in generation after generation.

In the 1930s, Langston Hughes wrote a poem, "Lenox Avenue Mural":

What happens to a dream deferred?
  Does it dry up
  like a raisin in the sun?
  Or fester like a sore—
  And then run?
Does it stink like rotten meat?
Or crust and sugar over—
like a syrupy sweet?

Maybe it just sags like a heavy load.

Or does it explode?

In a society of complex controls, both crude and refined, secret thoughts can often be found in the arts, and so it was in black society. Perhaps the blues, however pathetic, concealed anger; and the jazz, however joyful, portended rebellion. And then the poetry, the thoughts no longer so secret. In the 1920s, Claude McKay, one of the figures of what came to be called the "Harlem Renaissance," wrote a poem that Henry Cabot Lodge put in the *Congressional Record* as an example of dangerous currents among young blacks:

> If we must die, let it not be like hogs
> Hunted and penned in an inglorious spot. . . .
> Like men we'll face the murderous cowardly pack,
> Pressed to the wall, dying, but fighting back!

Countee Cullen's poem "Incident" evoked memories—all different, all the same—out of every black American's childhood:

> Once riding in old Baltimore,
> Heart-filled, head-filled with glee,
> I saw a Baltimorean
> Keep looking straight at me.
>
> Now I was eight and very small,
> And he was no whit bigger,
> And so I smiled, but he poked out
> His tongue, and called me, "Nigger."
>
> I saw the whole of Baltimore
> From May until December;
> Of all the things that happened there
> That's all that I remember.

At the time of the Scottsboro Boys incident, Cullen wrote a bitter poem noting that white poets had used their pens to protest in other cases of injustice, but now that blacks were involved, most were silent. His last stanza was:

> Surely, I said,
>   Now will the poets sing.
> But they have raised no cry.
>   I wonder why.

Even outward subservience—Uncle Tom behavior in real situations, the comic or fawning Negro on the stage, the self-ridicule, the caution—concealed resentment, anger, energy. The black poet Paul Laurence Dunbar, in the era of the black minstrel, around the turn of the century, wrote "We Wear the Mask":

> We wear the mask that grins and lies,
> It hides our cheeks and shades our eyes,—

> . . . We sing, but oh, the clay is vile
> Beneath our feet, and long the mile;
> But let the world dream otherwise,
> We wear the mask.

Two black performers of that time played the minstrel and satirized it at the same time. When Bert Williams and George Walker billed themselves as "Two Real Coons," they were, Nathan Huggins says, "intending to give style and comic dignity to a fiction that white men had created. . . ."

By the 1930s the mask was off for many black poets. Langston Hughes wrote "I, Too."

> I, too, sing America

> I am the darker brother.
> They send me to eat in the kitchen

When company comes,
But I laugh,
And eat well,
And grow strong.

Tomorrow,
I'll be at the table
When company comes. . . .

Gwendolyn Bennett wrote:

I want to see lithe Negro girls,
Etched dark against the sky
While sunset lingers. . . .

I want to hear the chanting
Around a heathen fire
Of a strange black race. . . .

I want to feel the surging
Of my sad people's soul
Hidden by a minstrel-smile.

There was Margaret Walker's prose-poem "For My People":

. . . Let a new earth rise. Let another world be born. Let a bloody
peace be written in the sky. Let a second generation full of courage
issue forth, let a people loving freedom come to growth, let a beauty
full of healing and a strength of final clenching be the pulsing in our
spirits and our blood. Let the martial songs be written, let the dirges
disappear. Let a race of men now rise and take control!

By the 1940s there was Richard Wright, a gifted novelist, a
black man. His autobiography of 1937, *Black Boy*, gave endless
insights: for instance, how blacks were set against one another,
when he told how he was prodded to fight another black boy for

the amusement of white men. *Black Boy* expressed unashamedly every humiliation and then:

> The white South said that it knew "niggers," and I was what the white South called a "nigger." Well, the white South had never known me—never known what I thought, what I felt. The white South said that I had a "place" in life. Well, I had never felt my "place"; or, rather, my deepest instincts had always made me reject the "place" to which the white South had assigned me. It had never occurred to me that I was in any way an inferior being. And no word that I had ever heard fall from the lips of southern white men had ever made me really doubt the worth of my own humanity.

It was all there in the poetry, the prose, the music, sometimes masked, sometimes unmistakably clear—the signs of a people unbeaten, waiting, hot, coiled.

In *Black Boy*, Wright told about the training of black children in America to keep them silent. But also:

> How do Negroes feel about the way they have to live? How do they discuss it when alone among themselves? I think this question can be answered in a single sentence. A friend of mine who ran an elevator once told me:
> "Lawd, man! Ef it wuzn't fer them polices 'n' them ol' lynch mobs, there wouldn't be nothin' but uproar down here!"

Richard Wright, for a time, joined the Communist party (he tells of this period of his life, and his disillusionment with the party, in *The God That Failed*). The Communist party was known to pay special attention to the problem of race equality. When the Scottsboro case unfolded in the 1930s in Alabama, it was the Communist party that had become associated with the defense of these young black men imprisoned, in the early years of the Depression, by southern injustice.

The party was accused by liberals and the NAACP of exploiting the issue for its own purposes, and there was a half-truth in it, but black people were realistic about the difficulty of having white allies who were pure in motive. The other half of the truth was that black Communists in the South had earned the admiration of blacks by their organizing work against enormous obstacles. There was Hosea Hudson, the black organizer of the unemployed in Birmingham, for instance. And in Georgia, in 1932, a nineteen-year-old black youth named Angelo Herndon, whose father died of miner's pneumonia, who had worked in mines as a boy in Kentucky, joined an Unemployment Council in Birmingham organized by the Communist party, and then joined the party. He wrote later:

> All my life I'd been sweated and stepped-on and Jim-Crowed. I lay on my belly in the mines for a few dollars a week, and saw my pay stolen and slashed, and my buddies killed. I lived in the worst section of town, and rode behind the "Colored" signs on streetcars, as though there was something disgusting about me. I heard myself called "nigger" and "darky" and I had to say "Yes, sir" to every white man, whether he had my respect or not.
>
> I had always detested it, but I had never known that anything could be done about it. And here, all of a sudden, I had found organizations in which Negroes and whites sat together, and worked together, and knew no difference of race or color. . . .

Herndon became a Communist party organizer in Atlanta. He and his fellow Communists organized block committees of Unemployment Councils in 1932 which got rent relief for needy people. They organized a demonstration to which a thousand people came, six hundred of them white, and the next day the city voted $6,000 in relief to the jobless. But soon after that Herndon was arrested, held incommunicado, and charged with violating a Georgia statute against insurrection. He recalled his trial:

> The state of Georgia displayed the literature that had been taken from my room, and read passages of it to the jury. They questioned me in great detail. Did I believe that the bosses and government

ought to pay insurance to unemployed workers? That Negroes should have complete equality with white people? Did I believe in the demand for the self-determination of the Black Belt—that the Negro people should be allowed to rule the Black Belt territory, kicking out the white landlords and government officials? Did I feel that the working-class could run the mills and mines and government? That it wasn't necessary to have bosses at all?

I told them I believed all of that—and more. . . .

Herndon was convicted and spent five years in prison until in 1937 the Supreme Court ruled unconstitutional the Georgia statute under which he was found guilty. It was men like him who represented to the Establishment a dangerous militancy among blacks, made more dangerous when linked with the Communist party.

There were others who made that same connection, magnifying the danger: Benjamin Davis, the black lawyer who defended Herndon at his trial; nationally renowned men like singer and actor Paul Robeson, and writer and scholar W. E. B. Du Bois, who did not hide their support and sympathy for the Communist party. The Negro was not as anti-Communist as the white population. He could not afford to be, his friends were so few—so that Herndon, Davis, Robeson, Du Bois, however their political views might be maligned by the country as a whole, found admiration for their fighting spirit in the black community.

The black militant mood, flashing here and there in the thirties, was reduced to a subsurface simmering during World War II, when the nation on the one hand denounced racism, and on the other hand maintained segregation in the armed forces and kept blacks in low-paying jobs. When the war ended, a new element entered the racial balance in the United States—the enormous, unprecedented upsurge of black and yellow people in Africa and Asia.

President Harry Truman had to reckon with this, especially as the cold war rivalry with the Soviet Union began, and the dark-skinned revolt of former colonies all over the world threatened to take Marxist form. Action on the race question was needed, not just to calm a black population at home emboldened by war promises, frustrated by the basic sameness of their condition. It was needed to present to the world a United States that could counter the continuous Communist thrust at the most flagrant failure of American society—the race question. What Du Bois had said long ago, unnoticed, now loomed large in 1945: "The problem of the 20th century is the problem of the color line."

President Harry Truman, in late 1946, appointed a Committee on Civil Rights, which recommended that the civil rights section of the Department of Justice be expanded, that there be a permanent Commission on Civil Rights, that Congress pass laws against lynching and to stop voting discrimination, and suggested new laws to end racial discrimination in jobs.

Truman's Committee was blunt about its motivation in making these recommendations. Yes, it said, there was "moral reason": a matter of conscience. But there was also an "economic reason"—discrimination was costly to the country, wasteful of its talent. And, perhaps most important, there was an international reason:

> Our position in the post-war world is so vital to the future that our smallest actions have far-reaching effects. . . . We cannot escape the fact that our civil rights record has been an issue in world politics. The world's press and radio are full of it. . . . Those with competing philosophies have stressed—and are shamelessly distorting—our shortcomings. . . . They have tried to prove our democracy an empty fraud, and our nation a consistent oppressor of underprivileged people. This may seem ludicrous to Americans, but it is sufficiently important to worry our friends. The United States is not so strong, the final triumph of the democratic ideal is not so inevitable that we can ignore what the world thinks of us or our record.

The United States was out in the world now in a way it had never been. The stakes were large—world supremacy. And, as Truman's Committee said: ". . . our smallest actions have far-reaching effects."

And so the United States went ahead to take small actions, hoping they would have large effects. Congress did not move to enact the legislation asked for by the Committee on Civil Rights. But Truman—four months before the presidential election of 1948, and challenged from the left in that election by Progressive party candidate Henry Wallace—issued an executive order asking that the armed forces, segregated in World War II, institute policies of racial equality "as rapidly as possible." The order may have been prompted not only by the election but by the need to maintain black morale in the armed forces, as the possibility of war grew. It took over a decade to complete the desegregation in the military.

Truman could have issued executive orders in other areas, but did not. The Fourteenth and Fifteenth Amendments, plus the set of laws passed in the late 1860s and early 1870s, gave the President enough authority to wipe out racial discrimination. The Constitution demanded that the President execute the laws, but no President had used that power. Neither did Truman. For instance, he asked Congress for legislation "prohibiting discrimination in interstate transportation facilities"; but specific legislation in 1887 already barred discrimination in interstate transportation and had never been enforced by executive action.

Meanwhile, the Supreme Court was taking steps—ninety years after the Constitution had been amended to establish racial equality—to move toward that end. During the war it ruled that the "white primary" used to exclude blacks from voting in the Democratic party primaries—which in the South were really the elections—was unconstitutional.

In 1954, the Court finally struck down the "separate but equal" doctrine that it had defended since the 1890s. The NAACP brought a series of cases before the Court to challenge segregation in the public schools, and now in *Brown* v. *Board of Education* the Court said the separation of schoolchildren "generates a feeling of inferiority . . . that may affect their hearts and minds in a way unlikely ever to be undone." In the field of public education, it said, "the doctrine of 'separate but equal' has no place." The Court did not insist on immediate change: a year later it said that segregated facilities should be integrated "with all deliberate speed." By 1965, ten years after the "all deliberate speed" guideline, more than 75 percent of the school districts in the South remained segregated.

Still, it was a dramatic decision—and the message went around the world in 1954 that the American government had outlawed segregation. In the United States too, for those not thinking about the customary gap between word and fact, it was an exhilarating sign of change.

What to others seemed rapid progress to blacks was apparently not enough. In the early 1960s black people rose in rebellion all over the South. And in the late 1960s they were engaging in wild insurrection in a hundred northern cities. It was all a surprise to those without that deep memory of slavery, that everyday presence of humiliation, registered in the poetry, the music, the occasional outbursts of anger, the more frequent sullen silences. Part of that memory was of words uttered, laws passed, decisions made, which turned out to be meaningless.

For such a people, with such a memory, and such daily recapitulation of history, revolt was always minutes away, in a timing mechanism which no one had set, but which might go off with some unpredictable set of events. Those events came, at the end of 1955, in the capital city of Alabama—Montgomery.

Three months after her arrest, Mrs. Rosa Parks, a forty-three-year-old seamstress, explained why she refused to obey the Montgomery law providing for segregation on city buses, why she decided to sit down in the "white" section of the bus:

> Well, in the first place, I had been working all day on the job. I was quite tired after spending a full day working. I handle and work on clothing that white people wear. That didn't come in my mind but this is what I wanted to know: when and how would we ever determine our rights as human beings? . . . It just happened that the driver made a demand and I just didn't feel like obeying his demand. He called a policeman and I was arrested and placed in jail. . . .

Montgomery blacks called a mass meeting. They voted to boycott all city buses. Car pools were organized to take Negroes to work; most people walked. The city retaliated by indicting one hundred leaders of the boycott, and sent many to jail. White segregationists turned to violence. Bombs exploded in four Negro churches. A shotgun blast was fired through the front door of the home of Dr. Martin Luther King, Jr., the twenty-seven-year-old Altanta-born minister who was one of the leaders of the boycott. King's home was bombed. But the black people of Montgomery persisted, and in November 1956, the Supreme Court outlawed segregation on local bus lines.

Montgomery was the beginning. It forecast the style and mood of the vast protest movement that would sweep the South in the next ten years: emotional church meetings, Christian hymns adapted to current battles, references to lost American ideals, the commitment to nonviolence, the willingness to struggle and sacrifice. A *New York Times* reporter described a mass meeting in Montgomery during the boycott:

> One after the other, indicted Negro leaders took the rostrum in a crowded Baptist church tonight to urge their followers to shun the city's buses and "walk with God."
>
> More than two thousand Negroes filled the church from basement to balcony and overflowed into the street. They chanted and sang; they shouted and prayed; they collapsed in the aisles and they sweltered in an eighty-five degree heat. They pledged themselves again and again to "passive resistance." Under this banner they have carried on for eighty days a stubborn boycott of the city's buses.

Martin Luther King at that meeting gave a preview of the oratory that would soon inspire millions of people to demand racial justice. He said the protest was not merely over buses but over things that "go deep down into the archives of history." He said:

> We have known humiliation, we have known abusive language, we have been plunged into the abyss of oppression. And we decided to

raise up only with the weapon of protest. It is one of the greatest glories of America that we have the right of protest.

If we are arrested every day, if we are exploited every day, if we are trampled over every day, don't ever let anyone pull you so low as to hate them. We must use the weapon of love. We must have compassion and understanding for those who hate us. We must realize so many people are taught to hate us that they are not totally responsible for their hate. But we stand in life at midnight, we are always on the threshold of a new dawn.

King's stress on love and nonviolence was powerfully effective in building a sympathetic following throughout the nation, among whites as well as blacks. But there were blacks who thought the message naïve, that while there were misguided people who might be won over by love, there were others who would have to be bitterly fought, and not always with nonviolence. Two years after the Montgomery boycott, in Monroe, North Carolina, an ex-marine named Robert Williams, the president of the local NAACP, became known for his view that blacks should defend themselves against violence, with guns if necessary. When local Klansmen attacked the home of one of the leaders of the Monroe NAACP, Williams and other blacks, armed with rifles, fired back. The Klan left. (The Klan was being challenged now with its own tactic of violence; a Klan raid on an Indian community in North Carolina was repelled by Indians firing rifles.)

Still, in the years that followed, southern blacks stressed nonviolence. On February 1, 1960, four freshmen at a Negro college in Greensboro, North Carolina, decided to sit down at the Woolworth's lunch counter downtown, where only whites ate. They were refused service, and when they would not leave, the lunch counter was closed for the day. The next day they returned, and then, day after day, other Negroes came to sit silently.

In the next two weeks, sit-ins spread to fifteen cities in five southern states. A seventeen-year-old sophomore at Spelman College in Atlanta, Ruby Doris Smith, heard about Greensboro:

When the student committee was formed ... I told my older sister ... to put me on the list. And when two hundred students were selected for the first demonstration I was among them. I went through the food line in the restaurant at the State Capitol with six other students, but when we got to the cashier she wouldn't take our money.... The Lieutenant-Governor came down and told us to leave. We didn't and went to the county jail.

In his Harlem apartment in New York, a young Negro teacher of mathematics named Bob Moses saw a photo in the newspapers of the Greensboro sit-inners. "The students in that picture had a certain look on their faces, sort of sullen, angry, determined. Before, the Negro in the South had always looked on the defensive, cringing. This time they were taking the initiative. They were kids my age, and I knew this had something to do with my own life."

There was violence against the sit-inners. But the idea of taking the initiative against segregation took hold. In the next twelve months, more than fifty thousand people, mostly black, some white, participated in demonstrations of one kind or another in a hundred cities, and over 3,600 people were put in jail. But by the end of 1960, lunch counters were open to blacks in Greensboro and many other places.

A year after the Greensboro incident, a northern-based group dedicated to racial equality—CORE (Congress of Racial Equality)—organized "Freedom Rides" in which blacks and whites traveled together on buses going through the South, to try to break the segregation pattern in interstate travel. Such segregation had long been illegal, but the federal government never enforced the law in the South; the President now was John F. Kennedy, but he too seemed cautious about the race question, concerned about the support of southern white leaders of the Democratic party.

The two buses that left Washington, D.C., on May 4, 1961, headed for New Orleans, never got there. In South Carolina, riders were beaten. In Alabama, a bus was set afire. Freedom Riders were attacked with fists and iron bars. The southern police did not interfere with any of this violence, nor did the federal government. FBI agents watched, took notes, did nothing.

At this point, veterans of the sit-ins, who had recently formed the Student Nonviolent Coordinating Committee (SNCC), dedicated to nonviolent but militant action for equal rights, organized another Freedom Ride, from Nashville to Birmingham. Before they started out, they called the Department of Justice in Washington, D.C., to ask for protection. As Ruby Doris Smith reported: ". . . the Justice Department said no, they couldn't protect anyone, but if something happened, they would investigate. You know how they do. . . ."

The racially mixed SNCC Freedom Riders were arrested in Birmingham, Alabama, spent a night in jail, were taken to the Tennessee border by police, made their way back to Birmingham, took a bus to Montgomery, and there were attacked by whites with fists and clubs, in a bloody scene. They resumed their trip, to Jackson, Mississippi.

By this time the Freedom Riders were in the news all over the world, and the government was anxious to prevent further violence. Attorney General Robert Kennedy, instead of insisting on their right to travel without being arrested, agreed to the Freedom Riders' being arrested in Jackson, in return for Mississippi police protection against possible mob violence. As Victor Navasky comments in *Kennedy Justice*, about Robert Kennedy: "He didn't hesitate to trade the freedom riders' constitutional right to interstate travel for Senator Eastland's guarantee of their right to live."

The Freedom Riders did not become subdued in jail. They resisted, protested, sang, demanded their rights. Stokely Carmichael recalled later how he and his fellow inmates were singing in the Parchman jail in Mississippi and the sheriff threatened to take away their mattresses:

I hung on to the mattress and said, "I think we have a right to them and I think you're unjust." And he said, "I don't want to hear all that shit, nigger," and started to put on the wristbreakers. I wouldn't move and started to sing "I'm Gonna Tell God How You Treat Me" and everybody started to sing it, and by this time Tyson was really to pieces. He called to the trusties, "Get him in there!" and he went out the door and slammed it, and left everybody else with their mattresses.

In Albany, Georgia, a small deep-South town where the atmosphere of slavery still lingered, mass demonstrations took place in the winter of 1961 and again in 1962. Of 22,000 black people in Albany, over a thousand went to jail for marching, assembling, to protest segregation and discrimination. Here, as in all the demonstrations that would sweep over the South, little black children participated—a new generation was learning to act. The Albany police chief, after one of the mass arrests, was taking the names of prisoners lined up before his desk. He looked up and saw a Negro boy about nine years old. "What's your name?" The boy looked straight at him and said: "Freedom, Freedom."

There is no way of measuring the effect of that southern movement on the sensibilities of a whole generation of young black people, or of tracing the process by which some of them became activists and leaders. In Lee County, Georgia, after the events of 1961–1962, a black teenager named James Crawford joined SNCC and began taking black people to the county courthouse to vote. One day, bringing a woman there, he was approached by the deputy registrar. Another SNCC worker took notes on the conversation:

REGISTRAR: What do you want?

CRAWFORD: I brought this lady down to register.

REGISTRAR: (after giving the woman a card to fill out and sending her outside in the hall) Why did you bring this lady down here?

CRAWFORD: Because she wants to be a first class citizen like y'all.

REGISTRAR: Who are you to bring people down to register?

CRAWFORD: It's my job.

REGISTRAR: Suppose you get two bullets in your head right now?

CRAWFORD: I got to die anyhow.

REGISTRAR: If I don't do it, I can get somebody else to do it. (No reply)

REGISTRAR: Are you scared?

CRAWFORD: No.

REGISTRAR: Suppose somebody came in that door and shoot you in the back of the head right now. What would you do?

CRAWFORD: I couldn't do nothing. If they shoot me in the back of the head there are people coming from all over the world.

REGISTRAR: What people?

CRAWFORD: The people I work for.

In Birmingham in 1963, thousands of blacks went into the streets, facing police clubs, tear gas, dogs, high-powered water hoses. And meanwhile, all over the deep South, the young people of SNCC, mostly black, a few white, were moving into communities in Georgia, Alabama, Mississippi, Arkansas. Joined by local black people, they were organizing, to register people to vote, to protest against racism, to build up courage against violence. The Department of Justice recorded 1412 demonstrations in three months of 1963. Imprisonment became commonplace, beatings became frequent. Many local people were afraid. Others came forward. A nineteen-year-old black student from Illinois named Carver Neblett, working for SNCC in Terrell County, Georgia, reported:

I talked with a blind man who is extremely interested in the civil rights movement. He has been keeping up with the movement from the beginning. Even though this man is blind he wants to learn all the questions on the literacy test. Imagine, while many are afraid that white men will burn our houses, shoot into them, or put us off their property, a blind man, seventy years old, wants to come to our meetings.

As the summer of 1964 approached, SNCC and other civil rights groups working together in Mississippi, and facing increasing violence, decided to call upon young people from other parts of the country for help. They hoped that would bring attention to the situation in Mississippi. Again and again in Mississippi and elsewhere, the FBI had stood by, lawyers for the Justice Department had stood by, while civil rights workers were beaten and jailed, while federal laws were violated.

On the eve of the Mississippi Summer, in early June 1964, the civil rights movement rented a theater near the White House, and a busload of black Mississippians traveled to Washington to testify publicly about the daily violence, the dangers facing the volunteers coming into Mississippi. Constitutional lawyers testified that the national government had the legal power to give protection against such violence. The transcript of this testimony was given to President Johnson and Attorney General Kennedy, accompanied by a request for a protective federal presence during the Mississippi Summer. There was no response.

Twelve days after the public hearing, three civil rights workers, James Chaney, a young black Mississippian, and two white volunteers, Andrew Goodman and Michael Schwerner, were arrested in Philadelphia, Mississippi, released from jail late at night, then seized, beaten with chains, and shot to death. Ultimately, an informer's testimony led to jail sentences for the sheriff and deputy sheriff and others. That came too late. The Mississippi murders had taken place after the repeated refusal of the national government, under Kennedy or Johnson, or any other President, to defend blacks against violence.

Dissatisfaction with the national government intensified. Later that summer, during the Democratic National Convention in Washington, Mississippi, blacks asked to be seated as part of the state delegation to represent the 40 percent of the state's population who were black. They were turned down by the liberal Democratic leadership, including vice-presidential candidate Hubert Humphrey.

Congress began reacting to the black revolt, the turmoil, the world publicity. Civil rights laws were passed in 1957, 1960, and 1964. They promised much, on voting equality, on employment equality, but were enforced poorly or ignored. In 1965, President Johnson sponsored and Congress passed an even stronger Voting Rights Law, this time ensuring on-the-spot federal protection of the right to register and vote. The effect on Negro voting in the South was dramatic. In 1952, a million southern blacks (20 percent of those eligible) registered to vote. In 1964 the number was 2 million—40 percent. By 1968, it was 3 million, 60 percent—the same percentage as white voters.

The federal government was trying—without making fundamental changes—to control an explosive situation, to channel anger into the traditional cooling mechanism of the ballot box, the polite petition, the officially endorsed quiet gathering. When black civil rights leaders planned a huge march on Washington in the summer of 1963 to protest the failure of the nation to solve the race problem, it was quickly embraced by President Kennedy and other national leaders, and turned into a friendly assemblage.

Martin Luther King's speech there thrilled 200,000 black and white Americans—"I have a dream. . . ." It was magnificent oratory, but without the anger that many blacks felt. When John Lewis, a young Alabama-born SNCC leader, much arrested, much beaten, tried to introduce a stronger note of outrage at the meeting, he was censored by the leaders of the march, who insisted he omit certain sentences critical of the national government and urging militant action.

Eighteen days after the Washington gathering, almost as if in deliberate contempt for its moderation, a bomb exploded in the basement of a black church in Birmingham and four girls attending a Sunday school class were killed. President Kennedy had praised the "deep fervor and quiet dignity" of the march, but the black militant Malcolm X was probably closer to the mood of the black community. Speaking in Detroit two months after the march on Washington and the Birmingham bombing, Malcolm X said, in his powerful, icy-clear, rhythmic style:

The Negroes were out there in the streets. They were talking about how they were going to march on Washington. . . . That they were going to march on Washington, march on the Senate, march on the White House, march on the Congress, and tie it up, bring it to a halt, not let the government proceed. They even said they were going out to the airport and lay down on the runway and not let any airplanes land. I'm telling you what they said. That was revolution. That was revolution. That was the black revolution.

It was the grass roots out there in the street. It scared the white man to death, scared the white power structure in Washington, D.C. to death; I was there. When they found out that this black steamroller was going to come down on the capital, they called in . . . these national Negro leaders that you respect and told them, "Call it off," Kennedy said. "Look you all are letting this thing go too far." And Old Tom said, "Boss, I can't stop it because I didn't start it." I'm telling you what they said. They said, "I'm not even in it, much less at the head of it." They said, "These Negroes are doing things on their own. They're running ahead of us." And that old shrewd fox, he said, "If you all aren't in it, I'll put you in it. I'll put you at the head of it. I'll endorse it. I'll welcome it. I'll help it. I'll join it."

This is what they did with the march on Washington. They joined it . . . became part of it, took it over. And as they took it over, it lost its militancy. It ceased to be angry, it ceased to be hot, it ceased to be uncompromising. Why, it even ceased to be a march. It became a picnic, a circus. Nothing but a circus, with clowns and all. . . .

No, it was a sellout. It was a takeover. . . . They controlled it so tight, they told those Negroes what time to hit town, where to stop, what signs to carry, what song to sing, what speech they could make, and what speech they couldn't make, and then told them to get out of town by sundown. . . .

The accuracy of Malcolm X's caustic description of the march on Washington is corroborated in the description from the other side—from the Establishment, by White House adviser Arthur Schlesinger, in his book *A Thousand Days*. He tells how Kennedy met with the civil rights leaders and said the march would "create an atmosphere of intimidation" just when Congress was considering civil rights bills. A. Philip Randolph replied: "The Negroes are already in the streets. It is very likely impossible to get them off. . . ." Schlesinger says: "The conference with the President did persuade the civil rights leaders that they should not lay siege to Capitol Hill." Schlesinger describes the Washington march admiringly and then concludes: "So in 1963 Kennedy moved to incorporate the Negro revolution into the democratic coalition. . . ."

But it did not work. The blacks could not be easily brought into "the democratic coalition" when bombs kept exploding in churches, when new "civil rights" laws did not change the root condition of black people. In the spring of 1963, the rate of unemployment for whites was 4.8 percent. For nonwhites it was 12.1 percent. According to government estimates, one-fifth of the white population was below the poverty line, and one-half of the black population was below that line. The civil rights bills emphasized voting, but voting was not a fundamental solution to racism or poverty. In Harlem, blacks who had voted for years still lived in rat-infested slums.

In precisely those years when civil rights legislation coming out of Congress reached its peak, 1964 and 1965, there were black outbreaks in every part of the country: in Florida, set off by the killing of a Negro woman and a bomb threat against a Negro high school; in Cleveland, set off by the killing of a white minister who sat in the path of a bulldozer to protest discrimination against blacks in construction work; in New York, set off by the fatal shooting of a fifteen-year-old Negro boy during a fight with an off-duty policeman. There were riots also in Rochester, Jersey City, Chicago, Philadelphia.

In August 1965, just as Lyndon Johnson was signing into law the strong Voting Rights Act, providing for federal registration of black voters to ensure their protection, the black ghetto in Watts, Los Angeles, erupted in the most violent urban outbreak since World War II. It was provoked by the forcible arrest of a young Negro driver, the clubbing of a bystander by police, the seizure of a young black woman falsely accused of spitting on the police.

There was rioting in the streets, looting and firebombing of stores. Police and National Guardsmen were called in; they used their guns. Thirty-four people were killed, most of them black, hundreds injured, four thousand arrested. Robert Conot, a West Coast journalist, wrote of the riot *(Rivers of Blood, Years of Darkness)*: "In Los Angeles the Negro was going on record that he would no longer turn the other cheek. That, frustrated and goaded, he would strike back, whether the response of violence was an appropriate one or no."

In the summer of 1966, there were more outbreaks, with rock throwing, looting, and fire bombing by Chicago blacks and wild shootings by the National Guard; three blacks were killed, one a thirteen-year-old boy, another a fourteen-year-old pregnant girl. In Cleveland, the National Guard was summoned to stop a commotion in the black community; four Negroes were shot to death, two by troopers, two by white civilians.

It seemed clear by now that the nonviolence of the southern movement, perhaps tactically necessary in the southern atmosphere, and effective because it could be used to appeal to national opinion against the segregationist South, was not enough to deal with the entrenched problems of poverty in the black ghetto. In 1910, 90 percent of Negroes lived in the South. But by 1965, mechanical cotton pickers harvested 81 percent of Mississippi Delta cotton. Between 1940 and 1970, 4 million blacks left the country for the city. By 1965, 80 percent of blacks lived in cities and 50 percent of the black people lived in the North.

There was a new mood in SNCC and among many militant blacks. Their disillusionment was expressed by a young black writer, Julius Lester:

> Now it is over. America has had chance after chance to show that it really meant "that all men are endowed with certain inalienable rights." . . . Now it is over. The days of singing freedom songs and the days of combating bullets and billy clubs with love. . . . Love is fragile and gentle and seeks a like response. They used to sing "I Love Everybody" as they ducked bricks and bottles. Now they sing:

Too much love,
Too much love,
Nothing kills a nigger like
Too much love.

In 1967, in the black ghettos of the country, came the greatest urban riots of American history. According to the report of the National Advisory Committee on Urban Disorders, they "involved Negroes acting against local symbols of white American society," symbols of authority and property in the black neighborhoods—rather than purely against white persons. The Commission reported eight major uprisings, thirty-three "serious but not major" outbreaks, and 123 "minor" disorders. Eighty-three died of gunfire, mostly in Newark and Detroit. "The overwhelming majority of the persons killed or injured in all the disorders were Negro civilians."

The "typical rioter," according to the Commission, was a young, high school dropout but "nevertheless, somewhat better educated than his non-rioting Negro neighbor" and "usually underemployed or employed in a menial job." He was "proud of his race, extremely hostile to both whites and middle-class Negroes and, although informed about politics, highly distrustful of the political system."

The report blamed "white racism" for the disorders, and identified the ingredients of the "explosive mixture which has been accumulating in our cities since the end of World War II":

Pervasive discrimination and segregation in employment, education, and housing . . . growing concentrations of impoverished Negroes in our major cities, creating a growing crisis of deteriorating facilities and services and unmet human needs. . . .

A new mood has sprung up among Negroes, particularly the young, in which self-esteem and enhanced racial pride are replacing apathy and submission to the "system."

But the Commission Report itself was a standard device of the system when facing rebellion: set up an investigating committee, issue a report; the words of the report, however strong, will have a soothing effect.

That didn't completely work either. "Black Power" was the new slogan—an expression of distrust of any "progress" given or conceded by whites, a rejection of paternalism. Few blacks (or whites) knew the statement of the white writer Aldous Huxley: "Liberties are not given, they are taken." But the idea was there, in Black Power. Also, a pride in race, an insistence on black independence, and often, on black separation to achieve this independence. Malcolm X was the most eloquent spokesman for this. After he was assassinated as he spoke on a public platform in February 1965, in a plan whose origins are still obscure, he became the martyr of this movement. Hundreds of thousands read his *Autobiography*. He was more influential in death than during his lifetime.

Martin Luther King, though still respected, was being replaced now by new heroes: Huey Newton of the Black Panthers, for instance. The Panthers had guns; they said blacks should defend themselves.

Malcolm X in late 1964 had spoken to black students from Mississippi visiting Harlem:

> You'll get freedom by letting your enemy know that you'll do anything to get your freedom; then you'll get it. It's the only way you'll get it. When you get that kind of attitude, they'll label you as a "crazy Negro," or they'll call you a "crazy nigger"—they don't say Negro. Or they'll call you an extremist or a subversive, or seditious, or a red or a radical. But when you stay radical long enough and get enough people to be like you, you'll get your freedom.

Congress responded to the riots of 1967 by passing the Civil Rights Act of 1968. Presumably it would make stronger the laws prohibiting violence against blacks; it increased the penalties against those depriving people of their civil rights. However, it said: "The provisions of this section shall not apply to acts or omissions on the part of law enforcement officers, members of the National Guard . . . or members of the Armed Forces of the

United States, who are engaged in suppressing a riot or civil disturbance. . . ."

Furthermore, it added a section—agreed to by liberal members of Congress in order to get the whole bill passed—that provided up to five years in prison for anyone traveling interstate or using interstate facilities (including mail and telephone) "to organize, promote, encourage, participate in, or carry on a riot." It defined a riot as an action by three or more people involving threats of violence. The first person prosecuted under the Civil Rights Act of 1968 was a young black leader of SNCC, H. Rap Brown, who had made a militant, angry speech in Maryland, just before a racial disturbance there. (Later the Act would be used against antiwar demonstrators in Chicago—the Chicago Eight.)

Martin Luther King himself became more and more concerned about problems untouched by civil rights laws—problems coming out of poverty. In the spring of 1968, he began speaking out, against the advice of some Negro leaders who feared losing friends in Washington, against the war in Vietnam. He connected war and poverty:

> . . . it's inevitable that we've got to bring out the question of the tragic mixup in priorities. We are spending all of this money for death and destruction, and not nearly enough money for life and constructive development . . . when the guns of war become a national obsession, social needs inevitably suffer.

King now became a chief target of the FBI, which tapped his private phone conversations, sent him fake letters, threatened him, blackmailed him, and even suggested once in an anonymous letter that he commit suicide. FBI internal memos discussed finding a black leader to replace King. As a Senate report on the FBI said in 1976, the FBI tried "to destroy Dr. Martin Luther King."

King was turning his attention to troublesome questions. He still insisted on nonviolence. Riots were self-defeating, he thought. But they did express a deep feeling that could not be ignored. And so, nonviolence, he said, "must be militant, massive nonviolence." He planned a "Poor People's Encampment" in Washington, this time not with the paternal approval of the President. And he went to Memphis, Tennessee, to support a strike of garbage workers in that city. There, standing on a balcony outside his hotel room, he was shot to death by an unseen marksman. The Poor People's Encampment went on, and then it was broken up by police action, just as the World War I veterans' Bonus Army of 1932 was dispersed.

The killing of King brought new urban outbreaks all over the country, in which thirty-nine people were killed, thirty-five of them black. Evidence was piling up that even with all of the civil rights laws now on the books, the courts would not protect blacks against violence and injustice:

1. In the 1967 riots in Detroit, three black teen-agers were killed in the Algiers Motel. Three Detroit policemen and a black private guard were tried for this triple murder. The defense conceded, a UPI dispatch said, that the four men had shot two of the blacks. A jury exonerated them.

2. In Jackson, Mississippi, in the spring of 1970, on the campus of Jackson State College, a Negro college, police laid down a 28-second barrage of gunfire, using shotguns, rifles, and a submachine gun. Four hundred bullets or pieces of buckshot struck the girls' dormitory and two black students were killed. A local grand jury found the attack "justified" and U.S. District Court Judge Harold Cox (a Kennedy appointee) declared that students who engage in civil disorders "must expect to be injured or killed."

3. In Boston in April 1970, a policeman shot and killed an unarmed black man, a patient in a ward in the Boston City Hospital, firing five shots after the black man snapped a towel at him. The chief judge of the municipal court of Boston exonerated the policeman.

4. In Augusta, Georgia, in May 1970, six Negroes were shot to death during looting and disorder in the city. The *New York Times* reported:

A confidential police report indicates that at least five of the victims were killed by the police. . . .

An eyewitness to one of the deaths said he had watched a Negro policeman and his white partner fire nine shots into the back of a man suspected of looting. They did not fire warning shots or ask him to stop running, said Charles A. Reid, a 38-year-old businessman. . . .

5. In April 1970, a federal jury in Boston found a policeman had used "excessive force" against two black soldiers from Fort Devens, and one of them required twelve stitches in his scalp; the judge awarded the servicemen $3 in damages.

These were "normal" cases, endlessly repeated in the history of the country, coming randomly but persistently out of a racism deep in the institutions, the mind of the country. But there was something else—a planned pattern of violence against militant black organizers, carried on by the police and the Federal Bureau of Investigation. On December 4, 1969, a little before five in the morning, a squad of Chicago police, armed with a submachine gun and shotguns, raided an apartment where Black Panthers lived. They fired at least eighty-two and perhaps two hundred rounds into the apartment, killing twenty-one-year-old Black Panther leader Fred Hampton as he lay in his bed, and another Black Panther, Mark Clark. Years later, it was discovered in a court proceeding that the FBI had an informer among the Panthers, and that they had given the police a floor plan of the apartment, including a sketch of where Fred Hampton slept.

Was the government turning to murder and terror because the concessions—the legislation, the speeches, the intonation of the civil rights hymn "We Shall Overcome" by President Lyndon Johnson—were not working? It was discovered later that the government in all the years of the civil rights movement, while making concessions through Congress, was acting through the FBI to harass and break up black militant groups. Between 1956 and 1971 the FBI concluded a massive Counterintelligence Program (known as COINTELPRO) that took 295 actions against black groups. Black militancy seemed stubbornly resistant to destruction. A secret FBI report to President Nixon in 1970 said "a recent poll indicates that approximately 25% of the black population has a great respect for the Black Panther Party, including 43% of blacks under 21 years of age." Was there fear that blacks would turn their attention from the controllable field of voting to the more dangerous arena of wealth and poverty—of class conflict? In 1966, seventy poor black people in Greenville, Mississippi, occupied an unused air force barracks, until they were evicted by the military. A local woman, Mrs. Unita Blackwell, said:

> I feel that the federal government have proven that it don't care about poor people. Everything that we have asked for through these years had been handed down on paper. It's never been a reality. We the poor people of Mississippi is tired. We're tired of it so we're going to build for ourselves, because we don't have a government that represents us.

Out of the 1967 riots in Detroit came an organization devoted to organizing black workers for revolutionary change. This was the League of Revolutionary Black Workers, which lasted until 1971 and influenced thousands of black workers in Detroit during its period of activity.

The new emphasis was more dangerous than civil rights, because it created the possibility of blacks and whites uniting on the issue of class exploitation. Back in November 1963, A. Philip Randolph had spoken to an AFL-CIO convention about the civil rights movement, and foreseen its direction: "The Negro's protest today is but the first rumbling of the 'under-class.' As the Negro has taken to the streets, so will the unemployed of all races take to the streets."

Attempts began to do with blacks what had been done historically with whites—to lure a small number into the system with economic enticements. There was talk of "black capitalism." Leaders of the NAACP and CORE were invited to the White

House. James Farmer of CORE, a former Freedom Rider and militant, was given a job in President Nixon's administration. Floyd McKissick of CORE received a $14 million government loan to build a housing development in North Carolina. Lyndon Johnson had given jobs to some blacks through the Office of Economic Opportunity; Nixon set up an Office of Minority Business Enterprise.

Chase Manhattan Bank and the Rockefeller family (controllers of Chase) took a special interest in developing "black capitalism." The Rockefellers had always been financial patrons of the Urban League, and a strong influence in black education through their support of Negro colleges in the South. David Rockefeller tried to persuade his fellow capitalists that while helping black businessmen with money might not be fruitful in the short run, it was necessary "to shape an environment in which the business can continue earning a profit four or five or ten years from now." With all of this, black business remained infinitesimally small. The largest black corporation (Motown Industries) had sales in 1974 of $45 million, while Exxon Corporation had sales of $42 billion. The total receipts of black-owned firms accounted for 0.3 percent of all business income.

There was a small amount of change and a lot of publicity. There were more black faces in the newspapers and on television, creating an impression of change—and siphoning off into the mainstream a small but significant number of black leaders.

Some new black voices spoke against this. Robert Allen (*Black Awakening in Capitalist America*) wrote:

If the community as a whole is to benefit, then the community as a whole must be organized to manage collectively its internal economy and its business relations with white America. Black business firms must be treated and operated as social property, belonging to the general black community, not as the private property of individual or limited groups of individuals. This necessitates the dismantling of capitalist property relations in the black community and their replacement with a planned communal economy.

A black woman, Patricia Robinson, in a pamphlet distributed in Boston in 1970 *(Poor Black Woman)*, tied male supremacy to capitalism and said the black woman "allies herself with the have-nots in the wider world and their revolutionary struggles." She said the poor black woman did not in the past "question the social and economic system" but now she must, and in fact, "she has begun to question aggressive male domination and the class society which enforces it, capitalism."

Another black woman, Margaret Wright, said she was not fighting for equality with men if it meant equality in the world of killing, the world of competition. "I don't want to compete on no damned exploitative level. I don't want to exploit nobody. . . . I want the right to be black and me. . . ."

The system was working hard, by the late sixties and early seventies, to contain the frightening explosiveness of the black upsurge. Blacks were voting in large numbers in the South, and in the 1968 Democratic Convention three blacks were admitted into the Mississippi delegation. By 1977, more than two thousand blacks held office in eleven southern states (in 1965 the number was seventy-two). There were two Congressmen, eleven state senators, ninety-five state representatives, 267 county commissioners, seventy-six mayors, 824 city council members, eighteen sheriffs or chiefs of police, 508 school board members. It was a dramatic advance. But blacks, with 20 percent of the South's population, still held less than 3 percent of the elective offices. A *New York Times* reporter, analyzing the new situation in 1977, pointed out that even where blacks held important city offices: "Whites almost always retain economic power." After Maynard Jackson, a black, became mayor of Atlanta, "the white business establishment continued to exert its influence."

Those blacks in the South who could afford to go to downtown restaurants and hotels were no longer barred because of their race. More blacks could go to colleges and universities, to law schools and medical schools. Northern cities were busing children back and forth in an attempt to create racially mixed schools, despite the racial segregation in housing. None of this, however, was halting what Frances Piven and Richard Cloward (*Poor People's Movements*) called "the destruction of the black lower class"—the unemployment, the deterioration of the ghetto, the rising crime, drug addiction, violence.

In the summer of 1977, the Department of Labor reported that the rate of unemployment among black youths was 34.8 percent. A small new black middle class of blacks had been created, and it raised the overall statistics for black income—but there was a great disparity between the newly risen middle-class black and the poor left behind. Despite the new opportunities for a small number of blacks, the median black family income of 1977 was only about 60 percent that of whites; blacks were twice as likely to die of diabetes; seven times as likely to be victims of homicidal violence rising out of the poverty and despair of the ghetto.

A *New York Times* report in early 1978 said: ". . . the places that experienced urban riots in the 1960's have, with a few exceptions, changed little, and the conditions of poverty have spread in most cities."

Statistics did not tell the whole story. Racism, always a national fact, not just a southern one, emerged in northern cities, as the federal government made concessions to poor blacks in a way that pitted them against poor whites for resources made scarce by the system. Blacks, freed from slavery to take their place under capitalism, had long been forced into conflict with whites for scarce jobs. Now, with desegregation in housing, blacks tried to move into neighborhoods where whites, themselves poor, crowded, troubled, could find in them a target for their anger. In the Boston *Globe*, November 1977:

> A Hispanic family of six fled their apartment in the Savin Hill section of Dorchester yesterday after a week of repeated stonings and window-smashings by a group of white youths, in what appears to have been racially motivated attacks, police said.

In Boston, the busing of black children to white schools, and whites to black schools, set off a wave of white neighborhood violence. The use of busing to integrate schools—sponsored by the government and the courts in response to the black movement—was an ingenious concession to protest. It had the effect of pushing poor whites and poor blacks into competition for the miserable inadequate schools which the system provided for all the poor.

Was the black population—hemmed into the ghetto, divided by the growth of a middle class, decimated by poverty, attacked by the government, driven into conflict with whites—under control? Surely, in the mid-seventies, there was no great black movement under way. Yet, a new black consciousness had been born and was still alive. Also, whites and blacks were crossing racial lines in the South to unite as a class against employers. In 1971, two thousand woodworkers in Mississippi, black and white, joined together to protest a new method of measuring wood that led to lower wages. In the textile mills of J. P. Stevens, where 44,000 workers were employed in eighty-five plants, mostly in the South, blacks and whites were working together in union activity. In Tifton, Georgia, and Milledgeville, Georgia, in 1977, blacks and whites served together on the union committees of their plants.

Would a new black movement go beyond the limits of the civil rights actions of the sixties, beyond the spontaneous urban riots of the seventies, beyond separatism to a coalition of white and black in a historic new alliance? There was no way of knowing this in 1978. In 1978, 6 million black people were unemployed. As Langston Hughes said, what happens to a dream deferred? Does it dry up, or does it explode? If it did explode, as it had in the past, it would come with a certain inevitability—out of the conditions of black life in America—and yet, because no one knew when, it would come as a surprise.

7

THE
IMPOSSIBLE VICTORY:
VIETNAM

From 1964 to 1972, the wealthiest and most powerful nation in the history of the world made a maximum military effort, with everything short of atomic bombs, to defeat a nationalist revolutionary movement in a tiny, peasant country—and failed. When the United States fought in Vietnam, it was organized modern technology versus organized human beings, and the human beings won.

In the course of that war, there developed in the United States the greatest antiwar movement the nation had ever experienced, a movement that played a critical part in bringing the war to an end.

It was another startling fact of the sixties.

In the fall of 1945 Japan, defeated, was forced to leave Indochina, the former French colony it had occupied at the start of the war. In the meantime, a revolutionary movement had grown there, determined to end colonial control and to achieve a new life for the peasants of Indochina. Led by a Communist named Ho Chi Minh, the revolutionists fought against the Japanese, and when they were gone held a spectacular celebration in Hanoi in late 1945, with a million people in the streets, and issued a Declaration of Independence. It borrowed from the Declaration of the Rights of Man and the Citizen, in the French Revolution, and from the American Declaration of Independence, and began: "All men are created equal. They are endowed by their Creator with certain inalienable rights; among these are Life, Liberty, and the pursuit of Happiness." Just as the Americans in 1776 had listed their grievances against the English King, the Vietnamese listed their complaints against French rule:

> They have enforced inhuman laws. . . . They have built more prisons than schools. They have mercilessly slain our patriots, they have drowned uprisings in rivers of blood. They have fettered public opinion. . . . They have robbed us of our rice fields, our mines, our forests, and our raw materials. . . .
>
> They have invented numerous unjustifiable taxes and reduced our people, especially our peasantry, to a state of extreme poverty. . . .
>
> . . . from the end of last year, to the beginning of this year . . . more than two million of our fellow-citizens died of starvation. . . .
>
> The whole Vietnamese people, animated by a common purpose, are determined to fight to the bitter end against any attempt by the French colonialists to reconquer their country.

The U.S. Defense Department study of the Vietnam war, intended to be "top secret" but released to the public by Daniel Ellsberg and Anthony Russo in the famous *Pentagon Papers* case, described Ho Chi Minh's work:

> . . . Ho had built the Viet Minh into the only Vietnam-wide political organization capable of effective resistance to either the Japanese or the French. He was the only Vietnamese wartime leader with a national following, and he assured himself wider fealty among the Vietnamese people when in August-September, 1945, he overthrew the Japanese . . . established the Democratic Republic of Vietnam,

and staged receptions for in-coming allied occupation forces. . . . For a few weeks in September, 1945, Vietnam was—for the first and only time in its modern history—free of foreign domination, and united from north to south under Ho Chi Minh. . . .

The Western powers were already at work to change this. England occupied the southern part of Indochina and then turned it back to the French. Nationalist China (this was under Chiang Kai-shek, before the Communist revolution) occupied the northern part of Indochina, and the United States persuaded it to turn that back to the French. As Ho Chi Minh told an American journalist: "We apparently stand quite alone. . . . We shall have to depend on ourselves."

Between October 1945 and February 1946, Ho Chi Minh wrote eight letters to President Truman, reminding him of the self-determination promises of the Atlantic Charter. One of the letters was sent both to Truman and to the United Nations:

> I wish to invite attention of your Excellency for strictly humanitarian reasons to following matter. Two million Vietnamese died of starvation during winter of 1944 and spring 1945 because of starvation policy of French who seized and stored until it rotted all available rice. . . . Three-fourths of cultivated land was flooded in summer 1945, which was followed by a severe drought; of normal harvest five-sixths was lost. . . . Many people are starving. . . . Unless great world powers and international relief organizations bring us immediate assistance we face imminent catastrophe. . . .

Truman never replied.

In October of 1946, the French bombarded Haiphong, a port in northern Vietnam, and there began the eight-year war between the Vietminh movement and the French over who would rule Vietnam. After the Communist victory in China in 1949 and the Korean war the following year, the United States began giving large amounts of military aid to the French. By 1954, the United States had given 300,000 small arms and machine guns, enough to equip the entire French army in Indochina, and $1 billion; all together, the U.S. was financing 80 percent of the French war effort.

Why was the United States doing this? To the public, the word was that the United States was helping to stop Communism in Asia, but there was not much public discussion. In the secret memoranda of the National Security Council (which advised the President on foreign policy) there was talk in 1950 of what came to be known as the "domino theory"—that, like a row of dominoes, if one country fell to Communism, the next one would do the same and so on. It was important therefore to keep the first one from falling.

A secret memo of the National Security Council in June 1952 also pointed to the chain of U.S. military bases along the coast of China, the Philippines, Taiwan, Japan, South Korea:

> Communist control of all of Southeast Asia would render the U.S. position in the Pacific offshore island chain precarious and would seriously jeopardize fundamental U.S. security interests in the Far East.

And:

> Southeast Asia, especially Malaya and Indonesia, is the principal world source of natural rubber and tin, and a producer of petroleum and other strategically important commodities. . . .

It was also noted that Japan depended on the rice of Southeast Asia, and Communist victory there would "make it extremely difficult to prevent Japan's eventual accommodation to communism."

In 1953, a congressional study mission reported: "The area of Indochina is immensely wealthy in rice, rubber, coal and iron ore. Its position makes it a strategic key to the rest of Southeast Asia." That year, a State Department memorandum said that the French were losing the war in Indochina, had failed "to win a sufficient native support," feared that a negotiated settlement "would mean the eventual loss to Communism not only of Indo-China but of the whole of Southeast Asia," and concluded: "If the French actually decided to withdraw, the U.S. would have to consider most seriously whether to take over in this area."

In 1954, the French, having been unable to win Vietnamese popular support, which was overwhelmingly behind Ho Chi Minh and the revolutionary movement, had to withdraw.

An international assemblage at Geneva presided over the peace agreement between the French and the Vietminh. It was agreed that the French would temporarily withdraw into the southern part of Vietnam, that the Vietminh would remain in the north, and that an election would take place in two years in a unified Vietnam to enable the Vietnamese to choose their own government.

The United States moved quickly to prevent the unification and to establish South Vietnam as an American sphere. It set up in Saigon as head of the government a former Vietnamese official named Ngo Dinh Diem, who had recently been living in New Jersey, and encouraged him not to hold the scheduled elections for unification. A memo in early 1954 of the Joint Chiefs of Staff said that intelligence estimates showed "a settlement based on free elections would be attended by almost certain loss of the Associated States [Laos, Cambodia, and Vietnam—the three parts of Indochina created by the Geneva Conference] to Communist control." Diem again and again blocked the elections requested by the Vietminh, and with American money and arms his government became more and more firmly established. As the *Pentagon Papers* put it: "South Viet Nam was essentially the creation of the United States."

The Diem regime became increasingly unpopular. Diem was a Catholic, and most Vietnamese were Buddhists; Diem was close to the landlords, and this was a country of peasants. His pretenses at land reform left things basically as they were. He replaced locally selected provincial chiefs with his own men, appointed in Saigon; by 1962, 88 percent of these provincial chiefs were military men. Diem imprisoned more and more Vietnamese who criticized the regime for corruption, for lack of reform.

Opposition grew quickly in the countryside, where Diem's apparatus could not reach well, and around 1958 guerrilla activities began against the regime. The Communist regime in Hanoi gave aid, encouragement, and sent people south—most of them southerners who had gone north after the Geneva accords—to support the guerrilla movement. In 1960, the National Liberation Front was formed in the South. It united the various strands of opposition to the regime; its strength came from South Vietnamese peasants, who saw it as a way of changing their daily lives. A U.S. government analyst named Douglas Pike, in his book *Viet Cong*, based on interviews with rebels and captured documents, tried to give a realistic assessment of what the United States faced:

> In the 2561 villages of South Vietnam, the National Liberation Front created a host of nation-wide socio-political organizations in a country where mass organizations . . . were virtually nonexistent. . . . Aside from the NLF there had never been a truly mass-based political party in South Vietnam.

Pike wrote: "The Communists have brought to the villages of South Vietnam significant social change and have done so largely by means of the communication process." That is, they were organizers much more than they were warriors. "What struck me most forcibly about the NLF was its totality as a social revolution first and as a war second." Pike was impressed with the mass involvement of the peasants in the movement. "The rural Vietnamese was not regarded simply as a pawn in a power struggle but as the active element in the thrust. He was the thrust." Pike wrote:

> The purpose of this vast organizational effort was . . . to restructure the social order of the village and train the villages to control themselves. This was the NLF's one undeviating thrust from the start.

Not the killing of ARVN (Saigon) soldiers, not the occupation of real estate, not the preparation for some great pitched battle . . . but organization in depth of the rural population through the instrument of self-control.

Pike estimated that the NLF membership by early 1962 stood at around 300,000. The *Pentagon Papers* said of this period: "Only the Viet Cong had any real support and influence on a broad base in the countryside."

When Kennedy took office in early 1961 he continued the policies of Truman and Eisenhower in Southeast Asia. Almost immediately, he approved a secret plan for various military actions in Vietnam and Laos, including the "dispatch of agents to North Vietnam" to engage in "sabotage and light harassment," according to the *Pentagon Papers*. Back in 1956, he had spoken of "the amazing success of President Diem" and said of Diem's Vietnam: "Her political liberty is an inspiration."

One day in June 1963, a Buddhist monk sat down in the public square in Saigon and set himself afire. More Buddhist monks began committing suicide by fire to dramatize their opposition to the Diem regime. Diem's police raided the Buddhist pagodas and temples, wounded thirty monks, arrested 1,400 people, and closed down the pagodas. There were demonstrations in the city. The police fired, killing nine people. Then, in Hué, the ancient capital, ten thousand demonstrated in protest.

Under the Geneva Accords, the United States was permitted to have 685 military advisers in southern Vietnam. Eisenhower secretly sent several thousand. Under Kennedy, the figure rose to sixteen thousand, and some of them began to take part in combat operations. Diem was losing. Most of the South Vietnam countryside was now controlled by local villagers organized by the NLF.

Diem was becoming an embarrassment, an obstacle to effective control over Vietnam. Some Vietnamese generals began plotting to overthrow his regime, staying in touch with a CIA man named Lucien Conein. Conein met secretly with American Ambassador

Henry Cabot Lodge, who was enthusiastically for the coup. Lodge reported to Kennedy's assistant, McGeorge Bundy, on October 25 *(Pentagon Papers):* "I have personally approved each meeting between General Tran Van Don and Conein who has carried out my orders in each instance explicitly." Kennedy seemed hesitant, but no move was made to warn Diem. Indeed, just before the coup, and just after he had been in touch through Conein with the plotters, Lodge spent a weekend with Diem at a seaside resort. When, on November 1, 1963, the generals attacked the presidential palace, Diem phoned Ambassador Lodge, and the conversation went as follows:

> Diem: Some units have made a rebellion and I want to know what is the attitude of the United States?
>
> Lodge: I do not feel well enough informed to be able to tell you. I have heard the shooting, but am not acquainted with all of the facts. Also it is 4:30 A.M. in Washington and the U.S. Government cannot possibly have a view.
>
> Diem: But you must have some general ideas. . . .

Lodge told Diem to phone him if he could do anything for his physical safety.

That was the last conversation any American had with Diem. He fled the palace, but he and his brother were apprehended by the plotters, taken out in a truck, and executed.

Earlier in 1963, Kennedy's Undersecretary of State, U. Alexis Johnson, was speaking before the Economic Club of Detroit:

> What is the attraction that Southeast Asia has exerted for centuries on the great powers flanking it on all sides? Why is it desirable, and why is it important? First, it provides a lush climate, fertile soil, rich natural resources, a relatively sparse population in most areas, and room to expand. The countries of Southeast Asia produce rich exportable surpluses such as rice, rubber, teak, corn, tin, spices, oil, and many others. . . .

This is not the language that was used by President Kennedy in his explanations to the American public. He talked of Communism and freedom. In a news conference February 14, 1962, he said: "Yes, as you know, the U.S. for more than a decade has been assisting the government, the people of Vietnam, to maintain their independence."

Three weeks after the execution of Diem, Kennedy himself was assassinated, and his Vice-President, Lyndon Johnson, took office.

The generals who succeeded Diem could not suppress the National Liberation Front. Again and again, American leaders expressed their bewilderment at the popularity of the NLF, at the high morale of its soldiers. The Pentagon historians wrote that when Eisenhower met with President-elect Kennedy in January 1961, he "wondered aloud why, in interventions of this kind, we always seemed to find that the morale of the Communist forces was better than that of the democratic forces." And General Maxwell Taylor reported in late 1964:

> The ability of the Viet-Cong continuously to rebuild their units and to make good their losses is one of the mysteries of the guerrilla war. . . . Not only do the Viet-Cong units have the recuperative powers of the phoenix, but they have an amazing ability to maintain morale. Only in rare cases have we found evidences of bad morale among Viet-Cong prisoners or recorded in captured Viet-Cong documents.

In early August 1964, President Johnson used a murky set of events in the Gulf of Tonkin, off the coast of North Vietnam, to launch full-scale war on Vietnam. Johnson and Secretary of Defense Robert McNamara told the American public there was an attack by North Vietnamese torpedo boats on American destroyers. "While on routine patrol in international waters," McNamara said, "the U.S. destroyer *Maddox* underwent an unprovoked attack." It later turned out that the Gulf of Tonkin episode was a fake, that the highest American officials had lied to the public—just as they had in the invasion of Cuba under Kennedy. In fact, the CIA had engaged in a secret operation attacking North Vietnamese coastal installations—so if there had been an attack it would not have been "unprovoked." It was not a "routine patrol," because the *Maddox* was on a special electronic spying mission. And it was not in international waters but in Vietnamese territorial waters. It turned out that no torpedoes were fired at the *Maddox*, as McNamara said. Another reported attack on another destroyer, two nights later, which Johnson called "open aggression on the high seas," seems also to have been an invention.

At the time of the incident, Secretary of State Rusk was questioned on NBC television:

REPORTER: What explanation, then, can you come up with for this unprovoked attack?

RUSK: Well, I haven't been able, quite frankly, to come to a fully satisfactory explanation. There is a great gulf of understanding, between that world and our world, ideological in character. They see what we think of as the real world in wholly different terms. Their very processes of logic are different. So that it's very difficult to enter into each other's minds across that great ideological gulf.

The Tonkin "attack" brought a congressional resolution, passed unanimously in the House, and with only two dissenting votes in the Senate, giving Johnson the power to take military action as he saw fit in Southeast Asia.

Two months before the Gulf of Tonkin incident, U.S. government leaders met in Honolulu and discussed such a resolution. Rusk said, in this meeting, according to the *Pentagon Papers*, that "public opinion on our Southeast Asia policy was badly divided in the United States at the moment and that, therefore, the President needed an affirmation of support."

The Tonkin Resolution gave the President the power to initiate hostilities without the declaration of war by Congress that the Constitution required. The Supreme Court, supposed to be the watchdog of the Constitution, was asked by a number of petitioners in the course of the Vietnam war to declare the war unconstitutional. Again and again, it refused even to consider the issue.

Immediately after the Tonkin affair, American warplanes began bombarding North Vietnam. During 1965, over 200,000 American soldiers were sent to South Vietnam, and in 1966, 200,000 more. By early 1968, there were more than 500,000 American troops there, and the U.S. Air Force was dropping bombs at a rate unequaled in history. Tiny glimmerings of the massive human suffering under this bombardment came to the outside world. On June 5, 1965, the *New York Times* carried a dispatch from Saigon:

As the Communists withdrew from Quangngai last Monday, United States jet bombers pounded the hills into which they were headed. Many Vietnamese—one estimate is as high as 500—were killed by the strikes. The American contention is that they were Vietcong soldiers. But three out of four patients seeking treatment in a Vietnamese hospital afterward for burns from napalm, or jellied gasoline, were village women.

On September 6, another press dispatch from Saigon:

In Bien Hoa province south of Saigon on August 15 United States aircraft accidentally bombed a Buddhist pagoda and a Catholic church . . . it was the third time their pagoda had been bombed in 1965. A temple of the Cao Dai religious sect in the same area had been bombed twice this year.

In another delta province there is a woman who has both arms burned off by napalm and her eyelids so badly burned that she cannot close them. When it is time for her to sleep her family puts a blanket over her head. The woman had two of her children killed in the air strike that maimed her.

Few Americans appreciate what their nation is doing to South

Vietnam with airpower . . . innocent civilians are dying every day in South Vietnam.

Large areas of South Vietnam were declared "free fire zones," which meant that all persons remaining within them—civilians, old people, children—were considered an enemy, and bombs were dropped at will. Villages suspected of harboring Viet Cong were subject to "search and destroy" missions—men of military age in the villages were killed, the homes were burned, the women, children, and old people were sent off to refugee camps. Jonathan Schell, in his book *The Village of Ben Suc*, describes such an operation: a village surrounded, attacked, a man riding on a bicycle shot down, three people picnicking by the river shot to death, the houses destroyed, the women, children, old people herded together, taken away from their ancestral homes.

The CIA in Vietnam, in a program called "Operation Phoenix," secretly, without trial, executed at least twenty thousand civilians in South Vietnam who were suspected of being members of the Communist underground. A pro-administration analyst wrote in the journal *Foreign Affairs* in January 1975: "Although the Phoenix program did undoubtedly kill or incarcerate many innocent civilians, it did also eliminate many members of the Communist infrastructure."

After the war, the release of records of the International Red Cross showed that in South Vietnamese prison camps, where at the height of the war 65,000 to 70,000 people were held and often beaten and tortured, American advisers observed and sometimes participated. The Red Cross observers found continuing, systematic brutality at the two principal Vietnamese POW camps—at Phu Quoc and Qui Nhon, where American advisers were stationed.

By the end of the Vietnam war, 7 million tons of bombs had been dropped on Vietnam, more than twice the total bombs dropped on Europe and Asia in World War II—almost one 500-pound bomb for every human being in Vietnam. It was estimated that there were 20 million bomb craters in the country. In addition, poisonous sprays were dropped by planes to destroy trees and any kind of growth—an area the size of the state of Massachusetts was covered with such poison. Vietnamese mothers reported birth defects in their children. Yale biologists, using the same poison (2,4,5,T) on mice, reported defective mice born and said they had no reason to believe the effect on humans was different.

On March 16, 1968, a company of American soldiers went into the hamlet of My Lai 4, in Quang Ngai province. They rounded up the inhabitants, including old people and women with infants in their arms. These people were ordered into a ditch, where they were methodically shot to death by American soldiers. The testimony of James Dursi, a rifleman, at the later trial of Lieutenant William Calley, was reported in the *New York Times*:

> Lieutenant Calley and a weeping rifleman named Paul D. Meadlo—the same soldier who had fed candy to the children before shooting them—pushed the prisoners into the ditch. . . .
>
> "There was an order to shoot by Lieutenant Calley, I can't remember the exact words—it was something like 'Start firing.'
>
> "Meadlo turned to me and said: 'Shoot, why don't you shoot?'
>
> "He was crying.
>
> "I said, 'I can't. I won't.'
>
> "Then Lieutenant Calley and Meadlo pointed their rifles into the ditch and fired.
>
> "People were diving on top of each other; mothers were trying to protect their children. . . ."

Journalist Seymour Hersh, in his book *My Lai 4*, writes:

> When Army investigators reached the barren area in November, 1969, in connection with the My Lai probe in the United States, they found mass graves at three sites, as well as a ditch full of bodies. It was estimated that between 450 and 500 people—most of them women, children and old men—had been slain and buried there.

The army tried to cover up what happened. But a letter began circulating from a GI named Ron Ridenhour, who had heard about the massacre. There were photos taken of the killing by an army photographer, Ronald Haeberle. Seymour Hersh, then working for an antiwar news agency in Southeast Asia called Dispatch News Service, wrote about it. The story of the massacre had appeared in May 1968 in two French publications, one called *Sud Vietnam en Lutte*, and another published by the North Vietnamese delegation to the peace talks in Paris—but the American press did not pay any attention.

Several of the officers in the My Lai massacre were put on trial, but only Lieutenant William Calley was found guilty. He was sentenced to life imprisonment, but his sentence was reduced twice; he served three years—Nixon ordered that he be under house arrest rather than a regular prison—and then was paroled. Thousands of Americans came to his defense. Part of it was in patriotic justification of his action as necessary against the "Communists." Part of it seems to have been a feeling that he was unjustly singled out in a war with many similar atrocities. Colonel Oran Henderson, who had been charged with covering up the My Lai killings, told reporters in early 1971: "Every unit of brigade size has its My Lai hidden someplace."

Indeed, My Lai was unique only in its details. Hersh reported a letter sent by a GI to his family, and published in a local newspaper:

Dear Mom and Dad:

Today we went on a mission and I am not very proud of myself, my friends, or my country. We burned every hut in sight!

It was a small rural network of villages and the people were incredibly poor. My unit burned and plundered their meager possessions. Let me try to explain the situation to you.

The huts here are thatched palm leaves. Each one has a dried mud bunker inside. These bunkers are to protect the families. Kind of like air raid shelters.

My unit commanders, however, chose to think that these bunkers are offensive. So every hut we find that has a bunker we are ordered to burn to the ground.

When the ten helicopters landed this morning, in the midst of these huts, and six men jumped out of each "chopper", we were firing the moment we hit the ground. We fired into all the huts we could. . . .

It is then that we burned these huts. . . . Everyone is crying, begging and praying that we don't separate them and take their husbands and fathers, sons and grandfathers. The women wail and moan.

Then they watch in terror as we burn their homes, personal possessions and food. Yes, we burn all rice and shoot all livestock.

The more unpopular became the Saigon government, the more desperate the military effort became to make up for this. A secret congressional report of late 1967 said the Viet Cong were distributing about five times more land to the peasants than the South Vietnamese government, whose land distribution program had come "to a virtual standstill." The report said: "The Viet Cong have eliminated landlord domination and reallocated lands owned by absentee landlords and the G.V.N. [Government of Viet Nam] to the landless and others who cooperate with Viet Cong authorities."

The unpopularity of the Saigon government explains the success of the National Liberation Front in infiltrating Saigon and other government-held towns in early 1968, without the people there warning the government. The NLF thus launched a surprise offensive (it was the time of "Tet," their New Year holiday) that carried them into the heart of Saigon, immobilized Tan San Nhut airfield, even occupied the American Embassy briefly. The offensive was beaten back, but it demonstrated that all the enormous firepower delivered on Vietnam by the United States had not destroyed the NLF, its morale, its popular support, its will to fight. It caused a reassessment in the American government, more doubts among the American people.

The massacre at My Lai by a company of ordinary soldiers was a small event compared with the plans of high-level military and civilian leaders to visit massive destruction on the civilian population of Vietnam. Assistant Secretary of Defense John McNaughton in early 1966, seeing that large-scale bombing of North Vietnam villages was not producing the desired result, suggested a different strategy. The air strikes on villages, he said, would "create a counterproductive wave of revulsion abroad and at home." He suggested instead:

> Destruction of locks and dams, however—if handled right—might . . . offer promise. It should be studied. Such destruction doesn't kill or drown people. By shallow-flooding the rice, it leads after a time to widespread starvation (more than a million?) unless food is provided—which we could offer to do "at the conference table." . . .

The heavy bombings were intended to destroy the will of ordinary Vietnamese to resist, as in the bombings of German and Japanese population centers in World War II—despite President Johnson's public insistence that only "military targets" were being bombed. The government was using language like "one more turn of the screw" to describe bombing. The CIA at one point in 1966 recommended a "bombing program of greater intensity," according to the *Pentagon Papers*, directed against, in the CIA's words, "the will of the regime as a target system."

Meanwhile, just across the border of Vietnam, in a neighboring country, Laos, where a right-wing government installed by the CIA faced a rebellion, one of the most beautiful areas in the world, the Plain of Jars, was being destroyed by bombing. This was not reported by the government or the press, but an American who lived in Laos, Fred Branfman, told the story in his book *Voices from the Plain of Jars*:

> Over 25,000 attack sorties were flown against the Plain of Jars from May, 1964, through September, 1969; over. 75,000 tons of bombs were dropped on it; on the ground, thousands were killed and wounded, tens of thousands driven underground, and the entire aboveground society leveled.

Branfman, who spoke the Laotian language and lived in a village with a Laotian family, interviewed hundreds of refugees from the bombing who poured into the capital city of Vientiane. He recorded their statements and preserved their drawings. A twenty-six-year-old nurse from Xieng Khouang told of her life in her village:

I was at one with the earth, the air, the upland fields, the paddy and the seedbeds of my village. Each day and night in the light of the moon I and my friends from the village would wander, calling out and singing, through forest and field, amidst the cries of the birds. During the harvesting and planting season, we would sweat and labor together, under the sun and the rain, contending with poverty and miserable conditions, continuing the farmer's life which has been the profession of our ancestors.

But in 1964 and 1965 I could feel the trembling of the earth and the shock from the sounds of arms exploding around my village. I began to hear the noise of airplanes, circling about in the heavens. One of them would stick its head down and, plunging earthward, loose a loud roar, shocking the heart as light and smoke covered everything so that one could not see anything at all. Each day we would exchange news with the neighboring villagers of the bombings that had occurred: the damaged houses, the injured and the dead. . . .

The holes! The holes! During that time we needed holes to save our lives. We who were young took our sweat and our strength, which should have been spent raising food in the ricefields and forests to sustain our lives, and squandered it digging holes to protect ourselves. . . .

One young woman explained why the revolutionary movement in Laos, the Neo Lao, attracted her and so many of her friends:

As a young girl, I had found that the past had not been very good, for men had mistreated and made fun of women as the weaker sex.

But after the Neo Lao party began to administer the region . . . it became very different . . . under the Neo Lao things changed psychologically, such as their teaching that women should be as brave as men. For example: although I had gone to school before, my elders advised me not to. They had said that it would not be useful for me as I could not hope to be a high ranking official after graduation, that only the children of the elite or rich could expect that.

But the Neo Lao said that women should have the same education as men, and they gave us equal privileges and did not allow anyone to make fun of us. . . .

And the old associations were changed into new ones. For example, most of the new teachers and doctors trained were women. And they changed the lives of the very poor. . . . For they shared the land of those who had many rice fields with those who had none.

A seventeen-year-old boy told about the Pathet Lao revolutionary army coming to his village:

Some people were afraid, mostly those with money. They offered cows to the Pathet Lao soldiers to eat, but the soldiers refused to take them. If they did take them, they paid a suitable price. The truth is that they led the people not to be afraid of anything.

Then they organized the election of village and canton chief, and the people were the ones who chose them. . . .

In September 1973, a former government official in Laos, Jerome Doolittle, wrote in the *New York Times*:

The Pentagon's most recent lies about bombing Cambodia bring back a question that often occurred to me when I was press attache at the American Embassy in Vientiane, Laos.

Why did we bother to lie?

When I first arrived in Laos, I was instructed to answer all press questions about our massive and merciless bombing campaign in that tiny country with: "At the request of the Royal Laotian Government, the United States is conducting unarmed reconnaissance flights accompanied by armed escorts who have the right to return if fired upon."

This was a lie. Every reporter to whom I told it knew it was a lie. Hanoi knew it was a lie. The International Control Commission knew it was a lie. Every interested Congressman and newspaper reader knew it was a lie. . . .

After all, the lies did serve to keep something from somebody, and the somebody was us.

By early 1968, the cruelty of the war began touching the conscience of many Americans. For many others, the problem was that the United States was unable to win the war, while 40,000 American soldiers were dead by this time, 250,000 wounded, with no end in sight. (The Vietnam casualties were many times this number.)

Lyndon Johnson had escalated a brutal war and failed to win it. His popularity was at an all-time low; he could not appear publicly without a demonstration against him and the war. The chant "LBJ, LBJ, how many kids did you kill today?" was heard in demonstrations throughout the country. In the spring of 1968 Johnson announced he would not run again for President, and that negotiations for peace would begin with the Vietnamese in Paris.

In the fall of 1968, Richard Nixon, pledging that he would get the United States out of Vietnam, was elected President. He began to withdraw troops; by February 1972, less than 150,000 were left. But the bombing continued. Nixon's policy was "Vietnamization"—the Saigon government, with Vietnamese ground troops, using American money and air power, would carry on the war. Nixon was not ending the war; he was ending the most unpopular aspect of it, the involvement of American soldiers on the soil of a faraway country.

In the spring of 1970, Nixon and Secretary of State Henry Kissinger launched an invasion of Cambodia, after a long bombardment that the government never disclosed to the public. The invasion not only led to an outcry of protest in the United States, it was a military failure, and Congress resolved that Nixon could not use American troops in extending the war without congressional approval. The following year, without American troops, the United States supported a South Vietnamese invasion of Laos. This too failed. In 1971, 800,000 tons of bombs were dropped by the United States on Laos, Cambodia, Vietnam. Meantime, the Saigon military regime, headed by President Nguyen Van Thieu, the last of a long succession of Saigon chiefs of state, was keeping thousands of opponents in jail.

Some of the first signs of opposition in the United States to the Vietnam war came out of the civil rights movement—perhaps because the experience of black people with the government led them to distrust any claim that it was fighting for freedom. On the very day that Lyndon Johnson was telling the nation in early August 1964 about the Gulf of Tonkin incident, and announcing the bombing of North Vietnam, black and white activists were gathering near Philadelphia, Mississippi, at a memorial service for the three civil rights workers killed there that summer. One of the speakers pointed bitterly to Johnson's use of force in Asia, comparing it with the violence used against blacks in Mississippi.

In mid-1965, in McComb, Mississippi, young blacks who had just learned that a classmate of theirs was killed in Vietnam distributed a leaflet:

No Mississippi Negroes should be fighting in Viet Nam for the White man's freedom, until all the Negro People are free in Mississippi.

Negro boys should not honor the draft here in Mississippi. Mothers should encourage their sons not to go. . . .

No one has a right to ask us to risk our lives and kill other Colored People in Santo Domingo and Viet Nam, so that the White American can get richer.

When Secretary of Defense Robert McNamara visited Mississippi and praised Senator John Stennis, a prominent racist, as a "man of very genuine greatness," white and black students marched in protest, with placards saying "In Memory of the Burned Children of Vietnam."

The Student Nonviolent Coordinating Committee declared in early 1966 that "the United States is pursuing an aggressive policy in violation of international law" and called for withdrawal from Vietnam. That summer, six members of SNCC were arrested for an invasion of an induction center in Atlanta. They were convicted and sentenced to several years in prison. Around the same time, Julian Bond, a SNCC activist who had just been elected to the Georgia House of Representatives, spoke out against the war and the draft, and the House voted that he not be seated because his statements violated the Selective Service Act and "tend to bring discredit to the House." The Supreme Court restored Bond to his seat, saying he had the right to free expression under the First Amendment.

One of the great sports figures of the nation, Muhammad Ali, the black boxer and heavyweight champion, refused to serve in what he called a "white man's war"; boxing authorities took away his title as champion. Martin Luther King, Jr., spoke out in 1967 at Riverside Church in New York:

> Somehow this madness must cease. We must stop now. I speak as a child of God and brother to the suffering poor of Vietnam. I speak for those whose land is being laid waste, whose homes are being destroyed, whose culture is being subverted. I speak for the poor of America who are paying the double price of smashed hopes at home and death and corruption in Vietnam. I speak as a citizen of the world, for the world as it stands aghast at the path we have taken. I speak as an American to the leaders of my own nation. The great initiative in this war is ours. The initiative to stop it must be ours.

Young men began to refuse to register for the draft, refused to be inducted if called. As early as May 1964 the slogan "We Won't Go" was widely publicized. Some who had registered began publicly burning their draft cards to protest the war. One, David O'Brien, burned his draft card in South Boston; he was convicted, and the Supreme Court overruled his argument that this was a protected form of free expression. In October of 1967 there were organized draft-card "turn-ins" all over the country; in San Francisco alone, three hundred draft cards were returned to the government. Just before a huge demonstration at the Pentagon that month, a sack of collected draft cards was presented to the Justice Department.

By mid-1965, 380 prosecutions were begun against men refusing to be inducted; by mid-1968 that figure was up to 3,305. At the end of 1969, there were 33,960 delinquents nationwide.

In May 1969 the Oakland induction center, where draftees reported from all of northern California, reported that of 4,400 men ordered to report for induction, 2,400 did not show up. In the first quarter of 1970 the Selective Service system, for the first time, could not meet its quota.

A Boston University graduate student in history, Philip Supina, wrote on May 1, 1968, to his draft board in Tucson, Arizona:

> I am enclosing the order for me to report for my pre-induction physical exam for the armed forces. I have absolutely no intention to report for that exam, or for induction, or to aid in any way the American war effort against the people of Vietnam. . . .

He ended his letter by quoting the Spanish philosopher Miguel Unamuno, who during the Spanish Civil War said: "Sometimes to be Silent is to Lie." Supina was convicted and sentenced to four years in prison.

Early in the war, there had been two separate incidents, barely noticed by most Americans. On November 2, 1965, in front of the Pentagon in Washington, as thousands of employees were streaming out of the building in the late afternoon, Norman Morrison, a thirty-two-year-old pacifist, father of three, stood below the third-floor windows of Secretary of Defense Robert McNamara, doused himself with kerosene, and set himself afire, giving up his life in protest against the war. Also that year, in Detroit, an eighty-two-year-old woman named Alice Herz burned herself to death to make a statement against the horror of Indochina.

A remarkable change in sentiment took place. In early 1965, when the bombing of North Vietnam began, a hundred people gathered on the Boston Common to voice their indignation. On October 15, 1969, the number of people assembled on the Boston Common to protest the war was 100,000. Perhaps 2 million people across the nation gathered that day in towns and villages that had never seen an antiwar meeting.

In the summer of 1965, a few hundred people had gathered in Washington to march in protest against the war: the first in line, historian Staughton Lynd, SNCC organizer Bob Moses, and long-time pacifist David Dellinger, were splattered with red paint by hecklers. But by 1970, the Washington peace rallies were drawing hundreds of thousands of people. In 1971, twenty thousand came to Washington to commit civil disobedience, trying to tie up Washington traffic to express their revulsion against the killing still going on in Vietnam. Fourteen thousand of them were arrested, the largest mass arrest in American history.

Hundreds of volunteers in the Peace Corps spoke out against the war. In Chile, ninety-two volunteers defied the Peace Corps director and issued a circular denouncing the war. Eight hundred former members of the Corps issued a statement of protest against what was happening in Vietnam.

The poet Robert Lowell, invited to a White House function, refused to come. Arthur Miller, also invited, sent a telegram to the White House: "When the guns boom, the arts die." Singer Eartha Kitt was invited to a luncheon on the White House lawn and shocked all those present by speaking out, in the presence of the President's wife, against the war. A teenager, called to the White House to accept a prize, came and criticized the war. In Hollywood, local artists erected a 60-foot Tower of Protest on Sunset Boulevard. At the National Book Award ceremonies in New York, fifty authors and publishers walked out on a speech by Vice-President Humphrey in a display of anger at his role in the war.

In London, two young Americans gate-crashed the American

ambassador's elegant Fourth of July reception and called out a toast: "To all the dead and dying in Vietnam." They were carried out by guards. In the Pacific Ocean, two young American seamen hijacked an American munitions ship to divert its load of bombs from airbases in Thailand. For four days they took command of the ship and its crew, taking amphetamine pills to stay awake until the ship reached Cambodian waters. The Associated Press reported in late 1972, from York, Pennsylvania: "Five antiwar activists were arrested by the state police today for allegedly sabotaging railroad equipment near a factory that makes bomb casings used in the Vietnam war."

Middle-class and professional people unaccustomed to activism began to speak up. In May 1970, the *New York Times* reported from Washington: "1000 'ESTABLISHMENT' LAWYERS JOIN WAR PROTEST." Corporations began to wonder whether the war was going to hurt their long-range business interests; the *Wall Street Journal* began criticizing the continuation of the war.

As the war became more and more unpopular, people in or close to the government began to break out of the circle of assent. The most dramatic instance was the case of Daniel Ellsberg.

Ellsberg was a Harvard-trained economist, a former marine officer, employed by the RAND Corporation, which did special, often secret research for the U.S. government. Ellsberg helped write the Department of Defense history of the war in Vietnam, and then decided to make the top-secret document public, with the aid of his friend, Anthony Russo, a former RAND Corporation man. The two had met in Saigon, where both had been affected, in different experiences, by direct sight of the war, and had become powerfully indignant at what the United States was doing to the people of Vietnam.

Ellsberg and Russo spent night after night, after hours, at a friend's advertising agency, duplicating the 7,000-page document. Then Ellsberg gave copies to various Congressmen and to the *New York Times*. In June 1971 the *Times* began printing selections from what came to be known as the *Pentagon Papers*. It created a national sensation.

The Nixon administration tried to get the Supreme Court to stop further publication, but the Court said this was "prior restraint" of the freedom of the press and thus unconstitutional. The government then indicted Ellsberg and Russo for violating the Espionage Act by releasing classified documents to unauthorized people; they faced long terms in prison if convicted. The judge, however, called off the trial during the jury deliberations, because the Watergate events unfolding at the time revealed unfair practices by the prosecution.

Ellsberg, by his bold act, had broken with the usual tactic of dissidents inside the government who bided their time and kept their opinions to themselves, hoping for small changes in policy. A colleague urged him not to leave the government because there he had "access," saying, "Don't cut yourself off. Don't cut your throat." Ellsberg replied: "Life exists outside the Executive Branch."

The antiwar movement, early in its growth, found a strange, new constituency: priests and nuns of the Catholic Church. Some of them had been aroused by the civil rights movement, others by their experiences in Latin America, where they saw poverty and injustice under governments supported by the United States. In the fall of 1967, Father Philip Berrigan (a Josephite priest who was a veteran of World War II), joined by artist Tom Lewis and friends David Eberhardt and James Mengel, went to the office of a draft board in Baltimore, Maryland, drenched the draft records with blood, and waited to be arrested. They were put on trial and sentenced to prison terms of two to six years.

The following May, Philip Berrigan—out on bail in the Baltimore case—was joined in a second action by his brother Daniel, a Jesuit priest who had visited North Vietnam and seen the effects of U.S. bombing. They and seven other people went into a draft board office in Catonsville, Maryland, removed records, and set them afire outside in the presence of reporters and onlookers. They were convicted and sentenced to prison, and became famous as the "Catonsville Nine." Dan Berrigan wrote a "Meditation" at the time of the Catonsville incident:

Our apologies, good friends, for the fracture of good order, the burning of paper instead of children, the angering of the orderlies in the front parlor of the charnel house. We could not, so help us God, do otherwise. . . . We say: killing is disorder, life and gentleness and community and unselfishness is the only order we recognize. For the sake of that order, we risk our liberty, our good name. The time is past when good men can remain silent, when obedience can segregate men from public risk, when the poor can die without defense.

When his appeals had been exhausted, and he was supposed to go to prison, Daniel Berrigan disappeared. While the FBI searched for him, he showed up at an Easter festival at Cornell University, where he had been teaching. With dozens of FBI men looking for him in the crowd, he suddenly appeared on stage. Then the lights went out, he hid inside a giant figure of the Bread and Puppet Theatre which was on stage, was carried out to a truck, and escaped to a nearby farmhouse. He stayed underground for four months, writing poems, issuing statements, giving secret interviews, appearing suddenly in a Philadelphia church to give a sermon and then disappearing again, baffling the FBI, until an informer's interception of a letter disclosed his whereabouts and he was captured and imprisoned.

The one woman among the Catonsville Nine, Mary Moylan, a former nun, also refused to surrender to the FBI. She was never found. Writing from underground, she reflected on her experience and how she came to it:

. . . We had all known we were going to jail, so we all had our toothbrushes. I was just exhausted. I took my little box of clothes and stuck it under the cot and climbed into bed. Now all the women in the Baltimore County jail were black—I think there was only one white. The women were waking me up and saying, "Aren't you going to cry?" I said, "What about?" They said, "You're in jail." And I said, "Yeah, I knew I'd be here." . . .

I was sleeping between two of these women, and every morning I'd wake up and they'd be leaning on their elbows watching me.

They'd say, "You slept all night." And they couldn't believe it. They were good. We had good times. . . .

I suppose the political turning point in my life came while I was in Uganda. I was there when American planes were bombing the Congo, and we were very close to the Congo border. The planes came over and bombed two villages in Uganda. . . . Where the hell did the American planes come in?

Later I was in Dar Es Salaam and Chou En-lai came to town. The American Embassy sent out letters saying that no Americans were to be on the street, because this was a dirty Communist leader; but I decided this was a man who was making history and I wanted to see him. . . .

When I came home from Africa I moved to Washington, and had to deal with the scene there and the insanity and brutality of the cops and the type of life that was led by most of the citizens of that city—70 percent black. . . .

And then Vietnam, and the napalm and the defoliants, and the bombings. . . .

I got involved with the women's movement about a year ago. . . .

At the time of Catonsville, going to jail made sense to me, partially because of the black scene—so many blacks forever filling the jails. . . . I don't think it's a valid tactic anymore. . . . I don't want to see people marching off to jail with smiles on their faces. I just don't want them going. The Seventies are going to be very difficult, and I don't want to waste the sisters and brothers we have by marching them off to jail and having mystical experiences or whatever they're going to have. . . .

The effect of the war and of the bold action of some priests and nuns was to crack the traditional conservatism of the Catholic community. On Moratorium Day 1969, at the Newton College of the Sacred Heart near Boston, a sanctuary of bucolic quiet and political silence, the great front door of the college displayed a huge painted red fist. At Boston College, a Catholic institution, six thousand people gathered that evening in the gymnasium to denounce the war.

Students were heavily involved in the early protests against the war. A survey by the Urban Research Corporation, for the first six months of 1969 only, and for only 232 of the nation's two thousand institutions of higher education, showed that at least 215,000 students had participated in campus protests, that 3,652 had been arrested, that 956 had been suspended or expelled. Even in the high schools, in the late sixties, there were five hundred underground newspapers. At the Brown University commencement in 1969, two-thirds of the graduating class turned their backs when Henry Kissinger stood up to address them.

The climax of protest came in the spring of 1970 when President Nixon ordered the invasion of Cambodia. At Kent State University in Ohio, on May 4, when students gathered to demonstrate against the war, National Guardsmen fired into the crowd. Four students were killed. One was paralyzed for life. Students at four hundred colleges and universities went on strike in protest. It was the first general student strike in the history of the United States. During that school year of 1969–1970, the FBI listed 1,785 student demonstrations, including the occupation of 313 buildings.

The commencement day ceremonies after the Kent State killings were unlike any the nation had ever seen. From Amherst, Massachusetts, came this newspaper report:

The 100th Commencement of the University of Massachusetts yesterday was a protest, a call for peace.

The roll of the funeral drum set the beat for 2600 young men and women marching "in fear, in despair and in frustration."

Red fists of protest, white peace symbols, and blue doves were stenciled on black academic gowns, and nearly every other senior wore an armband representing a plea for peace.

Student protests against the ROTC (Reserve Officers Training Program) resulted in the canceling of those programs in over forty colleges and universities. In 1966, 191,749 college students enrolled in ROTC. By 1973, the number was 72,459. The

ROTC was depended on to supply half the officers in Vietnam. In September 1973, for the sixth straight month, the ROTC could not fulfill its quota. One army official said: "I just hope we don't get into another war, because if we do, I doubt we could fight it."

The publicity given to the student protests created the impression that the opposition to the war came mostly from middle-class intellectuals. When some construction workers in New York attacked student demonstrators, the news was played up in the national media. However, a number of elections in American cities, including those where mostly blue-collar workers lived, showed that antiwar sentiment was strong in the working classes. For instance, in Dearborn, Michigan, an automobile manufacturing town, a poll as early as 1967 showed 41 percent of the population favored withdrawal from the Vietnam war. In 1970, in two counties in California where petitioners placed the issue on the ballot—San Francisco County and Marin County—referenda asking withdrawal of the U.S. forces from Vietnam received a majority vote.

In late 1970, when a Gallup poll presented the statement: "The United States should withdraw all troops from Vietnam by the end of next year," 65 percent of those questioned said, "Yes." In Madison, Wisconsin, in the spring of 1971, a resolution calling for an immediate withdrawal of U.S. forces from Southeast Asia won by 31,000 to 16,000 (in 1968 such a resolution had lost).

But the most surprising data were in a survey made by the University of Michigan. This showed that, throughout the Vietnam war, Americans with only a grade school education were much stronger for withdrawal from the war than Americans with a college education. In June 1966, of people with a college education, 27 percent were for immediate withdrawal from Vietnam; of people with only a grade school education, 41 percent were for immediate withdrawal. By September 1970, both groups were more antiwar: 47 percent of the college-educated were for withdrawal, and 61 percent of grade school graduates.

There is more evidence of the same kind. In an article in the

American Sociological Review (June 1968), Richard F. Hamilton found in his survey of public opinion: "Preferences for 'tough' policy alternatives are most frequent among the following groups, the highly educated, high status occupations, those with high incomes, younger persons, and those paying much attention to newspapers and magazines." And a political scientist, Harlan Hahn, doing a study of various city referenda on Vietnam, found support for withdrawal from Vietnam highest in groups of lower socioeconomic status. He also found that the regular polls, based on samplings, underestimated the opposition to the war among lower-class people.

All this was part of a general change in the entire population of the country. In August of 1965, 61 percent of the population thought the American involvement in Vietnam was not wrong. By May 1971 it was exactly reversed; 61 percent thought our involvement *was* wrong. Bruce Andrews, a Harvard student of public opinion, found that the people most opposed to the war were people over fifty, blacks, and women. He also noted that a study in the spring of 1964, when Vietnam was a minor issue in the newspapers, showed that 53 percent of college-educated people were willing to send troops to Vietnam, but only 33 percent of grade school-educated people were so willing.

It seems that the media, themselves controlled by higher-education, higher-income people who were more aggressive in foreign policy, tended to give the erroneous impression that working-class people were superpatriots for the war. Lewis Lipsitz, in a mid-1968 survey of poor blacks and whites in the South, paraphrased an attitude he found typical: "The only way to help the poor man is to get out of that war in Vietnam. . . . These taxes—high taxes—it's going over yonder to kill people with and I don't see no cause in it."

The capacity for independent judgement among ordinary Americans is probably best shown by the swift development of antiwar feeling among American GIs—volunteers and draftees who came mostly from lower-income groups. There had been, earlier in American history, instances of soldiers' disaffection from the war: isolated mutinies in the Revolutionary War, refusal of reenlistment in the midst of hostilities in the Mexican war, desertion and conscientious objection in World War I and World War II. But Vietnam produced opposition by soldiers and veterans on a scale, and with a fervor, never seen before.

It began with isolated protests. As early as June 1965, Richard Steinke, a West Point graduate in Vietnam, refused to board an aircraft taking him to a remote Vietnamese village. "The Vietnamese war," he said, "is not worth a single American life." Steinke was court-martialed and dismissed from the service. The following year, three army privates, one black, one Puerto Rican, one Lithuanian-Italian—all poor—refused to embark for Vietnam, denouncing the war as "immoral, illegal, and unjust." They were court-martialed and imprisoned.

In early 1967, Captain Howard Levy, an army doctor at Fort Jackson, South Carolina, refused to teach Green Berets, a Special Forces elite in the military. He said they were "murderers of women and children" and "killers of peasants." He was court-martialed on the grounds that he was trying to promote disaffection among enlisted men by his statements. The colonel who presided at the trial said: "The truth of the statements is not an issue in this case." Levy was convicted and sentenced to prison.

The individual acts multiplied: A black private in Oakland refused to board a troop plane to Vietnam, although he faced eleven years at hard labor. A navy nurse, Lieutenant Susan Schnall, was court-martialed for marching in a peace demonstration while in uniform, and for dropping antiwar leaflets from a plane on navy installations. In Norfolk, Virginia, a sailor refused to train fighter pilots because he said the war was immoral. An army lieutenant was arrested in Washington, D.C., in early 1968 for picketing the White House with a sign that said: "120,000 American Casualties—Why?" Two black marines, George Daniels and William Harvey, were given long prison sentences (Daniels, six years, Harvey, ten years, both later reduced) for talking to other black marines against the war.

As the war went on, desertions from the armed forces

mounted. Thousands went to Western Europe—France, Sweden, Holland. Most deserters crossed into Canada; some estimates were 50,000, others 100,000. Some stayed in the United States. A few openly defied the military authorities by taking "sanctuary" in churches, where, surrounded by antiwar friends and sympathizers, they waited for capture and court-martial. At Boston University, a thousand students kept vigil for five days and nights in the chapel, supporting an eighteen-year-old deserter, Ray Kroll.

Kroll's story was a common one. He had been inveigled into joining the army; he came from a poor family, was brought into court, charged with drunkenness, and given the choice of prison or enlistment. He enlisted. And then he began to think about the nature of the war.

On a Sunday morning, federal agents showed up at the Boston University chapel, stomped their way through aisles clogged with students, smashed down doors, and took Kroll away. From the stockade, he wrote back to friends: "I ain't gonna kill; it's against my will. . . ." A friend he had made at the chapel brought him books, and he noted a saying he had found in one of them: "What we have done will not be lost to all Eternity. Everything ripens at its time and becomes fruit at its hour."

The GI antiwar movement became more organized. Near Fort Jackson, South Carolina, the first "GI coffeehouse" was set up, a place where soldiers could get coffee and doughnuts, find antiwar literature, and talk freely with others. It was called the UFO, and lasted for several years before it was declared a "public nuisance" and closed by court action. But other GI coffeehouses sprang up in half a dozen other places across the country. An antiwar "bookstore" was opened near Fort Devens, Massachusetts, and another one at the Newport, Rhode Island, naval base.

Underground newspapers sprang up at military bases across the country; by 1970 more than fifty were circulating. Among them: *About Face* in Los Angeles; *Fed Up!* in Tacoma, Washington; *Short Times* at Fort Jackson; *Vietnam GI* in Chicago; *Graffiti* in Heidelberg, Germany; *Bragg Briefs* in North Carolina; *Last Harass* at Fort Gordon, Georgia; *Helping Hand* at Mountain

Home Air Base, Idaho. These newspapers printed antiwar articles, gave news about the harassment of GIs and practical advice on the legal rights of servicemen, told how to resist military domination.

Mixed with feeling against the war was resentment at the cruelty, the dehumanization, of military life. In the army prisons, the stockades, this was especially true. In 1968, at the Presidio stockade in California, a guard shot to death an emotionally disturbed prisoner for walking away from a work detail. Twenty-seven prisoners then sat down and refused to work, singing "We Shall Overcome." They were court-martialed, found guilty of mutiny, and sentenced to terms of up to fourteen years, later reduced after much public attention and protest.

The dissidence spread to the war front itself. When the great Moratorium Day demonstrations were taking place in October 1969 in the United States, some GIs in Vietnam wore black armbands to show their support. A news photographer reported that in a platoon on patrol near Da Nang, about half of the men were wearing black armbands. One soldier stationed at Cu Chi wrote to a friend on October 26, 1970, that separate companies had been set up for men refusing to go into the field to fight. "It's no big thing here anymore to refuse to go." The French newspaper *Le Monde* reported that in four months, 109 soldiers of the first air cavalry division were charged with refusal to fight. "A common sight," the correspondent for *Le Monde* wrote, "is the black soldier, with his left fist clenched in defiance of a war he has never considered his own."

Wallace Terry, a black American reporter for *Time* magazine, taped conversations with hundreds of black soldiers; he found bitterness against army racism, disgust with the war, generally low morale. More and more cases of "fragging" were reported in Vietnam—incidents where servicemen rolled fragmentation bombs under the tents of officers who were ordering them into combat, or against whom they had other grievances. The Pentagon reported 209 fraggings in Vietnam in 1970 alone.

Veterans back from Vietnam formed a group called Vietnam

Veterans Against the War. In December 1970, hundreds of them went to Detroit to what was called the "Winter Soldier" investigations, to testify publicly about atrocities they had participated in or seen in Vietnam, committed by Americans against Vietnamese. In April 1971 more than a thousand of them went to Washington, D.C., to demonstrate against the war. One by one, they went up to a wire fence around the Capitol, threw over the fence the medals they had won in Vietnam, and made brief statements about the war, sometimes emotionally, sometimes in icy, bitter calm.

In the summer of 1970, twenty-eight commissioned officers of the military, including some veterans of Vietnam, saying they represented about 250 other officers, announced formation of the Concerned Officers Movement against the war. During the fierce bombings of Hanoi and Haiphong, around Christmas 1972, came the first defiance of B-52 pilots who refused to fly those missions.

On June 3, 1973, the *New York Times* reported dropouts among West Point cadets. Officials there, the reporter wrote, "linked the rate to an affluent, less disciplined, skeptical, and questioning generation and to the anti-military mood that a small radical minority and the Vietnam war had created."

But most of the antiwar action came from ordinary GIs, and most of these came from lower-income groups—white, black, Native American, Chinese.

A twenty-year-old New York City Chinese-American named Sam Choy enlisted at seventeen in the army, was sent to Vietnam, was made a cook, and found himself the target of abuse by fellow GIs, who called him "Chink" and "gook" (the term for the Vietnamese) and said he looked like the enemy. One day he took a rifle and fired warning shots at his tormenters. "By this time I was near the perimeter of the base and was thinking of joining the Viet Cong; at least they would trust me."

Choy was taken by military police, beaten, court-martialed, sentenced to eighteen months of hard labor at Fort Leavenworth. "They beat me up every day, like a time clock." He ended his interview with a New York Chinatown newspaper saying: "One thing: I want to tell all the Chinese kids that the army made me sick. They made me so sick that I can't stand it."

A dispatch from Phu Bai in April 1972 said that fifty GIs out of 142 men in the company refused to go on patrol, crying: "This isn't our war!" The *New York Times* on July 14, 1973, reported that American prisoners of war in Vietnam, ordered by officers in the POW camp to stop cooperating with the enemy, shouted back: "Who's the enemy?" They formed a peace committee in the camp, and a sergeant on the committee later recalled his march from capture to the POW camp:

> Until we got to the first camp, we didn't see a village intact; they were all destroyed. I sat down and put myself in the middle and asked myself: Is this right or wrong? Is it right to destroy villages? Is it right to kill people en masse? After a while it just got to me.

Pentagon officials in Washington and navy spokesmen in San Diego announced, after the United States withdrew its troops from Vietnam in 1973, that the navy was going to purge itself of "undesirables"—and that these included as many as six thousand men in the Pacific fleet, "a substantial proportion of them black." All together, about 700,000 GIs had received less than honorable discharges. In the year 1973, one of every five discharges was "less than honorable," indicating something less than dutiful obedience to the military. By 1971, 177 of every 1,000 American soldiers were listed as "absent without leave," some of them three or four times. Deserters doubled from 47,000 in 1967 to 89,000 in 1971.

One of those who stayed, fought, but then turned against the war was Ron Kovic. His father worked in a supermarket on Long Island. In 1963, at the age of seventeen, he enlisted in the marines. Two years later, in Vietnam, at the age of nineteen, his spine was shattered by shellfire. Paralyzed from the waist down, he was put in a wheelchair. Back in the States, he observed the brutal treatment of wounded veterans in the veterans' hospitals, thought more and more about the war, and joined the Vietnam

Veterans Against the War. He went to demonstrations to speak against the war. One evening he heard actor Donald Sutherland read from the post–World War I novel by Dalton Trumbo, *Johnny Got His Gun*, about a soldier whose limbs and face were shot away by gunfire, a thinking torso who invented a way of communicating with the outside world and then beat out a message so powerful it could not be heard without trembling.

> Sutherland began to read the passage and something I will never forget swept over me. It was as if someone was speaking for everything I ever went through in the hospital. . . . I began to shake and I remember there were tears in my eyes.

Kovic demonstrated against the war, and was arrested. He tells his story in *Born on the Fourth of July*:

> They help me back into the chair and take me to another part of the prison building to be booked.
>
> "What's your name?" the officer behind the desk says.
>
> "Ron Kovic," I say. "Occupation, Vietnam veteran against the war."
>
> "What?" he says sarcastically, looking down at me.
>
> "I'm a Vietnam veteran against the war," I almost shout back.
>
> "You should have died over there," he says. He turns to his assistant. "I'd like to take this guy and throw him off the roof."
>
> They fingerprint me and take my picture and put me in a cell. I have begun to wet my pants like a little baby. The tube has slipped out during my examination by the doctor. I try to fall asleep but even though I am exhausted, the anger is alive in me like a huge hot stone in my chest. I lean my head up against the wall and listen to the toilets flush again and again.

Kovic and the other veterans drove to Miami to the Republican National Convention in 1972, went into the Convention Hall, wheeled themselves down the aisles, and as Nixon began his acceptance speech shouted, "Stop the bombing! Stop the war!"

Delegates cursed them: "Traitor!" and Secret Service men hustled them out of the hall.

In the fall of 1973, with no victory in sight and North Vietnamese troops entrenched in various parts of the South, the United States agreed to accept a settlement that would withdraw American troops and leave the revolutionary troops where they were, until a new elected government would be set up including Communist and non-Communist elements. But the Saigon government refused to agree, and the United States decided to make one final attempt to bludgeon the North Vietnamese into submission. It sent waves of B-52s over Hanoi and Haiphong, destroying homes and hospitals, killing unknown numbers of civilians. The attack did not work. Many of the B-52s were shot down, there was angry protest all over the world—and Kissinger went back to Paris and signed very much the same peace agreement that had been agreed on before.

The United States withdrew its forces, continuing to give aid to the Saigon government, but when the North Vietnamese launched attacks in early 1975 against the major cities in South Vietnam, the government collapsed. In late April 1975, North Vietnamese troops entered Saigon. The American embassy staff fled, along with many Vietnamese who feared Communist rule, and the long war in Vietnam was over. Saigon was renamed Ho Chi Minh City, and both parts of Vietnam were unified as the Democratic Republic of Vietnam.

Traditional history portrays the end of wars as coming from the initiatives of leaders—negotiations in Paris or Brussels or Geneva or Versailles—just as it often finds the coming of war a response to the demand of "the people." The Vietnam war gave clear evidence that at least for that war (making one wonder about the others) the political leaders were the last to take steps to end the war—"the people" were far ahead. The President was always far behind. The Supreme Court silently turned away from cases challenging the Constitutionality of the war. Congress was years behind public opinion.

In the spring of 1971, syndicated columnists Rowland Evans

and Robert Novak, two firm supporters of the war, wrote regretfully of a "sudden outbreak of anti-war emotionalism" in the House of Representatives, and said: "The anti-war animosities now suddenly so pervasive among House Democrats are viewed by Administration backers as less anti-Nixon than as a response to constituent pressures."

It was only after the intervention in Cambodia ended, and only after the nationwide campus uproar over that invasion, that Congress passed a resolution declaring that American troops should not be sent into Cambodia without its approval. And it was not until late 1973, when American troops had finally been removed from Vietnam, that Congress passed a bill limiting the power of the President to make war without congressional consent; even there, in that "War Powers Resolution," the President could make war for sixty days on his own without a congressional declaration.

The administration tried to persuade the American people that the war was ending because of its decision to negotiate a peace—not because it was losing the war, not because of the powerful antiwar movement in the United States. But the government's own secret memoranda all through the war testify to its sensitivity at each stage about "public opinion" in the United States and abroad. The data is in the *Pentagon Papers*.

In June of 1964, top American military and State Department officials, including Ambassador Henry Cabot Lodge, met in Honolulu. "Rusk stated that public opinion on our SEA policy was badly divided and that, therefore, the President needed an affirmation of support." Diem had been replaced by a general named Khanh. The Pentagon historians write: "Upon his return to Saigon on June 5 Ambassador Lodge went straight from the airport to call on General Khanh . . . the main thrust of his talk with Khanh was to hint that the United States Government would in the immediate future be preparing U.S. public opinion for actions against North Vietnam." Two months later came the Gulf of Tonkin affair.

On April 2, 1965, a memo from CIA director John McCone

suggested that the bombing of North Vietnam be increased because it was "not sufficiently severe" to change North Vietnam's policy. "On the other hand . . . we can expect increasing pressure to stop the bombing . . . from various elements of the American public, from the press, the United Nations and world opinion." The U.S. should try for a fast knockout before this opinion could build up, McCone said.

Assistant Secretary of Defense John McNaughton's memo of early 1966 suggested destruction of locks and dams to create mass starvation, because "strikes at population targets" would "create a counterproductive wave of revulsion abroad and at home." In May 1967, the Pentagon historians write: "McNaughton was also very deeply concerned about the breadth and intensity of public unrest and dissatisfaction with the war . . . especially with young people, the underprivileged, the intelligentsia and the women." McNaughton worried: "Will the move to call up 20,000 Reserves . . . polarize opinion to the extent that the 'doves' in the United States will get out of hand—massive refusals to serve, or to fight, or to cooperate, or worse?" He warned:

There may be a limit beyond which many Americans and much of the world will not permit the United States to go. The picture of the world's greatest superpower killing or seriously injuring 1000 noncombatants a week, while trying to pound a tiny backward nation into submission, on an issue whose merits are hotly disputed, is not a pretty one. It could conceivably produce a costly distortion in the American national consciousness.

That "costly distortion" seems to have taken place by the spring of 1968, when, with the sudden and scary Tet offensive of the National Liberation Front, Westmoreland asked President Johnson to send him 200,000 more troops on top of the 525,000 already there. Johnson asked a small group of "action officers" in the Pentagon to advise him on this. They studied the situation and concluded that 200,000 troops would totally Americanize the war and would not strengthen the Saigon government because:

"The Saigon leadership shows no signs of a willingness—let alone an ability—to attract the necessary loyalty or support of the people." Furthermore, the report said, sending troops would mean mobilizing reserves, increasing the military budget. There would be more U.S. casualties, more taxes. And:

> This growing disaffection accompanied as it certainly will be, by increased defiance of the draft and growing unrest in the cities because of the belief that we are neglecting domestic problems, runs great risks of provoking a domestic crisis of unprecedented proportions.

The "growing unrest in the cities" must have been a reference to the black uprisings that had taken place in 1967—and showed the link, whether blacks deliberately made it or not—between the war abroad and poverty at home.

The evidence from the *Pentagon Papers* is clear—that Johnson's decision in the spring of 1968 to turn down Westmoreland's request, to slow down for the first time the escalation of the war, to diminish the bombing, to go to the conference table, was influenced to a great extent by the actions Americans had taken in demonstrating their opposition to the war.

When Nixon took office, he too tried to persuade the public that protest would not affect him. But he almost went berserk when one lone pacifist picketed the White House. The frenzy of Nixon's actions against dissidents—plans for burglaries, wiretapping, mail openings—suggests the importance of the antiwar movement in the minds of national leaders.

One sign that the ideas of the antiwar movement had taken hold in the American public was that juries became more reluctant to convict antiwar protesters, and local judges too were treating them differently. In Washington, by 1971, judges were dismissing charges against demonstrators in cases where two years before they almost certainly would have been sent to jail. The antiwar groups who had raided draft boards—the Baltimore Four, the Catonsville Nine, the Milwaukee Fourteen, the Boston Five, and more—were receiving lighter sentences for the same crimes.

The last group of draft board raiders, the "Camden 28," were priests, nuns, and laypeople who raided a draft board in Camden, New Jersey, in August 1971. It was essentially what the Baltimore Four had done four years earlier, when all were convicted and Phil Berrigan got six years in prison. But in this instance, the Camden defendants were acquitted by the jury on all counts. When the verdict was in, one of the jurors, a fifty-three-year-old black taxi driver from Atlantic City named Samuel Braithwaite, who had spent eleven years in the army, left a letter for the defendants:

> To you, the clerical physicians with your God-given talents, I say, well done. Well done for trying to heal the sick irresponsible men, men who were chosen by the people to govern and lead them. These men, who failed the people, by raining death and destruction on a hapless country. . . . You went out to do your part while your brothers remained in their ivory towers watching . . . and hopefully some day in the near future, peace and harmony may reign to people of all nations.

That was in May of 1973. The American troops were leaving Vietnam. C. L. Sulzberger, the *New York Times* correspondent (a man close to the government), wrote: "The U.S. emerges as the big loser and history books must admit this. . . . We lost the war in the Mississippi valley, not the Mekong valley. Successive American governments were never able to muster the necessary mass support at home."

In fact, the United States had lost the war in both the Mekong Valley and the Mississippi Valley. It was the first clear defeat to the global American empire formed after World War II. It was administered by revolutionary peasants abroad, and by an astonishing movement of protest at home.

Back on September 26, 1969, President Richard Nixon, noting the growing antiwar activity all over the country, announced that "under no circumstance will I be affected whatever by it."

But nine years later, in his *Memoirs*, he admitted that the antiwar movement caused him to drop plans for an intensification of the war: "Although publicly I continued to ignore the raging antiwar controversy. . . . I knew, however, that after all the protests and the Moratorium, American public opinion would be seriously divided by any military escalation of the war." It was a rare presidential admission of the power of public protest.

From a long-range viewpoint, something perhaps even more important had happened. The rebellion at home was spreading beyond the issue of war in Vietnam.

8

SURPRISES

Helen Keller had said in 1911: "We vote? What does that mean?" And Emma Goldman around the same time: "Our modern fetish is universal suffrage." After 1920, women were voting, as men did, and their subordinate condition had hardly changed.

Right after women got the vote, the measure of their social progress can be seen in an advice column written by Dorothy Dix that appeared in newspapers all over the country. The woman should not merely be a domestic drudge, she said:

> . . . a man's wife is the show window where he exhibits the measure of his achievement. . . . The biggest deals are put across over luncheon tables; . . . we meet at dinner the people who can push our fortunes. . . . The woman who cultivates a circle of worthwhile people, who belongs to clubs, who makes herself interesting and agreeable . . . is a help to her husband.

Robert and Helen Lynd, studying Muncie, Indiana (*Middletown*), in the late twenties, noted the importance of good looks and dress in the assessment of women. Also, they found that when men spoke frankly among themselves they were "likely to speak of women as creatures purer and morally better than men but as relatively impractical, emotional, unstable, given to prejudice, easily hurt, and largely incapable of facing facts or doing hard thinking."

A writer in early 1930, boosting the beauty business, started off a magazine article with the sentence: "The average American woman has sixteen square feet of skin." He went on to say that there were forty thousand beauty shops in the country, and that $2 billion was spent each year on cosmetics for women—but this was insufficient: "American women are not yet spending even one-fifth of the amount necessary to improve their appearance." He then gave an itemized list of the "annual beauty needs of every woman": twelve hot-oil treatments, fifty-two facials, twenty-six eyebrow plucks, etc.

It seems that women have best been able to make their first escape from the prison of wifeliness, motherhood, femininity, housework, beautification, isolation, when their services have been desperately needed—whether in industry, or in war, or in social movements. Each time practicality pulled the woman out of her prison—in a kind of work-parole program—the attempt was made to push her back once the need was over, and this led to women's struggle for change.

World War II had brought more women than ever before out of the home into work. By 1960, 36 percent of all women sixteen and older—23 million women—worked for paid wages. But although 43 percent of women with school-age children worked, there were nursery schools for only 2 percent—the rest had to work things out themselves. Women were 50 percent of the voters—but (even by 1967) they held 4 percent of the state legislative seats, and 2 percent of the judgeships. The median income of the working woman was about one-third that of the man. And attitudes toward women did not seem to have changed much since the twenties.

"There is no overt anti-feminism in our society in 1964," wrote feminist and sociologist Alice Rossi, "not because sex equality has been achieved, but because there is practically no feminist spark left among American women."

In the civil rights movement of the sixties, the signs of a collective stirring began to appear. Women took the place they customarily took in social movements, in the front lines—as privates, not generals. In the office of the Student Nonviolent Coordinating Committee in Atlanta, a Spelman College student named Ruby Doris Smith, who had been jailed during the sit-ins, expressed her anger at the way women were relegated to the routine office work, and she was joined in her protest by two white women in SNCC, Sandra Hayden and Mary King. The men in SNCC listened to them respectfully, read the position paper they had put together asserting their rights, but did not do very much. Ella Baker, a veteran fighter from Harlem, now organizing in the South, knew the pattern: "I knew from the beginning that as a woman, an older woman in a group of ministers who are accustomed to having women largely as supporters, there was no place for me to have come into a leadership role."

Nevertheless, women played a crucial role in those early dangerous years of organizing in the South, and were looked on with admiration. Many of these were older women like Ella Baker, and Amelia Boynton in Selma, Alabama, and "Mama Dolly" in Albany, Georgia. Younger women—Gloria Richardson in Maryland, Annelle Ponder in Mississippi—were not only active, but leaders. Women of all ages demonstrated, went to jail. Mrs. Fannie Lou Hamer, a sharecropper in Ruleville, Mississippi, became legendary as organizer and speaker. She sang hymns; she walked picket lines with her familiar limp (as a child she contracted polio). She roused people to excitement at mass meetings: "I'm sick an' tired o' bein' sick an' tired!"

Around the same time, white, middle-class, professional women were beginning to speak up. A pioneering, early book, strong and influential, was Betty Friedan's *The Feminine Mystique*.

Just what was the problem that has no name? What were the words women used when they tried to express it? Sometimes a woman would say "I feel empty somehow . . . incomplete." Or she would say, "I feel as if I don't exist." Sometimes. . . . "A tired feeling . . . I get so angry with the children it scares me. . . . I feel like crying without any reason."

Friedan wrote out of her experience as a middle-class housewife, but what she spoke about touched something inside all women:

> The problem lay buried, unspoken for many years in the minds of American women. It was a strange stirring, a sense of dissatisfaction, a yearning that women suffered in the middle of the twentieth century in the United States. Each suburban wife struggled with it alone. As she made the beds, shopped for groceries, matched slip-cover material, ate peanut butter sandwiches with her children, chauffeured Cub Scouts and Brownies, lay beside her husband at night—she was afraid to ask even of herself the silent question—"Is this all?"...
>
> But on an April morning in 1959, I heard a mother of four, having coffee with four other mothers in a suburban development fifteen miles from New York, say in a tone of quiet desperation, "the problem." And the others knew, without words, that she was not talking about a problem with her husband, or her children, or her home. Suddenly they realized they all shared the same problem, the problem that has no name. They began, hesitantly, to talk about it. Later, after they had picked up their children at nursery school and taken them home to nap, two of the women cried, in sheer relief, just to know they were not alone.

The "mystique" that Friedan spoke of was the image of the woman as mother, as wife, living through her husband, through her children, giving up her own dreams for that. She concluded: "The only way for a woman, as for a man, to find herself, to know herself as a person, is by creative work of her own."

In the summer of 1964, in McComb, Mississippi, at a Freedom House (a civil rights headquarters where people worked and lived together) the women went on strike against the men who wanted them to cook and make beds while the men went around in cars organizing. The stirring that Friedan spoke of was true of women everywhere, it seemed.

By 1969, women were 40 percent of the entire labor force of the United States, but a substantial number of these were secretaries, cleaning women, elementary school teachers, saleswomen, waitresses, and nurses. One out of every three working women had a husband earning less than $5,000 a year.

What of the women who didn't have jobs? They worked very hard, at home, but this wasn't looked on as work, because in a capitalist society (or perhaps in any modern society where things and people are bought and sold for money), if work is not paid for, not given a money value, it is considered valueless. Women began to think more about this fact in the 1960s, and Margaret Benston wrote about it ("The Political Economy of Women's Liberation"). Women doing housework were people outside the modern economic system, therefore they were like serfs or peasants, she said.

The women who worked in the typical "woman's job"—secretary, receptionist, typist, salesperson, cleaning woman, nurse— were treated to the full range of humiliations that men in subordinate positions faced at work, plus another set of humiliations stemming from being a woman: gibes at their mental processes, sexual jokes and aggression, invisibility except as sexual objects, cold demands for more efficiency. A commercial "Guide to Clerical Times Standards" printed a question-and-answer column:

> **Q.** I'm a businessman, and my secretary seems to move entirely too slowly. How many times a minute should she be able to open and close a file drawer?
>
> **A.** Exactly 25 times. Times for other "open and close operations" . . . are .04 minutes for opening or closing a folder, and .026 minutes for opening a standard center desk drawer. If you're worried about her "chair activity," clock her against these standards: "Got up from chair," .033 minutes; "turn in swivel chair," .009 minutes.

A woman factory worker in New Bedford, Massachusetts, in the early seventies, in a medium-sized corporation whose president's dividends from the corporation in 1970 amounted to $325,000, wrote in an organizing newspaper that 9 percent of the workers in her department were women, but all the supervisors were men.

A few years ago I was suspended for three days from work because my children were still young and I had to take time off when they were sick. . . . They want people who keep quiet, squeal on one another, and are very good little robots. The fact that many have to take nerve pills before starting their day, and a week doesn't go by that there aren't two or three people who break down and cry, doesn't mean a thing to them.

She added: "But times are changing, and from now on, more people will speak out and demand from their so-called bosses that they be treated the way the bosses themselves would like to be treated."

Times indeed were changing. Around 1967, women in the various movements—civil rights, Students for a Democratic Society, antiwar groups—began meeting as women, and in early 1968, at a women's antiwar meeting in Washington, hundreds of women carrying torches paraded to the Arlington National Cemetery and staged "The Burial of Traditional Womanhood." At this point, and later too, there was some disagreement among women, and even more among men, on whether women should battle on specifically women's issues, or just take part in general movements against racism, war, capitalism. But the idea of a feminist focus grew.

In the fall of 1968, a group called Radical Women attracted national attention when they protested the selection of Miss America, which they called "an image that oppresses women." They all threw bras, girdles, curlers, false eyelashes, wigs, and other things they called "women's garbage" into a Freedom Trash Can. A sheep was crowned Miss America. More important, people were beginning to speak of "Women's Liberation."

Some of the New York Radical Women shortly afterward formed WITCH (Women's International Terrorist Conspiracy from Hell), and its members, dressed as witches, appeared suddenly on the floor of the New York Stock Exchange. A leaflet put out by WITCH in New York said:

WITCH lives and laughs in every woman. She is the free part of each of us, beneath the shy smiles, the acquiescence to absurd male domination, the make-up or flesh-suffocating clothes our sick society demands. There is no "joining" WITCH. If you are a woman and dare to look within yourself, you are a WITCH. You make your own rules.

WITCH in Washington, D.C., protested at the United Fruit Company for the corporation's activities in the Third World and its treatment of its women office workers. In Chicago it protested the firing of a radical feminist teacher named Marlene Dixon.

Poor women, black women, expressed the universal problem of women in their own way. In 1964 Robert Coles (*Children of Crisis*) interviewed a black woman from the South recently moved to Boston, who spoke of the desperation of her life, the difficulty of finding happiness: "To me, having a baby inside me is the only time I'm really alive."

Without talking specifically about their problems as women, many women, among the poor, did as they had always done, quietly organized neighborhood people to right injustices, to get needed services. In the mid-1960s, ten thousand black people in a community in Atlanta called Vine City joined together to help one another: they set up a thrift shop, a nursery, a medical clinic, monthly family suppers, a newspaper, a family counseling service. One of the organizers, Helen Howard, told Gerda Lerner (*Black Women in White America*) about it:

I organized this neighborhood organization, two men and six ladies started it. That was a hard pull. A lot of people joined in later. For about five months we had meetings pretty near every night. We learned how to work with other people. . . . A lot of people were afraid to really do anything. You were afraid to go to the city hall or ask for anything. You didn't even ask the landlord for anything, you were afraid of him. Then we had meetings and then we weren't afraid so much anymore. . . .

The way we got this playground: we blocked off the street, wouldn't let anything come through. We wouldn't let the trolley bus come through. The whole neighborhood was in it. Took record players and danced; it went on for a week. We didn't get arrested, they was too many of us. So then the city put up this playground for the kids. . . .

A woman named Patricia Robinson wrote a pamphlet called *Poor Black Woman*, in which she connected the problems of women with the need for basic social change:

Rebellion by poor black women, the bottom of a class hierarchy heretofore not discussed, places the question of what kind of society will the poor black woman demand and struggle for. Already she demands the right to have birth control, like middle class black and white women. She is aware that it takes two to oppress and that she and other poor people no longer are submitting to oppression, in this case genocide. She allies herself with the have-nots in the wider world and their revolutionary struggles. She had been forced by historical conditions to withdraw the children from male dominance and to educate and support them herself. In this very process, male authority and exploitation are seriously weakened. Further, she realizes that the children will be used as all poor children have been used through history—as poorly paid mercenaries fighting to keep or put an elite group in power. Through these steps . . . she has begun to question aggressive male domination and the class society which enforces it, capitalism.

In 1970, Dorothy Bolden, a laundry worker in Atlanta and mother of six, told why in 1968 she began organizing women doing housework, into the National Domestic Workers Union. She said: "I think women should have a voice in making decisions in their community for betterment. Because this woman in the slum is scuffling hard, and she's got a very good intelligent mind to do things, and she's been overlooked for so many years. I think she should have a voice."

Women tennis players organized. A woman fought to be a jockey, won her case, became the first woman jockey. Women artists picketed the Whitney Museum, charging sex discrimination in a sculptors' show. Women journalists picketed the Gridiron Club in Washington, which excluded women. By the start of 1974, women's studies programs existed at seventy-eight institutions, and about two thousand courses on women were being offered at about five hundred campuses.

Women's magazines and newspapers began appearing, locally and nationally, and books on women's history and the movement came out in such numbers that some bookstores had special sections for them. The very jokes on television, some sympathetic, some caustic, showed how national was the effect of the movement. Certain television commercials, which women felt humiliated them, were eliminated after protest.

In 1967, after lobbying by women's groups, President Johnson signed an executive order banning sex discrimination in federally connected employment, and in the years that followed, women's groups demanded that this be enforced. Over a thousand suits were initiated by NOW (National Organization for Women, formed in 1966) against U.S. corporations charging sex discrimination.

The right to abortion became a major issue. Before 1970, about a million abortions were done every year, of which only about ten thousand were legal. Perhaps a third of the women having illegal abortions—mostly poor people—had to be hospitalized for complications. How many thousands died as a result of these illegal abortions no one really knows. But the illegalization of abortion clearly worked against the poor, for the rich could manage either to have their baby or to have their abortion under safe conditions.

Court actions to do away with the laws against abortions were begun in over twenty states between 1968 and 1970, and public opinion grew stronger for the right of women to decide for themselves without government interference. In the book *Sisterhood Is Powerful,* an important collection of women's writing around

1970, an article by Lucinda Cisler, "Unfinished Business: Birth Control," said that "abortion is a woman's right . . . no one can veto her decision and compel her to bear a child against her will. . . ." In the spring of 1969 a Harris poll showed that 64 percent of those polled thought the decision on abortion was a private matter.

Finally, in early 1973, the Supreme Court decided (*Roe* v. *Wade, Doe* v. *Bolton*) that the state could prohibit abortions only in the last three months of pregnancy, that it could regulate abortion for health purposes during the second three months of pregnancy, and during the first three months, a woman and her doctor had the right to decide.

There was a push for child care centers, and although women did not succeed in getting much help from government, thousands of cooperative child care centers were set up.

Women also began to speak openly, for the first time, about the problem of rape. Each year, fifty thousand rapes were reported and many more were unreported. Women began taking self-defense courses. There were protests against the way police treated women, interrogated them, insulted them, when women filed rape charges. A book by Susan Brownmiller, *Against Our Will*, was widely read— it is a powerful, indignant history and analysis of rape, suggesting self-defense, individual or collective:

> Fighting back. On a multiplicity of levels, that is the activity we must engage in, together, if we—women—are to redress the imbalance and rid ourselves and men of the ideology of rape. Rape can be eradicated, not merely controlled or avoided on an individual basis, but the approach must be long-range and cooperative, and must have the understanding and good will of many men as well as women. . . .

Many women were active in trying to get a Constitutional amendment, ERA (Equal Rights Amendment), passed by enough states. But it seemed clear that even if it became law, it would not be enough, that what women had accomplished had come through organization, action, protest. Even where the law was helpful it was helpful only if backed by action. Shirley Chisholm, a black Congresswoman, said:

> The law cannot do it for us. We must do it for ourselves. Women in this country must become revolutionaries. We must refuse to accept the old, the traditional roles and stereotypes. . . . We must replace the old, negative thoughts about our femininity with positive thoughts and positive action. . . .

Perhaps the most profound effect of the women's movement of the sixties—beyond the actual victories on abortion, in job equality—was called "consciousness raising," often done in "women's groups," which met in homes all across the country. This meant the rethinking of roles, the rejection of inferiority, the confidence in self, a bond of sisterhood, a new solidarity of mother and daughter. The Atlanta poet Esta Seaton wrote "Her Life":

> This is the picture that keeps forming in my mind:
> my young mother, barely seventeen,
> cooking their Kosher dinner on the coal stove,
> that first winter in Vermont,
> and my father, mute in his feelings
> except when he shouted,
> eating to show his love.
>
> Fifty years later her blue eyes would grow cold
> with the shock of that grey house
> and the babies one after another
> and the doctor who said
> "If you don't want any more children
> move out of the house."

For the first time, the sheer biological uniqueness of women was openly discussed. Some theorists (Shulamith Firestone, in *The Dialectics of Sex*, for instance) thought this was more fundamental to their oppression than any particular economic system. It was liberating to talk frankly about what had for so long been secret, hidden, cause for shame and embarrassment: menstruation, masturbation, menopause, abortion, lesbianism.

One of the most influential books to appear in the early seventies was a book assembled by eleven women in the Boston Women's Health Book Collective called *Our Bodies, Ourselves*. It contained an enormous amount of practical information, on women's anatomy, on sexuality and sexual relationships, on lesbianism, on nutrition and health, on rape, self-defense, venereal disease, birth control, abortion, pregnancy, childbirth, and menopause. More important even than the information, the charts, the photos, the candid exploration of the previously unmentioned, was the mood of exuberance throughout the book, the enjoyment of the body, the happiness with the new-found understanding, the new sisterhood with young women, middle-aged women, older women. They quoted the English suffragette Christabel Pankhurst:

> Remember the dignity
> of your womanhood.
> Do not appeal,
> do not beg,
> do not grovel.
> Take courage
> join hands,
> stand beside us.
> Fight with us. . . .

The fight began, many women were saying, with the body, which seemed to be the beginning of the exploitation of women— as sex plaything (weak and incompetent), as pregnant woman (helpless), as middle-aged woman (no longer considered beautiful), as older woman (to be ignored, set aside). A biological prison had been created by men and society. As Adrienne Rich said *(Of Woman Born)*: "Women are controlled by lashing us to our bodies." She wrote:

I have a very clear, keen memory of myself the day after I was married: I was sweeping a floor. Probably the floor did not really need to be swept; probably I simply did not know what else to do with myself. But as I swept that floor I thought: "Now I am a woman. This is an age-old action, this is what women have always done." I felt I was bending to some ancient form, too ancient to question. *This is what women have always done.*

As soon as I was visibly and clearly pregnant, I felt, for the first time in my adolescent and adult life, not-guilty. The atmosphere of approval in which I was bathed—even by strangers on the street, it seemed—was like an aura I carried with me, in which doubts, fears, misgivings met with absolute denial. *This is what women have always done.. . .*

Rich said women could use the body "as a resource, rather than a destiny." Patriarchal systems, she said, whether under capitalism or "socialism," limited women's bodies to their own needs. She discussed the training of passivity in women. Generations of schoolgirls were raised on *Little Women*, where Jo is told by her mother: "I am angry nearly every day of my life, Jo; but I have learned not to show it; and I still hope to learn not to feel it, though it may take me another forty years to do so."

Male doctors used instruments to bring out children, replacing the sensitive hands of midwives, in the era of "anesthetized, technologized childbirth." Rich disagreed with her fellow feminist Firestone, who wanted to change the biological inevitability of childbirth, because it is painful and a source of subordination; she wants, under different social conditions, to make childbirth a source of physical and emotional joy.

One could not talk of Freud's ignorance of women, Rich said, as his one "blind spot," which implied that in other matters his vision was clear; such ignorance distorts all. There is a dilemma of the body:

I know no woman—virgin, mother, lesbian, married, celibate—whether she earns her keep as a housewife, a cocktail waitress, or a scanner of brain waves—for whom her body is not a fundamental problem: its clouded meaning, its fertility, its desire, its so-called frigidity, its bloody speech, its silences, its changes and mutilations, its rapes and ripenings.

Her reply to this: the "repossession of our bodies . . . a world in which every woman is the presiding genius of her own body" as a basis for bringing forth not just children but new visions, new meanings, a new world.

For most women who were not intellectuals, the question was even more immediate: how to eliminate hunger, suffering, subordination, humiliation, in the here and now. A woman named Johnnie Tillmon wrote in 1972:

> I'm a woman. I'm a black woman. I'm a poor woman. I'm a fat woman. I'm a middle-aged woman. And I'm on welfare. . . . I have raised six children. . . . I grew up in Arkansas . . . worked there for fifteen years in a laundry . . . moved to California. . . . In 1963 I got too sick to work anymore. Friends helped me to go on welfare. . . .
>
> Welfare's like a traffic accident. It can happen to anybody, but especially it happens to women.
>
> And that is why welfare is a women's issue. For a lot of middle-class women in this country, Women's Liberation is a matter of concern. For women on welfare it's a matter of survival.

Welfare, she said, was like "a supersexist marriage. You trade in *a* man for *the* man. . . . *The* man runs everything . . . controls your money. . . ." She and other welfare mothers organized a National Welfare Rights Organization. They urged that women be paid for their work—housekeeping, child rearing. ". . . No woman can be liberated, until all women get off their knees."

In the problem of women was the germ of a solution, not only for their oppression, but for everybody's. The control of women in society was ingeniously effective. It was not done directly by the state. Instead, the family was used—men to control women, women to control children, all to be preoccupied with one another, to turn to one another for help, to blame one another for trouble, to do violence to one another when things weren't going right. Why could this not be turned around? Could women liberating themselves, children freeing themselves, men and women beginning to understand one another, find the source of their common oppression outside rather than in one another? Perhaps then they could create nuggets of strength in their own relationships, millions of pockets of insurrection. They could revolutionize thought and behavior in exactly that seclusion of family privacy which the system had counted on to do its work of control and indoctrination. And together, instead of at odds—male, female, parents, children—they could undertake the changing of society itself.

It was a time of uprisings. If there could be rebellion inside that most subtle and complex of prisons—the family—it was reasonable that there be rebellions in the most brutal and obvious of prisons: the penitentiary system itself. In the sixties and early seventies, those rebellions multiplied. They also took on an unprecedented political character and the ferocity of class war, coming to a climax at Attica, New York, in September of 1971.

The prison had arisen in the United States as an attempt at Quaker reform, to replace mutilation, hanging, exile—the traditional punishments during colonial times. The prison was intended, through isolation, to produce repentence and salvation, but prisoners went insane and died in that isolation. By midnineteenth century, the prison was based on hard labor, along with various punishments: sweat boxes, iron yokes, solitary. The approach was summed up by the warden at the Ossining, New York, penitentiary: "In order to reform a criminal you must first break his spirit." That approach persisted.

Prison officials would convene annually to congratulate themselves on the progress being made. The president of the American Correctional Association, delivering the annual address in 1966, described the new edition of the *Manual of Correctional Standards*: "It permits us to linger, if we will, at the gates of correctional Valhalla—with an abiding pride in the sense of a job superbly done! We may be proud, we may be satisfied, we may be content." He said this just after, in the midst of, and just before the most intense series of prison uprisings the country had ever seen.

There had always been prison riots. A wave of them in the 1920s ended with a riot at Clinton, New York, a prison of 1,600 inmates, which was suppressed with three prisoners killed. Between 1950 and 1953 more than fifty major riots occurred in American prisons. In the early 1960s, prisoners on a work gang in Georgia smashing rocks used the same sledgehammers to break their legs, to call attention to their situation of daily brutality.

At San Quentin prison in California, which housed four thousand prisoners, there was a series of revolts in the late sixties: a race riot in 1967, a united black-white general strike in early 1968 that shut down almost all the prison industries, and then a second strike that summer.

At the Queens House of Detention on Long Island in New York in the fall of 1970, prisoners took over the jail, took hostages, issued demands. The prisoners' negotiating committee included four blacks, one Puerto Rican, one white; they demanded immediate bail hearings on forty-seven cases that they said were examples of racism in the granting of bail. Judges came inside the prison, granted some paroles and reductions, and the hostages were released. But when the prisoners continued to hold out, police stormed the jail with tear gas and clubs and the revolt was over.

Around the same time, in November 1970, in Folsom prison in California, a work stoppage began which became the longest prison strike in the history of the United States. Most of the 2,400 prisoners held out in their cells for nineteen days, without food, in the face of threats and intimidation. The strike was broken with a combination of force and deception, and four of the prisoners were sent on a fourteen-hour ride to another prison, shackled and naked on the floor of a van. One of the rebels wrote: ". . . the spirit of awareness has grown. . . . The seed has been planted. . . ."

The prisons in the United States had long been an extreme reflection of the American system itself: the stark life differences between rich and poor, the racism, the use of victims against one another, the lack of resources of the underclass to speak out, the endless "reforms" that changed little. Dostoevski once said: "The degree of civilization in a society can be judged by entering its prisons."

It had long been true, and prisoners knew this better than anyone, that the poorer you were the more likely you were to end up in jail. This was not just because the poor committed more crimes. In fact, they did. The rich did not have to commit crimes to get what they wanted; the laws were on their side. But when the rich did commit crimes, they often were not prosecuted, and if they were they could get out on bail, hire clever lawyers, get better treatment from judges. Somehow, the jails ended up full of poor black people.

In 1969, there were 502 convictions for tax fraud. Such cases, called "white-collar crimes," usually involve people with a good deal of money. Of those convicted, 20 percent ended up in jail. The fraud averaged $190,000 per case; their sentences averaged seven months. That same year, for burglary and auto theft (crimes of the poor) 60 percent ended up in prison. The auto thefts averaged $992; the sentences averaged eighteen months. The burglaries averaged $321; the sentences averaged thirty-three months.

Willard Gaylin, a psychiatrist, relates (*Partial Justice*) a case which, with changes in details, could be multiplied thousands of times. He had just interviewed seventeen Jehovah's Witnesses who refused to register for the draft during the Vietnam war, and all had received two-year sentences. He came to a young black man who had notified his draft board he could not in conscience cooperate with the draft because he was repelled by the violence of the Vietnam war. He received a five-year sentence. Gaylin writes: "Hank's was the first five-year sentence I had encountered. He was also the first black man." There were additional factors:

"How was your hair then?" I asked.

"Afro."

"And what were you wearing?"

"A dashiki."

"Don't you think that might have affected your sentence?"

"Of course."

"Was it worth a year or two of your life?" I asked.

"That's all of my life," he said, looking at me with a combination of dismay and confusion. "Man, don't you know! That's what it's all about! Am I free to have my style, am I free to have my hair, am I free to have my skin?"

"Of course," I said. "You're right."

Gaylin found enormous discretion given to judges in the handing out of sentences. In Oregon, of thirty-three men convicted of violating the draft law, eighteen were put on probation. In southern Texas, of sixteen men violating the same law, none was put on probation, and in southern Mississippi, every defendant was convicted and given the maximum of five years. In one part of the country (New England), the average sentence for all crimes was eleven months; in another part (the South), it was seventy-eight months. But it wasn't simply a matter of North and South. In New York City, one judge handling 673 persons brought before him for public drunkenness (all poor; the rich get drunk behind closed doors) discharged 531 of them. Another judge, handling 566 persons on the same charge, discharged one person.

With such power in the hands of the courts, the poor, the black, the odd, the homosexual, the hippie, the radical are not likely to get equal treatment before judges who are almost uniformly white, upper middle class, orthodox.

While in any one year (1972, for instance) perhaps 375,000 people will be in jail (county or city) or in prisons (state or federal), and 54,000 in juvenile detention, there will also be 900,000 under probation and 300,000 on parole—a total of 1,600,000 people affected by the criminal justice system. Considering turnover, in any one year, several million people will come in and go out of this system. It is a population largely invisible to middle-class America, but if 20 million blacks could be invisible for so long, why not four or five million "criminals"? A study by the Children's Defense Fund (Thomas Cottle, *Children in Jail*) in the mid-seventies revealed that more than 900,000 young people under eighteen are jailed in the course of a year.

Anyone trying to describe the reality of prison falters. A man in Walpole prison in Massachusetts wrote:

> Every program that we get is used as a weapon against us. The right to go to school, to go to church, to have visitors, to write, to go to the movies. They all end up being weapons of punishment. None of the programs are *ours*. Everything is treated as a privilege that can be taken away from us. The result is insecurity—a frustration that keeps eating away at you.

Another Walpole prisoner:

> I haven't eaten in the mess hall for four years. I just couldn't take it any more. You'd go into the serving line in the morning and 100 or 200 cockroaches would go running away from the trays. The trays were grimy and the food was raw or had dirt or maggots in it.
>
> Many a night I'd go hungry, living on peanut butter and sandwiches, getting a loaf of bread here or a hunk of bologna there. Other guys couldn't do that because they didn't have my connections or they didn't have money for the canteen.

Communication with the outside world was difficult. Guards would tear up letters. Others would be intercepted and read. Jerry Sousa, a prisoner at Walpole in 1970, sent two letters—one to a judge, the other to the parole board—to tell about a beating by guards. They went unanswered. Eight years later, at a court hearing, he discovered the prison authorities had intercepted them, never sent them out.

The families suffered with the prisoner: "During the last lock-up my four-year-old son sneaked off into the yard and picked me a flower. A guard in the tower called the warden's office and a deputy came in with the State Police at his side. He announced that if any child went into the yard and picked another flower, all visits would be terminated."

The prison rebellions of the late sixties and early seventies had a distinctly different character than the earlier ones. The prisoners in the Queens House of Detention referred to themselves as "revolutionaries." All over the country, prisoners were obviously affected by the turmoil in the country, the black revolt, the youth upsurge, the antiwar movement.

The events of those years underlined what prisoners already sensed—that whatever crimes they had committed, the greatest crimes were being committed by the authorities who maintained the prisons, by the government of the United States. The law was being broken daily by the President, sending bombers to kill, sending men to be killed, outside the Constitution, outside the "highest law of the land." State and local officials were violating the civil rights of black people, which was against the law, and were not being prosecuted for it.

Literature about the black movement, books on the war, began to seep into the prisons. The example set in the streets by blacks, by antiwar demonstrators, was exhilarating—against a lawless system, defiance was the only answer.

It was a system which sentenced Martin Sostre, a fifty-two-year-old black man running an Afro-Asian bookstore in Buffalo, New York, to twenty-five to thirty years in prison for allegedly selling $15 worth of heroin to an informer who later recanted his testimony. The recantation did not free Sostre—he could find no court, including the Supreme Court of the United States, to revoke the judgment. He spent eight years in prison, was beaten ten times by guards, spent three years in solitary confinement, battling and defying the authorities all the way until his release. Such injustice deserved only rebellion.

There had always been political prisoners—people sent to jail for belonging to radical movements, for opposing war. But now a new kind of political prisoner appeared—the man, or woman, convicted of an ordinary crime, who, in prison, became awakened politically. Some prisoners began making connections between their personal ordeal and the social system. They then turned not to individual rebellion but to collective action. They became concerned—amid an environment whose brutality demanded concentration on one's own safety, an atmosphere of cruel rivalry—for the rights, the safety of others.

George Jackson was one of these new political prisoners. In Soledad prison, California, on an indeterminate sentence for a $70 robbery, having already served ten years of it, Jackson became a revolutionary. He spoke with a fury that matched his condition:

This monster—the monster they've engendered in me will return to torment its maker, from the grave, the pit, the profoundest pit. Hurl me into the next existence, the descent into hell won't turn me. . . . I'm going to charge them reparations in blood. I'm going to charge them like a maddened, wounded, rogue male elephant, ears flared, trunk raised, trumpet blaring. . . . War without terms.

A prisoner like this would not last. And when his book *Soledad Brother* became one of the most widely read books of black militancy in the United States—by prisoners, by black people, by white people—perhaps this ensured he would not last.

All my life I've done exactly what I wanted to do just when I wanted, no more, perhaps less sometimes, but never any more, which explains why I had to be jailed. . . . I never adjusted. I haven't adjusted even yet, with half of my life already in prison.

He knew what might happen:

Born to a premature death, a menial, subsistence-wage worker, odd-job man, the cleaner, the caught, the man under hatches, without bail—that's me, the colonial victim. Anyone who can pass the civil service examination today can kill me tomorrow . . . with complete immunity.

In August 1971 he was shot in the back by guards at San Quentin prison while he was allegedly trying to escape. The state's story (analyzed by Eric Mann in *Comrade George*) was full of holes. Prisoners in jails and state prisons all over the country knew, even before the final autopsy was in, even before later disclosures suggested a government plot to kill Jackson, that he had been murdered for daring to be a revolutionary in prison. Shortly after Jackson's death, there was a chain of rebellions around the country, in San Jose Civic Center jail, in Dallas county jail, in Suffolk county jail in Boston, in Cumberland county jail in Bridgeton, New Jersey, in Bexar county jail in San Antonio, Texas.

The most direct effect of the George Jackson murder was the rebellion at Attica prison in September 1971—a rebellion that came from long, deep grievances, but that was raised to boiling point by the news about George Jackson. Attica was surrounded by a 30-foot wall, 2 feet thick, with fourteen gun towers. Fifty-four percent of the inmates were black; 100 percent of the guards were white. Prisoners spent fourteen to sixteen hours a day in their cells, their mail was read, their reading material restricted, their visits from families conducted through a mesh screen, their medical care disgraceful, their parole system inequitable, racism everywhere. How perceptive the prison administration was about these conditions can be measured by the comment of the superintendent of Attica, Vincent Mancusi, when the uprising began: "Why are they destroying their home?"

Most of the Attica prisoners were there as a result of plea bargaining. Of 32,000 felony indictments a year in New York State, 4,000 to 5,000 were tried. The rest (about 75 percent) were disposed of by deals made under duress, called "plea bargaining," described as follows in the Report of the Joint Legislative Committee on Crime in New York:

> The final climactic act in the plea bargaining procedure is a charade which in itself has aspects of dishonesty which rival the original crime in many instances. The accused is made to assert publicly his

guilt on a specific crime, which in many cases he has not committed; in some cases he pleads guilty to a non-existing crime. He must further indicate that he is entering his plea freely . . . and that he is not doing so because of any promises . . . made to him.

In plea bargaining, the accused pleads guilty, whether he is or not, and saves the state the trouble of a trial in return for the promise of a less severe punishment.

When Attica prisoners were up for parole, the average time of their hearing, including the reading of the file and deliberation among the three members, was 5.9 minutes. Then the decision was handed out, with no explanation.

The official report on the Attica uprising tells how an inmate-instructed sociology class there became a forum for ideas about change. Then there was a series of organized protest efforts, and in July an inmate manifesto setting forth a series of moderate demands, after which "tensions at Attica had continued to mount," culminating in a day of protest over the killing of George Jackson at San Quentin, during which few inmates ate at lunch and dinner and many wore black armbands.

On September 9, 1971, a series of conflicts between prisoners and guards ended with a group of inmates breaking through a gate with a defective weld and taking over one of the four prison yards, with forty guards as hostages. Then followed five days in which the prisoners set up a remarkable community in the yard. A group of citizen-observers, invited by the prisoners, included *New York Times* columnist Tom Wicker, who wrote *(A Time to Die)*: "The racial harmony that prevailed among the prisoners—it was absolutely astonishing. . . . That prison yard was the first place I have ever seen where there was no racism." One black prisoner later said: "I never thought whites could really get it on. . . . But I can't tell you what the yard was like, I actually cried it was so close, everyone so together. . . ."

After five days, the state lost patience. Governor Nelson Rockefeller approved a military attack on the prison (see Cinda

Firestone's stunning film *Attica*). National Guardsmen, prison guards, and local police went in with automatic rifles, carbines, and submachine guns in a full-scale assault on the prisoners, who had no firearms. Thirty-one prisoners were killed. The first stories given the press by prison authorities said that nine guards held hostage had their throats slashed by the prisoners during the attack. The official autopsies almost immediately showed this to be false: the nine guards died in the same hail of bullets that killed the prisoners.

The effects of Attica are hard to measure. Two months after the revolt at Attica, men at Norfolk prison in Massachusetts began to organize. On November 8, 1971, armed guards and state troopers, in a surprise raid, moved into the cells at Norfolk, pulled out sixteen men, and shipped them out. A prisoner described the scene:

> Between one and two last night I was awakened (I've been a light sleeper since Vietnam) and I looked out my window. There were troopers. And screws. Lots. Armed with sidearms, and big clubs. They were going into dorms and taking people, all kinds of people. . . .
>
> They took a friend of mine. . . . Being pulled outside in our underwear, at 1:30, in bare feet by two troopers and a housescrew. Looking at those troops, with guns, and masks and clubs, with the moon shining off the helmets and the hate that you could see in their faces. Thinking that this is where these guys live, with the guns and the hate, and the helmets and masks, and you, you're trying to wake up, flashing on Kent State and Jackson, and Chicago. And Attica. Most of all, Attica. . . .

That same week at Concord prison in Massachusetts, another raid. It was as if everywhere, in the weeks and months after Attica, the authorities were taking preventive action to break up organizing efforts among the prisoners. Jerry Sousa, a young leader of the prison reform movement at Concord, was taken away, dumped into Walpole in the middle of the night, and immediately put into Nine Block, the dreaded segregation unit. He had been there only a short time when he managed to get a report out to friends. The content of this report tells much about what was happening before and after Attica to the thinking of prisoners:

> We are writing a somber report regarding the circumstances and events leading up to and surrounding the death of prisoner Joseph Chesnulavich which occurred here an hour ago in Nine Block.
>
> Since Christmas eve, vicious prison guards here in Nine Block have created a reign of terror directed toward us prisoners. Four of us have been beaten, one who was prisoner Donald King.
>
> In an attempt to escape constant harassment and inhuman treatment, prisoner George Hayes ate razor blades and prisoner Fred Ahern swallowed a needle . . . they both were rushed to Mass General Hospital.
>
> This evening at 6 P.M. prison guards Baptist, Sainsbury, and Montiega turned a fire extinguisher containing a chemical foam on Joe then slammed the solid steel door sealing him in his cell and walked away, voicing threats of, "We'll get that punk."
>
> At 9:25 P.M. Joe was found dead. . . . Prison authorities as well as news media will label little Joe's death a suicide, but the men here in Block Nine who witnessed this murder know. But are we next?

What was happening was the organization of prisoners—the caring of prisoners for one another, the attempt to take the hatred and anger of individual rebellion and turn it into collective effort for change. On the outside, something new was also happening, the development of prison support groups all over the country, the building of a body of literature about prisons. There were more studies of crime and punishment, a growing movement for the abolition of prisons on the grounds that they did not prevent crime or cure it, but expanded it. Alternatives were discussed: community houses in the short run (except for the incorrigibly violent); guaranteed minimum economic security, in the long run.

The prisoners were thinking about issues beyond prison, victims other than themselves and their friends. In Walpole prison a statement asking for American withdrawal from Vietnam was circulated; it was signed by every single prisoner—an amazing organizing feat by a handful of inmates. One Thanksgiving day there, most of the prisoners, not only in Walpole but in three other prisons, refused to eat the special holiday meal, saying they wanted to bring attention to the hungry all over the United States.

Prisoners worked laboriously on lawsuits, and some victories were won in the courts. The publicity around Attica, the community of support, had its effect. Although the Attica rebels were indicted on heavy charges and faced double and triple life terms, the charges were finally dropped. But in general, the courts declared their unwillingness to enter the closed, controlled world of the prison, and so the prisoners remained as they had been so long, on their own.

Even where an occasional "victory" came in the courts it turned out, on close reading, to leave things not much different. In 1973 (*Procunier* v. *Martinez*) the U.S. Supreme Court declared unconstitutional certain mail censorship regulations of the California Department of Corrections. But when one looked closely, the decision, with all its proud language about "First Amendment liberties," said: ". . . we hold that censorship of prison mail is justified if the following criteria are met. . . ." When the censorship could be said to "further an important or substantial government interest" or where it was in the "substantial governmental interests of security, order, and rehabilitation," censorship would be allowed.

In 1978 the Supreme Court ruled that the news media do not have guaranteed rights of access to jails and prisons. It ruled also that prison authorities could forbid inmates to speak to one another, assemble, or spread literature about the formation of a prisoners' union.

It became clear—and prisoners seemed to know this from the start—that their condition would not be changed by law, but by

protest, organization, resistance, the creation of their own culture, their own literature, the building of links with people on the
outside. There were more outsiders now who knew about prisons. Tens of thousands of Americans had spent time behind bars
in the civil rights and antiwar movements. They had learned
about the prison system and could hardly forget their experiences. There was a basis now for breaking through the long isolation of the prisoners from the community and finding support
there. In the mid-seventies, this was beginning to happen.

It was a time of upsurge. Women, guarded in their very
homes, rebelled. Prisoners, put out of sight and behind bars,
rebelled. The greatest surprise was still to come.

It was thought that the Indians, once the only occupants of the
continent, then pushed back and annihilated by the white
invaders, would not be heard from again. In the last days of the
year 1890, shortly after Christmas, the last massacre of Indians
took place at Pine Ridge, South Dakota, near Wounded Knee
Creek. Sitting Bull, the great Sioux leader, had just been assassinated by Indian police in the pay of the United States, and the
remaining Sioux sought refuge at Pine Ridge, 120 men and 230
women and children, surrounded by U.S. cavalry, with two
Hotchkiss guns—capable of hurling shells over 2 miles—on a rise
overlooking the camp. When the troopers ordered the Indians to
turn over their weapons, one of them fired his rifle. The soldiers
then let loose with their carbines, and the big guns on the hill
shelled the tepees. When it was over between 200 and 300 of the
original 350 men, women, and children were dead. The twenty-
five soldiers who died were mostly hit by their own shrapnel or
bullets, since the Indians had only a few guns.

The Indian tribes, attacked, subdued, starved out, had been
divided up by putting them on reservations where they lived in
poverty. In 1887, an Allotment Act tried to break up the reservations into small plots of land owned by individual Indians, to turn
them into American-type small farmers—but much of this land
was taken by white speculators, and the reservations remained.

Then, during the New Deal, with a friend of the Indians, John Collier, in charge of the Bureau of Indian Affairs, there was an attempt to restore tribal life. But in the decades that followed, no fundamental change took place. Many Indians stayed on the impoverished reservations. The younger ones often left. An Indian anthropologist said: "An Indian reservation is the most complete colonial system in the world that I know about."

For a time, the disappearance or amalgamation of the Indians seemed inevitable—only 300,000 were left at the turn of the century, from the original million or more in the area of the United States. But then the population began to grow again, as if a plant left to die refused to do so, began to flourish. By 1960 there were 800,000 Indians, half on reservations, half in towns all over the country.

The autobiographies of Indians show their refusal to be absorbed by the white man's culture. One wrote:

Oh, yes, I went to the white man's schools. I learned to read from school books, newspapers, and the Bible. But in time I found that these were not enough. Civilized people depend too much on manmade printed pages. I turn to the Great Spirit's book which is the whole of his creation. . . .

A Hopi Indian named Sun Chief said:

I had learned many English words and could recite part of the Ten Commandments. I knew how to sleep on a bed, pray to Jesus, comb my hair, eat with a knife and fork, and use a toilet. . . . I had also learned that a person thinks with his head instead of his heart.

Chief Luther Standing Bear, in his 1933 autobiography, *From the Land of the Spotted Eagle*, wrote:

True, the white man brought great change. But the varied fruits of his civilization, though highly colored and inviting, are sickening and deadening. And if it be the part of civilization to maim, rob, and thwart, then what is progress?

I am going to venture that the man who sat on the ground in his tipi meditating on life and its meaning, accepting the kinship of all creatures, and acknowledging unity with the universe of things, was infusing into his being the true essence of civilization. . . .

As the civil rights and antiwar movements developed in the 1960s, Indians were already gathering their energy for resistance, thinking about how to change their situation, beginning to organize. In 1961, five hundred tribal and urban Indian leaders met in Chicago. Out of this came another gathering of university-educated young Indians who formed the National Indian Youth Council. Mel Thom, a Paiute Indian, their first president, wrote:

> There is increased activity over on the Indian side. There are disagreements, laughing, singing, outbursts of anger, and occasionally some planning. . . . Indians are gaining confidence and courage that their cause is right.
>
> The struggle goes on. . . . Indians are gathering together to deliberate their destiny. . . .

Around this time, Indians began to approach the United States government on an embarrassing topic: treaties. In his widely read 1969 book, *Custer Died for Your Sins*, Vine Deloria, Jr., noted that President Lyndon Johnson talked about America's "commitments," and President Nixon talked about Russia's failure to respect treaties. He said: "Indian people laugh themselves sick when they hear these statements."

The United States government had signed more than four hundred treaties with Indians and violated every single one. For instance, back in George Washington's administration, a treaty was signed with the Iroquois of New York: "The United States acknowledge all the land within the aforementioned boundaries to be the property of the Seneka nation. . . ." But in the early sixties, under President Kennedy, the United States ignored the treaty and built a dam on this land, flooding most of the Seneca reservation.

Resistance was already taking shape in various parts of the country. In the state of Washington, there was an old treaty taking land from the Indians but leaving them fishing rights. This became unpopular as the white population grew and wanted the fishing areas exclusively for themselves. When state courts closed river areas to Indian fishermen, in 1964, Indians had "fish-ins" on the Nisqually River, in defiance of the court orders, and went to jail, hoping to publicize their protest.

A local judge the following year ruled that the Puyallup tribe did not exist, and its members could not fish on the river named for them, the Puyallup River. Policemen raided Indian fishing groups, destroyed boats, slashed nets, manhandled people, arrested seven Indians. A Supreme Court ruling in 1968 confirmed Indian rights under the treaty but said a state could "regulate all fishing" if it did not discriminate against Indians. The state continued to get injunctions and to arrest Indians fishing. They were doing to the Supreme Court ruling what whites in the South had done with the Fourteenth Amendment for many years—ignoring it. Protests, raids, arrests, continued into the early seventies.

Some of the Indians involved in the fish-ins were veterans of the Vietnam war. One was Sid Mills, who was arrested in a fish-in at Frank's Landing on the Nisqually River in Washington on October 13, 1968. He made a statement:

I am a Yakima and Cherokee Indian, and a man. For two years and four months, I've been a soldier in the United States Army. I served in combat in Vietnam—until critically wounded. . . . I hereby renounce further obligation in service or duty to the United States Army.

My first obligation now lies with the Indian People fighting for the lawful Treaty to fish in usual and accustomed water of the Nisqually, Columbia and other rivers of the Pacific Northwest, and in serving them in this fight in any way possible. . . .

My decision is influenced by the fact that we have already buried

Indian fishermen returned dead from Vietnam, while Indian fishermen live here without protection and under steady attack. . . .

Just three years ago today, on October 13, 1965, 19 women and children were brutalized by more than 45 armed agents of the State of Washington at Frank's Landing on the Nisqually river in a vicious, unwarranted attack. . . .

Interestingly, the oldest human skeletal remains ever found in the Western Hemisphere were recently uncovered on the banks of the Columbia River—the remains of Indian fishermen. What kind of government or society would spend millions of dollars to pick upon our bones, restore our ancestral life patterns, and protect our ancient remains from damage—while at the same time eating upon the flesh of our living People . . . ?

We will fight for our rights.

Indians fought back not only with physical resistance, but also with the artifacts of white culture—books, words, newspapers. In 1968, members of the Mohawk Nation at Akwesasne, on the St. Lawrence River between the United States and Canada, began a remarkable newspaper, *Akwesasne Notes*, with news, editorials, poetry, all flaming with the spirit of defiance. Mixed in with all that was an irrepressible humor. Vine Deloria, Jr., wrote:

Every now and then I am impressed with the thinking of the non-Indian. I was in Cleveland last year and got to talking with a non-Indian about American history. He said that he was really sorry about what had happened to Indians, but that there was a good reason for it. The continent had to be developed and he felt that Indians had stood in the way, and thus had had to be removed. "After all," he remarked, "what did you do with the land when you had it?" I didn't understand him until later when I discovered that the Cuyahoga River running through Cleveland is inflammable. So many combustible pollutants are dumped into the river that the inhabitants have to take special precautions during the summer to avoid setting it on fire. After reviewing the argument of my non-Indian friend I decided that he was probably correct. Whites had made better use of the land. How many Indians could have thought of creating an inflammable river?

In 1969, November 9, there took place a dramatic event which focused attention on Indian grievances as nothing else had. It burst through the invisibility of previous local Indian protests and declared to the entire world that the Indians still lived and would fight for their rights. On that day, before dawn, seventy-eight Indians landed on Alcatraz Island in San Francisco Bay and occupied the island. Alcatraz was an abandoned federal prison, a hated and terrible place nicknamed "The Rock." In 1964 some young Indians had occupied it to establish an Indian university, but they were driven off and there was no publicity.

This time, it was different. The group was led by Richard Oakes, a Mohawk who directed Indian Studies at San Francisco State College, and Grace Thorpe, a Sac and Fox Indian, daughter of Jim Thorpe, the famous Indian college football star and Olympic runner, jumper, hurdler. More Indians landed, and by the end of November nearly six hundred of them, representing more than fifty tribes, were living on Alcatraz. They called themselves "Indians of All Tribes" and issued a proclamation, "We Hold the Rock." In it they offered to buy Alcatraz in glass beads and red cloth, the price paid Indians for Manhattan Island over three hundred years earlier. They said:

We feel that this so-called Alcatraz Island is more than suitable for an Indian reservation, as determined by the white man's own standards. By this we mean that this place resembles most Indian reservations in that:

1. It is isolated from modern facilities, and without adequate means of transportation.
2. It has no fresh running water.
3. It has inadequate sanitation facilities.
4. There are no oil or mineral rights.
5. There is no industry and so unemployment is very great.
6. There are no health care facilities.

7. The soil is rocky and non-productive; and the land does not support game.
8. There are no educational facilities.
9. The population has always exceeded the land base.
10. The population has always been held as prisoners and dependent upon others.

They announced they would make the island a center for Native American Studies for Ecology: "We will work to de-pollute the air and waters of the Bay Area . . . restore fish and animal life. . . ."

In the months that followed, the government cut off telephones, electricity, and water to Alcatraz Island. Many of the Indians had to leave, but others insisted on staying. A year later they were still there, and they sent out a message to "our brothers and sisters of all races and tongues upon our Earth Mother":

> We are still holding the Island of Alcatraz in the true names of Freedom, Justice and Equality, because you, our brothers and sisters of this earth, have lent support to our just cause. We reach out our hands and hearts and send spirit messages to each and every one of you—WE HOLD THE ROCK. . . .
>
> We have learned that violence breeds only more violence and we therefore have carried on our occupation of Alcatraz in a peaceful manner, hoping that the government of these United States will also act accordingly. . . .
>
> We are a proud people! We are Indians! We have observed and rejected much of what so-called civilization offers. We are Indians! We will preserve our traditions and ways of life by educating our own children. We are Indians! We will join hands in a unity never before put into practice. We are Indians! Our Earth Mother awaits our voices.
>
> We are Indians Of All Tribes! WE HOLD THE ROCK!

Six months later, federal forces invaded the island and physically removed the Indians living there.

It had been thought that the Navajo Indians would not be

heard from again. In the mid-1800s, United States troops under "Kit" Carson burned Navajo villages, destroyed their crops and orchards, forced them from their lands. But in the Black Mesa of New Mexico they never surrendered. In the late 1960s, the Peabody Coal Company began strip mining on their land—a ruthless excavation of the topsoil. The company pointed to a "contract" signed with some Navajos. It was reminiscent of the "treaties" signed with some Indians in the past that took away all Indian land.

One hundred and fifty Navajos met in the spring of 1969 to declare that the strip mining would pollute the water and the air, destroy the grazing land for livestock, use up their scarce water resources. A young woman pointed to a public relations pamphlet put out by the Peabody Coal Company, showing fishing lakes, grassland, trees, and said: "We're not going to have anything like those you see in the pictures. . . . What is the future going to be like for our children, our children's children?" An elderly Navajo woman, one of the organizers of the meeting, said, "Peabody's monsters are digging up the heart of our mother earth, our sacred mountain, and we also feel the pains. . . . I have lived here for years and I'm not about to move."

The Hopi Indians were also affected by the Peabody operations. They wrote to President Nixon in protest:

Today the sacred lands where the Hopi live are being desecrated by men who seek coal and water from our soil that they may create more power for the whiteman's cities. . . . The Great Spirit said not to allow this to happen. . . . The Great Spirit said not to take from the Earth—not to destroy living things. . . .

It is said by the Great Spirit that if a gourd of ashes is dropped upon the Earth, that many men will die and that the end of this way of life is near at hand. We interpret this as the dropping of atomic bombs on Hiroshima and Nagasaki. We do not want to see this happen to any place or any nation again, but instead we should turn all this energy for peaceful uses, not for war. . . .

In the fall of 1970, a magazine called *La Raza*, one of the countless local publications coming out of the movements of those years to supply information ignored in the regular media, told about the Pit River Indians of northern California. Sixty Pit Indians occupied land they said belonged to them; they defied the Forest Services when ordered to leave. One of them, Darryl B. Wilson, later recalled: "As the flames danced orange making the trees come to life, and the cold creeped out of the darkness to challenge the speaking fire, and our breath came in small clouds, we spoke." They asked the government by what treaty it claimed the land. It could point to none. They cited a federal statute *(25 USCA 194)* that where there was a land dispute between Indian and white "the burden of proof falls on the white man."

They had built a quonset hut, and the marshals told them it was ugly and ruined the landscape. Wilson wrote later:

> The whole world is rotting. The water is poisoned, the air polluted, the politics deformed, the land gutted, the forest pillaged, the shores ruined, the towns burned, the lives of the people destroyed . . . and the federals spent the best part of October trying to tell us the quonset hut was "ugly"!
>
> To us it was beautiful. It was the beginning of our school. The meeting place. Home for our homeless. A sanctuary for those needing rest. Our church. Our headquarters. Our business office. Our symbol of approaching freedom. And it still stands.
>
> It was also the center for the reviving of our stricken, diluted and separated culture. Our beginning. It was our sun rising on a clear spring day when the sky holds no clouds. It was a good and pure thing for the heart to look upon. That small place on earth. Our place.

But 150 marshals came, with machine guns, shotguns, rifles, pistols, riot sticks, Mace, dogs, chains, manacles. "The old people were frightened. The young questioned bravery. The small children were like a deer that has been shot by the thunder stick.

Hearts beat fast as though a race was just run in the heat of summer." The marshals began swinging their riot sticks, and blood
started flowing. Wilson grabbed one marshal's club, was thrown
down, manacled, and while lying face down on the ground was
struck behind the head several times. A sixty-six-year-old man
was beaten into unconsciousness. A white reporter was arrested,
his wife beaten. They were all thrown into trucks and taken away,
charged with assaulting state and federal officers and cutting
trees—but not with trespassing, which might have brought into
question the ownership of the land. When the episode was all
over, they were still defiant.

Indians who had been in the Vietnam war made connections.
At the "Winter Soldier Investigations" in Detroit, where Vietnam
veterans testified about their experiences, an Oklahoma Indian
named Evan Haney told about his:

> The same massacres happened to the Indians 100 years ago. Germ
> warfare was used then. They put smallpox in the Indians' blan-
> kets. . . .
>
> I got to know the Vietnamese people and I learned they were just
> like us. . . . What we are doing is destroying ourselves and the world.
>
> I have grown up with racism all my life. When I was a child, watch-
> ing cowboys and Indians on TV, I would root for the cavalry, not the
> Indians. It was that bad. I was that far toward my own destruction. . . .
>
> Though 50 percent of the children at the country school I attended
> in Oklahoma were Indians, nothing in school, on television, or on the
> radio taught anything about Indian culture. There were no books on
> Indian history, not even in the library. . . .
>
> But I knew something was wrong. I started reading and learning
> my own culture. . . .
>
> I saw the Indian people at their happiest when they went to Alca-
> traz or to Washington to defend their fishing rights. They at last felt
> like human beings.

Indians began to do something about their "own destruction"—the annihilation of their culture. In 1969, at the First

Convocation of American Indian Scholars, Indians spoke indignantly of either the ignoring or the insulting of Indians in textbooks given to little children all over the United States. That year the Indian Historian Press was founded. It evaluated four hundred textbooks in elementary and secondary schools and found that not one of them gave an accurate depiction of the Indian.

A counterattack began in the schools. In early 1971, forty-five Indian students at Copper Valley School, in Glennalen, Alaska, wrote a letter to their Congressman opposing the Alaska oil pipeline as ruinous to the ecology, a threat to the "peace, quiet and security of our Alaska."

Other Americans were beginning to pay attention, to rethink their own learning. The first motion pictures attempting to redress the history of the Indian appeared: one was *Little Big Man*, based on a novel by Thomas Berger. More and more books appeared on Indian history, until a whole new literature came into existence. Teachers became sensitive to the old stereotypes, threw away the old textbooks, started using new material. In the spring of 1977 a teacher named Jane Califf, in the New York City elementary schools, told of her experiences with fourth and fifth grade students. She brought into class the traditional textbooks and asked the students to locate the stereotypes in them. She read aloud from Native American writers and articles from *Akwesasne Notes*, and put protest posters around the room. The children then wrote letters to the editors of the books they had read:

> Dear Editor,
>   I don't like your book called *The Cruise of Christopher Columbus*. I didn't like it because you said some things about Indians that weren't true. . . . Another thing I didn't like was on page 69, it says that Christopher Columbus invited the Indians to Spain, but what really happened was that he stole them!
>
>   censearly, Raymond Miranda

On Thanksgiving Day 1970, at the annual celebration of the landing of the Pilgrims, the authorities decided to do something different: invite an Indian to make the celebratory speech. They found a Wampanoag Indian named Frank James and asked him to speak. But when they saw the speech he was about to deliver, they decided they did not want it. His speech, not heard at Plymouth, Massachusetts, on that occasion, said, in part (the whole speech is in *Chronicles of American Indian Protest*):

> I speak to you as a Man—a Wampanoag Man. . . . It is with mixed emotions that I stand here to share my thoughts. . . . The Pilgrims had hardly explored the shores of Cape Cod four days before they had robbed the graves of my ancestors, and stolen their corn, wheat, and beans. . . .
>
> Our spirit refuses to die. Yesterday we walked the woodland paths and sandy trails. Today we must walk the macadam highways and roads. We are uniting. We're standing not in our wigwams but in your concrete tent. We stand tall and proud and before too many moons pass we'll right the wrongs we have allowed to happen to us. . . .

For Indians there has never been a clear line between prose and poetry. When an Indian studying in New Mexico was praised for his poetry he said, "In my tribe we have no poets. Everyone talks in poetry." There are, however, "poems," collected in William Brandon's *The Last Americans* and in *The Way* by Shirley Hill Witt and Stan Steiner.

An Ashinabe "spring poem" translated by Gerald Vizenor:

> as my eyes
> look across the prairie
> i feel the summer
> in the spring

"Snow the Last" by Joseph Concha:

> Snow comes last
> for it quiets down everything

This from a fifth-year group in a Special Navajo Program in the year 1940, called "It is Not!"

The Navajo Reservation a lonesome place?
It is Not!
The skies are sunny,
Clear blue,
Or grey with rain.
Each day is gay—
in Nature's way.
It is not a lonesome place at all.
A Navajo house shabby and small?
It is Not!
Inside there's love,
Good laughter,
And Big Talk.
But best—
it's home
With an open door
And room for all
A Castle could have no more.

In March of 1973 came a powerful affirmation that the Indians of North America were still alive. On the site of the 1890 massacre, on Pine Ridge reservation, several hundred Oglala Sioux and friends returned to the village of Wounded Knee to occupy it as a symbol of the demand for Indian land, Indian rights. The history of that event, in the words of the participants, has been captured in a rare book published by *Akwesasne Notes* (*Voices from Wounded Knee*, 1973).

In the 1970s, 54 percent of the adult males on the Pine Ridge reservation were unemployed, one-third of the families were on welfare or pensions, alcoholism was widespread, and suicide rates were high. The life expectancy of an Oglala Sioux was forty-six years. Just before the Wounded Knee occupation, there was violence at the town of Custer. An Indian named Wesley Bad Heart

Bull was killed by a white gas station attendant. The man was let out on $5,000 bond and indicted for manslaughter, facing a possible ten-year term. A gathering of Indians to protest this led to a clash with police. The murder victim's mother, Mrs. Sarah Bad Heart Bull, was arrested, on charges that called for a maximum sentence of thirty years.

On February 27, 1973, about three hundred Oglala Sioux, many of them members of the new militant organization called the American Indian Movement (AIM), entered the village of Wounded Knee and declared it liberated territory. Ellen Moves Camp later said: "We decided that we did need the American Indian Movement in here because our men were scared, they hung to the back. It was mostly the women that went forward and spoke out."

Within hours, more than two hundred FBI agents, federal marshals, and police of the Bureau of Indian Affairs surrounded and blockaded the town. They had armored vehicles, automatic rifles, machine guns, grenade launchers, and gas shells, and soon began firing. Gladys Bissonette said three weeks later: "Since we are here, in Wounded Knee, we've been shot at, over and over, always after dark. But last night we were hit the hardest. I guess the Great Spirit is with us, and no bullets find their way into our bodies. We ran through a hail of bullets one night. . . . We're going to hold our stand until we are completely an independent sovereign nation, Oglala Sioux Nation."

After the siege began, food supplies became short. Indians in Michigan sent food via a plane that landed inside the encampment. The next day FBI agents arrested the pilot and a doctor from Michigan who had hired the plane. In Nevada, eleven Indians were arrested for taking food, clothing, and medical supplies to South Dakota. In mid-April three more planes dropped 1,200 pounds of food, but as people scrambled to gather it up, a government helicopter appeared overhead and fired down on them while groundfire came from all sides. Frank Clearwater, an Indian man lying on a cot inside a church, was hit by a bullet. When his wife accompanied him to a hospital, she was arrested and jailed. Clearwater died.

There were more gun battles, another death. Finally, a negotiated peace was signed, in which both sides agreed to disarm (the Indians had refused to disarm while surrounded by armed men, recalling the 1890 massacre). The United States government promised to investigate Indian affairs, and a presidential commission would reexamine the 1868 treaty. The siege ended and 120 occupiers were arrested. The U.S. government then said that it had reexamined the 1868 treaty, found it valid, but that it was superseded by the U.S. power of "eminent domain"—the government's power to take land.

The Indians had held out for seventy-one days, creating a marvelous community inside the besieged territory. Communal kitchens were set up, a health clinic, and hospital. A Navajo Vietnam veteran:

> There's a tremendous amount of coolness considering that we're outgunned.... But people stay because they believe; they have a cause. That's why we lost in Viet Nam, cause there was no cause. We were fighting a rich man's war, for the rich man.... In Wounded Knee, we're doing pretty damn good, morale-wise. Because we can still laugh.

Messages of support had come to Wounded Knee from Australia, Finland, Germany, Italy, Japan, England. One message came from some of the Attica brothers, two of whom were Indians: "You fight for our Earth Mother and Her Children. Our spirits fight with you!" Wallace Black Elk replied: "Little Wounded Knee is turned into a giant world."

After Wounded Knee, in spite of the deaths, the trials, the use of the police and courts to try to break the movement, the Native American movement continued.

In the Akwesasne community itself, which put out *Akwesasne Notes*, the Indians had always insisted their territory was separate, not to be invaded by the white man's law. One day New York State police gave three traffic tickets to a Mohawk Indian truck driver, and a council of Indians met with a police lieutenant. At first, he insisted that he had to follow orders and give out tickets, even in Akwesasne territory, although he obviously was trying to be reasonable. He finally agreed that they would not arrest an Indian in the territory or even outside of it without first having a meeting with the Mohawk council. The lieutenant then sat down and lit a cigar. Indian Chief Joahquisoh, a distinguished-looking man with long hair, rose and addressed the lieutenant with a serious voice. "There is one more thing before you go," he said looking straight at the lieutenant. "I want to know," he said slowly, "if you've got an extra cigar." The meeting ended in laughter.

Akwesasne Notes continued to publish. On its poetry page, late autumn, 1976, appeared poems reflecting the spirit of the times. Ila Abernathy wrote:

> I am grass growing and the shearer of grass,
> I am the willow and the splitter of laths,
> weaver and the thing woven, marriage of willow and grass.
> I am frost on the land and the land's life,
> breath and beast and the sharp rock underfoot;
> in me the mountain lives, and the owl strikes,
> and I in them. I am the sun's twin,
> mover of blood and the blood lost,
> I am the deer and the deer's death;
> I am the burr in your conscience:
> acknowledge me.

And Buffy Sainte-Marie:

> You think I have visions
> because I am an Indian.
>
> I have visions because
> there are visions to be seen.

In the sixties and seventies, it was not just a women's movement, a prisoner's movement, an Indian movement. There was general revolt against oppressive, artificial, previously unquestioned ways of living. It touched every aspect of personal life: childbirth, childhood, love, sex, marriage, dress, music, art, sports, language, food, housing, religion, literature, death, schools.

The new temper, the new behavior, shocked many Americans. It created tensions. Sometimes it was seen as a "generation gap"—the younger generation moving far away from the older one in its way of life. But it seemed after a while to be not so much a matter of age—some young people remained "straight" while some middle-aged people were changing their ways and old people were beginning to behave in ways that astounded others.

Sexual behavior went through startling changes. Premarital sex was no longer a matter for silence. Men and women lived together outside of marriage, and struggled for words to describe the other person when introduced: "I want you to meet my . . . friend." Married couples candidly spoke of their affairs, and books appeared discussing "open marriage." Masturbation could be talked about openly, even approvingly. Homosexuality was no longer concealed. "Gay" men and "gay" women—lesbians—organized to combat discrimination against them, to give themselves a sense of community, to overcome shame and isolation.

All this was reflected in the literature and in the mass media. Court decisions overruled the local banning of books that were erotic or even pornographic. A new literature appeared (*The Joy of Sex* and others) to teach men and women how sexual fulfillment could be attained. The movies now did not hesitate to show nudity, although the motion picture industry, wanting to preserve principle as well as profit, set up a classification system (R for Restricted, X for prohibited to children). The language of sex became more common both in literature and in ordinary conversation.

All this was connected with new living arrangements. Especially among young people, communal living arrangements flourished. A few were truly communes—that is, based on the sharing of money and decisions, creating a community of intimacy, affection, trust. Most were practical arrangements for sharing the rent, with varying degrees of friendship and intimate association among the participants. It was no longer unusual for men and women to be "roommates"—in groups of two or three or larger, and without sexual relations—as practical, unself-conscious arrangements.

The most important thing about dress in the cultural change of the sixties was the greater informality. For women it was a continuation of the historic feminist movement's insistence on discarding of "feminine," hampering clothes. Many women stopped wearing bras. The restrictive "girdle"—almost a uniform of the forties and fifties—became rare. Young men and women dressed more nearly alike, in jeans, in discarded army uniforms. Men stopped wearing neckties, women of all ages wore pants more often—unspoken homage to Amelia Bloomer.

There was a new popular music of protest. Pete Seeger had been singing protest songs since the forties, but now he came into his own, his audiences much larger. Bob Dylan and Joan Baez, singing not only protest songs, but songs reflecting the new abandon, the new culture, became popular idols. A middle-aged woman on the West Coast, Malvina Reynolds, wrote and sang songs that fit her socialist thinking and her libertarian spirit, as well as her critique of the modern commercial culture. Everybody now, she sang, lived in "little boxes" and they "all came out just the same."

Bob Dylan was a phenomenon unto himself: powerful songs of protest, personal songs of freedom and self-expression. In an angry song, "Masters of War," he hopes that one day they will die and he will follow their casket "in the pale afternoon." "A Hard Rain's A-Gonna Fall" recounts the terrible stories of the last decades, of starvation and war, and tears, and dead ponies, and poisoned waters, and damp, dirty prisons—"It's a hard rain's a-gonna fall." Dylan sang a bitter antiwar song, "With God on Our Side," and one about the killer of the black activist Medgar Evers, "Only a Pawn in Their Game." He offered a challenge to the old, hope to the new, for "The Times They Are A-Changin'."

The Catholic upsurge against the war was part of a general revolt inside the Catholic Church, which had for so long been a bulwark of conservatism, tied to racism, jingoism, war. Priests and nuns resigned from the church, opened their lives to sex, got married and had children—sometimes without bothering to leave the church officially. True, there was still enormous popularity for the old-time religious revivalists, and Billy Graham commanded the obedience of millions, but now there were small swift currents against the mainstream.

There was a new suspicion of big business, of profiteering as the motive for ruining the environment. There was a reexamination of the "death industry," of moneymaking funerals and profitable tombstones, as in Jessica Mitford's *The American Way of Death*.

With the loss of faith in big powers—business, government, religion—there arose a stronger belief in self, whether individual or collective. The experts in all fields were now looked at skeptically: the belief grew that people could figure out for themselves what to eat, how to live their lives, how to be healthy. There was suspicion of the medical industry and campaigns against chemical preservatives, valueless foods, advertising. By now the scientific evidence of the evils of smoking—cancer, heart disease—was so powerful that the government barred advertising of cigarettes on television and in newspapers.

Traditional education began to be reexamined. The schools had taught whole generations the values of patriotism, of obeying authority, and had perpetuated ignorance, even contempt for people of other nations, races, Native Americans, women. Not just the content of education was challenged, but the style—the formality, the bureaucracy, the insistence on subordination to authority. This made only a small dent in the formidable national system of orthodox education, but it was reflected in a new generation of teachers all over the country, and a new literature to sustain them: Jonathan Kozol, *Death at an Early Age*; George

Denison, *The Lives of Children*; Ivan Illich, *De-schooling Society*.

Never in American history had more movements for change been concentrated in so short a span of years. But the system in the course of two centuries had learned a good deal about the control of people. In the mid-seventies, it went to work.

9

THE SEVENTIES: UNDER CONTROL?

In the early seventies, the system seemed out of control—it could not hold the loyalty of the public. As early as 1970, according to the University of Michigan's Survey Research Center, "trust in government" was low in every section of the population. And there was a significant difference by class. Of professional people, 40 percent had "low" political trust in the government; of unskilled blue-collar workers, 66 percent had "low" trust.

Public opinion surveys in 1971—after seven years of intervention in Vietnam—showed an unwillingness to come to the aid of other countries, assuming they were attacked by Communist-backed forces. Even for countries allied to the United States in the North Atlantic Treaty Organization, or Mexico, right on our southern border, there was no majority opinion for intervening with American troops. As for Thailand, if it were under Communist attack, only 12 percent of whites interrogated would send troops, 4 percent of nonwhites would do so.

In the summer of 1972, antiwar people in the Boston area were picketing Honeywell Corporation. The literature they distributed pointed out that Honeywell was producing antipersonnel weapons used in Vietnam, like the deadly cluster bomb that had riddled thousands of Vietnamese civilians with painful, hard-to-extricate pellets. About six hundred ballots were given to the Honeywell employees, asking if they thought that Honeywell should discontinue making these weapons. Of the 231 persons who returned the ballots, 131 said that Honeywell should stop, 88 said it should not. They were invited to make comments. A typical "no" comment: "Honeywell is not responsible for what the Department of Defense does with the goods it buys. . . ." A typical "yes" comment: "How may we have pride in our work when the entire basis for this work is immoral?"

The Survey Research Center of the University of Michigan had been posing the question: "Is the government run by a few big interests looking out for themselves?" The answer in 1964 had been "yes" from 26 percent of those polled; by 1972 the answer was "yes" from 53 percent of those polled. An article in the *American Political Science Review* by Arthur H. Miller, reporting on the extensive polling done by the Survey Research Center, said that the polls showed "widespread, basic discontent and political alienation." He added (political scientists often took on the worries of the Establishment): "What is startling and somewhat alarming is the rapid degree of change in this basic attitude over a period of only six years."

More voters than ever before refused to identify themselves as either Democrats or Republicans. Back in 1940, 20 percent of those polled called themselves "independents." In 1974, 34 percent called themselves "independents."

The courts, the juries, and even judges were not behaving as usual. Juries were acquitting radicals: Angela Davis, an acknowledged Communist, was acquitted by an all-white jury on the West Coast. Black Panthers, whom the government had tried in every way to malign and destroy, were freed by juries in several trials. A judge in western Massachusetts threw out a case against a young activist, Sam Lovejoy, who had toppled a 500-foot tower erected by a utility company trying to set up a nuclear plant. In Washington, D.C., in August 1973, a Superior Court judge refused to sentence six men charged with unlawful entry who had stepped from a White House tour line to protest the bombing of Cambodia.

Undoubtedly, much of this national mood of hostility to government and business came out of the Vietnam war, its 55,000 casualties, its moral shame, its exposure of government lies and atrocities. On top of this came the political disgrace of the Nixon administration in the scandals that came to be known by the one-word label "Watergate," and which led to the historic resignation from the presidency—the first in American history—of Richard Nixon in August 1974.

It began during the presidential campaign in June of 1972, when five burglars, carrying wiretapping and photo equipment, were caught in the act of breaking into the offices of the Democratic National Committee, in the Watergate apartment complex of Washington, D.C. One of the five, James McCord, Jr., worked for the Nixon campaign; he was "security" officer for the Committee to Re-elect the President (CREEP). Another of the five had an address book in which was listed the name of E. Howard Hunt, and Hunt's address was listed as the White House. He was assistant to Charles Colson, who was special counsel to President Nixon.

Both McCord and Hunt had worked for many years for the CIA. Hunt had been the CIA man in charge of the invasion of Cuba in 1961, and three of the Watergate burglars were veterans of the invasion. McCord, as CREEP security man, worked for the chief of CREEP, John Mitchell, the Attorney General of the United States.

Thus, due to an unforeseen arrest by police unaware of the high-level connections of the burglars, information was out to the public before anyone could stop it, linking the burglars to important officials in Nixon's campaign committee, to the CIA, and to Nixon's Attorney General. Mitchell denied any connection with the burglary, and Nixon, in a press conference five days after the event, said "the White House has had no involvement whatever in this particular incident."

What followed the next year, after a grand jury in September indicted the Watergate burglars—plus Howard Hunt and G. Gordon Liddy—was that, one after another, lesser officials of the Nixon administration, fearing prosecution, began to talk. They gave information in judicial proceedings, to a Senate investigating committee, to the press. They implicated not only John Mitchell, but Robert Haldeman and John Ehrlichman, Nixon's highest White House aides, and finally Richard Nixon himself—in not only the Watergate burglaries, but a whole series of illegal actions against political opponents and antiwar activists. Nixon and his aides lied again and again as they tried to cover up their involvement.

These facts came out in the various testimonies:

1. Attorney General John Mitchell controlled a secret fund of $350,000 to $700,000—to be used against the Democratic party—for forging letters, leaking false news items to the press, stealing campaign files.

2. Gulf Oil Corporation, ITT (International Telephone and Telegraph), American Airlines, and other huge American corporations had made illegal contributions, running into millions of dollars, to the Nixon campaign.

3. In September of 1971, shortly after the *New York Times* printed Daniel Ellsberg's copies of the top-secret *Pentagon Papers*, the administration planned and carried out—Howard Hunt and Gordon Liddy themselves doing it—the burglary of the office of Ellsberg's psychiatrist, looking for Ellsberg's records.

4. After the Watergate burglars were caught, Nixon secretly pledged to give them executive clemency if they were imprisoned, and suggested that up to a million dollars be given them to keep them quiet. In fact, $450,000 was given to them, on Erlichman's orders.

5. Nixon's nominee for head of the FBI (J. Edgar Hoover had recently died), L. Patrick Gray, revealed that he had turned over the FBI records on its investigation of the Watergate burglary to Nixon's legal assistant, John Dean, and that

Attorney General Richard Kleindienst (Mitchell had just resigned, saying he wanted to pursue his private life) had ordered him not to discuss Watergate with the Senate Judiciary Committee.

6. Two former members of Nixon's cabinet—John Mitchell and Maurice Stans—were charged with taking $250,000 from a financier named Robert Vesco in return for his help with a Securities and Exchange Commission investigation of Vesco's activities.

7. It turned out that certain material had disappeared from FBI files—material from a series of illegal wiretaps ordered by Henry Kissinger, placed on the telephones of four journalists and thirteen government officials—and was in the White House safe of Nixon's adviser John Erlichman.

8. One of the Watergate burglars, Bernard Barker, told the Senate committee that he had also been involved in a plan to physically attack Daniel Ellsberg while Ellsberg spoke at an antiwar rally in Washington.

9. A deputy director of the CIA testified that Haldeman and Ehrlichman told him it was Nixon's wish that the CIA tell the FBI not to pursue its investigation beyond the Watergate burglary.

10. Almost by accident, a witness told the Senate committee that President Nixon had tapes of all personal conversations and phone conversations at the White House. Nixon at first refused to turn over the tapes, and when he finally did, they had been tampered with: eighteen and a half minutes of one tape had been erased.

11. In the midst of all this, Nixon's Vice-President, Spiro Agnew, was indicted in Maryland for receiving bribes from Maryland contractors in return for political favors, and resigned from the vice-presidency in October 1973. Nixon appointed Congressman Gerald Ford to take Agnew's place.

12. Over $10 million in government money had been used by Nixon on his private homes in San Clemente and Key Biscayne on grounds of "security," and he had illegally taken—

with the aid of a bit of forgery—a $576,000 tax deduction for
some of his papers.

13. It was disclosed that for over a year in 1969–1970 the U.S. had
engaged in a secret, massive bombing of Cambodia, which it
kept from the American public and even from Congress.

It was a swift and sudden fall. In the November 1972 presidential election, Nixon and Agnew had won 60 percent of the
popular vote and carried every state except Massachusetts, defeat-
ing an antiwar candidate, Senator George McGovern. By June of
1973 a Gallup poll showed 67 percent of those polled thought
Nixon was involved in the Watergate break-in or lied to cover up.

By the fall of 1973 eight different resolutions had been introduced in the House of Representatives for the impeachment of
President Nixon. The following year a House committee drew up
a bill of impeachment to present it to a full House. Nixon's advisers told him it would pass the House by the required majority and
then the Senate would vote the necessary two-thirds majority to
remove him from office. On August 8, 1974, Nixon resigned.

Six months before Nixon resigned, the business magazine
Dun's Review reported a poll of three hundred corporation executives. Almost all had voted for Nixon in 1972, but now a majority
said he should resign. "Right now, 90% of Wall Street would
cheer if Nixon resigns," said a vice-president of Merrill Lynch
Government Securities. When he did, there was relief in all sec-
tors of the Establishment.

Gerald Ford, taking Nixon's office, said: "Our long national
nightmare is over." Newspapers, whether they had been for or
against Nixon, liberal or conservative, celebrated the successful,
peaceful culmination of the Watergate crisis. "The system is
working," said a long-time strong critic of the Vietnam war, *New
York Times* columnist Anthony Lewis. The two journalists who
had much to do with investigating and exposing Nixon, Carl
Bernstein and Bob Woodward of the Washington *Post*, wrote that
with Nixon's departure, there might be "restoration." All of this
was in a mood of relief, of gratitude.

No respectable American newspaper said what was said by Claude Julien, editor of *Le Monde Diplomatique* in September 1974. "The elimination of Mr. Richard Nixon leaves intact all the mechanisms and all the false values which permitted the Watergate scandal." Julien noted that Nixon's Secretary of State, Henry Kissinger, would remain at his post—in other words, that Nixon's foreign policy would continue. "That is to say," Julien wrote, "that Washington will continue to support General Pinochet in Chile, General Geisel in Brazil, General Stroessner in Paraguay, etc. . . ."

Months after Julien wrote this, it was disclosed that top Democratic and Republican leaders in the House of Representatives had given secret assurance to Nixon that if he resigned they would not support criminal proceedings against him. One of them, the ranking Republican of the Judiciary Committee, said: "We had all been shuddering about what two weeks of televised floor debates on impeachment would do, how it would tear the country apart and affect foreign policy." The *New York Times*'s articles that reported on Wall Street's hope for Nixon's resignation quoted one Wall Street financier as saying that if Nixon resigned: "What we will have is the same play with different players."

When Gerald Ford, a conservative Republican who had supported all of Nixon's policies, was nominated for President, a liberal Senator from California, Alan Cranston, spoke for him on the floor, saying he had polled many people, Republicans and Democrats, and found "an almost startling consensus of conciliation that is developing around him." When Nixon resigned and Ford became President, the *New York Times* said: "Out of the despair of Watergate has come an inspiring new demonstration of the uniqueness and strength of the American democracy." A few days later the *Times* wrote happily that the "peaceful transfer of power" brought "a cleansing sense of relief to the American people."

In the charges brought by the House Committee on Impeachment against Nixon, it seemed clear that the committee did not want to emphasize those elements in his behavior which were found in other Presidents and which might be repeated in the future. It stayed clear of Nixon's dealings with powerful corporations; it did not mention the bombing of Cambodia. It concentrated on things peculiar to Nixon, not on fundamental policies continuous among American Presidents, at home and abroad.

The word was out: get rid of Nixon, but keep the system. Theodore Sorensen, who had been an adviser to President Kennedy, wrote at the time of Watergate: "The underlying causes of the gross misconduct in our law-enforcement system now being revealed are largely personal, not institutional. Some structural changes are needed. All the rotten apples should be thrown out. But save the barrel."

Indeed, the barrel was saved. Nixon's foreign policy remained. The government's connections to corporate interests remained. Ford's closest friends in Washington were corporate lobbyists. Alexander Haig, who had been one of Nixon's closest advisers, who had helped in "processing" the tapes before turning them over to the public, and who gave the public misinformation about the tapes, was appointed by President Ford to be head of the armed forces of the North Atlantic Treaty Organization. One of Ford's first acts was to pardon Nixon, thus saving him from possible criminal proceedings and allowing him to retire with a huge pension in California.

The Establishment had cleansed itself of members of the club who had broken the rules—but it took some pains not to treat them too harshly. Those few who received jail sentences got short terms, were sent to the most easygoing federal institutions available, and were given special privileges not given to ordinary prisoners. Richard Kleindienst pleaded guilty; he got a $100 fine and one month in jail, which was suspended.

That Nixon would go, but that the power of the President to do anything he wanted in the name of "national security" would stay—this was underscored by a Supreme Court decision in July 1974. The Court said Nixon had to turn over his White House tapes to the special Watergate prosecutor. But at the same time it affirmed "the confidentiality of Presidential communications," which it could not uphold in Nixon's case, but which remained as a general principle when the President made a "claim of need to protect military, diplomatic or sensitive national security secrets."

The televised Senate Committee hearings on Watergate stopped suddenly before the subject of corporate connections was reached. It was typical of the selective coverage of important events by the television industry: bizarre shenanigans like the Watergate burglary were given full treatment, while instances of ongoing practice—the My Lai massacre, the secret bombing of Cambodia, the work of the FBI and CIA—were given the most fleeting attention. Dirty tricks against the Socialist Workers party, the Black Panthers, other radical groups, had to be searched for in a few newspapers. The whole nation heard the details of the quick break-in at the Watergate apartment; there was never a similar television hearing on the long-term break-in in Vietnam.

In the trial of John Mitchell and Maurice Stans for obstruction of justice in impeding a Securities and Exchange Commission investigation of Robert Vesco (a contributor to Nixon), George Bradford Cook, former general counsel of the SEC, testified that on November 13, 1972, he crouched in a Texas rice field while on a goose hunt with Maurice Stans, and told him he wanted to be chairman of the SEC. For this, he would cut out a critical paragraph in the SEC charges against Vesco that referred to Vesco's $200,000 secret contribution to the Nixon campaign.

Corporate influence on the White House is a permanent fact of the American system. Most of it is wise enough to stay within the law; under Nixon they took chances. An executive in the meatpacking industry said during the Watergate events that he had been approached by a Nixon campaign official and told that while a $25,000 contribution would be appreciated, "for $50,000 you get to talk to the President."

Many of these corporations gave money to both sides, so that whichever won they would have friends in the administration. Chrysler Corporation urged its executives to "support the party and candidate of their choice," and then collected the checks from them and delivered the checks to Republican or Democratic campaign committees.

International Telephone and Telegraph was an old hand at giving money on both sides. In 1960 it had made illegal contributions to Bobby Baker, who worked with Democratic Senators, including Lyndon Johnson. A senior vice-president of ITT was quoted by one of his assistants as saying the board of directors "have it set up to 'butter' both sides so we'll be in good position whoever wins." And in 1970, an ITT director, John McCone, who also had been head of the CIA, told Henry Kissinger, Secretary of State, and Richard Helms, CIA director, that ITT was willing to give $1 million to help the U.S. government in its plans to overthrow the Allende government in Chile.

In 1971 ITT planned to take over the $1½ billion Hartford Fire Insurance Company—the largest merger in corporate history. The antitrust division of the Justice Department moved to prosecute ITT for violating the antitrust laws. However, the prosecution did not take place and ITT was allowed to merge with Hartford. It was all settled out of court, in a secret arrangement in which ITT agreed to donate $400,000 to the Republican party. It seemed that Richard Kleindienst, deputy Attorney General, had six meetings with an ITT director named Felix Rohatyn, and then brought in the head of the antitrust division, Richard McLaren, who was persuaded by Rohatyn that to stop the merger would cause a "hardship" for ITT stockholders. McLaren agreed. He was later appointed a federal judge.

One of the items not mentioned in the impeachment charges and never televised in the Senate hearings was the way the government cooperated with the milk industry. In early 1971 the Secretary of Agriculture announced the government would not increase its price supports for milk—the regular subsidy to the big milk producers. Then the Associated Milk Producers began giving money to the Nixon campaign, met in the White House with Nixon and the Secretary of Agriculture, gave more money, and the secretary announced that "new analysis" made it necessary to raise milk price supports from $4.66 to $4.93 a hundredweight. More contributions were made, until the total exceeded $400,000. The price increases added $500 million to the profits of dairy farmers (mostly big corporations) at the expense of consumers.

Whether Nixon or Ford or any Republican or Democrat was President, the system would work pretty much the same way. A Senate subcommittee investigating multinational corporations revealed a document (given passing mention in a few newspapers) in which oil company economists discussed holding back production of oil to keep prices up. ARAMCO—the Arabian-American Oil Corporation, 75 percent of whose stock was held by American oil companies and 25 percent by Saudi Arabia—had made $1 profit on a barrel of oil in 1973. In 1974 it was making $4.50. None of this would be affected by who was President.

Even in the most diligent of investigations in the Watergate affair, that of Archibald Cox, a special prosecutor later fired by Nixon, the corporations got off easy. American Airlines, which admitted making illegal contributions to the Nixon campaign, was fined $5,000; Goodyear was fined $5,000; 3M Corporation was fined $3,000. A Goodyear official was fined $1,000; a 3M official was fined $500. The *New York Times* (October 20, 1973) reported:

> Mr. Cox charged them only with the misdemeanor of making illegal contributions. The misdemeanor, under the law, involved "nonwillful" contributions. The felony count, involving willful contributions, is punishable by a fine of $10,000 and/or a two-year jail term; the misdemeanor by a $1000 fine and/or a one-year jail term.
>
> Asked at the courthouse here how the two executives—who had admitted making the payments—could be charged with making nonwilling contributions, Mr. McBride [Cox's staff] replied: "That's a legal question which frankly baffles me as well."

With Gerald Ford in office, the long continuity in American policy was maintained. He continued Nixon's policy of aid to the

Saigon regime, apparently still hoping that the Thieu government would remain stable. The head of a congressional committee, John Calkins, visiting South Vietnam just around the time of
Nixon's fall from office, reported:

> The South Vietnamese Army shows every sign of being an effective
> and spirited security force. . . .
>
> Oil exploration will begin very soon. Tourism can be encouraged
> by continued security of scenic and historic areas and by the erection
> of a new Hyatt Hotel. . . .
>
> South Vietnam needs foreign investment to finance these and
> other developments. . . . She has a large labor pool of talented,
> industrious people whose cost of labor is far less than Hong Kong,
> Singapore, or even Korea or Taiwan. . . .
>
> I also feel there is much profit to be made there. The combina-
> tion of serving both God and Mammon had proved attractive to
> Americans and others in the past. . . . Vietnam can be the next "take
> off" capitalistic showplace in Asia.

In the spring of 1975, everything that radical critics of American policy in Vietnam had been saying—that without American
troops, the Saigon government's lack of popular support would be
revealed—came true. An offensive by North Vietnamese troops,
left in the South by terms of the 1973 truce, swept through town
after town.

Ford continued to be optimistic. He was the last of a long line
of government officials and journalists who promised victory.
(Secretary of Defense Robert McNamara, February 19, 1963:
"Victory is in sight." General William Westmoreland, November
15, 1967: "I have never been more encouraged in my four years in
Vietnam." Columnist Joseph Alsop, November 1, 1972: "Hanoi
has accepted near-total defeat.") On April 16, 1975, Ford said: "I
am absolutely convinced if Congress made available $722 million
in military assistance by the time I asked—or sometime shortly
thereafter—the South Vietnamese could stabilize the military situation in Vietnam today."

Two weeks later, April 29, 1975, the North Vietnamese moved into Saigon, and the war was over.

Most of the Establishment had already—despite Ford and a few stalwarts—given up on Vietnam. What they worried about was the readiness of the American public now to support other military actions overseas. There were trouble signs in the months before the defeat in Vietnam.

In early 1975 Senator John C. Culver of Iowa was unhappy that Americans would not fight for Korea: "He said that Vietnam had taken a mighty toll on the national will of the American people." Shortly before that, Secretary of Defense James Schlesinger, speaking to the Georgetown Center for Strategic and International Studies, was reported as being "generally gloomy," saying that "the world no longer regarded American military power as awesome."

In March 1975 a Catholic organization, making a survey of American attitudes on abortion, learned other things. To the statement: "The people running this country (government, political, church and civic leaders) don't tell us the truth," more than 83 percent agreed.

New York Times international correspondent C. L. Sulzberger, a consistent supporter of government cold-war foreign policy, wrote in a troubled mood in early 1975 from Ankara, Turkey, that "the glow has worn off from the era of the Truman Doctrine" (when military aid was given to Greece and Turkey). He added: "And one cannot say that the bleak outlook here is balanced by any brilliant United States successes in Greece, where a vast mob recently battered the United States Embassy." He concluded, "There must be something seriously wrong with the way we present ourselves these days." The problem, according to Sulzberger, was not the United States' behavior, but the way this behavior was presented to the world.

It was a few months after these reports, in April of 1975, that Secretary of State Kissinger, invited to be commencement speaker at the University of Michigan, was faced with petitions protesting the invitation, because of Kissinger's role in the Vietnam war. Also a counter-commencement program was planned. He withdrew. It was a low time for the administration. Vietnam was "lost" (the very word supposed it was ours to lose). Kissinger was quoted that April (by Washington *Post* columnist Tom Braden): "The U.S. must carry out some act somewhere in the world which shows its determination to continue to be a world power."

The following month came the *Mayaguez* affair.

The *Mayaguez* was an American cargo ship sailing from South Vietnam to Thailand in mid-May 1975, just three weeks after the victory of the revolutionary forces in Vietnam. When it came close to an island in Cambodia, where a revolutionary regime had just taken power, the ship was stopped by the Cambodians, taken to a port at a nearby island, and the crew removed to the mainland. The crew later described their treatment as courteous: "A man who spoke English greeted us with a handshake and welcomed us to Cambodia." The press reported: "Captain Miller and his men all say they were never abused by their captors. There were even accounts of kind treatment—of Cambodian soldiers feeding them first and eating what the Americans left, of the soldiers giving the seamen the mattresses off their beds." But the Cambodians did ask the crew about spying and the CIA.

President Ford sent a message to the Cambodian government to release the ship and crew, and when thirty-six hours had elapsed and there was no response (the message had been given to the Chinese liaison mission in Washington, but was returned the next day, "ostensibly undelivered," one press account said), he began military operations—U.S. planes bombed Cambodian ships. They strafed the very boat that was taking the American sailors to the mainland.

The men had been detained on a Monday morning. On Wednesday evening the Cambodians released them—putting them on a fishing boat headed for the American fleet. That afternoon, knowing the seamen had been taken off Tang Island, Ford nevertheless ordered a marine assault on Tang Island. That assault began about 7:15 Wednesday evening, but an hour earlier the crewmen were already headed back to the American fleet.

About 7:00 P.M. the release had been announced on the radio in Bangkok. Indeed, the boat carrying the returned crewmen was spotted by a U.S. reconnaissance plane that signaled them.

Not mentioned in any press account at the time or in any government statement was a fact that emerged in October 1976 when the General Accounting Office made a report on the *Mayaguez* affair: the U.S. had received a message from a Chinese diplomat saying China was using its influence with Cambodia on the ship "and expected it to be released soon." This message was received fourteen hours before the marine assault began.

No American soldier was hurt by the Cambodians. The marines invading Tang Island, however, met unexpectedly tough resistance, and of two hundred invaders, one-third were soon dead or wounded (this exceeded the casualty rate in the World War II invasion of Iwo Jima). Five of eleven helicopters in the invasion force were blown up or disabled. Also, twenty-three Americans were killed in a helicopter crash over Thailand on their way to participate in the action, a fact the government tried to keep secret. All together, forty-one Americans were killed in the military actions ordered by Ford. There were thirty-nine sailors on the *Mayaguez*. Why the rush to bomb, strafe, attack? Why, even after the ship and crew were recovered, did Ford order American planes to bomb the Cambodian mainland, with untold Cambodian casualties? What could justify such a combination of moral blindness and military bungling?

The answer to this came soon: It was necessary to show the world that giant America, defeated by tiny Vietnam, was still powerful and resolute. The *New York Times* reported on May 16, 1975:

> Administration officials, including Secretary of State Henry Kissinger and Secretary of Defense James Schlesinger, were said to have been eager to find some dramatic means of underscoring President Ford's stated intention to "maintain our leadership on a world-wide basis." The occasion came with the capture of the vessel. . . . Administration officials . . . made it clear that they welcomed the opportunity. . . .

Another press dispatch from Washington, in the midst of the *Mayaguez* events, said: "High-ranking sources familiar with military strategy and planning said privately that the seizure of the vessel might provide the test of American determination in Southeast Asia that, they asserted, the U.S. had been seeking since the collapse of allied governments in South Vietnam and Cambodia."

Columnist James Reston wrote: "In fact, the Administration almost seems grateful for the opportunity to demonstrate that the President can act quickly. . . . Officials here have been bridling over a host of silly taunts about the American 'paper tiger' and hope the Marines have answered the charge."

It was not surprising that Secretary of Defense Schlesinger called it a "very successful operation," done "for purposes that were necessary for the well-being of this society." But why would the prestigious *Times* columnist James Reston, a strong critic of Nixon and Watergate, call the *Mayaguez* operation "melodramatic and successful"? And why would the *New York Times*, which had criticized the Vietnam war, talk about the "admirable efficiency" of the operation?

What seemed to be happening was that the Establishment—Republicans, Democrats, newspapers, television—was closing ranks behind Ford and Kissinger, and behind the idea that American authority must be asserted everywhere in the world.

Congress at this time behaved much as it had done in the early years of the Vietnam war, like a flock of sheep. Back in 1973, in a mood of fatigue and disgust with the Vietnam war, Congress had passed a War Powers Act that required the President, before taking military action, to consult with Congress. In the *Mayaguez* affair, Ford ignored this—he had several aides make phone calls to eighteen Congressmen to inform them that military action was under way. But, as I. F. Stone said (he was the maverick journalist who published the anti-Establishment *I. F. Stone's Weekly*), "Congress raped as easily as it did in the Tonkin Gulf affair." Congressman Robert Drinan of Massachusetts was an exception. Senator McGovern, Nixon's presidential opponent in 1976 and long-time antiwar critic, opposed the action. So did Senator Gaylord Nelson of Wisconsin. Senator Edward Brooke raised questions. Senator Edward Kennedy did not speak out, nor did other Senators who during the Vietnam war had influenced Congress to ban further military action in Indochina but now said their own legislation did not apply.

Secretary of State Kissinger would say: "We are forced into this." When Kissinger was asked why the U.S. was risking the lives of the *Mayaguez* seamen by firing on ships in the area without knowing where they were, he called it a "necessary risk."

Kissinger also said the incident "ought to make clear that there are limits beyond which the United States cannot be pushed, that the United States is prepared to defend those interests, and that it can get public support and congressional support for these actions."

Indeed, Congressmen, Democrats as well as Republicans, who had been critical of the Vietnam war now seemed anxious to pull things together in a unified show of strength to the rest of the world. A week before the *Mayaguez* affair (two weeks before Saigon fell), fifty-six Congressmen had signed a statement saying: "Let no nation read the events in Indochina as the failure of the American will." One of them was a black Congressman from Georgia, Andrew Young.

It was a complex process of consolidation that the system undertook in 1975. It included old-type military actions, like the *Mayaguez* affair, to assert authority in the world and at home. There was also a need to satisfy a disillusioned public that the system was criticizing and correcting itself. The standard way was to conduct publicized investigations that found specific culprits but left the system intact. Watergate had made both the FBI and the CIA look bad—breaking the laws they were sworn to uphold, cooperating with Nixon in his burglary jobs and illegal wiretapping. In 1975, congressional committees in the House and Senate began investigations of the FBI and CIA.

The CIA inquiry disclosed that the CIA had gone beyond its original mission of gathering intelligence and was conducting secret operations of all kinds. For instance, back in the 1950s, it had administered the drug LSD to unsuspecting Americans to test its effects: one American scientist, given such a dose by a CIA agent, leaped from a New York hotel window to his death in the 1950s.

The CIA had also been involved in assassination plots against Castro of Cuba and other heads of state. It had introduced African swine fever virus into Cuba in 1971, bringing disease and then slaughter to 500,000 pigs. A CIA operative told a reporter he delivered the virus from an army base in the Canal Zone to anti-Castro Cubans.

It was also learned from the investigation that the CIA—with the collusion of a secret Committee of Forty headed by Henry Kissinger—had worked to "destabilize" the Chilean government headed by Salvadore Allende, a Marxist who had been elected president in one of the rare free elections in Latin America. ITT, with large interests in Cuba, played a part in this operation. When in 1974 the American ambassador to Chile, David Popper, suggested to the Chilean junta (which, with U.S. aid, had over-thrown Allende) that they were violating human rights, he was rebuked by Kissinger, who sent word: "Tell Popper to cut out the political science lectures."

The investigation of the FBI disclosed many years of illegal actions to disrupt and destroy radical groups and left-wing groups of all kinds. The FBI had sent forged letters, engaged in burglaries (it admitted to ninety-two between 1960 and 1966), opened mail illegally, and, in the case of Black Panther leader Fred Hampton, seems to have conspired in murder.

Valuable information came out of the investigations, but it was just enough, and in just the right way—moderate press coverage, little television coverage, thick books of reports with limited readership—to give the impression of an honest society correct-ing itself.

The investigations themselves revealed the limits of govern-ment willingness to probe into such activities. The Church Com-mittee, set up by the Senate, conducted its investigations with the cooperation of the agencies being investigated and, indeed, submitted its findings on the CIA to the CIA to see if there was material that the Agency wanted omitted. Thus, while there was much valuable material in the report, there is no way of knowing how much more there was—the final report was a compromise between committee diligence and CIA caution.

The Pike Committee, set up in the House of Representatives, made no such agreement with the CIA or FBI, and when it issued its final report, the same House that had authorized its investigation voted to keep the report secret. When the report was leaked via a CBS newscaster, Daniel Schorr, to the *Village Voice* in New York, it was never printed by the important newspapers in the country—the *Times*, the Washington *Post*, or others. Schorr was suspended by CBS. It was another instance of cooperation between the mass media and the government in instances of "national security."

The Church Committee, in its report of CIA attempts to assassinate Fidel Castro and other foreign leaders, revealed an interesting point of view. The committee seemed to look on the killing of a head of state as an unpardonable violation of some gentlemen's agreement among statesmen, much more deplorable than military interventions that killed ordinary people. The Committee wrote, in the introduction to its assassination report:

> Once methods of coercion and violence are chosen, the probability of loss of life is always present. There is, however, a significant difference between a cold-blooded, targeted, intentional killing of an individual foreign leader and other forms of intervening in the affairs of foreign nations.

The Church Committee uncovered CIA operations to secretly influence the minds of Americans:

> The CIA is now using several hundred American academics (administrators, faculty members, graduate students engaged in teaching) who, in addition to providing leads and, on occasion, making intro-

ductions for intelligence purposes, write books and other material to be used for propaganda purposes abroad. . . . These academics are located in over 100 American colleges, universities and related institutions. At the majority of institutions, no one other than the individual concerned is aware of the CIA link. At the others, at least one university official is aware of the operational use of academics on his campus. . . . The CIA considers these operational relationships within the U.S. academic community as perhaps its most sensitive domestic area and has strict controls governing these operations. . . .

In 1961 the chief of the CIA's Covert Action Staff wrote that books were "the most important weapon of strategic propaganda." The Church Committee found that more than a thousand books were produced, subsidized, or sponsored by the CIA before the end of 1967.

When Kissinger testified before the Church Committee about the bombing of Laos, orchestrated by the CIA as a secret activity, he said: "I do not believe in retrospect that it was a good national policy to have the CIA conduct the war in Laos. I think we should have found some other way of doing it." There was no indication that anyone on the Committee challenged this idea—that what was done should have been done, but by another method.

Thus, in 1974–1975, the system was acting to purge the country of its rascals and restore it to a healthy, or at least to an acceptable, state. The resignation of Nixon, the succession of Ford, the exposure of bad deeds by the FBI and CIA—all aimed to regain the badly damaged confidence of the American people. However, even with these strenuous efforts, there were still many signs in the American public of suspicion, even hostility, to the leaders of government, military, big business.

Two months after the end of the Vietnam war, only 20 percent of Americans polled thought the collapse of the Saigon government was a threat to United States security.

June 14, 1975, was Flag Day, and President Gerald Ford spoke at Fort Benning, Georgia, where the army staged a march symbolizing its involvement in thirteen wars. Ford commented that he was glad to see so many flags, but a reporter covering the event wrote: "Actually, there were few American flags to be seen near the President's reviewing stand. One, held aloft by demonstrators, bore an inked-in inscription saying, 'No more genocide in our name.' It was torn down by spectators as their neighbors applauded."

That July the Lou Harris poll, looking at the public's confidence in the government from 1966 to 1975, reported that confidence in the military during that period had dropped from 62 percent to 29 percent, in business from 55 percent to 18 percent, in both President and Congress from 42 percent to 13 percent. Shortly after that, another Harris poll reported "65% of Americans oppose military aid abroad because they feel it allows dictatorships to maintain control over their population."

Perhaps much of the general dissatisfaction was due to the economic state of most Americans. Inflation and unemployment had been rising steadily since 1973, which was the year when, according to a Harris poll, the number of Americans feeling "alienated" and "disaffected" with the general state of the country climbed (from 29 percent in 1966) to over 50 percent. After Ford succeeded Nixon, the percentage of "alienated" was 55 percent. The survey showed that people were troubled most of all by inflation.

In the fall of 1975 a *New York Times* survey of 1,559 persons, and interviews with sixty families in twelve cities, showed "a substantial decline in optimism about the future." The *Times* reported:

> Inflation, the apparent inability of the country to solve its economic problems, and a foreboding that the energy crisis will mean a permanent step backward for the nation's standard of living have made inroads into Americans' confidence, expectations, and aspirations. . . .
>
> Pessimism about the future is particularly acute among those who earn less than $7000 annually, but it is also high within families whose annual incomes range from $10,000 to $15,000. . . .
>
> There is also concern that . . . no longer will hard work and a

conscientious effort to save money bring them a nice home in the suburbs. . . .

Even higher-income people, the survey found, "are not as optimistic now as they were in past years, indicating that discontent is moving up from the lower middle-income to higher economic levels."

Around the same time, that fall of 1975, public opinion analysts testifying before a congressional committee reported, according to the *New York Times*, "that public confidence in the Government and in the country's economic future is probably lower than it has ever been since they began to measure such things scientifically."

Government statistics suggested the reasons. The Census Bureau reported that from 1974 to 1975 the number of Americans "legally" poor (that is, below an income of $5,500) had risen 10 percent and was now 25.9 million people. Also, the unemployment rate, which had been 5.6 percent in 1974, had risen to 8.3 percent in 1975, and the number of people who exhausted their unemployment benefits increased from 2 million in 1974 to 4.3 million in 1975.

Government figures, however, generally underestimated the amount of poverty, set the "legally" poor level too low, and underestimated the amount of unemployment. For instance, if 16.6 percent of the population averaged six months of unemployment during 1975, or 33.2 percent averaged three months of unemployment, the "average annual figure" given by the government was 8.3 percent, which sounded better.

In the year 1976, with a presidential election approaching, there was worry in the Establishment about the public's faith in the system. William Simon, Secretary of the Treasury under both Nixon and Ford (before then an investment banker earning over $2 million a year), spoke in the fall of 1976 to a Business Council meeting in Hot Springs, Virginia. He said that when "so much of the world is lurching towards socialism or totalitarianism" it was urgent to make the American business system understood, because "private enterprise is losing by default—in many of our schools, in much of the communications media, and in a growing portion of the public consciousness." His speech could well be taken to represent the thinking of the American corporate elite:

> Vietnam, Watergate, student unrest, shifting moral codes, the worst recession in a generation, and a number of other jarring cultural shocks have all combined to create a new climate of questions and doubt. . . . It all adds up to a general malaise, a society-wide crisis of institutional confidence. . . .

Too often, Simon said, Americans "have been taught to distrust the very word profit and the profit motive that makes our prosperity possible, to somehow feel this system, that has done more to alleviate human suffering and privation than any other, is somehow cynical, selfish, and amoral." We must, Simon said, "get across the human side of capitalism."

As the United States prepared in 1976 to celebrate the bicentennial of the Declaration of Independence, a group of intellectuals and political leaders from Japan, the United States, and Western Europe, organized into "The Trilateral Commission," issued a report. It was entitled "The Governability of Democracies." Samuel Huntington, a political science professor at Harvard University and long-time consultant to the White House on the war in Vietnam, wrote the part of the report that dealt with the United States. He called it "The Democratic Distemper" and identified the problem he was about to discuss: "The 1960's witnessed a dramatic upsurge of democratic fervor in America." In the sixties, Huntington wrote, there was a huge growth of citizen participation "in the forms of marches, demonstrations, protest movements, and 'cause' organizations." There were also "markedly higher levels of self-consciousness on the part of blacks, Indians, Chicanos, white ethnic groups, students and women, all of whom became mobilized and organized in new ways. . . ." There was a "marked expansion of white-collar unionism," and all this added up to "a reassertion of equality as a goal in social, economic and political life."

Huntington pointed to the signs of decreasing government

authority: The great demands in the sixties for equality had transformed the federal budget. In 1960 foreign affairs spending was 53.7 percent of the budget, and social spending was 22.3 percent. By 1974 foreign affairs took 33 percent and social spending 31 percent. This seemed to reflect a change in public mood: In 1960 only 18 percent of the public said the government was spending too much on defense, but in 1969 this jumped to 52 percent.

Huntington was troubled by what he saw:

> The essence of the democratic surge of the 1960's was a general challenge to existing systems of authority, public and private. In one form or another, this challenge manifested itself in the family, the university, business, public and private associations, politics, the governmental bureaucracy, and the military services. People no longer felt the same obligation to obey those whom they had previously considered superior to themselves in age, rank, status, expertise, character, or talents.

All this, he said, "produced problems for the governability of democracy in the 1970's. . . ."

Critical in all this was the decline in the authority of the President. And:

> To the extent that the United States was governed by anyone during the decades after World War II, it was governed by the President acting with the support and cooperation of key individuals and groups in the executive office, the federal bureaucracy, Congress, and the more important businesses, banks, law firms, foundations, and media, which constitute the private sector's "Establishment."

This was probably the frankest statement ever made by an Establishment adviser.

Huntington further said that the President, to win the election, needed the support of a broad coalition of people. However: "The day after his election, the size of his majority is almost—if not entirely—irrelevant to his ability to govern the country. What counts then is his ability to mobilize support from the leaders of key institutions in a society and government. . . . This coalition must include key people in Congress, the executive branch, and the private-sector 'Establishment.'" He gave examples:

> Truman made a point of bringing a substantial number of non-partisan soldiers, Republican bankers, and Wall Street lawyers into his Administration. He went to the existing sources of power in the country to get help he needed in ruling the country. Eisenhower in part inherited this coalition and was in part almost its creation. . . . Kennedy attempted to re-create a somewhat similar structure of alliances.

What worried Huntington was the loss in governmental authority. For instance, the opposition to Vietnam had brought the abolition of the draft. "The question necessarily arises, however, whether if a new threat to security should materialize in the future (as it inevitably will at some point), the government will possess the authority to command the resources, as well as the sacrifices, which are necessary to meet that threat."

Huntington saw the possible end of that quarter century when "the United States was the hegemonic power in a system of world order." His conclusion was that there had developed "an excess of democracy," and he suggested "desirable limits to the extension of political democracy."

Huntington was reporting all this to an organization that was very important to the future of the United States. The Trilateral Commission was organized in early 1973 by David Rockefeller and Zbigniew Brzezinski. Rockefeller was an official of the Chase Manhattan Bank and a powerful financial figure in the United States and the world; Brzezinski, a Columbia University professor, specialized in international relations and was a consultant to the State Department. As reported in the *Far Eastern Economic Review* (March 25, 1977) by Robert Manning:

The initiative for the Commission came entirely from Rockefeller. According to George Franklin, the Commission's executive secretary, Rockefeller "was getting worried about the deteriorating relations between the United States, Europe and Japan." Franklin explained that Rockefeller began to present his ideas to another elite fraternity: ". . . at the Bilderberg Group—a very distinguished Anglo-American group which has been meeting for a long time— Mike Blumenthal said he thought things were in a very serious condition in the world and couldn't some kind of private group do more about it? . . . So then David again made his proposal. . . ." Then Brzezinski, a close friend of Rockefeller's, carried the Rockefeller-funded ball and organized the Commission.

It seems probable that the "very serious condition" mentioned as the reason for the Trilateral Commission was the need for greater unity among Japan, Western Europe, and the United States in the face of a much more complicated threat to tricontinental capitalism than a monolithic Communism: revolutionary movements in the Third World. These movements had directions of their own.

The Trilateral Commission wanted also to deal with another situation. Back in 1967, George Ball, who had been Undersecretary of State for economic affairs in the Kennedy administration and who was director of Lehman Brothers, a large investment banking firm, told members of the International Chamber of Commerce:

In these twenty postwar years, we have come to recognize in action, though not always in words, that the political boundaries of nation-states are too narrow and constricted to define the scope and activities of modern business.

To show the growth of international economics for United States corporations, one would only have to note the situation in banking. In 1960 there were eight United States banks with foreign branches; in 1974 there were 129. The assets of these overseas branches amounted to $3.5 billion in 1960, $155 billion in 1974.

The Trilateral Commission apparently saw itself as helping to create the necessary international links for the new multinational economy. Its members came from the highest circles of politics, business, and the media in Western Europe, Japan, and the United States. They were from Chase Manhattan, Lehman Brothers, Bank of America, Banque de Paris, Lloyd's of London, Bank of Tokyo, etc. Oil, steel, auto, aeronautic, and electric industries were represented. Other members were from *Time* magazine, the Washington *Post*, the Columbia Broadcasting System, *Die Zeit*, the *Japan Times*, *The Economist* of London, and more.

1976 was not only a presidential election year—it was the much-anticipated year of the bicentennial celebration, and it was filled with much-publicized events all over the country. The great effort that went into the celebration suggests that it was seen as a way of restoring American patriotism, invoking the symbols of history to unite people and government and put aside the protest mood of the recent past.

But there did not seem to be great enthusiasm for it. When the 200th anniversary of the Boston Tea Party was celebrated in Boston, an enormous crowd turned out, not for the official celebration, but for the "People's Bi-Centennial" countercelebration, where packages marked "Gulf Oil" and "Exxon" were dumped into the Boston Harbor, to symbolize opposition to corporate power in America.

10

CARTER-REAGAN-BUSH: THE BIPARTISAN CONSENSUS

Halfway through the twentieth century, the historian Richard Hofstadter, in his book *The American Political Tradition*, examined our important national leaders, from Jefferson and Jackson to Herbert Hoover and the two Roosevelts—Republicans and Democrats, liberals and conservatives. Hofstadter concluded that "the range of vision embraced by the primary contestants in the major parties has always been bounded by the horizons of property and enterprise. . . . They have accepted the economic virtues of capitalist culture as necessary qualities of man. . . . That culture has been intensely nationalistic. . . ."

Coming to the end of the century, observing its last twenty-five years, we have seen exactly that limited vision Hofstadter talked about—a capitalistic encouragement of enormous fortunes alongside desperate poverty, a nationalistic acceptance of war and preparations for war. Governmental power swung from Republicans to Democrats and back again, but neither party showed itself capable of going beyond that vision.

After the disastrous war in Vietnam came the scandals of Watergate. There was a deepening economic insecurity for much of the population, along with environmental deterioration, and a growing culture of violence and family disarray. Clearly, such fundamental problems could not be solved without bold changes in the social and economic structure. But no major party candidates proposed such changes. The "American political tradition" held fast.

In recognition of this, perhaps only vaguely conscious of this, voters stayed away from the polls in large numbers, or voted without enthusiasm. More and more they declared, if only by nonparticipation, their alienation from the political system. In 1960, 63 percent of those eligible to vote voted in the presidential election. By 1976, this figure had dropped to 53 percent. In a CBS News and *New York Times* survey, over half of the respondents said that public officials didn't care about people like them. A typical response came from a plumber: "The President of the United States isn't going to solve our problems. The problems are too big."

There was a troubling incongruity in the society. Electoral politics dominated the press and television screens, and the doings of presidents, members of Congress, Supreme Court justices, and other officials were treated as if they constituted the history of the country. Yet there was something artificial in all this, something pumped up, a straining to persuade a skeptical public that this was all, that they must rest their hopes for the future in Washington politicians, none of whom were inspiring because it seemed that behind the bombast, the rhetoric, the promises, their major concern was their own political power.

The distance between politics and the people was reflected clearly in the culture. In what was supposed to be the best of the media, uncontrolled by corporate interest—that is, in *public* television, the public was largely invisible. On the leading political forum on public television, the nightly "MacNeil-Lehrer Report," the public was uninvited, except as viewer of an endless parade of Congressmen, Senators, government bureaucrats, experts of various kinds.

On commercial radio, the usual narrow band of consensus, excluding fundamental criticism, was especially apparent. In the mid-1980s, with Ronald Reagan as President, the "fairness doctrine" of the Federal Communications Commission, requiring air time for dissenting views, was eliminated. By the 1990s, "talk radio" had perhaps 20 million listeners, treated to daily tirades from right-wing talk-show "hosts," with left-wing guests uninvited.

A citizenry disillusioned with politics and with what pretended to be intelligent discussions of politics turned its attention (or had its attention turned) to entertainment, to gossip, to ten thousand schemes for self-help. Those at its margins became violent, finding scapegoats within one's group (as with poor-black on poor-black violence), or against other races, immigrants, demonized foreigners, welfare mothers, minor criminals (standing in for untouchable major criminals).

There were other citizens, those who tried to hold on to ideas and ideals still remembered from the sixties and early seventies, not just by recollecting but by acting. Indeed, all across the country there was a part of the public unmentioned in the media, ignored by political leaders—energetically active in thousands of local groups around the country. These organized groups were campaigning for environmental protection or women's rights or decent health care (including anguished concern about the horrors of AIDS) or housing for the homeless, or against military spending.

This activism was unlike that of the sixties, when the surge of protest against race segregation and war became an overwhelming national force. It struggled uphill, against callous political leaders, trying to reach fellow Americans most of whom saw little hope in either the politics of voting or the politics of protest.

The presidency of Jimmy Carter, covering the years 1977 to 1980, seemed an attempt by one part of the Establishment, that represented in the Democratic party, to recapture a disillusioned citizenry. But Carter, despite a few gestures toward black people and the poor, despite talk of "human rights" abroad, remained within the historic political boundaries of the American system, protecting corporate wealth and power, maintaining a huge military machine that drained the national wealth, allying the United States with right-wing tyrannies abroad.

Carter seemed to be the choice of that international group of powerful influence-wielders—the Trilateral Commission. Two founding members of the commission, according to the *Far Eastern Economic Review*—David Rockefeller and Zbigniew Brzezinski—thought Carter was the right person for the presidential election of 1976 given that "the Watergate-plagued Republican Party was a sure loser. . . ."

Carter's job as President, from the point of view of the Establishment, was to halt the rushing disappointment of the American people with the government, with the economic system, with disastrous military ventures abroad. In his campaign, he tried to speak to the disillusioned and angry. His strongest appeal was to blacks, whose rebellion in the late sixties was the most frightening challenge to authority since the labor and unemployed upsurges in the thirties.

His appeal was "populist"—that is, he appealed to various elements of American society who saw themselves beleaguered by the powerful and wealthy. Although he himself was a millionaire peanut grower, he presented himself as an ordinary American farmer. Although he had been a supporter of the Vietnam war until its end, he presented himself as a sympathizer with those who had been against the war, and he appealed to many of the young rebels of the sixties by his promise to cut the military budget.

In a much-publicized speech to lawyers, Carter spoke out against the use of the law to protect the rich. He appointed a black woman, Patricia Harris, as Secretary of Housing and Urban Development, and a black civil rights veteran, Andrew Young, as ambassador to the United Nations. He gave the job of heading the domestic youth service corps to a young former antiwar activist, Sam Brown.

His most crucial appointments, however, were in keeping with the Trilateral Commission report of Harvard political scientist Samuel Huntington, which said that, whatever groups voted for a president, once elected "what counts then is his ability to mobilize support from the leaders of key institutions." Brzezinski, a traditional cold war intellectual, became Carter's National Security Adviser. His Secretary of Defense, Harold Brown, had, during the Vietnam war, according to the *Pentagon Papers*, "envisaged the elimination of virtually all the constraints under which the bombing then operated." His Secretary of Energy, James Schlesinger, as Secretary of Defense under Nixon, was described by a member of the Washington press corps as showing "an almost missionary drive in seeking to reverse a downward trend in the defense budget." Schlesinger was also a strong proponent of nuclear energy.

His other cabinet appointees had strong corporate connections. A financial writer wrote, not long after Carter's election: "So far, Mr. Carter's actions, commentary, and particularly his Cabinet appointments, have been highly reassuring to the business community." Veteran Washington correspondent Tom Wicker wrote: "The available evidence is that Mr. Carter so far is opting for Wall Street's confidence."

Carter did initiate more sophisticated policies toward governments that oppressed their own people. He used United Nations Ambassador Andrew Young to build up good will for the United States among the black African nations, and urged that South Africa liberalize its policies toward blacks. A peaceful settlement in South Africa was necessary for strategic reasons; South Africa was used for radar tracking systems. Also, it had important U.S. corporate investments and was a critical source of needed raw materials (diamonds, especially). Therefore, what the United States needed was a stable government in South Africa; the continued oppression of blacks might create civil war.

The same approach was used in other countries—combining practical strategic needs with the advancement of civil rights. But because the chief motivation was practicality, not humanity, there was a tendency toward token changes—as in Chile's release of a few political prisoners. When Congressman Herman Badillo introduced in Congress a proposal that required the U.S. representatives to the World Bank and other international financial institutions to vote against loans to countries that systematically violated essential rights, by the use of torture or imprisonment without trial, Carter sent a personal letter to every Congressman urging the defeat of this amendment. It won a voice vote in the House, but lost in the Senate.

Under Carter, the United States continued to support, all over the world, regimes that engaged in imprisonment of dissenters, torture, and mass murder: in the Philippines, in Iran, in Nicaragua, and in Indonesia, where the inhabitants of East Timor were being annihilated in a campaign bordering on genocide.

The *New Republic* magazine, presumably on the liberal side of the Establishment, commented approvingly on the Carter policies: ". . . American foreign policy in the next four years will essentially extend the philosophies developed . . . in the Nixon-Ford years. This is not at all a negative prospect. . . . There should be continuity. It is part of history. . . ."

Carter had presented himself as a friend of the movement against the war, but when Nixon mined Haiphong harbor and resumed bombing of North Vietnam in the spring of 1973, Carter urged that "we give President Nixon our backing and support—whether or not we agree with specific decisions." Once elected, Carter declined to give aid to Vietnam for reconstruction, despite the fact that the land had been devastated by American bombing. Asked about this at a press conference, Carter replied that there was no special obligation on the United States to do this because "the destruction was mutual."

Considering that the United States had crossed half the globe with an enormous fleet of bombers and 2 million soldiers, and after eight years left a tiny nation with over a million dead and its land in ruins, this was an astounding statement.

One Establishment intention, perhaps, was that future generations see the war not as it appeared in the Defense Department's own *Pentagon Papers*—as a ruthless attack on civilian populations for strategic military and economic interests—but as an unfortunate error. Noam Chomsky, one of the leading antiwar intellectuals during the Vietnam period, looked in mid-1978 at how the history of the war was being presented in the major media and wrote that they were "destroying the historical record and supplanting it with a more comfortable story . . . reducing 'lessons' of the war to the socially neutral categories of error, ignorance, and cost."

The Carter administration clearly was trying to end the disillusionment of the American people after the Vietnam war by following foreign policies more palatable, less obviously aggressive. Hence, the emphasis on "human rights," the pressure on South Africa and Chile to liberalize their policies. But on close examination, these more liberal policies were designed to leave intact the power and influence of American military and American business in the world.

The renegotiation of the Panama Canal treaty with the tiny Central American republic of Panama was an example. The canal saved American companies $1.5 billion a year in delivery costs, and the United States collected $150 million a year in tolls, out of which it paid the Panama government $2.3 million dollars, while maintaining fourteen military bases in the area.

Back in 1903 the United States had engineered a revolution against Colombia, set up the new tiny republic of Panama in Central America, and dictated a treaty giving the United States military bases, control of the Panama Canal, and sovereignty "in perpetuity." The Carter administration in 1977, responding to anti-American protests in Panama, decided to renegotiate the treaty. The *New York Times* was candid about the Canal: "We stole it, and removed the incriminating evidence from our history books."

By 1977 the canal had lost military importance. It could not accommodate large tankers or aircraft carriers. That, plus the anti-American riots in Panama, led the Carter administration, over conservative opposition, to negotiate a new treaty which called for a gradual removal of U.S. bases (which could easily be relocated elsewhere in the area). The canal's legal ownership would be turned over to Panama after a period. The treaty also contained vague language which could be the basis for American military intervention under certain conditions.

Whatever Carter's sophistication in foreign policy, certain fundamentals operated in the late sixties and the seventies. American corporations were active all over the world on a scale never seen before. There were, by the early seventies, about three hundred U.S. corporations, including the seven largest banks, which earned 40 percent of their net profits outside the United States. They were called "multinationals," but actually 98 percent of their top executives were Americans. As a group, they now constituted the third-largest economy in the world, next to the United States and the Soviet Union.

The relationship of these global corporations with the poorer countries had long been an exploiting one, it was clear from U.S. Department of Commerce figures. Whereas U.S. corporations in Europe between 1950 and 1965 invested $8.1 billion and made $5.5 billion in profits, in Latin America they invested $3.8 billion and made $11.2 billion in profits, and in Africa they invested $5.2 billion and made $14.3 billion in profits.

It was the classical imperial situation, where the places with natural wealth became victims of more powerful nations whose power came from that seized wealth. American corporations depended on the poorer countries for 100 percent of their diamonds, coffee, platinum, mercury, natural rubber, and cobalt. They got 98 percent of their manganese from abroad, 90 percent of their chrome and aluminum. And 20 to 40 percent of certain imports (platinum, mercury, cobalt, chrome, manganese) came from Africa.

Another fundamental of foreign policy, whether Democrats or Republicans were in the White House, was the training of foreign military officers. The Army had a "School of the Americas" in the Canal Zone, from which thousands of military leaders in Latin America had graduated. Six of the graduates, for instance, were in the Chilean military junta that overthrew the democratically elected Allende government in 1973. The American commandant of the school told a reporter: "We keep in touch with our graduates and they keep in touch with us."

And yet the United States cultivated a reputation for being generous with its riches. Indeed, it had frequently given aid to disaster victims. This aid, however, often depended on political loyalty. In one six-year drought in West Africa, 100,000 Africans died of starvation. A report by the Carnegie Endowment said the Agency for International Development (AID) of the United States had been inefficient and neglectful in giving aid to nomads in the Sahel area of West Africa, an area covering six countries. The response of AID was that those countries had "no close historical, economic, or political ties to the United States."

In early 1975 the press carried a dispatch from Washington: "Secretary of State Henry A. Kissinger has formally initiated a policy of selecting for cutbacks in American aid those nations that have sided against the U.S. in votes in the United Nations. In some cases the cutbacks involve food and humanitarian relief."

Most aid was openly military, and by 1975, the United States exported $9.5 billion in arms. The Carter administration promised to end the sale of arms to repressive regimes, but when it took office the bulk of the sales continued.

And the military continued to take a huge share of the national budget. When Carter was running for election, he told the Democratic Platform Committee: "Without endangering the defense of our nation or commitments to our allies, we can reduce present defense expenditures by about 5 to 7 billion dollars annually." But his first budget proposed not a decrease but an increase of $10 billion for the military. Indeed, he proposed that the U.S. spend a thousand billion dollars (a trillion dollars) in the next five years on its military forces. And the administration had just announced that the Department of Agriculture would save $25 million a year by no longer giving free second helpings of milk to 1.4 million needy schoolchildren who got free meals in school.

If Carter's job was to restore faith in the system, here was his greatest failure—solving the economic problems of the people. The price of food and the necessities of life continued to rise faster than wages were rising. Unemployment remained officially at 6 or 8 percent; unofficially, the rates were higher. For certain key groups in the population—young people, and especially young black people—the unemployment rate was 20 or 30 percent.

It soon became clear that blacks in the United States, the group most in support of Carter for President, were bitterly disappointed with his policies. He opposed federal aid to poor people who needed abortions, and when it was pointed out to him that this was unfair, because rich women could get abortions with ease, he replied: "Well, as you know, there are many things in life that are not fair, that wealthy people can afford and poor people cannot."

Carter's "populism" was not visible in his administration's relationship to the oil and gas interests. It was part of Carter's "energy plan" to end price regulation of natural gas for the consumer. The largest producer of natural gas was Exxon Corporation, and the largest blocs of private stock in Exxon were owned by the Rockefeller family.

Early in Carter's administration, the Federal Energy Administration found that Gulf Oil Corporation had overstated by $79.1 million its costs for crude oil obtained from foreign affiliates. It then passed on these false costs to consumers. In the summer of 1978 the administration announced that "a compromise" had been made with Gulf Oil in which Gulf agreed to pay back $42.2 million. Gulf informed its stockholders that "the payments will not affect earnings since adequate provision was made in prior years."

The lawyer for the Energy Department who worked out the compromise with Gulf said it had been done to avoid a lengthy and costly lawsuit. Would the lawsuit have cost the $36.9 million dropped in the compromise? Would the government have considered letting off a bank robber without a jail term in return for half the loot? The settlement was a perfect example of what Carter had told a meeting of lawyers during his presidential campaign—that the law was on the side of the rich.

The fundamental facts of maldistribution of wealth in America were clearly not going to be affected by Carter's policies, any more than by previous administrations, whether conservative or liberal. According to Andrew Zimbalist, an American economist writing in *Le Monde Diplomatique* in 1977, the top 10 percent of the American population had an income thirty times that of the bottom tenth; the top 1 percent of the nation owned 33 percent of the wealth. The richest 5 percent owned 83 percent of the personally owned corporate stock. The one hundred largest corporations (despite the graduated income tax that misled people into thinking the very rich paid at least 50 percent in taxes) paid an average of 26.9 percent in taxes, and the leading oil companies paid 5.8 percent in taxes (Internal Revenue Service figures for 1974). Indeed, 244 individuals who earned over $200,000 paid no taxes.

In 1979, as Carter weakly proposed benefits for the poor, and Congress strongly turned them down, a black woman, Marian Wright Edelman, director of the Children's Defense Fund in Washington, pointed to some facts. One of every seven American children (10 million altogether) had no known regular source of primary health care. One of every three children under seventeen (18 million altogether) had never seen a dentist. In an article on the *New York Times* op-ed page, she wrote:

> The Senate Budget Committee recently . . . knocked off $88 million from a modest $288 million Administration request to improve the program that screens and treats children's health problems. At the same time the Senate found $725 million to bail out Litton Industries and to hand to the Navy at least two destroyers ordered by the Shah of Iran.

Carter approved tax "reforms" which benefited mainly the corporations. Economist Robert Lekachman, writing in *The Nation*, noted the sharp increase in corporate profits (44 percent) in the last quarter of 1978 over the previous year's last quarter. He wrote: "Perhaps the President's most outrageous act occurred last November when he signed into law an $18 billion tax reduction, the bulk of whose benefits accrue to affluent individuals and corporations."

In 1979, while the poor were taking cuts, the salary of the chairman of Exxon Oil was being raised to $830,000 a year and that of the chairman of Mobil Oil to over a million dollars a year. That year, while Exxon's net income rose 56 percent to more than $4 billion, three thousand small independent gasoline stations went out of business.

Carter made some efforts to hold onto social programs, but this was undermined by his very large military budgets. Presumably, this was to guard against the Soviet Union, but when the Soviet Union invaded Afghanistan in 1979, Carter could take only symbolic actions, like reinstituting the draft, or calling for a boycott of the 1980 Moscow Olympics.

On the other hand, American weaponry was used to support dictatorial regimes battling left-wing rebels abroad. A report by the Carter administration to Congress in 1977 was blunt, saying that "a number of countries with deplorable records of human rights observance are also countries where we have important security and foreign policy interests."

Thus, Carter asked Congress in the spring of 1980 for $5.7 million in credits for the military junta fighting off a peasant rebellion in El Salvador. In the Philippines, after the 1978 National Assembly elections, President Ferdinand Marcos imprisoned ten of the twenty-one losing opposition candidates; many prisoners were tortured, many civilians were killed. Still, Carter urged Congress to give Marcos $300 million in military aid for the next five years.

In Nicaragua, the United States had helped maintain the Somoza dictatorship for decades. Misreading the basic weakness of that regime, and the popularity of the revolution against it, the Carter administration continued its support for Somoza until close to the regime's fall in 1979.

In Iran, toward the end of 1978, the long years of resentment against the Shah's dictatorship culminated in mass demonstrations. On September 8, 1978, hundreds of demonstrators were massacred by the Shah's troops. The next day, according to a UPI dispatch from Teheran, Carter affirmed his support for the Shah:

> Troops opened fire on demonstrators against the Shah for the third straight day yesterday and President Jimmy Carter telephoned the royal palace to express support for Shah Mohammad Reza Pahlevi, who faced the worst crisis of his 37-year reign. Nine members of parliament walked out on a speech by Iran's new premier, shouting that his hands were "stained with blood" in the crackdown on conservative Moslems and other protesters.

On December 13, 1978, Nicholas Gage reported for the *New York Times*:

> The staff of the United States Embassy here has been bolstered by dozens of specialists flown in to back an effort to help the Shah against a growing challenge to his rule according to embassy sources. . . . The new arrivals, according to the embassy sources, include a number of Central Intelligence Agency specialists on Iran, in addition to diplomats and military personnel.

In early 1979, as the crisis in Iran was intensifying, the former chief analyst on Iran for the CIA told *New York Times* reporter Seymour Hersh that "he and his colleagues knew of the tortures of Iranian dissenters by Savaki, the Iranian secret police set up during the late 1950s by the Shah with help from the CIA." Furthermore, he told Hersh that a senior CIA official was involved in instructing officials in Savaki on torture techniques.

It was a popular, massive revolution, and the Shah fled. The Carter administration later accepted him into the country, presumably for medical treatment, and the anti-American feelings of the revolutionaries reached a high point. On November 4, 1979, the U.S. embassy in Teheran was taken over by student militants who, demanding that the Shah be returned to Iran for punishment, held fifty-two embassy employees hostage.

For the next fourteen months, with the hostages still held in the embassy compound, that issue took the forefront of foreign news in the United States and aroused powerful nationalist feelings. When Carter ordered the Immigration and Naturalization Service to start deportation proceedings against Iranian students who lacked valid visas, the *New York Times* gave cautious but clear approval. Politicians and the press played into a general hysteria. An Iranian-American girl who was slated to give a high school commencement address was removed from the program. The bumper sticker "Bomb Iran" appeared on autos all over the country.

It was a rare journalist bold enough to point out, as Alan Richman of the Boston *Globe* did when the fifty-two hostages were released alive and apparently well, that there was a certain lack of proportion in American reactions to this and other violations of human rights: "There were 52 of them, a number easy to comprehend. It wasn't like 15,000 innocent people permanently disappearing in Argentina.... They [the American hostages] spoke our language. There were 3000 people summarily shot in Guatemala last year who did not."

The hostages were still in captivity when Jimmy Carter faced Ronald Reagan in the election of 1980. That fact, and the economic distress felt by many, were largely responsible for Carter's defeat.

Reagan's victory, followed eight years later by the election of George Bush, meant that another part of the Establishment, lacking even the faint liberalism of the Carter presidency, would be in charge. The policies would be more crass—cutting benefits to poor people, lowering taxes for the wealthy, increasing the military budget, filling the federal court system with conservative judges, actively working to destroy revolutionary movements in the Caribbean.

The dozen years of the Reagan-Bush presidency transformed the federal judiciary, never more than moderately liberal, into a predominantly conservative institution. By the fall of 1991, Reagan and Bush had filled more than half of the 837 federal judgeships, and appointed enough right-wing justices to transform the Supreme Court.

In the seventies, with liberal justices William Brennan and Thurgood Marshall in the lead, the Court had declared death penalties unconstitutional, had supported (in *Roe* v. *Wade*) the right of women to choose abortions, and had interpreted the civil rights law as permitting special attention to blacks and women to make up for past discrimination (affirmative action).

William Rehnquist, first named to the Supreme Court by Richard Nixon, was made Chief Justice by Ronald Reagan. In the Reagan-Bush years, the Rehnquist Court made a series of decisions that weakened *Roe* v. *Wade*, brought back the death penalty, reduced the rights of detainees against police powers, prevented doctors in federally supported family planning clinics from giving women information on abortions, and said that poor people could be forced to pay for public education (education was not "a fundamental right").

Justices William Brennan and Thurgood Marshall were the last of the Court's liberals. Old and ill, though reluctant to give up the fight, they retired. The final act to create a conservative Supreme Court was President Bush's nomination to replace Marshall. He chose a black conservative, Clarence Thomas. Despite dramatic testimony from a former colleague, a young black law professor named Anita Hill, that Thomas had sexually harassed her, Thomas was approved by the Senate and now the Supreme Court moved even more decisively to the right.

With conservative federal judges, with pro-business appointments to the National Labor Relations Board, judicial decisions and board findings weakened a labor movement already troubled by a decline in manufacturing. Workers who went out on strike found themselves with no legal protection. One of the first acts of the Reagan administration was to dismiss from their jobs, en masse, striking air traffic controllers. It was a warning to future strikers, and a sign of the weakness of a labor movement which in the thirties and forties had been a powerful force.

Corporate America became the greatest beneficiary of the

Reagan-Bush years. In the sixties and seventies an important environmental movement had grown in the nation, horrified at the poisoning of the air, the seas and rivers, and the deaths of thousands each year as a result of work conditions. After a mine explosion in West Virginia killed seventy-eight miners in November 1968 there had been angry protest in the mine district, and Congress passed the Coal Mine Health and Safety Act of 1969. Nixon's Secretary of Labor spoke of "a new national passion, passion for environmental improvement."

The following year, yielding to strong demands from the labor movement and consumer groups, but also seeing it as an opportunity to win the support of working-class voters, President Nixon had signed the Occupational Safety and Health Act of 1970. This was an important piece of legislation, establishing a universal right to a safe and healthy workplace, and creating an enforcement machinery. Reflecting on this years later, Herbert Stein, who had been the chairman of Nixon's Council of Economic Advisers, lamented that "the juggernaut of environmental regulation proved not to be controllable by the Nixon administration."

While President Jimmy Carter came into office praising the OSHA program, he was also eager to please the business community. The woman he appointed to head OSHA, Eula Bingham, fought for strong enforcement of the act, and was occasionally successful. But as the American economy showed signs of trouble, with oil prices, inflation, and unemployment rising, Carter seemed more and more concerned about the difficulties the act created for business. He became an advocate of removing regulations on corporations and giving them more leeway, even if this was hurtful to labor and to consumers. Environmental regulation became more and more a victim of "cost-benefit" analysis, in which regulations protecting the health and safety of the public became secondary to how costly this would be for business.

Under Reagan and Bush this concern for "the economy," which was a short-hand term for corporate profit, dominated any concern for workers or consumers. President Reagan proposed to replace tough enforcement of environmental laws by a "voluntary" approach, leaving it to businesses to decide for themselves what they would do. He appointed as head of OSHA a businessman who was hostile to OSHA's aims. One of his first acts was to order the destruction of 100,000 government booklets pointing out the dangers of cotton dust to textile workers.

Political scientist William Grover (*The President as Prisoner*), evaluating environmental policy under Carter and Reagan as part of his penetrating "structural critique" of both presidents, concluded:

> OSHA appears caught in a cycle of liberal presidents—who want to retain some health and safety regulatory programs, but who also need economic growth for political survival—and conservative presidents, who focus almost exclusively on the growth side of the equation. Such a cycle will always tend to subordinate the need for safe and healthful workplaces to . . . ensuring that commitment to OSHA will only be as strong as the priorities of business will allow.

George Bush presented himself as the "environmental president," and pointed with pride to his signing of the Clean Air Act of 1990. But two years after that act was passed, it was seriously weakened by a new rule of the Environmental Protection Agency that allowed manufacturers to increase by 245 tons a year hazardous pollutants in the atmosphere.

Furthermore, little money was allocated for enforcement. Contaminated drinking water had caused over 100,000 illnesses between 1971 and 1985, according to an EPA report. But in Bush's first year in office, while the EPA received 80,000 complaints of contaminated drinking water, only one in a hundred was investigated. And in 1991 and 1992, according to a private environmental group, the National Resources Defense Council, there were some 250,000 violations of the Safe Water Drinking Act (which had been passed during the Nixon administration).

Shortly after Bush took office, a government scientist prepared testimony for a Congressional committee on the dangerous effects of industrial uses of coal and other fossil fuels in contributing to "global warming," a depletion of the earth's protective ozone layer. The White House changed the testimony, over the scientist's objections, to minimize the danger (Boston *Globe*, October 29, 1990). Again, business worries about regulation seemed to override the safety of the public.

The ecological crisis in the world had become so obviously serious that Pope John Paul II felt the need to rebuke the wealthy classes of the industrialized nations for creating that crisis: "Today, the dramatic threat of ecological breakdown is teaching us the extent to which greed and selfishness, both individual and collective, are contrary to the order of creation."

At international conferences to deal with the perils of global warming, the European Community and Japan proposed specific levels and timetables for carbon dioxide emissions, in which the United States was the leading culprit. But, as the *New York Times* reported in the summer of 1991, "the Bush Administration fears that . . . it would hurt the nation's economy in the short term for no demonstrable long-term climatic benefit." Scientific opinion was quite clear on the long-term benefit, but this was not as important as "the economy"—that is, the needs of corporations.

Evidence became stronger by the late eighties that renewable energy sources (water, wind, sunlight) could produce more usable energy than nuclear plants, which were dangerous and expensive, and produced radioactive wastes that could not be safely disposed of. Yet the Reagan and Bush administrations made deep cuts (under Reagan, a 90 percent cut) in research into renewable energy possibilities.

In June 1992 more than a hundred countries participated in the Earth Summit environmental conference in Brazil. Statistics showed that the armed forces of the world were responsible for two-thirds of the gases that depleted the ozone layer. But when it was suggested that the Earth Summit consider the effects of the military on environmental degradation, the United States delegation objected and the suggestion was defeated.

Indeed, the preservation of a huge military establishment and the retention of profit levels of oil corporations appeared to be twin objectives of the Reagan-Bush administrations. Shortly after Ronald Reagan took office, twenty-three oil industry executives contributed $270,000 to redecorate the White House living quarters. According to the Associated Press:

> The solicitation drive ... came four weeks after the President decontrolled oil prices, a decision worth $2 billion to the oil industry ... Jack Hodges of Oklahoma City, owner of Core Oil and Gas Company, said: "The top man of this country ought to live in one of the top places. Mr. Reagan has helped the energy business."

While he built up the military (allocations of over a trillion dollars in his first four years in office), Reagan tried to pay for this with cuts in benefits for the poor. There would be $140 billion of cuts in social programs through 1984 and an increase of $181 billion for "defense" in the same period. He also proposed tax cuts of $190 billion (most of this going to the wealthy).

Despite the tax cuts and the military appropriations, Reagan insisted he would still balance the budget because the tax cuts would so stimulate the economy as to generate new revenue. Nobel Prize–winning economist Wassily Leontief remarked dryly: "This is not likely to happen. In fact, I personally guarantee that it will not happen."

Indeed, Department of Commerce figures showed that periods of lowered corporate taxes (1973–1975, 1979–1982) did not at all show higher capital investment, but a steep drop. The sharpest rise of capital investment (1975–1979) took place when corporate taxes were slightly higher than they had been the preceding five years.

The human consequences of Reagan's budget cuts went deep. For instance, Social Security disability benefits were terminated for 350,000 people. A man injured in an oil field accident was forced to go back to work, the federal government overruling both the company doctor and a state supervisor who testified that he was too disabled to work. The man died, and federal officials said, "We have a P.R. problem." A war hero of Vietnam, Roy Benavidez, who had been presented with the Congressional Medal of Honor by Reagan, was told by Social Security officials that the shrapnel pieces in his heart, arms, and leg did not prevent him from working. Appearing before a Congressional committee, he denounced Reagan.

Unemployment grew in the Reagan years. In the year 1982, 30 million people were unemployed all or part of the year. One result was that over 16 million Americans lost medical insurance, which was often tied to holding a job. In Michigan, where the unemployment rate was the highest in the country, the infant death rate began to rise in 1981.

New requirements eliminated free school lunches for more than one million poor children, who depended on the meal for as much as half of their daily nutrition. Millions of children entered the ranks of the officially declared "poor" and soon a quarter of the nation's children—twelve million—were living in poverty. In parts of Detroit, one-third of the children were dying before their first birthday, and the *New York Times* commented: "Given what's happening to the hungry in America, this Administration has cause only for shame."

Welfare became an object of attack: aid to single mothers with children through the AFDC (Aid to Families with Dependent Children) program, food stamps, health care for the poor through Medicaid. For most people on welfare (the benefits differed from state to state) this meant $500 to $700 a month in aid, leaving them well below the poverty level of about $900 a month. Black children were four times as likely as white children to grow up on welfare.

Early in the Reagan administration, responding to the argument that government aid was not needed, that private enterprise would take care of poverty, a mother wrote to her local newspaper:

I am on Aid to Families with Dependent Children, and both my children are in school. . . . I have graduated from college with distinction, 128th in a class of over 1000, with a B.A. in English and sociology. I have experience in library work, child care, social work and counseling.

I have been to the CETA office. They have nothing for me. . . . I also go every week to the library to scour the newspaper Help Wanted ads. I have kept a copy of every cover letter that I have sent out with my resume; the stack is inches thick. I have applied for jobs paying as little as $8000 a year. I work part-time in a library for $3.50 an hour, welfare reduces my allotment to compensate. . . .

It appears we have employment offices that can't employ, governments that can't govern and an economic system that can't produce jobs for people ready to work. . . .

Last week I sold my bed to pay for the insurance on my car, which, in the absence of mass transportation, I need to go job hunting. I sleep on a piece of rubber foam somebody gave me.

So this is the great American dream my parents came to this country for: Work hard, get a good education, follow the rules, and you will be rich. I don't want to be rich. I just want to be able to feed my children and live with some semblance of dignity. . . ."

Democrats often joined Republicans in denouncing welfare programs. Presumably, this was done to gain political support from a middle-class public that believed they were paying taxes to support teenage mothers and people they thought too lazy to work. Much of the public did not know, and were not informed by either political leaders or the media, that welfare took a tiny part of the taxes, and military spending took a huge chunk of it. Yet, the public's attitude on welfare was different from that of the two major parties. It seemed that the constant attacks on welfare by politicians, reported endlessly in the press and on television, did not succeed in eradicating a fundamental generosity felt by most Americans.

A *New York Times*/CBS News poll conducted in early 1992 showed that public opinion on welfare changed depending on how the question was worded. If the word "welfare" was used, 44 percent of those questioned said too much was being spent on welfare (while 50 percent said either that the right amount was being spent, or that too little was being spent. But when the question was about "assistance to the poor," only 13 percent thought too much was being spent, and 64 percent thought too little was being spent.

This suggested that both parties were trying to manufacture an antihuman-needs mood by constant derogatory use of the word "welfare," and then to claim they were acting in response to public opinion. The Democrats as well as the Republicans had strong connections to wealthy corporations. Kevin Phillips, a Republican analyst of national politics, wrote in 1990 that the Democratic Party was "history's second-most enthusiastic capitalist party."

Phillips pointed out that the greatest beneficiaries of government policy during the Republican presidencies of Ronald Reagan and George Bush were the superrich: "It was the truly wealthy, more than anyone else, who flourished under Reagan. . . . The 1980s were the triumph of upper America . . . the political ascendancy of the rich, and a glorification of capitalism, free markets, and finance."

When government policy enriched the already rich, it was not called welfare. This was not as obvious as the monthly checks to the poor; it most often took the form of generous changes in the tax system.

In *America: Who Really Pays The Taxes?*, two investigative reporters with the *Philadelphia Inquirer,* Donald Barlett and James Steele, traced the path by which tax rates for the very rich got lower and lower. It was not the Republicans but the Democrats— the Kennedy-Johnson administrations—who, under the guise of "tax reform," first lowered the World War II–era rate of 91 percent on incomes over $400,000 a year to 70 percent. During the Carter Administration (though over his objections) Democrats and Republicans in Congress joined to give even more tax breaks to the rich.

The Reagan administration, with the help of Democrats in Congress, lowered the tax rate on the very rich to 50 percent and in 1986 a coalition of Republicans and Democrats sponsored another "tax reform" bill that lowered the top rate to 28 percent. Barlett and Steele noted that a schoolteacher, a factory worker, and a billionaire could all pay 28 percent. The idea of a "progressive" income in which the rich paid at higher rates than everyone else was now almost dead.

As a result of all the tax bills from 1978 to 1990, the net worth of the "Forbes 400," chosen as the richest in the country by *Forbes Magazine* (advertising itself as "capitalist tool"), was tripled. About $70 billion a year was lost in government revenue, so that in those thirteen years the wealthiest 1 percent of the country gained a trillion dollars.

As William Greider pointed out, in his remarkable book *Who Will Tell The People? The Betrayal of American Democracy*:

For those who blame Republicans for what has happened and believe that equitable taxation will be restored if only the Democrats can win back the White House, there is this disquieting fact: The turning point on tax politics, when the monied elites first began to win big, occurred in 1978 with the Democratic party fully in power and well before Ronald Reagan came to Washington. Democratic majorities have supported this great shift in tax burden every step of the way.

Not only did the income tax become less progressive during the last decades of the century, but the Social Security tax became more *regressive*. That is, more and more was deducted from the salary checks of the poor and middle classes, but when salaries reached $42,000 no more was deducted, By the early 1990s, a middle-income family earning $37,800 a year paid 7.65 percent of its income in Social Security taxes. A family earning ten times as much, $378,000 paid 1.46 percent of its income in Social Security taxes.

The result of these higher payroll taxes was that three-fourths of all wage earners paid more each year through the Social Security tax than through the income tax. Embarrassingly for the Democratic party, which was supposed to be the party of the working class, those higher payroll taxes had been put in motion under the administration of Jimmy Carter.

In a two-party system, if *both* parties ignore public opinion, there is no place voters can turn. And in the matter of taxation, it has been clear that American citizens have wanted taxes that are truly progressive. William Greider informs us that shortly after World War II, when rates on the very rich were up to 90 percent, a Gallup poll showed that 85 percent of the public thought the federal tax code was "fair." But by 1984, when all those tax "reforms" had been put into effect by Democrats and Republicans, a public opinion survey by the Internal Revenue Service found that 80 percent of those polled agreed with the statement: "The present tax system benefits the rich and is unfair to the ordinary working man and woman."

By the end of the Reagan years, the gap between rich and poor in the United States had grown dramatically. Where in 1980, the chief executive officers (CEOs) of corporations made forty times as much in salary as the average factory worker, by 1989 they were making ninety-three times as much. In the dozen years from 1977 to 1989, the before-tax income of the richest 1 percent rose 77 percent; meanwhile, for the poorest two-fifths of the population, there was no gain at all, indeed a small decline.

And because of favorable changes for the rich in the tax structure, the richest 1 percent, in the decade ending in 1990, saw their after-tax income increase 87 percent. In the same period, the after-tax income of the lower four-fifths of the population either went down 5 percent (at the poorest level) or went up no more than 8.6 percent.

While everybody at the lower levels was doing worse, there were especially heavy losses for blacks, Hispanics, women, and the young. The general impoverishment of the lowest-income groups that took place in the Reagan-Bush years hit black families hardest, with their lack of resources to start with and with racial discrimination facing them in jobs. The victories of the civil rights movement had opened up spaces for some African-Americans, but left others far behind.

At the end of the eighties, at least a third of African-American families fell below the official poverty level, and black unemployment seemed fixed at two and a half times that of whites, with young blacks out of work at the rate of 30 to 40 percent. The life expectancy of blacks remained at least ten years lower than that of whites. In Detroit, Washington, and Baltimore, the mortality rate for black babies was higher than in Jamaica or Costa Rica.

Along with poverty came broken homes, family violence, street crime, drugs. In Washington, D.C., with a concentrated population of black poor within walking distance of the marbled buildings of the national government, 42 percent of young black men between the ages of eighteen and thirty-five were either in jail, or out on probation or parole. The crime rate among blacks, instead of being seen as a crying demand for the elimination of poverty, was used by politicians to call for the building of more prisons.

The 1954 Supreme Court decision in *Brown* v. *Board of Education* had begun the process of desegregating schools. But poverty kept black children in ghettos and many schools around the country remained segregated by race and class. Supreme Court decisions in the seventies determined that there need be no equalization of funds for poor school districts and rich school districts (*San Antonio Independent School District* v. *Rodriguez*) and that the busing of children need not take place between wealthy suburbs and inner cities (*Milliken* v. *Bradley*).

To admirers of free enterprise and laissez-faire, those people were poor who did not work and produce, and so had themselves to blame for their poverty. They ignored the fact that women taking care of children on their own were working very hard indeed. They did not ask why babies who were not old enough to show their work skills should be penalized—to the point of death—for growing up in a poor family.

Ironically, it was Republican Kevin Phillips who, analyzing the Reagan years, wrote: "Less and less wealth was going to people who produced something . . . disproportionate rewards to society's economic, legal and cultural manipulators—from lawyers to financial advisers."

In the mid-eighties, a major scandal began to emerge in

Washington. The deregulation of the savings and loan banks begun in the Carter administration had continued under Reagan, leading to risky investments which drained the assets of the banks, leaving them owing billions of dollars to depositors, which the government had insured.

As the years went by and the problem was kept behind a screen, it was going to take more and more money to pay depositors and bail out these banks. The figure began to reach $200 billion. During the 1988 presidential campaign, the Democratic candidate Michael Dukakis was restrained from pointing the finger at the Republican administration because the Democrats in Congress were heavily involved in bringing about and then covering up the situation. So the voters were kept in the dark.

The enormous drain of money from the treasury for defense had once been declared by President Eisenhower to be a "theft" from human needs. But it was accepted by both parties, as Democrats competed with Republicans to show the electorate how "tough" they were.

Jimmy Carter as president had proposed a $10 billion increase in the military budget, an enactment of exactly what Eisenhower had described. All of the huge military budgets of the post–World War II period, from Truman to Reagan and Bush, were approved overwhelmingly by both Democrats and Republicans.

The spending of trillions of dollars to build up nuclear and non-nuclear forces was justified by fears that the Soviet Union, also building up its military forces, would invade Western Europe. But George Kennan, the former ambassador to the Soviet Union and one of the theoreticians of the cold war, said this fear had no basis in reality. And Harry Rositzke, who worked for the CIA for twenty-five years and was at one time CIA director of espionage operations against the Soviet Union, wrote in the 1980s: "In all of my years in government and since I have never seen an intelligence estimate that shows how it would be profitable to Soviet interests to invade Western Europe or to attack the United States."

However, the creation of such a fear in the public mind was useful in arguing for the building of frightful and superfluous weapons. For instance, the *Trident* submarine, which was capable of firing hundreds of nuclear warheads, cost $1.5 billion. It was totally useless except in a nuclear war, in which case it would only add several hundred warheads to the tens of thousands already available. That $1.5 billion was enough to finance a five-year program of child immunization around the world against deadly diseases, and prevent five million deaths (Ruth Sivard, *World Military and Social Expenditures 1987–1988*).

In the mid-1980s, an analyst with the Rand Corporation, which did research for the Defense Department, told an interviewer in an unusually candid statement, that the enormous number of weapons was unnecessary from a military point of view, but were useful to convey a certain *image* at home and abroad:

> If you had a strong president, a strong secretary of defense they could temporarily go to Congress and say, "We're only going to build what we need. . . . And if the Russians build twice as many, tough." But it would be unstable politically. . . . And it is therefore better for our own domestic stability as well as international perceptions to insist that we remain good competitors even though the objective significance of the competition is . . . dubious.

In 1984, the CIA admitted that it had exaggerated Soviet military expenditures, that since 1975 it had claimed Soviet military spending was growing by 4 to 5 percent each year when the actual figure was 2 percent. Thus, by misinformation, even deception, the result was to inflate military expenditures.

One of the favorite military programs of the Reagan administration was the Star Wars program, in which billions were spent, supposedly to build a shield in space to stop enemy nuclear missiles in midair. But the first three tests of the technology failed. A fourth test was undertaken, with government funding for the program at stake. There was another failure, but Reagan's Secretary of Defense, Caspar Weinberger, approved the faking of results to show that the test had succeeded.

When the Soviet Union began to disintegrate in 1989, and

there was no longer the familiar "Soviet threat," the military budget was reduced somewhat, but still remained huge, with support from both Democrats and Republicans. In 1992, the head of the House Armed Services Committee, Les Aspin, a Democrat, proposed, in view of the new international situation, that the military budget be cut by 2%, from $281 billion to $275 billion.

That same year, as Democrats and Republicans both supported minor cuts in the military budget, a public opinion survey done for the National Press Club showed that 59 percent of American voters wanted a 50 percent cut in defense spending over the next five years.

It seemed that both parties had failed in persuading the citizenry that the military budget should continue at its high level. But they continued to ignore the public they were supposed to represent. In the summer of 1992, Congressional Democrats and Republicans joined to vote against a transfer of funds from the military budget to human needs, and voted to spend $120 billion to "defend" Europe, which everyone acknowledged was no longer in danger—if it ever had been—from Soviet attack.

Democrats and Republicans had long been joined in a "bipartisan foreign policy," but in the Reagan-Bush years the United States government showed a special aggressiveness in the use of military force abroad. This was done either directly in invasions, or through both overt and covert support of right-wing tyrannies that cooperated with the United States.

Reagan came into office just after a revolution had taken place in Nicaragua, in which a popular Sandinista movement (named after the 1920s revolutionary hero Augusto Sandino) overthrew the corrupt Somoza dynasty (long supported by the United States). The Sandinistas, a coalition of Marxists, left-wing priests, and assorted nationalists, set about to give more land to the peasants and to spread education and health care among the poor.

The Reagan administration, seeing in this a "Communist" threat, but even more important, a challenge to the long U.S. control over governments in Central America, began immediately to work to overthrow the Sandinista government. It waged a secret war by having the CIA organize a counterrevolutionary force (the "contras"), many of whose leaders were former leaders of the hated National Guard under Somoza.

The contras seemed to have no popular support inside Nicaragua and so were based next door in Honduras, a very poor country dominated by the United States. From Honduras they moved across the border, raiding farms and villages, killing men, women and children, committing atrocities. A former colonel with the contras, Edgar Chamorro, testified before the World Court:

> We were told that the only way to defeat the Sandinistas was to use the tactics the agency [the CIA] attributed to Communist insurgencies elsewhere: kill, kidnap, rob, and torture. . . . Many civilians were killed in cold blood. Many others were tortured, mutilated, raped, robbed, or otherwise abused. . . . When I agreed to join . . . I had hoped that it would be an organization of Nicaraguans. . . . [It] turned out to be an instrument of the U.S. government. . . .

There was a reason for the secrecy of the U.S. actions in Nicaragua; public opinion surveys showed that the American public was opposed to military involvement there. In 1984, the CIA, using Latin American agents to conceal its involvement, put mines in the harbors of Nicaragua to blow up ships. When information leaked out, Secretary of Defense Weinberger told ABC news: "The United States is not mining the harbors of Nicaragua."

Later that year Congress, responding perhaps to public opinion and the memory of Vietnam, made it illegal for the United States to support "directly or indirectly, military or paramilitary operations in Nicaragua." The Reagan administration decided to ignore this law and to find ways to fund the contras secretly, looking for "third-party support." Reagan himself solicited funds from Saudi Arabia, at least $32 million. The friendly dictatorship in Guatemala was used to get arms surreptitiously to the contras. Israel, dependent on U.S. aid and always dependable for support, was also used.

In 1986, a story appearing in a Beirut magazine created a sensation: that weapons had been sold by the United States to Iran (supposedly an enemy), that in return Iran had promised to release hostages being held by extremist Moslems in Lebanon, and that profits from the sale were being given to the contras to buy arms.

When asked about this at a press conference in November 1986, President Reagan told four lies: that the shipment to Iran consisted of a few token antitank missiles (in fact, 2,000), that the United States didn't condone shipments by third parties, that weapons had not been traded for hostages, and that the purpose of the operation was to promote a dialogue with Iranian moderates. In reality, the purpose was a double one: to free hostages and get credit for that, and to help the contras.

The previous month, when a transport plane that had carried arms to the contras was downed by Nicaraguan gunfire and the American pilot captured, the lies had multiplied. Assistant Secretary of State Elliot Abrams lied. Secretary of State Shultz lied ("no connection with the U.S. government at all"). Evidence mounted that the captured pilot was working for the CIA.

The whole Iran-contra affair became a perfect example of the double line of defense of the American Establishment. The first defense is to deny the truth. If exposed, the second defense is to investigate, but not too much; the press will publicize, but they will not get to the heart of the matter.

Once the scandal was out in the open, neither the Congressional investigating committees nor the press nor the trial of Colonel Oliver North, who oversaw the contra aid operation, got to the critical questions: What is U.S. foreign policy all about? How are the president and his staff permitted to support a terrorist group in Central America to overthrow a government that, whatever its faults, is welcomed by its own people as a great improvement over the terrible governments the U.S. has supported there for years? What does the scandal tell us about democracy, about freedom of expression, about an open society?

Out of the much-publicized "contragate" scandal came no

powerful critique of secrecy in government or of the erosion of democracy by actions taken in secret by a small group of men safe from the scrutiny of public opinion. The media, in a country priding itself on its level of education and information, kept the public informed only on the most superficial level.

The limits of Democratic party criticism of the affair were revealed by a leading Democrat, Senator Sam Nunn of Georgia, who, as the investigation was getting under way, said: "We must, all of us, help the President restore his credibility in foreign affairs."

A few Democrats were critical, which was deplored by a Harvard professor, James Q. Wilson, who was a member of Reagan's Foreign Intelligence Advisory Board. Wilson looked back nostalgically to a "bipartisan consensus" (the equivalent of the one-party system in a totalitarian state). He worried most about "a lack of resolve to act like a great power."

It became clear that President Reagan and Vice-President Bush were involved in what became known as the Iran-contra affair. But their underlings scrupulously kept them out of it, illustrating the familiar government device of "plausible denial," in which the top official, shielded by subordinates, can plausibly deny involvement. Although Congressman Henry Gonzalez of Texas introduced a resolution for the impeachment of Reagan, it was quickly suppressed in Congress.

Neither Reagan nor Bush were indicted. Rather, the Congressional committee put the lesser culprits on the witness stand and several of them were indicted. One (Robert McFarlane, a former National Security Adviser to Reagan) tried to commit suicide. Another, Colonel Oliver North, stood trial for lying to Congress, was found guilty, but was not sentenced to prison. Reagan retired in peace and Bush became the next president of the United States.

In an ironic twist, an obscure citizen of the tiny town of Odon, Indiana, became a tangential actor in the Iran-contra controversy. This was a young man named Bill Breeden, a former minister who lived in a tepee in the woods with his wife and two children, teaching the children at home. Breeden's home town of Odon was also the home town of Admiral John Poindexter, McFarlane's successor as Reagan's National Security Adviser, who was heavily involved in the illegal activities of the Iran-contra affair.

One day Bill Breeden noticed that the town, to show its pride in its "home boy," had renamed one of its streets "John Poindexter Street." Breeden, a pacifist and critic of U.S. foreign policy, indignant at what he thought was a celebration of immoral behavior in government, stole the sign. He announced that he was holding it for "ransom"—$30 million, the amount of money that had been given to Iran for transfer to the contras.

He was apprehended, put on trial, and spent a few days in jail. As it turned out, Bill Breeden was the only person to be imprisoned as a result of the Iran-contra affair.

The Iran-contra affair was only one of the many instances in which the government of the United States violated its own laws in pursuit of some desired goal in foreign policy.

Toward the end of the Vietnam war, in 1973, Congress, seeking to limit the presidential power that had been used so ruthlessly in Indochina, passed the War Powers Act, which said:

"The President, in every possible instance, shall consult with Congress before introducing United States Armed Forces into hostilities or into situations where imminent involvement in hostilities is clearly indicated by the circumstances."

Almost immediately, President Gerald Ford violated the act when he ordered the invasion of a Cambodian island and the bombing of a Cambodian town in retaliation for the temporary detention of American merchant seamen on the ship *Mayaguez*. He did not consult Congress before he gave the attack orders.

In the fall of 1982, President Reagan sent American marines into a dangerous situation in Lebanon, where a civil war was raging, again ignoring the requirements of the War Powers Act. The following year, over two hundred of those marines were killed when a bomb was exploded in their barracks by terrorists.

Shortly after that, in October 1983 (with some analysts concluding this was done to take attention away from the Lebanon disaster), Reagan sent U.S. forces to invade the tiny Caribbean island of Grenada. Again, Congress was notified, but not consulted. The reasons given to the American people for this invasion (officially called Operation Urgent Fury) were that a recent coup that had taken place in Grenada put American citizens (students at a medical school on the island) in danger; and that the United States had received an urgent request from the Organization of Eastern Caribbean States to intervene.

An unusually pointed article in the *New York Times* on October 29, 1983, by correspondent Bernard Gwertzman demolished those reasons:

> The formal request that the U.S. and other friendly countries provide military help was made by the Organization of Eastern Caribbean States last Sunday at the request of the United States, which wanted to show proof that it had been requested to act under terms of that group's treaty. The wording of the formal request, however, was drafted in Washington and conveyed to the Caribbean leaders by special American emissaries.
>
> Both Cuba and Grenada, when they saw that American ships were heading for Grenada, sent urgent messages promising that American students were safe and urging that an invasion not occur. . . . There is no indication that the Administration made a determined effort to evacuate the Americans peacefully. . . . Officials have acknowledged that there was no inclination to try to negotiate with the Grenadian authorities. . . . "We got there just in time," the President said. . . . A major point in the dispute is whether in fact the Americans on the island were in such danger as to warrant an invasion. No official has produced firm evidence that the Americans were being mistreated or that they would not be able to leave if they wanted.

The real reason for the invasion, one high American official told Gwertzman, was that the United States should show (determined to overcome the sense of defeat in Vietnam) that it was a truly powerful nation: "What good are maneuvers and shows of force, if you never use it?"

The connection between U.S. military intervention and the promotion of capitalist enterprise had always been especially crass in the Caribbean. As for Grenada, an article in the *Wall Street Journal* eight years after the military invasion (October 29, 1991) spoke of "an invasion of banks" and noted that St. George's, the capital of Grenada, with 7500 people, had 118 offshore banks, one for every 64 residents. "St. George's has become the Casablanca of the Caribbean, a fast-growing haven for money laundering, tax evasion and assorted financial fraud. . . ."

After a study of various U.S. military interventions, political scientist Stephen Shalom (*Imperial Alibis*) concluded that people in the invaded countries died "not to save U.S. nationals, who would have been far safer without U.S. intervention, but so that Washington might make clear that it ruled the Caribbean and that it was prepared to engage in a paroxysm of violence to enforce its will." He continued:

> There have been some cases where American citizens were truly in danger: for example, the four churchwomen who were killed by government-sponsored death squads in El Salvador in 1980. But there was no U.S. intervention there, no Marine landings, no protective bombing raids. Instead Washington backed the death squad regime with military and economic aid, military training, intelligence sharing, and diplomatic support.

The historic role of the United States in El Salvador, where 2 percent of the population owned 60 percent of the land, was to make sure governments were in power there that would support U.S. business interests, no matter how this impoverished the great majority of people. Popular rebellions that would threaten these business arrangements were to be opposed. When a popular uprising in 1932 threatened the military government, the United States sent a cruiser and two destroyers to stand by while the government massacred thirty thousand Salvadorans.

The administration of Jimmy Carter did nothing to reverse this history. It wanted reform in Latin America, but not revolution that would threaten U.S. corporate interests. In 1980, Richard Cooper, a State Department expert on economic affairs, told Congress that a more equitable distribution of wealth was desirable. "However, we also have an enormous stake in the continuing smooth functioning in the economic system. . . . Major changes in the system can . . . have important implications for our own welfare."

In February 1980 El Salvador Catholic Archbishop Oscar Romero sent a personal letter to President Carter, asking him to stop military aid to El Salvador. Not long before that, the National Guard and National Police had opened fire on a crowd of protesters in front of the Metropolitan Cathedral and killed twenty-four people. But the Carter administration continued the aid. The following month Archbishop Romero was assassinated.

There was mounting evidence that the assassination had been ordered by Roberto D'Aubuisson, a leader of the right wing. But D'Aubuisson had the protection of Nicolas Carranza, a deputy minister of defense, who at the time was receiving $90,000 a year from the CIA. And Elliot Abrams, ironically Assistant Secretary of State for Human Rights, declared that D'Aubuisson "was not involved in murder."

When Reagan became President, military aid to the El Salvador government rose steeply. From 1946 to 1979, total military aid to El Salvador was $16.7 million. In Reagan's first year in office, the figure rose to $82 million.

Congress was sufficiently embarrassed by the killings in El Salvador to require that before any more aid was given the President must certify that progress in human rights was taking place. Reagan did not take this seriously. On January 28, 1982, there were reports of a government massacre of peasants in several villages. The following day, Reagan certified that the Salvadoran government was making progress in human rights. Three days after certification, soldiers stormed the homes of poor people in San Salvador, dragged out twenty people, and killed them.

When, at the end of 1983, Congress passed a law to continue the requirement of certification, Reagan vetoed it.

The press was especially timid and obsequious during the Reagan years, as Mark Hertsgaard documents in his book *On Bended Knee*. When journalist Raymond Bonner continued to report on the atrocities in El Salvador, and on the U.S. role, the *New York Times* removed him from his assignment. Back in 1981 Bonner had reported on the massacre of hundreds of civilians in the town of El Mozote, by a battalion of soldiers trained by the United States. The Reagan administration scoffed at the account, but in 1992, a team of forensic anthropologists began unearthing skeletons from the site of the massacre, most of them children; the following year a UN commission confirmed the story of the massacre at El Mozote.

The Reagan administration, which did not appear at all offended by military juntas governing in Latin America (Guatemala, El Salvador, Chile) if they were "friendly" to the United States, became very upset when a tyranny was hostile, as was the government of Muammar Khadafi in Libya. In 1986, when unknown terrorists bombed a discotheque in West Berlin, killing a U.S. serviceman, the White House immediately decided to retaliate. Khadafi was probably responsible for various acts of terrorism over the years, but there was no real evidence that in this case he was to blame.

Reagan was determined to make a point. Planes were sent over the capital city of Tripoli with specific instructions to aim at Khadafi's house. The bombs fell on a crowded city; perhaps a hundred people were killed, it was estimated by foreign diplomats in Tripoli. Khadafi was not injured, but an adopted daughter of his was killed.

Professor Stephen Shalom, analyzing this incident, writes (*Imperial Alibis*): "If terrorism is defined as politically motivated violence perpetrated against non-combatant targets, then one of the most serious incidents of international terrorism of the year was precisely this U.S. raid on Libya."

Early in the presidency of George Bush, there came the most dramatic developments on the international scene since the end of World War II. In the year 1989, with a dynamic new leader, Mikhail Gorbachev, at the head of the Soviet Union, the long suppressed dissatisfaction with "dictatorships of the proletariat" which had turned out to be dictatorships *over* the proletariat erupted all through the Soviet bloc.

There were mass demonstrations in the Soviet Union and in the countries of Eastern Europe which had been long dominated by the Soviet Union. East Germany agreed to unite with West Germany, and the wall separating East Berlin from West Berlin, long a symbol of the tight control of its citizens by East Germany, was dismantled in the presence of wildly exultant citizens of both Germanies. In Czechoslovakia, a new non-Communist government came into being, headed by a playwright and former imprisoned dissident named Vaclav Havel. In Poland, Bulgaria, Hungary, a new leadership emerged, promising freedom and democracy. And remarkably, all this took place without civil war, in response to overwhelming popular demand.

In the United States, the Republican party claimed that the hard-line policies of Reagan and the increase in military expenditures had brought down the Soviet Union. But the change had begun much earlier, after the death of Stalin in 1953, and especially with the leadership of Nikita Khrushchev. A remarkably open discussion had been initiated.

But the continued hard line of the United States became an obstacle to further liberalization, according to former ambassador to the Soviet Union George Kennan, who wrote that "the general effect of cold war extremism was to delay rather than hasten the great change that overtook the Soviet Union by the end of the 1980s." While the press and politicians in the United States exulted over the collapse of the Soviet Union, Kennan pointed out that, not only did American policies delay this collapse, but these cold war policies were carried on at a frightful cost to the American people:

We paid with forty years of enormous and otherwise unnecessary military expenditures. We paid through the cultivation of nuclear weaponry to the point where the vast and useless nuclear arsenal had become (and remains today) a danger to the very environment of the planet. . . .

The sudden collapse of the Soviet Union left the political leadership of the United States unprepared. Military interventions had been undertaken in Korea and Vietnam with enormous loss of life, also in Cuba and the Dominican Republic, and huge amounts of military aid had been given all over the world—in Europe, Africa, Latin America, the Middle East, Asia—on the supposition that this was necessary to deal with a Communist menace emanating from the Soviet Union. Several trillion dollars had been taken from American citizens in the form of taxes to maintain a huge nuclear and nonnuclear arsenal and military bases all over the world—all primarily justified by the "Soviet threat."

Here then was an opportunity for the United States to reconstruct its foreign policy, and to free hundreds of billions of dollars a year from the budget to be used for constructive, healthy projects.

But this did not happen. Along with the exultation "We have won the cold war" came a kind of panic: "What can we do to maintain our military establishment?"

It became clearer now, although it had been suspected, that United States foreign policy was not simply based on the existence of the Soviet Union, but was motivated by fear of revolution in various parts of the world. The radical social critic Noam Chomsky had long maintained that "the appeal to security was largely fraudulent, the Cold War framework having been employed as a device to justify the suppression of independent nationalism—whether in Europe, Japan, or the Third World" (*World Orders Old and New*).

The fear of "independent nationalism" was that this would jeopardize powerful American economic interests. Revolutions in Nicaragua or Cuba or El Salvador or Chile were threats to United Fruit, Anaconda Copper, International Telephone and

Telegraph, and others. Thus, foreign interventions presented to the public as "in the national interest" were really undertaken for special interests, for which the American people were asked to sacrifice their sons and their tax dollars.

The CIA now had to prove it was still needed. The *New York Times* (February 4, 1992) declared that "in a world where the postwar enemy has ceased to exist, the C.I.A. and its handful of sister agencies, with their billion-dollar satellites and mountains of classified documents, must somehow remain relevant in the minds of Americans."

The military budget remained huge. The cold war budget of $300 billion was reduced by 7 percent to $280 billion. The Chairman of the Joint Chiefs of Staff, Colin Powell, said: "I want to scare the hell out of the rest of the world. I don't say that in a bellicose way."

As if to prove that the gigantic military establishment was still necessary, the Bush administration, in its four-year term, launched two wars: a "small" one against Panama and a massive one against Iraq.

Coming into office in 1989, George Bush was embarrassed by the new defiant posture of Panama's dictator, General Manuel Noriega. Noriega's regime was corrupt, brutal, authoritarian, but President Reagan and Vice-President Bush had overlooked this because Noriega was useful to the United States. He cooperated with the CIA in many ways, such as offering Panama as a base for contra operations against the Sandinista government of Nicaragua and meeting with Colonel Oliver North to discuss sabotage targets in Nicaragua. When he was director of the CIA in 1976–1977, Bush had protected Noriega.

But by 1987 Noriega's usefulness was over, his activities in the drug trade were in the open, and he became a convenient target for an administration which wanted to prove that the United States, apparently unable to destroy the Castro regime or the Sandinistas or the revolutionary movement in El Salvador, was still a power in the Caribbean.

Claiming that it wanted to bring Noriega to trial as a drug

trafficker (he had been indicted in Florida on that charge) and also that it needed to protect U.S. citizens (a military man and his wife had been threatened by Panamanian soldiers), the United States invaded Panama in December 1989, with 26,000 troops.

It was a quick victory. Noriega was captured and brought to Florida to stand trial (where he was subsequently found guilty and sent to prison). But in the invasion, neighborhoods in Panama City were bombarded and hundreds, perhaps thousands of civilians were killed. It was estimated that 14,000 were homeless. Writer Mark Hertsgaard noted that even if the official Pentagon figure of several hundred civilian casualties was correct, this meant that in Panama the U.S. had killed as many people as did the Chinese government in its notorious attack on student demonstrators at Tiananmen Square in Beijing six months earlier. A new president friendly to the United States was installed in Panama, but poverty and unemployment remained, and in 1992 the *New York Times* reported that the invasion and removal of Noriega "failed to stanch the flow of illicit narcotics through Panama."

The United States, however, succeeded in one of its aims, to reestablish its strong influence over Panama. The *Times* reported: "The President [of Panama] and his key aides and the American Ambassador, Deane Hinton, have breakfast together once a week in a meeting that many Panamanians view as the place where important decisions are taken."

Liberal Democrats (John Kerry and Ted Kennedy of Massachusetts, and many others) declared their support of the military action. The Democrats were being true to their historic role as supporters of military intervention, anxious to show that foreign policy was bipartisan. They seemed determined to show they were as tough (or as ruthless) as the Republicans.

But the Panama operation was on too small a scale to accomplish what both the Reagan and Bush administrations badly wanted: to overcome the American public's abhorrence, since Vietnam, of foreign military interventions.

Two years later, the Gulf War against Iraq presented such an opportunity. Iraq, under the brutal dictatorship of Saddam Hussein, had taken over its small but oil-rich neighbor, Kuwait, in August 1990.

George Bush needed something at this point to boost his popularity among American voters. The *Washington Post* (October 16, 1990) had a front-page story headline: "Poll Shows Plunge in Public Confidence: Bush's Rating Plummets." The *Post* reported (October 28): "Some observers in his own party worry that the president will be forced to initiate combat to prevent further erosion of his support at home."

On October 30, a secret decision was made for war against Iraq. The United Nations had responded to the invasion of Kuwait by establishing sanctions against Iraq. Witness after witness testified before Congressional committees in the fall of 1990 that the sanctions were having an effect and should continue. Secret CIA testimony to the Senate affirmed that Iraq's imports and exports had been reduced by more than 90 percent because of the sanctions.

But after the November elections brought gains for the Democrats in Congress, Bush doubled American military forces in the Gulf, to 500,000, creating what was now clearly an offensive force rather than a defensive one. According to Elizabeth Drew, a writer for the *New Yorker*, Bush's aide John Sununu "was telling people that a short successful war would be pure political gold for the President and would guarantee his re-election."

Historian Jon Wiener, analyzing the domestic context of the war decision shortly afterward, wrote that "Bush abandoned sanctions and chose war because his time frame was a political one set by the approaching 1992 presidential elections."

That and the long-time U.S. wish to have a decisive voice in the control of Middle East oil resources were the crucial elements in the decision to go to war against Iraq. Shortly after the war, as representatives of the thirteen oil-producing nations were about to gather in Geneva, the business correspondent of the *New York Times* wrote: "By virtue of its military victory the United States is likely to have more influence in the Organization of Petroleum

Exporting Countries than any industrial nation has ever exercised."

But those motives were not presented to the American public. It was told that the United States wanted to liberate Kuwait from Iraqi control. The major media dwelled on this as a reason for war, without noting that other countries had been invaded without the United States showing such concern (East Timor by Indonesia, Iran by Iraq, Lebanon by Israel, Mozambique by South Africa; to say nothing of countries invaded by the United States itself—Grenada, Panama).

The justification for war that seemed most compelling was that Iraq was on its way to building a nuclear bomb, but the evidence for this was very weak. Before the crisis over Kuwait, Western intelligence sources had estimated it would take Iraq three to ten years to build a nuclear weapon. Even if Iraq could build a bomb in a year or two, which was the most pessimistic estimate, it had no delivery system to send it anywhere. Besides, Israel already had nuclear weapons. And the United States had perhaps 30,000 of them. The Bush administration was trying hard to develop a paranoia in the nation about an Iraqi bomb which did not yet exist.

Bush seemed determined to go to war. There had been several chances to negotiate an Iraqi withdrawal from Kuwait right after the invasion, including an Iraqi proposal reported on August 29 by *Newsday* correspondent Knut Royce. But there was no response from the United States. When Secretary of State James Baker went to Geneva to meet with Iraqi foreign minister Tariq Aziz, the instruction from Bush was "no negotiations."

Despite months of exhortation from Washington about the dangers of Saddam Hussein, surveys showed that less than half of the public favored military action.

In January 1991, Bush, apparently feeling the need for support, asked Congress to give him the authority to make war. This was not a *declaration* of war, as called for by the Constitution; but since Korea and Vietnam, that provision of the Constitution seemed dead, and even the "strict constructionists" on the Supreme Court who prided themselves on taking the words of the Constitution literally and seriously would not intervene.

The debate in Congress was lively. (At one point, a Senate speech was interrupted by protesters in the balcony shouting "No blood for oil!" The protesters were hustled out by guards.) It is likely that Bush was sure of having enough votes, or he would have launched the invasion without Congressional approval; after all, the precedent for ignoring Congress and the Constitution had been set in Korea, Vietnam, Grenada, and Panama.

The Senate voted for military action by only a few votes. The House supported the resolution by a larger majority. However, once Bush ordered the attack on Iraq, both houses, with just a few dissents, Democrats as well as Republicans, voted to "support the war and support the troops."

It was in mid-January 1991, after Saddam Hussein defied an ultimatum to leave Kuwait, that the U.S. launched its air war against Iraq. It was given the name Desert Storm. The government and the media had conjured up a picture of a formidable military power, but Iraq was far from that. The U.S. Air Force had total control of the air, and could bomb at will.

Not only that, U.S. officials had virtual total control of the airwaves. The American public was overwhelmed with television photos of "smart bombs" and confident statements that laser bombs were being guided with perfect precision to military targets. The major networks presented all of these claims without question or criticism.

This confidence in "smart bombs" sparing civilians may have contributed to a shift in public opinion, from being equally divided on going to war, to perhaps 85 percent support for the invasion. Perhaps more important in winning over public support was that once American military were engaged, it seemed to many people who had previously opposed military action that to criticize it now meant betraying the troops who were there. All over the nation yellow ribbons were displayed as a symbol of support for the forces in Iraq.

In fact, the public was being deceived about how "smart" the bombs being dropped on Iraqi towns were. After talking with former intelligence and Air Force officers, a correspondent for the Boston *Globe* reported that perhaps 40 percent of the laser-guided bombs dropped in Operation Desert Storm missed their targets.

John Lehman, Secretary of the Navy under President Reagan, estimated there had been thousands of civilian casualties. The Pentagon officially had no figure on this. A senior Pentagon official told the *Globe*, "To tell you the truth, we're not really focusing on this question."

A Reuters dispatch from Iraq described the destruction of a seventy-three-room hotel in a town south of Baghdad, and quoted an Egyptian witness: "They hit the hotel, full of families, and then they came back to hit it again." Reuters reported that the air raids on Iraq first used laser-guided bombs, but within a few weeks turned to B-52s, which carried conventional bombs, meaning more indiscriminate bombing.

American reporters were kept from seeing the war close-up, and their dispatches were subject to censorship. Apparently recalling how press reports of civilian casualties had affected public opinion during the Vietnam war, the U.S. government was taking no chances this time.

A *Washington Post* reporter complained about the control of information, writing (January 22, 1991):

> The bombing has involved . . . dozens of high-flying B-52 bombers equipped with huge, unguided munitions. But the Pentagon has not allowed interviews with B-52 pilots, shown videotapes of their actions or answered any questions about the operations of an aircraft that is the most deadly and least accurate in the armada of more than 2000 U.S. and allied planes in the Persian Gulf region. . . .

In mid-February, U.S. planes dropped bombs on an air raid shelter in Baghdad at four in the morning, killing 400 to 500 people. An Associated Press reporter who was one of few allowed to go to the site said: "Most of the recovered bodies were charred and mutilated beyond recognition. Some clearly were children." The Pentagon claimed it was a military target, but the AP reporter on the scene said: "No evidence of any military presence could be seen inside the wreckage." Other reporters who inspected the site agreed.

After the war, fifteen Washington news bureau chiefs complained in a joint statement that the Pentagon exercised "virtual total control . . . over the American press" during the Gulf War.

But while it was happening, leading television news commentators behaved as if they were working for the United States government. For instance, CBS correspondent Dan Rather, perhaps the most widely seen of the TV newsmen, reported from Saudi Arabia on a film showing a laser bomb (this one dropped by British aircraft in support of the American war) hitting a marketplace and killing civilians. Rather's only comment was: "We can be sure that Saddam Hussein will make propaganda of these casualties."

When the Soviet government tried to negotiate an end to the war, bringing Iraq out of Kuwait before the ground war could get under way, top CBS correspondent Lesley Stahl asked another reporter: "Isn't this the nightmare scenario? Aren't the Soviets trying to stop us?" (Ed Siegel, TV reporter for the Boston *Globe*, February 23, 1991).

The final stage of the war, barely six weeks after it had begun, was a ground assault which, like the air war, encountered virtually no resistance. With victory certain and the Iraqi army in full flight, U.S. planes kept bombing the retreating soldiers who clogged the highway out of Kuwait City. A reporter called the scene "a blazing hell . . . a gruesome testament. . . . To the east and west across the sand lay the bodies of those fleeing."

A Yale professor of military history, Michael Howard, writing in the *New York Times* (January 28, 1991), quoted the military strategist Clausewitz approvingly: "The fact that a bloody slaughter is a horrifying act must make us take war more seriously, but not provide an excuse for gradually blunting our swords in the name of humanity." Howard went on to say: "In this conflict of wills, the bottom line remains a readiness to kill and be killed. . . ."

The human consequences of the war became shockingly clear after its end, when it was revealed that the bombings of Iraq had caused starvation, disease, and the deaths of tens of thousands of children. A U.N. team visiting Iraq immediately after the war reported that "the recent conflict has wrought near-apocalyptic results upon the infrastructure. . . . Most means of modern life support have been destroyed or rendered tenuous. . . ."

A Harvard medical team reporting in May said that child mortality had risen steeply, and that 55,000 more children died in the first four months of the year (the war lasted from January 15 to February 28) than in a comparable period the year before.

The director of a pediatric hospital in Baghdad told a *New York Times* reporter that on the first night of the bombing campaign the electricity was knocked out: "Mothers grabbed their children out of incubators, took intravenous tubes out of their arms. Others were removed from oxygen tents and they ran to the basement, where there was no heat. I lost more than 40 prematures in the first 12 hours of the bombing."

Although in the course of the war Saddam Hussein had been depicted by U.S. officials and the press as another Hitler, the war ended short of a march into Baghdad, leaving Hussein in power. It seemed that the United States had wanted to weaken him, but not to eliminate him, in order to keep him as a balance against Iran. In the years before the Gulf War, the United States had sold arms to both Iran and Iraq, at different times favoring one or the other as part of the traditional "balance of power" strategy.

Therefore, as the war ended, the United States did not support Iraqi dissidents who wanted to overthrow the regime of Saddam Hussein. A *New York Times* dispatch from Washington, datelined March 26, 1991, reported: "President Bush has decided to let President Saddam Hussein put down rebellions in his country without American intervention rather than risk the splintering of Iraq, according to official statements and private briefings today."

This left the Kurdish minority, which was rebelling against Saddam Hussein, helpless. And anti-Hussein elements among the

Iraqi majority were also left hanging. The *Washington Post* reported (May 3, 1991): "Major defections from the Iraqi military were in the offing in March at the height of the Kurdish rebellion, but never materialized because the officers concluded the U.S. would not back the uprising. . . ."

The man who had been Jimmy Carter's National Security Adviser, Zbigniew Brzezinski, a month after the end of the Gulf War, gave a cold assessment of the pluses and minuses of the event. "The benefits are undeniably impressive. First, a blatant act of aggression was rebuffed and punished. . . . Second, U.S military power is henceforth likely to be taken more seriously. . . . Third, the Middle East and Persian Gulf region is now clearly an American sphere of preponderance."

Brzezinski, however, was concerned about "some negative consequences." One of them was that "the very intensity of the air assault on Iraq gives rise to concern that the conduct of the war may come to be seen as evidence that Americans view Arab lives as worthless. . . . And that raises the moral question of the proportionality of response."

His point about Arab lives being seen as "worthless" was underlined by the fact that the war provoked an ugly wave of anti-Arab racism in the United States, with Arab-Americans insulted or beaten or threatened with death. There were bumper stickers that said "I don't brake for Iraqis." An Arab-American businessman was beaten in Toledo, Ohio.

Brzezinski's measured assessment of the Gulf War could be taken as close to representing the view of the Democratic Party. It went along with the Bush administration. It was pleased with the results. It had some misgivings about civilian casualties. But it did not constitute an opposition.

President George Bush was satisfied. As the war ended, he declared on a radio broadcast: "The specter of Vietnam has been buried forever in the desert sands of the Arabian peninsula."

The Establishment press very much agreed. The two leading news magazines, *Time* and *Newsweek*, had special editions hailing the victory in the war, noting there had been only a few hundred

American casualties, without any mention of Iraqi casualties. A *New York Times* editorial (March 30, 1991) said: "America's victory in the Persian Gulf war . . . provided special vindication for the U.S. Army, which brilliantly exploited its firepower and mobility and in the process erased memories of its grievous difficulties in Vietnam."

A black poet in Berkeley, California, June Jordan, had a different view: "I suggest to you it's a hit the same way that crack is, and it doesn't last long."

11

THE UNREPORTED RESISTANCE

In the early 1990s, a writer for the *New Republic* magazine, reviewing with approval in the *New York Times* a book about the influence of dangerously unpatriotic elements among American intellectuals, warned his readers of the existence of "a permanent adversarial culture" in the United States.

It was an accurate observation. Despite the political consensus of Democrats and Republicans in Washington which set limits on American reform, making sure that capitalism was in place, that national military strength was maintained, that wealth and power remained in the hands of a few, there were millions of Americans, probably tens of millions, who refused, either actively or silently, to go along. Their activities were largely unreported by the media. They constituted this "permanent adversarial culture."

The Democratic party was more responsive to these Americans, on whose votes it depended. But its responsiveness was limited by its own captivity to corporate interests, and its domestic reforms were severely limited by the system's dependency on militarism and war. Thus, President Lyndon Johnson's War on Poverty in the sixties became a victim of the war in Vietnam, and

Jimmy Carter could not go far so long as he insisted on a huge outlay of money for the military, much of this to stockpile more nuclear weapons.

As these limits became clear in the Carter years, a small but determined movement against nuclear arms began to grow. The pioneers were a tiny group of Christian pacifists who had been active against the Vietnam war (among them were a former priest, Philip Berrigan, and his wife, Elizabeth McAlister, a former nun). Again and again, members of this group would be arrested for engaging in nonviolent acts of dramatic protest against nuclear war at the Pentagon and the White House—trespassing on forbidden areas, pouring their own blood on symbols of the war machine.

In 1980, small delegations of peace activists from all over the country maintained a series of demonstrations at the Pentagon, in which over a thousand people were arrested for acts of nonviolent civil disobedience.

In September of that year, Philip Berrigan, his brother Daniel (the Jesuit priest and poet), Molly Rush (a mother of six), Anne Montgomery (a nun and counselor to young runaways and prostitutes in Manhattan), and four of their friends made their way past a guard in the General Electric Plant at King of Prussia, Pennsylvania, where nose cones for nuclear missiles were manufactured. They used sledgehammers to smash two of the nose cones and smeared their own blood over missile parts, blueprints, and furniture. Arrested, sentenced to years in prison, they said they were trying to set an example to do as the Bible suggested, to beat swords into plowshares.

They pointed to the huge allocations of taxpayers' money to corporations producing weaponry: "G.E. drains $3 million a day from the public treasury—an enormous larceny against the poor." Before their trial (they came to be known as the Plowshares Eight), Daniel Berrigan had written in the *Catholic Worker*:

I know of no sure way of predicting where things will go from there, whether others will hear and respond, or how quickly or slowly. Or whether the act will fail to vitalize others, will come to a grinding halt then and there, its actors stigmatized or dismissed as fools. One swallows dry and takes a chance.

In fact, the movement did not come to a halt. Over the next decade, a national movement against nuclear weapons developed, from a small number of men and women willing to go to jail to make others stop and think to millions of Americans frightened at the thought of nuclear holocaust, indignant at the billions of dollars spent on weaponry while people were in need of life's necessities.

Even the very Middle-American Pennsylvania jurors who convicted the Plowshares Eight showed remarkable sympathy with their actions. One juror, Michael DeRosa, told a reporter, "I didn't think they really went to commit a crime. They went to protest." Another, Mary Ann Ingram, said the jury argued about that: "We . . . really didn't want to convict them on anything. But we had to because of the way the judge said the thing you can use is what you get under the law." She added: "These people are not criminals. Here are people who are trying to do some good for the country. But the judge said nuclear power wasn't the issue."

Reagan's huge military budget was to provoke a national movement against nuclear weapons. In the election of 1980 that brought him into the Presidency, local referenda in three districts in western Massachusetts permitted voters to say whether they believed in a mutual Soviet-American halt to testing, production, and deployment of all nuclear weapons, and wanted Congress to devote those funds instead to civilian use. Two peace groups had worked for months on the campaign and all three districts approved the resolution (94,000 to 65,000), even those that voted for Reagan as President. Similar referenda received majority votes between 1978 and 1981 in San Francisco, Berkeley, Oakland, Madison, and Detroit.

Women were in the forefront of the new antinuclear movement. Randall Forsberg, a young specialist in nuclear arms, organized the Council for a Nuclear Weapons Freeze, whose simple program—a mutual Soviet-American freeze on the production of new nuclear weapons—began to catch on throughout the country. Shortly after Reagan's election, two thousand women assembled in Washington, marched on the Pentagon, and surrounded it in a great circle, linking arms or stretching to hold the ends of brightly colored scarves. One hundred forty women were arrested for blocking the Pentagon entrance.

A small group of doctors began to organize meetings around the country to teach citizens the medical consequences of nuclear war. They were the core of the Physicians for Social Responsibility, and Dr. Helen Caldicott, the group's president, became one of the most powerful and eloquent national leaders of the movement. At one of their public symposia, Howard Hiatt, dean of the Harvard School of Public Health, gave a graphic description of the results of one twenty-megaton nuclear bomb falling on Boston. Two million people would die. Survivors would be burned, blinded, crippled. In a nuclear war there would be 25 million severe burn cases in the nation, yet all existing facilities could take care of only 200 cases.

At a national meeting of Catholic bishops early in the Reagan administration, the majority opposed any use of nuclear weapons. In November 1981, there were meetings on 151 college campuses around the country on the issue of nuclear war. And at local elections in Boston that month, a resolution calling for increased federal spending on social programs "by reducing the amount of our tax dollars spent on nuclear weapons and programs of foreign intervention" won a majority in every one of Boston's twenty-two wards, including both white and black working-class districts.

On June 12, 1982, the largest political demonstration in the history of the country took place in Central Park, New York City. Close to a million people gathered to express their determination to bring an end to the arms race.

Scientists who had worked on the atom bomb added their voices to the growing movement. George Kistiakowsky, a Harvard University chemistry professor who had worked on the first atomic bomb, and later was science adviser to President Eisenhower, became a spokesman for the disarmament movement. His last public remarks, before his death from cancer at the age of eighty-two, were in an editorial for the *Bulletin of Atomic Scientists* in December 1982. "I tell you as my parting words: Forget the channels. There simply is not enough time left before the world explodes. Concentrate instead on organizing, with so many others of like mind, a mass movement for peace such as there has not been before."

By the spring of 1983, the nuclear freeze had been endorsed by 368 city and county councils across the country, by 444 town meetings and 17 state legislatures, and by the House of Representatives. A Harris poll at this time indicated that 79 percent of the population wanted a nuclear freeze agreement with the Soviet Union. Even among evangelical Christians—a group of 40 million people presumed to be conservative and pro-Reagan—a Gallup poll sampling showed 60 percent favoring a nuclear freeze.

A year after the great Central Park demonstration, there were over three thousand antiwar groups around the country. And the antinuclear feeling was being reflected in the culture—in books, magazine articles, plays, motion pictures. Jonathan Schell's impassioned book against the arms race, *The Fate of the Earth*, became a national best-seller. A documentary film on the arms race made in Canada was forbidden to enter the country by the Reagan administration, but a federal court ordered it admitted.

In less than three years, there had come about a remarkable change in public opinion. At the time of Reagan's election, nationalist feeling—drummed up by the recent hostage crisis in Iran and by the Russian invasion of Afghanistan—was strong; the University of Chicago's National Opinion Research Center found that only 12 percent of those it polled thought too much was being spent on arms. But when it took another poll in the spring of 1982, that figure rose to 32 percent. And in the spring of 1983, a *New York Times*/CBS News poll found that the figure had risen again, to 48 percent.

Antimilitarist feeling expressed itself also in resistance to the draft. When President Jimmy Carter, responding to the Soviet

Union's invasion of Afghanistan, called for the registration of young men for a military draft, more than 800,000 men (10 percent) failed to register. One mother wrote to the *New York Times*:

> To the Editor: Thirty-six years ago I stood in front of the crematorium. The ugliest force in the world had promised itself that I should be removed from the cycle of life—that I should never know the pleasure of giving life. With great guns and great hatred, this force thought itself the equal of the force of life.
>
> I survived the great guns, and with every smile of my son, they grow smaller. It is not for me, sir, to offer my son's blood as lubricant for the next generation of guns. I remove myself and my own from the cycle of death.
>
> Isabella Leitner

Former Nixon aide Alexander Haig warned, in an interview in the French journal *Politique Internationale*, that there might reappear in the U.S. the conditions that forced President Nixon to stop the draft. "There is a Jane Fonda on every doorstep," he said.

One of the young men who refused to register, James Peters, wrote an open letter to President Carter:

> Dear Mr. President: On July 23, 1980, I . . . am expected to report to my local post office for the purpose of registering with the Selective Service System. I hereby inform you, Mr. President, that I will not register on July 23, or at any time thereafter. . . . We have tried militarism, and it has failed the human race in every way imaginable.

Once he was in office, Ronald Reagan hesitated to renew draft registration, because, as his Secretary of Defense, Caspar Weinberger, explained, "President Reagan believes that resuming the draft to meet manpower problems would lead to public unrest comparable to that in the sixties and seventies." William Beecher, a former Pentagon reporter, wrote in November 1981 that Reagan was "obviously concerned, even alarmed, by the mounting voices of discontent and suspicion over emerging U.S. nuclear strategy both in the streets of Europe and more recently on American campuses."

Hoping to intimidate this opposition, the Reagan administration began to prosecute draft resisters. One of those facing prison was Benjamin Sasway, who cited U.S. military intervention in El Salvador as a good reason not to register for the draft.

Aroused by Sasway's civil disobedience, a right-wing columnist (William A. Rusher, of the *National Review*) wrote indignantly that one heritage of the sixties was a new generation of antiwar teachers:

> Almost certainly there was a teacher, or teachers, who taught Benjamin Sasway to look at American society as a hypocritical, exploitative, materialistic roadblock on the path of human progress. The generation of the Vietnam protesters is now in its early thirties, and the academicians among them are already ensconced in the faculties of the country's high schools and colleges. . . . What a pity our jurisprudence doesn't allow us to reach and penalize the real architects of this sort of destruction!

Reagan's policy of giving military aid to the dictatorship of El Salvador was not accepted quietly around the nation. He had barely taken office when the following report appeared in the Boston *Globe*:

> It was a scene reminiscent of the 1960s, a rally of students in Harvard Yard shouting antiwar slogans, a candlelight march through the streets of Cambridge. . . . 2000 persons, mostly students, gathered to protest U.S. involvement in El Salvador. . . . Students from Tufts, MIT, Boston University and Boston College, the University of Massachusetts, Brandeis, Suffolk, Dartmouth, Northeastern, Vassar, Yale and Simmons were represented.

During commencement exercises that spring of 1981 at Syracuse University, when Reagan's Secretary of State, Alexander Haig, was given an honorary doctorate in "public service," two hundred students and faculty turned their backs on the presentation. During Haig's address, the press reported, "Nearly every pause in Mr. Haig's fifteen-minute address was punctuated by chants: 'Human needs, not military greed!' 'Get out of El Salvador!' 'Washington guns killed American nuns!'"

The last slogan was a reference to the execution in the fall of 1980 of four American nuns by Salvadoran soldiers. Thousands of people in El Salvador were being murdered each year by "death squads" sponsored by a government armed by the United States, and the American public was beginning to pay attention to events in this tiny Central American country.

As has been true generally in the making of U.S. foreign policy, there was no pretense at democracy. Public opinion was simply ignored. A *New York Times*/CBS News poll in the spring of 1982 reported that only 16 percent of its sampling favored Reagan's program of sending military and economic aid to El Salvador.

In the spring of 1983, it was disclosed that an American physician named Charles Clement was working with the Salvadoran rebels. As an Air Force pilot in Southeast Asia, he had become disillusioned with U.S. policy there, having seen firsthand that his government was lying, and refused to fly any more missions. The Air Force response was to commit him to a psychiatric hospital, then to discharge him as psychologically unfit. He went to medical school, and then volunteered to be a doctor with the guerrillas in El Salvador.

There was much talk in the American press in the early eighties about the political cautiousness of a new generation of college students concerned mostly with their own careers. But when, at the Harvard commencement of June 1983, Mexican writer Carlos Fuentes criticized American intervention in Latin America, and said, "Because we are your true friends, we will not permit you to conduct yourselves in Latin American affairs as the Soviet Union conducts itself in Central European and Central Asian affairs," he was interrupted twenty times by applause and received a standing ovation when finished.

Among my own students at Boston University, I did not find the pervasive selfishness and unconcern with others that the media kept reporting, in deadening repetition, about the students of the eighties. In the journals they kept, I found the following comments:

A male student: "Do you think anything good that has happened in the world had anything to do with government? I work in Roxbury [a black neighborhood]. I know the government doesn't work. Not for the people of Roxbury, and not for the people anywhere. It works for people with money."

A graduate of a Catholic high school: "America to me is a society, a culture. America is my home; if someone were to rob that *culture* from me, then perhaps there would be reason to resist. I will not die, however, to defend the honor of the *government*."

A young woman: "As a white middle class person I've never felt discriminated against at all. But I'll say this: If anyone ever tried to make me sit in a different schoolroom, use a different bathroom, or anything like that, I would knock them right on their ass. . . . The people are the last ones that need their rights stated on paper, for if they're abused or injusticed by government or authority, they can act on the injustice directly. . . . When you look at the . . . statements of rights and laws, it's really government and authority and institutions and corporations that need laws and rights to insulate them from the physicality, the directness of the people."

Beyond the campuses, out in the country, there was opposition to government policy, not widely known. A report from Tucson, Arizona, early in the Reagan presidency described "demonstrators, mainly middle-aged," protesting at the Federal Building against U.S. involvement in El Salvador. Over a thousand people in Tucson marched in a procession and attended a mass to commemorate the anniversary of the assassination of Archbishop Oscar Romero, who had spoken out against the Salvadoran death squads.

Over 60,000 Americans signed pledges to take action of some

sort, including civil disobedience, if Reagan moved to invade Nicaragua. When the President instituted a blockade of the tiny country to try to force its government out of power, there were demonstrations around the country. In Boston alone, 550 people were arrested protesting the blockade.

During Reagan's presidency, there were hundreds of actions throughout the nation against his policies in South Africa. He obviously did not want to see the white ruling minority of South Africa displaced by the radical African National Congress, which represented the black majority. Chester Crocker, Assistant Secretary of State for African Affairs, in his memoirs, called Reagan "insensitive" to the conditions under which blacks lived there. Public opinion was strong enough to cause Congress to legislate economic sanctions against the South African Government in 1986, overriding Reagan's veto.

Reagan's cuts in social services were felt on the local level as vital needs could not be taken care of, and there were angry reactions. In the spring and summer of 1981, residents of East Boston took to the streets; for fifty-five nights they blocked major thoroughfares and the Sumner Tunnel during rush hour, in order to protest cutbacks in funds for fire, police, and teachers. The police superintendent, John Doyle, said: "Maybe these people are starting to take lessons from the protests of the sixties and seventies." The Boston *Globe* reported: "The demonstrators in East Boston were mostly middle-aged, middle- or working-class people who said they had never protested anything before."

The Reagan administration took away federal funds for the arts, suggesting that the performing arts seek help from private donors. In New York, two historic Broadway theaters were razed to make way for a luxury fifty-story hotel, after two hundred theater people demonstrated, picketing, reading plays and singing songs, refusing to disperse when ordered by police. Some of the nation's best-known theater personalities were arrested, including producer Joseph Papp, actresses Tammy Grimes, Estelle Parsons, and Celeste Holm, actors Richard Gere and Michael Moriarty.

The budget cuts spurred strikes across the country, often by groups unaccustomed to striking. In the fall of 1982, United Press International reported:

> Angered by layoffs, salary cuts and uncertainty about job security, more schoolteachers throughout the country have decided to go on strike. Teachers' strikes last week in seven states, from Rhode Island to Washington, have idled more than 300,000 students.

Surveying a series of news events in the first week of January 1983, David Nyhan of the Boston *Globe* wrote: "There is something brewing in the land that bodes ill for those in Washington who ignore it. People have moved from the frightened state to the angry stage and are acting out their frustrations in ways that will test the fabric of civil order." He gave some examples:

> In Little Washington, Pennsylvania, in early 1983, when a 50-year-old computer science teacher who led a teachers' strike was sent to jail, 2000 people demonstrated outside the jailhouse in his support, and the Pittsburgh *Post-Gazette* called it "the largest crowd in Washington County since the 1794 Whiskey Rebellion."
>
> When unemployed or bankrupt home owners in the Pittsburgh area could no longer make mortgage payments, and foreclosure sales were scheduled, 60 pickets jammed the courthouse to protest the auction, and Allegheny sheriff Eugene Coon halted the proceedings.
>
> The foreclosure of a 320-acre wheat farm in Springfield, Colorado, was interrupted by 200 angry farmers, who had to be dispersed by tear gas and Mace.

When Reagan arrived in Pittsburgh in April 1983 to make a speech, 3000 people, many of them unemployed steelworkers, demonstrated against him, standing in the rain outside his hotel. Demonstrations by the unemployed were taking place in Detroit, Flint, Chicago, Cleveland, Los Angeles, Washington—over twenty cities in all.

Just around that time, Miami blacks rioted against police brutality; they were reacting against their general deprivation as well. The unemployment rate among young African-Americans had risen above 50 percent, and the Reagan administration's only response to poverty was to build more jails. Understanding that blacks would not vote for him, Reagan tried, unsuccessfully, to get Congress to eliminate a crucial section of the Voting Rights Act of 1965, which had been very effective in safeguarding the right of blacks to vote in Southern states.

Reagan's policies clearly joined the two issues of disarmament and social welfare. It was guns versus children, and this was expressed dramatically by the head of the Children's Defense Fund, Marian Wright Edelman, in a commencement speech at the Milton Academy in Massachusetts in the summer of 1983:

> You are graduating into a nation and world teetering on the brink of moral and economic bankruptcy. Since 1980, our President and Congress have been turning our national plowshares into swords and been bringing good news to the rich at the expense of the poor. . . . Children are the major victims. Our misguided national and world choices are literally killing children daily. . . . Yet governments throughout the world, led by our own, spend over $600 billion a year on arms, while an estimated 1 billion of our world's people live in poverty and 600 million are under- or unemployed. Where is the human commitment and political will to find the relative pittance of money needed to protect children?

She urged her listeners: "Pick a piece of the problem that you can help solve while trying to see how your piece fits into the broader social change puzzle."

Her words seemed to represent a growing mood that worried the Reagan administration. It withdrew some of its proposed cutbacks, and Congress eliminated others. When, in its second year, the administration proposed $9 billion in cuts in support for children and poor families, Congress accepted only $1 billion. The Washington correspondent of the *New York Times* reported:

"Political concerns about the fairness of Mr. Reagan's programs have forced the Administration to curtail its efforts to make further cutbacks in programs for the poor."

The repeated elections of Republican candidates, Reagan in 1980 and 1984, George Bush in 1988, were treated by the press with words like "landslide" and "overwhelming victory." They were ignoring four facts: that roughly half the population, though eligible to vote, did not; that those who did vote were limited severely in their choices to the two parties that monopolized the money and the media; that as a result many of their votes were cast without enthusiasm; and that there was little relationship between voting for a candidate and voting for specific policies.

In 1980 Reagan received 51.6 percent of the popular vote, while Jimmy Carter received 41.7 percent and John Anderson (a liberal Republican running on a third-party ticket) received 6.7 percent. Only 54 percent of the voting-age population voted, so that—of the total eligible to vote—27 percent voted for Reagan.

A survey by the *New York Times* found that only 11 percent of those who voted for Reagan did so because "he's a real conservative." Three times as many said they voted for him because "it is time for a change."

For a second term, running against former Vice-President Walter Mondale, Reagan won 59 percent of the popular vote, but with half the electorate not voting, he had 29 percent of the voting population.

In the 1988 election, with Vice-President George Bush running against Democrat Michael Dukakis, Bush's 54 percent victory added up to 27 percent of the eligible voters.

Because our peculiar voting arrangements allow a small margin of popular votes to become a huge majority of electoral votes, the media can talk about "overwhelming victory," thus deceiving their readers and disheartening those who don't look closely at the statistics. Could one say from these figures that "the American people" wanted Reagan, or Bush, as President? One could certainly say that more voters preferred the Republican candidates to their opponents. But even more seemed to want neither

candidate. Nevertheless, on the basis of these slim electoral plu-
ralities, Reagan and Bush would claim that "the people" had spoken.

Indeed, when the people did speak about issues, in surveys of
public opinion, they expressed beliefs to which neither the Republican nor Democratic parties paid attention.

For instance, both parties, through the eighties and early
nineties, kept strict limits on social programs for the poor, on the
grounds that this would require more taxes, and "the people" did
not want higher taxes.

This was certainly true as a general proposition, that Americans wanted to pay as little in taxes as possible. But when they
were asked if they would be willing to pay higher taxes for specific purposes like health and education, they said yes, they
would. For instance, a 1990 poll of Boston area voters showed
that 54 percent of them would pay more taxes if that would go
toward cleaning up the environment.

And when higher taxes were presented in class terms, rather
than as a general proposal, people were quite clear. A *Wall Street
Journal*/NBC News poll in December 1990 showed that 84 percent of the respondents favored a surtax on millionaires (this provision was dropped around that time from a Democratic-Republi-
can budget compromise). Even though 51 percent of the respondents were in favor of *raising* the capital gains tax, neither major
party favored that.

A Harris/Harvard School of Public Health poll of 1989
showed that most Americans (61 percent) favored a Canadian-
type health system, in which the government was the single payer
to doctors and hospitals, bypassing the insurance companies, and
offering universal medical coverage to everyone. Neither the
Democratic nor the Republican party adopted that as its program, although both insisted they wanted to "reform" the health
system.

A survey by the Gordon Black Corporation for the National
Press Club in 1992 found that 59 percent of all voters wanted a
50 percent cut in defense spending in five years. Neither of the

major parties was willing to make major cuts in the military budget.

How the public felt about government aid to the poor seemed to depend on how the question was put. Both parties, and the media, talked incessantly about the "welfare" system, that it was not working, and the word "welfare" became a signal for opposition. When people were asked (a *New York Times*/CBS News poll of 1992) if more money should be allocated to welfare, 23 percent said no. But when the same people were asked, should the government help the poor, 64 percent said yes.

This was a recurring theme. When, at the height of the Reagan presidency, in 1987, people were asked if the government should guarantee food and shelter to needy people, 62 percent answered yes.

Clearly, there was something amiss with a political system, supposed to be democratic, in which the desires of the voters were repeatedly ignored. They could be ignored with impunity so long as the political system was dominated by two parties, both tied to corporate wealth. An electorate forced to choose between Carter and Reagan, or Reagan and Mondale, or Bush and Dukakis could only despair (or decide not to vote) because neither candidate was capable of dealing with a fundamental economic illness whose roots were deeper than any single presidency.

That illness came from a fact which was almost never talked about: that the United States was a class society, in which 1 percent of the population owned 33 percent of the wealth, with an underclass of 30 to 40 million people living in poverty. The social programs of the sixties—Medicare and Medicaid, food stamps, etc.—did not do much more than maintain the historic American maldistribution of resources.

While the Democrats would give more help to the poor than the Republicans, they were not capable (indeed, not really desirous) of seriously tampering with an economic system in which corporate profit comes before human need.

There was no important national movement for radical change, no social democratic (or democratic socialist) party such as existed in countries in Western Europe, Canada, and New Zealand. But there were a thousand signs of alienation, voices of protest, local actions in every part of the country to call attention to deep-felt grievances, to demand that some injustice be remedied.

For instance, the Citizens' Clearinghouse for Hazardous Wastes in Washington, D.C., which had been formed early in the Reagan administration by housewife and activist Lois Gibbs, reported that it was giving help to 8000 local groups around the country. One of these groups, in Oregon, brought a series of successful lawsuits to force the Environmental Protection Agency to do something about unsafe drinking water in the Bull Run reservoir near Portland.

In Seabrook, New Hampshire, there were years of persistent protest against a nuclear power plant which residents considered a danger to themselves and their families. Between 1977 and 1989, over 3500 people were arrested in these protests. Ultimately, the plant, plagued by financial problems and opposition, had to shut down.

Fear of nuclear accidents was intensified by disastrous events at Three Mile Island in Pennsylvania in 1979 and by an especially frightening calamity in Chernobyl in the Soviet Union in 1986. All of this was having an effect on the once-booming nuclear industry. By 1994, the Tennessee Valley Authority had stopped the construction of three nuclear plants, which the *New York Times* called "the symbolic death notice for the current generation of reactors in the United States."

In Minneapolis, Minnesota, thousands of people demonstrated year after year against the Honeywell Corporation's military contracts, and between 1982 and 1988 over 1800 people were arrested.

Furthermore, when those who engaged in such civil disobedience were brought into court, they often found sympathetic support from juries, winning acquittals from ordinary citizens who seemed to understand that even if they had technically broken the law, they had done so in a good cause.

In 1984, a group of Vermont citizens (the "Winooski Forty-four") refused to leave the hallway outside a U.S. Senator's office, protesting his votes to give arms to the Nicaraguan contras. They were arrested, but at their trial they were treated sympathetically by the judge and acquitted by the jury.

At another trial shortly after, a number of people (including activist Abbie Hoffman and Amy Carter, daughter of former President Jimmy Carter) were charged with blocking CIA recruiters at the University of Massachusetts. They called to the witness stand ex-CIA agents who told the jury that the CIA had engaged in illegal and murderous activities all around the world. The jury acquitted them.

One juror, a woman hospital worker, said later: "I was not familiar with the CIA's activities. . . . I was shocked. . . . I was kind of proud of the students." Another juror said: "It was very educational." The county district attorney, prosecuting the case, concluded: "If there is a message, it was that this jury was composed of middle America. . . . Middle America doesn't want the CIA doing what they are doing."

In the South, while there was no great movement comparable to the civil rights movement of the Sixties, there were hundreds of local groups organizing poor people, white and black. In North Carolina, Linda Stout, the daughter of a mill worker who had died of industrial poisons, coordinated a multiracial network of 500 textile workers, farmers, maids—most of them low-income women of color—in the Piedmont Peace Project.

The historic Highlander Folk School in Tennessee, which had nurtured so many black and white activists throughout the South, was now joined by other folk schools and popular education centers.

Anne Braden, a veteran of racial and labor struggles in the South, was still organizing, leading the Southern Organizing Committee for Economic and Social Justice. The group gave help in local actions: to 300 African-Americans in Tift County, Georgia, who were protesting the existence of a chemical plant which was making them sick; to Native Americans in Cherokee

County, North Carolina, who were organizing to stop a polluted landfill.

Back in the sixties, Chicano farm workers, people of Mexican descent who came to work and live mostly in California and the Southwestern states, rebelled against their feudal working conditions. They went out on strike and organized a national boycott of grapes, under the leadership of Cesar Chavez. Soon farmworkers were organizing in other parts of the country.

In the seventies and eighties, their struggles against poverty and discrimination continued. The Reagan years hit them hard, as it did poor people all over the country. By 1984, 42 percent of all Latino children and one-fourth of the families lived below the poverty line.

Copper miners in Arizona, mostly Mexican, went on strike against the Phelps-Dodge company after it cut wages, benefits, and safety measures in 1983. They were attacked by National Guardsmen and state troopers, by tear gas and helicopters, but held out for three years until a combination of governmental and corporate power finally defeated them.

There were victories too. In 1985, 1700 cannery workers, most of them Mexican women, went on strike in Watsonville, California, and won a union contract with medical benefits. In 1990 workers who had been laid off from the Levi Strauss company in San Antonio because the company was moving to Costa Rica called a boycott, organized a hunger strike, and won concessions. In Los Angeles, Latino janitors went on strike in 1990 and despite police attacks, won recognition of their union, a pay raise, and sick benefits.

Latino and Latina activists (not necessarily Chicano, which refers to those of Mexican ancestry), through the eighties and early nineties, campaigned for better labor conditions, for representation in local government, for tenants' rights, for bilingual education in the schools. Kept out of the media, they organized a bilingual radio movement, and by 1991 had fourteen Latino stations in the country, twelve of them bilingual.

In New Mexico, Latinos fought for land and water rights

against real estate developers who tried to throw them off land they had lived on for decades. In 1988 there was a confrontation, and the people organized an armed occupation, built bunkers for protection against attack, and won support from other communities in the Southwest; finally, a court ruled in their favor.

Abnormal rates of cancer for farmworkers in California aroused the Chicano community. Cesar Chavez of the United Farm Workers fasted for thirty-five days in 1988 to call attention to these conditions. There were now United Farm Workers unions in Texas, Arizona, and other states.

The importation of Mexican workers for low wages, under terrible conditions, spread from the Southwest to other parts of the country. By 1991, 80,000 Latinos lived in North Carolina, 30,000 in north Georgia. The Farm Labor Organizing Committee, which had won a difficult strike in the Ohio tomato fields in 1979, the largest agricultural strike ever in the Midwest, brought thousands of farmworkers together in several Midwest states.

As the Latino population of the country kept growing, it soon matched the 12 percent of the population that was African-American and began to have a distinct effect on American culture. Much of its music, art, and drama was much more consciously political and satirical than mainstream culture.

The Border Arts workshop was formed in 1984 by artists and writers in San Diego and Tijuana, and its work dealt powerfully with issues of racism and injustice. In Northern California, Teatro Campesino and Teatro de la Esperanza performed for working people all over the country, turning schoolhouses, churches, and fields into theaters.

Latinos were especially conscious of the imperial role the United States had played in Mexico and the Caribbean, and many of them became militant critics of U.S. policy toward Nicaragua, El Salvador, and Cuba. In 1970 a great march in Los Angeles against the Vietnam war, which had been attacked by police, left three Chicanos dead.

When the Bush administration was preparing for war against Iraq in the summer of 1990, thousands of people in Los Angeles marched along the same route they had taken twenty years before, when they were protesting the Vietnam war. As Elizabeth Martinez wrote (*500 Years of Chicano History in Pictures*):

> Before and during President Bush's war in the Persian Gulf many people—including Raza [literally "race"; a term adopted by Latino activists]—had doubts about it or were opposed. We had learned some lessons about wars started in the name of democracy that turned out to benefit only the rich and powerful. Raza mobilized to protest this war of mass murder, even faster than the U.S. war in Vietnam, though we could not stop it.

In 1992, a fund-raising group which came out of the Vietnam war called Resist made donations to 168 organizations around the country—community groups, peace groups, Native American groups, prisoners' rights organizations, health and environmental groups.

A new generation of lawyers, schooled in the sixties, constituted a small but socially conscious minority within the legal profession. They were in court defending the poor and the helpless, or bringing suit against powerful corporations. One law firm used its talent and energy to defend whistleblowers—men and women who were fired because they "blew the whistle" on corporate corruption that victimized the public.

The women's movement, which had managed to raise the consciousness of the whole nation on the issue of sexual equality, faced a powerful backlash in the eighties. The Supreme Court's defense of abortion rights in its 1973 *Roe* v. *Wade* decision aroused a pro-life movement that had strong supporters in Washington. Congress passed, and the Supreme Court later let stand, a law that eliminated federal medical benefits to help poor women pay for abortions. But the National Organization of Women and other groups remained strong; in 1989, a Washington rally for what had come to be known as the right to choose drew over 300,000 people. When, in 1994 and 1995, abortion clinics were attacked and several supporters murdered, the conflict became grimly intense.

The rights of gay and lesbian Americans had come vividly to the forefront in the Seventies with radical changes in ideas about sexuality and freedom. The gay movement then became a visible presence in the nation, with parades, demonstrations, campaigns for the elimination of state statutes discriminating against homosexuals. One result was a growing literature about the hidden history of gay life in the United States and in Europe.

In 1994, there was a Stonewall 25 march in Manhattan, which commemorated an event homosexuals regarded as a turning point: twenty-five years earlier, gay men fought back vigorously against a police raid on the Stonewall bar in Greenwich Village. In the early nineties, gay and lesbian groups campaigned more openly, more determinedly, against discrimination, and for more attention to the scourge of AIDS, which they claimed was being given only marginal attention by the national government.

In Rochester, New York, a local campaign achieved an unprecedented decision barring military recruiters from a school district because of the Defense Department discrimination against gay soldiers.

The labor movement in the eighties and nineties was considerably weakened by the decline of manufacturing, by the flight of factories to other countries, by the hostility of the Reagan administration and its appointees on the National Labor Relations Board. Yet organizing continued, especially among white collar workers and low-income people of color. The AFL-CIO put on hundreds of new organizers to work among Latinos, African-Americans, and Asian-Americans.

Rank-and-file workers in old, stagnant unions began to rebel. In 1991, the notoriously corrupt leadership of the powerful Teamsters Union was voted out of office by a reform slate. The new leadership immediately became a force in Washington, and took the lead in working for independent political coalitions outside the two major parties. But the labor movement as a whole, much diminished, was struggling for survival.

Against the overwhelming power of corporate wealth and governmental authority, the spirit of resistance was kept alive in the early nineties, often by small-scale acts of courage and defiance. On the West Coast, a young activist named Keith McHenry and hundreds of others were arrested again and again for distributing free food to poor people without a license. They were part of a program called Food Not Bombs. More Food Not Bombs groups sprang up in communities around the country.

In 1992, a New York group interested in revising traditional ideas about American history received approval from the New York City Council to put up thirty metal plaques high on lampposts around the city. One of them, placed opposite the Morgan corporate headquarters, identified the famous banker J.P. Morgan as a Civil War "draft dodger." In fact, Morgan had avoided the draft and profited in business deals with the government during the war. Another plaque, placed near the Stock Exchange, portrayed a suicide and carried the label "Advantage of an Unregulated Free Market."

The general disillusionment with government during the Vietnam years and the Watergate scandals, the exposure of antidemocratic actions by the FBI and the CIA, led to resignations from government and open criticism by former employees.

A number of former CIA officials left the agency, and wrote books critical of its activities. John Stockwell, who had headed the CIA operation in Angola, resigned, wrote a book exposing the CIA's activities, and lectured all over the country about his experiences. David MacMichael, a historian and former CIA specialist, testified at trials on behalf of people who had protested government policy in Central America.

FBI Agent Jack Ryan, a twenty-one-year veteran of the bureau, was fired when he refused to investigate peace groups. He was deprived of his pension and for some time had to live in a shelter for homeless people.

Sometimes the war in Vietnam, which had ended in 1975, came back to public attention in the eighties and nineties through people who had been involved in the conflicts of that day. Some of them had since made dramatic turnabouts in their thinking. John Wall, who prosecuted Dr. Benjamin Spock and four others in Boston for "conspiring" to obstruct the draft, showed up at a dinner honoring the defendants in 1994, saying the trial had changed his ideas.

Even more striking was the statement by Charles Hutto, a U.S. soldier who had participated in the atrocity known as the My Lai massacre, in which a company of American soldiers shot to death women and children by the hundreds in a tiny Vietnamese village. Interviewed in the eighties, Hutto told a reporter:

> I was nineteen years old, and I'd always been told to do what the grown-ups told me to do. . . . But now I'll tell my sons, if the government calls, to go, to serve their country, but to use their own judgment at times . . . to forget about authority . . . to use their own conscience. I wish somebody had told me that before I went to Vietnam. I didn't know. Now I don't think there should be even a thing called war . . . cause it messes up a person's mind.

It was this legacy of the Vietnam war—the feeling among a great majority of Americans that it was a terrible tragedy, a war that should not have been fought—that plagued the Reagan and Bush administrations, which still hoped to extend American power around the world.

In 1985, when George Bush was Vice-President, former Defense Secretary James Schlesinger had warned the Senate Foreign Relations Committee: "Vietnam brought a sea change in domestic attitudes . . . a breakdown in the political consensus behind foreign policy. . . ."

When Bush became President, he was determined to overcome what came to be called the Vietnam syndrome—the resistance of the American people to a war desired by the Establishment. And so, he launched the air war against Iraq in mid-January 1991 with overwhelming force, so the war could be over quickly, before there was time for a national antiwar movement to develop.

The signs of a possible movement were there in the months of the prewar buildup. On Halloween, 600 students marched through downtown Missoula, Montana, shouting "Hell no, we won't go!" In Shreveport, Louisiana, despite the *Shreveport Journal*'s front-page headline: "Poll Favors Military Action," the story was that 42 percent of the respondents thought the U.S. should "initiate force" and 41 percent said "wait and see."

The November 11, 1990, Veterans Parade in Boston was joined by a group called Veterans for Peace, carrying signs: "No More Vietnams. Bring 'Em Home Now" and "Oil and Blood Do Not Mix, Wage Peace." The Boston *Globe* reported that "the protesters were greeted with respectful applause and, at some places, strong demonstrations of support by onlookers." One of those onlookers, a woman named Mary Belle Dressler, said: "Personally, parades that honor the military are somewhat troublesome to me because the military is about war, and war is troublesome to me."

Most Vietnam veterans were supporting military action, but there was a strong dissident minority. In one survey that showed 53 percent of the veterans polled saying they would gladly serve in the Gulf War, 37 percent said they would not.

Perhaps the most famous Vietnam veteran, Ron Kovic, author of *Born on the Fourth of July*, made a thirty-second television speech as Bush moved toward war. In the appeal, broadcast on 200 television stations in 120 cities across the country, he asked all citizens to "stand up and speak out" against war. "How many more Americans coming home in wheelchairs—like me—will it take before we learn?"

That November of 1990, several months into the Kuwait crisis, college students in St. Paul, Minnesota, demonstrated against war. The local press reported:

It was a full-blown antiwar demonstration with mothers pushing kids in strollers, college professors and grade school teachers carrying signs, peace activists bedecked in peace symbols, and hundreds of students from a dozen schools singing, beating drums and chanting, "Hey, hey, ho ho, we won't fight for Amoco."

Ten days before the bombing began, at a town meeting in Boulder, Colorado, with 800 people present, the question was put: "Do you support Bush's policy for war?" Only four people raised their hands. A few days before the war began, 4000 people in Santa Fe, New Mexico, blocked a four-lane highway for an hour, asking that there be no war. Residents said this was larger than any demonstration in the Vietnam era.

On the eve of war, 6000 people marched through Ann Arbor, Michigan, to ask for peace. On the night the war began, 5000 people gathered in San Francisco to denounce the war and formed a human chain around the Federal Building. Police broke the chain by swinging their clubs at the hands of the protesters. But the San Francisco Board of Supervisors passed a resolution declaring the city and county a sanctuary for those who for "moral, ethical or religious reasons cannot participate in war."

The night before Bush gave the order to launch the bombing, a seven-year-old girl in Lexington, Massachusetts, told her mother she wanted to write a letter to the President. Her mother suggested it was late and she should write the next day. "No, tonight," the girl said. She was still learning to write, so she dictated a letter:

> Dear President Bush. I don't like the way you are behaving. If you would make up your mind there won't be a war we won't have to have peace vigils. If you were in a war you wouldn't want to get hurt. What I'm saying is: I don't want any fighting to happen. Sincerely yours. Serena Kabat.

After the bombing of Iraq began along with the bombardment of public opinion, the polls showed overwhelming support for Bush's action, and this continued through the six weeks of the war. But was it an accurate reflection of the citizenry's long-term feelings about war? The split vote in the polls just before the war reflected a public still thinking its opinion might have an effect. Once the war was on, and clearly irreversible, in an atmosphere charged with patriotic fervor (the president of the United Church of Christ spoke of "the steady drumbeat of war messages"), it was not surprising that a great majority of the country would declare its support.

Nevertheless, even with little time to organize, and with the war over very fast, there was an opposition—a minority for sure, but a determined one, and with the potential to grow. Compared to the first months of the military escalation in Vietnam, the movement against the Gulf War expanded with extraordinary speed and vigor.

That first week of the war, while it was clear most Americans were supporting Bush's action, tens of thousands of people took to the streets in protest, in towns and cities all over the country. In Athens, Ohio, over 100 people were arrested, as they clashed with a prowar group. In Portland, Maine, 500 marched wearing white arm bands or carrying white paper crosses with one word, "Why?," written in red.

At the University of Georgia, 70 students opposed to the war held an all-night vigil, and in the Georgia Legislature, Representative Cynthia McKinnon made a speech attacking the bombing of Iraq, leading many of the other legislators to walk off the floor. She held her ground, and it seemed that there had been at least some change in thinking since Representative Julian Bond was expelled from the very same legislature for criticizing the war in Vietnam during the 1960s. At a junior high school in Newton, Massachusetts, 350 students marched to city hall to present a petition to the mayor declaring their opposition to the war in the Gulf. Clearly, many were trying to reconcile their feelings about war with their sympathy for soldiers sent to the Middle East. A student leader, Carly Baker, said: "We don't think bloodshed is the right way. We are supporting the troops and are proud of them, but we don't want war."

In Ada, Oklahoma, while East Central Oklahoma State University was "adopting" two National Guard units, two young women sat quietly on top of the concrete entrance gate with signs that read "Teach Peace . . . Not War." One of them, Patricia Biggs, said: "I don't think we should be over there. I don't think it's about justice and liberty, I think it's about economics. The big oil corporations have a lot to do with what is going on over there. . . . We are risking people's lives for money."

Four days after the United States launched its air attack, 75,000 people (the estimate of the Capitol Police) marched in Washington, rallying near the White House to denounce the war. In Southern California, Ron Kovic addressed 6000 people who chanted "Peace Now!" In Fayetteville, Arkansas, a group supporting military policy was confronted by the Northwest Arkansas Citizens Against War, who marched carrying a flag-draped coffin and a banner that read "Bring Them Home Alive."

Another disabled Vietnam veteran, a professor of history and political science at York College in Pennsylvania named Philip Avillo, wrote in a local newspaper: "Yes, we need to support our men and women under arms. But let's support them by bringing them home; not by condoning this barbarous, violent policy." In Salt Lake City, hundreds of demonstrators, many with children, marched through the city's main streets chanting antiwar slogans.

In Vermont, which had just elected Socialist Bernie Sanders to Congress, over 2000 demonstrators disrupted a speech by the governor at the state house, and in Burlington, Vermont's largest city, 300 protesters walked through the downtown area, asking shop owners to close their doors in solidarity.

On January 26, nine days after the beginning of the war, over 150,000 people marched through the streets of Washington, D.C., and listened to speakers denounce the war, including the movie stars Susan Sarandon and Tim Robbins. A woman from Oakland, California, held up the folded American flag that was given to her when her husband was killed in Vietnam, saying, "I learned the hard way there is no glory in a folded flag."

Labor unions had supported the war in Vietnam for the most part, but after the bombing started in the Gulf, eleven affiliates of the AFL-CIO, including some of its more powerful unions—like steel, auto, communications, chemical workers—spoke out against the war.

The black community was far less enthusiastic than the rest of the country about what the U.S. Air Force was doing to Iraq. An ABC News/*Washington Post* poll in early February, 1991, found that support for the war was 84 percent among whites, but only 48 percent among African-Americans.

When the war had been going on for a month, with Iraq devastated by the incessant bombing, there were feelers from Saddam Hussein that Iraq would withdraw from Kuwait if the United States would stop its attacks. Bush rejected the idea, and a meeting of black leaders in New York sharply criticized him, calling the war "an immoral and unspiritual diversion . . . a blatant evasion of our domestic responsibilities."

In Selma, Alabama, which had been the scene of bloody police violence against civil rights marchers twenty-six years before, a meeting to observe the anniversary of that "bloody Sunday" demanded that "our troops be brought home alive to fight for justice at home."

The father of a twenty-one-year-old Marine in the Persian Gulf, Alex Molnar, wrote an angry open letter, published in the *New York Times*, to President Bush:

Where were you, Mr. President, when Iraq was killing its own people with poison gas? Why, until the recent crisis, was it business as usual with Saddam Hussein, the man you now call a Hitler? Is the American "way of life" that you say my son is risking his life for the continued "right" of Americans to consume 25 to 30 percent of the world's oil? . . . I intend to support my son and his fellow soldiers by doing everything I can to oppose any offensive American military action in the Persian Gulf.

There were courageous individual acts by citizens, speaking out in spite of threats.

Peg Mullen, of Brownsville, Texas, whose son had been killed by "friendly fire" in Vietnam, organized a busload of mothers to protest in Washington, in spite of a warning that her house would be burned down if she persisted.

The actress Margot Kidder ("Lois Lane" in the *Superman* films), despite the risk to her career, spoke out eloquently against the war.

A basketball player for Seton Hall University in New Jersey

refused to wear the American flag on his uniform, and when he became the object of derision for this, he left the team and the university, and returned to his native Italy.

More tragically, a Vietnam veteran in Los Angeles set fire to himself and died, to protest the war.

In Amherst, Massachusetts, a young man carrying a cardboard peace sign knelt on the town common, poured two cans of flammable fluid on himself, struck two matches, and died in the flames. Two hours later, students from nearby universities gathered on the common for a candlelight vigil, and placed peace signs at the site of death. One of the signs read, "Stop this crazy war."

There was no time, as there had been during the Vietnam conflict, for a large antiwar movement to develop in the military. But there were men and women who defied their commanders and refused to participate in the war.

When the first contingents of U.S. troops were being sent to Saudi Arabia, in August of 1990, Corporal Jeff Patterson, a twenty-two-year-old Marine stationed in Hawaii, sat down on the runway of the airfield and refused to board a plane bound for Saudi Arabia. He asked to be discharged from the Marine Corps:

> I have come to believe that there are no justified wars.... I began to question exactly what I was doing in the Marine Corps about the time I began to read about history. I began to read up on America's support for the murderous regimes of Guatemala, Iran under the Shah, and El Salvador.... I object to the military use of force against any people, anywhere, any time.

Fourteen Marine Corps reservists at Camp Lejeune, North Carolina, filed for conscientious objector status, despite the prospect of a court-martial for desertion. A lance corporal in the Marines, Erik Larsen, issued a statement:

> I declare myself a conscientious objector. Here is my sea bag full of personal gear. Here is my gas mask. I no longer need them. I am no

longer a Marine. . . . It, to me, is embarrassing to fight for a way of life in which basic human needs, like a place to sleep, one hot meal a day and some medical attention, cannot even be met in our nation's capital.

Corporal Yolanda Huet-Vaughn, a physician who was a captain in the Army Reserve Medical Corps, a mother of three young children, and a member of the Physicians for Social Responsibility, was called to active duty in December 1990, a month before the start of the war. She replied: "I am refusing orders to be an accomplice in what I consider an immoral, inhumane and unconstitutional act, namely an offensive military mobilization in the Middle East." She was court-martialed, convicted of desertion, and sentenced to 2½ years in prison.

Another soldier, Stephanie Atkinson of Murphysboro, Illinois, refused to report for active duty, saying she thought the U.S. military was in the Persian Gulf solely for economic reasons. She was first placed under house arrest, then given a discharge under "other than honorable conditions."

An Army physician named Harlow Ballard, stationed at Fort Devens in Massachusetts, refused to follow an order to go to Saudi Arabia. "I would rather go to jail than support this war," he said. "I don't believe there is any such thing as a just war."

Over a thousand reservists declared themselves conscientious objectors. A twenty-three-year-old Marine Corps reservist named Rob Calabro was one of them. "My father tells me that he's ashamed of me, he screams at me that he's embarrassed by me. But I believe that killing people is morally wrong. I believe I'm serving my country more by being true to my conscience than by living a lie."

An information network sprang up during the Gulf War to tell what was not being told in the major media. There were alternative newspapers in many cities. There were over a hundred community radio stations, able to reach only a fraction of those tuned in to the major networks but the only sources, during the Gulf War, of critical analyses of the war. An ingenious radio person in

Boulder, Colorado, named David Barsamian recorded a speech by Noam Chomsky made at Harvard—a devastating critique of the war. He then sent the cassette out to his network of community stations, which were eager for a point of view different from the official one. Two young men in New Jersey then transcribed the talk, put it in pamphlet form, in a shape easily photocopied, and placed the pamphlets in bookstores all over the country.

After "victorious" wars there is almost always a sobering effect, as the war fervor wears off, and citizens assess the costs and wonder what was gained. War fever was at its height in February 1991. In that month, when people being polled were reminded of the huge costs of the war, only 17 percent said the war was not worth it. Four months later, in June, the figure was 30 percent. In the months that followed, Bush's support in the nation dropped steeply, as economic conditions deteriorated. (And in 1992, with the war spirit evaporated, Bush went down to defeat.)

After the disintegration of the Soviet bloc began in 1989, there had been talk in the United States of a "peace dividend," the opportunity to take billions of dollars from the military budget and use it for human needs. The war in the Gulf became a convenient excuse for the government determined to stop such talk. A member of the Bush administration said: "We owe Saddam a favor. He saved us from the peace dividend" (*New York Times*, March 2, 1991).

But the idea of a peace dividend could not be stifled so long as Americans were in need. Shortly after the war, historian Marilyn Young warned:

> The U.S. can destroy Iraq's highways, but not build its own; create the conditions for epidemic in Iraq, but not offer health care to millions of Americans. It can excoriate Iraqi treatment of the Kurdish minority, but not deal with domestic race relations; create homelessness abroad but not solve it here; keep a half million troops drug free as part of a war, but refuse to fund the treatment of millions of drug addicts at home. . . . We shall lose the war after we have won it.

In 1992, the limits of military victory became apparent during the quincentennial celebrations of Columbus's arrival in the Western Hemisphere. Five hundred years ago Columbus and his fellow conquerors had wiped out the native population of Hispaniola. This was followed during the next four centuries by the methodical destruction of Indian tribes by the United States government as it marched across the continent. But now, there was a dramatic reaction.

The Indians—the Native Americans—had become a visible force since the sixties and seventies, and in 1992 were joined by other Americans to denounce the quincentennial celebrations. For the first time in all the years that the country had celebrated Columbus Day, there were nationwide protests against honoring a man who had kidnapped, enslaved, mutilated, murdered the natives who greeted his arrival with gifts and friendship.

Preparations for the quincentennial began on both sides of the controversy. Official commissions, nationally and in the states, were set up long before the year of the quincentennial.

This spurred action by Native Americans. In the summer of 1990 350 Indians, representatives from all over the hemisphere, met in Quito, Ecuador, at the first intercontinental gathering of indigenous people in the Americas, to mobilize against the glorification of the Columbus conquest.

The following summer, in Davis, California, over a hundred Native Americans gathered for a follow-up meeting to the Quito conference. They declared October 12, 1992, International Day of Solidarity with Indigenous People, and resolved to inform the king of Spain that the replicas of Columbus's three ships, the *Niña*, *Pinta*, and *Santa Maria*, "will not receive permission from the Native Nations to land in the western hemisphere unless he apologizes for the original incursion 500 years ago. . . ."

The movement grew. The largest ecumenical body in the United States, the National Council of Churches, called on Christians to refrain from celebrating the Columbus quincentennial, saying, "What represented newness of freedom, hope and opportunity for some was the occasion for oppression, degradation and genocide for others."

The National Endowment for the Humanities funded a traveling exhibition called "First Encounter," which romanticized the Columbus conquest. When the exhibition opened at the Florida Museum of National History, Michelle Diamond, a freshman at the University of Florida, climbed aboard a replica of one of Columbus's ships with a sign reading "Exhibit Teaches Racism." She said: "It's a human issue—not just a Red [Indian] issue." She was arrested and charged with trespassing, but demonstrations continued for sixteen days against the exhibit.

A newspaper called *Indigenous Thought* began publication in early 1991 to create a link among all the counter-Columbus quincentenary activities. It carried articles by Native Americans about current struggles over land stolen by treaty.

In Corpus Christi, Texas, Indians and Chicanos joined to protest the city's celebrations of the quincentennial. A woman named Angelina Mendez spoke for the Chicanos: "The Chicano nation, in solidarity with our Indian brothers and sisters to the north, come together with them on this day to denounce the atrocity the U.S. government proposes in reenacting the arrival of the Spanish, more specifically the arrival of Cristóbal Colón, to the shores of this land."

The Columbus controversy brought an extraordinary burst of educational and cultural activity. A professor at the University of California at San Diego, Deborah Small, put together an exhibit of over 200 paintings on wood panels called "1492." She juxtaposed words from Columbus's diary with blown-up fragments from sixteenth-century engravings to dramatize the horrors that accompanied Columbus's arrival in the hemisphere. A reviewer wrote that "it does remind us, in the most vivid way, of how the coming of Western-style civilization to the New World doesn't provide us with a sunny tale."

When President Bush attacked Iraq in 1991, claiming that he was acting to end the Iraqi occupation of Kuwait, a group of

Native Americans in Oregon distributed a biting and ironic "open letter":

> Dear President Bush. Please send your assistance in freeing our small nation from occupation. This foreign force occupied our lands to steal our rich resources. They used biological warfare and deceit, killing thousands of elders, children and women in the process. As they overwhelmed our land, they deposed our leaders and people of our own government, and in its place, they installed their own government systems that yet today control our daily lives in many ways. As in your own words, the occupation and overthrow of one small nation . . . is one too many. Sincerely, An American Indian.

The publication *Rethinking Schools*, which represented socially conscious schoolteachers all over the country, printed a 100-page book called *Rethinking Columbus*, featuring articles by Native Americans and others, a critical review of children's books on Columbus, a listing of resources for people wanting more information on Columbus, and more reading material on counter-quincentenary activities. In a few months, 200,000 copies of the book were sold.

A Portland, Oregon, teacher named Bill Bigelow, who helped put together *Rethinking Schools*, took a year off from his regular job to tour the country in 1992, giving workshops to other teachers, so that they could begin to tell those truths about the Columbus experience that were omitted from the traditional books and class curricula.

One of Bigelow's own students wrote to the publisher Allyn and Bacon with a critique of their history text *The American Spirit*:

> I'll just pick one topic to keep it simple. How about Columbus. No, you didn't lie, but saying, "Though they had a keen interest in the peoples of the Caribbean, Columbus and his crews were never able to live peacefully among them," makes it seem as if Columbus did no wrong. The reason for not being able to live peacefully is that he and

crew took slaves and killed thousands of Indians for not bringing enough gold.

Another student wrote: "It seemed to me as if the publishers had just printed up some 'glory story' that was supposed to make us feel more patriotic about our country. . . . They want us to look at our country as great and powerful and forever right. . . ."

A student named Rebecca wrote: "Of course, the writers of the books probably think it's harmless enough—what does it matter who discovered America, really. . . . But the thought that I have been lied to all my life about this, and who knows what else, really makes me angry."

A group was formed on the West Coast called Italian-Americans Against Christopher Columbus, saying: "When Italian-Americans identify with Native people . . . we are bringing ourselves, each of us, closer to possible change in the world."

In Los Angeles, a high school student named Blake Lindsey went before the city council to argue against celebrating the quincentennial. She spoke to the council about the genocide of the Arawaks, but she got no official response. However, when she told her story on a talk show, a woman phoned in who said she was from Haiti: "The girl is right. We have no Indians left. At our last uprising in Haiti people destroyed the statue of Columbus. Let's have statues for the aborigines."

There were counter-Columbus activities all over the country, unmentioned in the press or on television. In Minnesota alone, a listing of such activities for 1992 reported dozens of workshops, meetings, films, art shows. At Lincoln Center in New York City, on October 12, there was a performance of Leonard Lehrmann's *New World: An Opera About What Columbus Did to the Indians.* In Baltimore, there was a multimedia show about Columbus. In Boston and then in a national tour, the Underground Railway Theater performed *The Christopher Columbus Follies* to packed audiences.

The protests, the dozens of new books that were appearing about Indian history, the discussions taking place all over the country, were bringing about an extraordinary transformation in the educational world. For generations, exactly the same story had been told all American schoolchildren about Columbus, a romantic, admiring story. Now, thousands of teachers around the country were beginning to tell that story differently.

This aroused anger among defenders of the old history, who derided what they called a movement for "political correctness" and "multiculturalism." They resented the critical treatment of Western expansion and imperialism, which they considered an attack on Western civilization. Ronald Reagan's Secretary of Education, William Bennett, had called Western civilization "our common culture . . . its highest ideas and aspirations."

A much-publicized book by a philosopher named Allan Bloom, *The Closing of the American Mind*, expressed horror at what the social movements of the sixties had done to change the educational atmosphere of American universities. To him Western civilization was the high point of human progress, and the United States its best representative: "America tells one story: the unbroken, ineluctable progress of freedom and equality. From its first settlers and its political foundings on, there has been no dispute that freedom and equality are the essence of justice for us."

In the civil rights movement, black people disputed that claim of America's standing for "freedom and equality." The women's movement had disputed that claim, too. And now, in 1992, Native Americans were pointing to the crimes of Western civilization against their ancestors. They were recalling the communitarian spirit of the Indians Columbus met and conquered, trying to tell the history of those millions of people who were here before Columbus, giving the lie to what a Harvard historian (Perry Miller) had called "the movement of European culture into the vacant wilderness of America."

As the United States entered the nineties, the political system, whether Democrats or Republicans were in power, remained in the control of those who had great wealth. The main instruments of information were also dominated by corporate wealth. The country was divided, though no mainstream political leader would speak of it, into classes of extreme wealth and extreme poverty, separated by an insecure and jeopardized middle class.

Yet, there was, unquestionably, though largely unreported, what a worried mainstream journalist had called "a permanent adversarial culture" which refused to surrender the possibility of a more equal, more humane society. If there was hope for the future of America, it lay in the promise of that refusal.

THE
CLINTON PRESIDENCY
AND THE
CRISIS OF DEMOCRACY

President Bill Clinton was reelected in 1996 with a distinct lack of voter enthusiasm. As was true in 1992 (when 19 percent of the voters showed their distaste for both parties by voting for a third-party candidate, Ross Perot), the electorate was clearly not happy about its choices. Half of the eligible voters stayed away from the polls, and of those who did vote, only 49 percent chose Clinton over his lackluster opponent, Robert Dole. One bumper sticker read: "If God had intended us to vote, he would have given us candidates."

At his second inauguration ceremony, Clinton spoke of the nation at the edge of "a new century, in a new millennium." He said, "We need a new government for a new century." But it was apparent from his weak support at the polls that Americans had seen nothing in Clinton's first four years to justify the claim that there would be a "new government."

It happened that the inauguration coincided with the nation-wide celebration of the birthday of Martin Luther King, Jr., and Clinton invoked King's name several times in his address. The two men, however, represented very different social philosophies.

By the time King was assassinated in 1968, he had come to believe that our economic system was fundamentally unjust and needed radical transformation. He spoke of "the evils of capital-ism" and asked for "a radical redistribution of economic and polit-ical power."

On the other hand, as major corporations gave money to the Democratic Party on an unprecedented scale, Clinton demon-strated clearly, in the four years of his first term in office, his total confidence in "the market system" and "private enterprise." Dur-ing the 1992 campaign, the chief executive officer of Martin Marietta Corporation noted: "I think the Democrats are moving more toward business and business is moving more toward the Democrats."

Martin Luther King's reaction to the buildup of military power had been the same as his reaction to the Vietnam war. "This mad-ness must cease." And: ". . . the evils of racism, economic exploita-tion, and militarism are all tied together. . . ."

Clinton was willing to recall King's "dream" of racial equality, but not his dream of a society rejecting violence. Even though the Soviet Union was no longer a military threat, he insisted that the United States must keep its armed forces dispersed around the globe, prepare for "two regional wars," and continue the mili-tary budget at cold war levels.

Clinton had become the Democratic Party candidate in 1992 with a formula not for social change but for electoral victory: Move the party closer to the center. This meant doing just enough for blacks, women, and working people to keep their sup-port, while trying to win over white conservative voters with a program of toughness on crime and a strong military.

Once in office, Clinton appointed more people of color to government posts than his Republican predecessors. But if any prospective or actual appointees became too bold, Clinton abandoned them quickly.

His Secretary of Commerce, Ronald Brown (who was killed in a plane crash), was black, and a corporate lawyer, and Clinton was clearly pleased with him. On the other hand, Lani Guinier, a black legal scholar who was up for a job with the Civil Rights Division of the Justice Department, was abandoned when conservatives objected to her strong ideas on matters of racial equality and voter representation. And when Surgeon General Joycelyn Elders, a black, made the controversial suggestion that masturbation was a proper subject in sex education, Clinton asked her to resign.

He showed the same timidity in the two appointments he made to the Supreme Court, making sure that Ruth Bader Ginsburg and Stephen Breyer would be moderate enough to be acceptable to Republicans as well as to Democrats. He was not willing to fight for a strong liberal to follow in the footsteps of Thurgood Marshall or William Brennan, who had recently left the Court. Breyer and Ginsburg both defended the constitutionality of capital punishment, and upheld drastic restrictions on the use of habeas corpus. Both voted with the most conservative judges on the Court to uphold the "constitutional right" of Boston's St. Patrick's Day parade organizers to exclude gay marchers.

In choosing judges for the lower federal courts, Clinton showed himself no more likely to appoint liberals than the Republican Gerald Ford had in the seventies. According to a three-year study published in the *Fordham Law Review* in early 1996, Clinton's appointments made "liberal" decisions in less than half their cases. The *New York Times* noted that, while Reagan and Bush had been willing to fight for judges who would reflect their philosophies, "Mr. Clinton, in contrast, has been quick to drop judicial candidates if there is even a hint of controversy."

Clinton was eager to show he was "tough" on matters of "law and order." Running for president in 1992 while still governor of

Arkansas, he flew back to Arkansas to oversee the execution of a mentally retarded man on death row. And early in his administration, he and Attorney General Janet Reno approved an FBI attack on a group of religious zealots who were armed and ensconced in a building complex in Waco, Texas. The attack resulted in a fire that swept through the compound, killing at least 86 men, women, and children.

Early in his first term Clinton signed legislation cutting funds for state resource centers that supplied lawyers to indigent prisoners. The result, according to Bob Herbert writing in the *New York Times*, was that a man facing the death penalty in Georgia had to appear at a habeas corpus proceeding without a lawyer.

In 1996, the President signed legislation that made it more difficult for judges to put prison systems under special masters to ensure the improvement of terrible prison conditions. He also approved a new statute withholding federal funds for legal services where lawyers used those funds to handle class action suits (such suits were important for challenging assaults on civil liberties).

The "Crime Bill" of 1996, which both Republicans and Democrats in Congress voted for overwhelmingly, and which Clinton endorsed with enthusiasm, dealt with the problem of crime by emphasizing punishment, not prevention. It extended the death penalty to a whole range of criminal offenses, and provided $8 billion for the building of new prisons.

All this was to persuade voters that politicians were "tough on crime." But, as criminologist Todd Clear wrote in the *New York Times* ("Tougher Is Dumber") about the new crime bill, harsher sentencing since 1973 had added 1 million people to the prison population, giving the United States the highest rate of incarceration in the world, and yet violent crime continued to increase. "Why," Clear asked, "do harsh penalties seem to have so little to do with crime?" A crucial reason is that "police and prisons have virtually no effect on the sources of criminal behavior." He pointed to those sources: "About 70 percent of prisoners in New York State come from eight neighborhoods in New York City. These neighborhoods suffer profound poverty, exclusion, marginalization and despair. All these things nourish crime."

Those holding political power—whether Clinton or his Republican predecessors—had something in common. They sought to keep their power by diverting the anger of citizens to groups without the resources to defend themselves. As H. L. Mencken, the acerbic social critic of the 1920s, put it: "The whole aim of practical politics is to keep the populace alarmed by menacing it with an endless series of hobgoblins, all of them imaginary."

Criminals were among these hobgoblins. Also immigrants, people on "welfare," and certain governments—Iraq, North Korea, Cuba. By turning attention to them, by inventing or exaggerating their dangers, the failures of the American system could be concealed.

Immigrants were a convenient object of attack, because as nonvoters their interests could be safely ignored. It was easy for politicians to play upon the xenophobia that has erupted from time to time in American history: the anti-Irish prejudices of the mid-nineteenth century; the continual violence against Chinese who had been brought in to work on the railroads; the hostility toward immigrants from eastern and southern Europe that led to the restrictive immigration laws of the 1920s.

The reform spirit of the sixties had led to an easing of restrictions on immigration, but in the nineties, Democrats and Republicans alike played on the economic fears of working Americans. Jobs were being lost because corporations were firing employees to save money ("downsizing") or moving plants out of the country to more profitable situations. Immigrants, especially the large numbers coming over the southern border from Mexico, were blamed for taking jobs from citizens of the United States, for receiving government benefits, for causing higher taxes on American citizens.

Both major political parties joined to pass legislation, which Clinton then signed, to remove welfare benefits (food stamps, payments to elderly and disabled people) from not only illegal but legal immigrants. By early 1997, letters were going out to close to

1 million legal immigrants, who were poor, old, or disabled, warning them that their food stamps and cash payments would be cut off in a few months unless they became citizens.

For perhaps half a million legal immigrants, passing the tests required for becoming a citizen was quite impossible—they could not read English, were sick or disabled or just too old to learn. An immigrant from Portugal living in Massachusetts told a reporter, through an interpreter: "Every day, we are afraid the letter will come. What will we do if we lose our checks? We will starve. Oh, my God. It will not be worth living."

Illegal immigrants, fleeing poverty in Mexico, began to face harsher treatment in the early nineties. Thousands of border guards were added. A Reuters dispatch from Mexico City (April 3, 1997) said about the tougher policy: "Any crackdown against illegal immigration automatically angers Mexicans, millions of whom migrate, legally and illegally, across the 2000-mile border to the United States in search of jobs each year."

Hundreds of thousands of Central Americans who had fled death squads in Guatemala and El Salvador while the United States was giving military aid to those governments now faced deportation because they had never been deemed "political" refugees. To admit that these cases were political would have given the lie to U.S. claims at the time that those repressive regimes were improving their human rights record and therefore deserved to continue receiving military aid.

In early 1996, the Congress and the President joined to pass an "Anti-Terrorism and Effective Death Penalty Act," allowing deportation of any immigrant ever convicted of a crime, no matter how long ago or how serious. Lawful permanent residents who had married Americans and now had children were not exempt. The *New York Times* reported that July that "hundreds of long-term legal residents have been arrested since the law passed."

The new government policy toward immigrants, far from fulfilling Clinton's promise of "a new government for a new century," was a throwback to the notorious Alien and Sedition Laws of the eighteenth century, and the McCarthy-era McCarran-Walter Act of the 1950s. It was hardly in keeping with the grand claim inscribed on the Statue of Liberty: "Give me your tired, your poor, your huddled masses yearning to breathe free, the wretched refuse of your teeming shore. Send these, the homeless, tempest-tossed to me. I lift my lamp beside the golden door."

In the summer of 1996 (apparently seeking the support of "centrist" voters for the coming election), Clinton signed a law to end the federal government's guarantee, created under the New Deal, of financial help to poor families with dependent children. This was called "welfare reform," and the law itself had the deceptive title of "Personal Responsibility and Work Opportunity Reconciliation Act of 1996." Its aim was to force poor families receiving federal cash benefits (many of them single mothers with children) to go to work, by cutting off their benefits after two years, limiting lifetime benefits to five years, and allowing people without children to get food stamps for only three months in any three-year period.

The *Los Angeles Times* reported: "As legal immigrants lose access to Medicaid, and families battle a new five-year limit on cash benefits . . . health experts anticipate a resurgence of tuberculosis and sexually transmitted diseases. . . ." The aim of the welfare cuts was to save $50 billion over a five-year period (less than the cost of a planned new generation of fighter planes). Even the *New York Times*, a supporter of Clinton during the election, said that the provisions of the new law "have nothing to do with creating work but everything to do with balancing the budget by cutting programs for the poor."

There was a simple but overwhelming problem with cutting off benefits to the poor to force them to find jobs. There were not jobs available for all those who would lose their benefits. In New York City in 1990, when 2000 jobs were advertised in the Sanitation Department at $23,000 a year, 100,000 people applied. Two years later in Chicago, 7000 people showed up for 550 jobs at Stouffer's, a restaurant chain. In Joliet, Illinois, 2000 showed up at Commonwealth Edison at 4:30 A.M. to apply for jobs that did not yet exist. In early 1997, 4000 people lined up for 700 jobs at the Roosevelt Hotel in Manhattan. It was estimated that at the existing rate of job growth in New York, with 470,000 adults on welfare, it would take twenty-four years to absorb those thrown off the rolls.

What the Clinton administration steadfastly refused to do was to establish government programs to create jobs, as had been done in the New Deal era, when billions were spent to give employment to several million people, from construction workers and engineers to artists and writers.

"The era of big government is over," Clinton proclaimed as he ran for president, seeking votes on the supposition that Americans supported the Republican position that government was spending too much for social programs. But both parties were misreading public opinion.

The press was often complicit in this. When, in the midyear election of 1994, only 37 percent of the electorate went to the polls, and slightly more than half voted Republican, the media reported this as a "revolution." A headline in the *New York Times* read "Public Shows Trust in GOP Congress," suggesting that the American people were supporting the Republican agenda of less government. But in the story below that headline, a *New York Times*/CBS News public opinion survey found that 65 percent of those polled said that "it is the responsibility of government to take care of people who can't take care of themselves."

Clinton and the Republicans, in joining against "big government," were aiming only at social services. The other manifestations of big government—huge contracts to military contractors and generous subsidies to corporations—continued at exorbitant levels.

"Big government" had, in fact, begun with the Founding Fathers, who deliberately set up a strong central government to protect the interests of the bondholders, the slave owners, the land speculators, the manufacturers. For the next two hundred years, the American government continued to serve the interests of the wealthy and powerful, offering millions of acres of free land to the railroads, setting high tariffs to protect manufacturers, giving tax breaks to oil corporations, and using its armed forces to suppress strikes and rebellions.

It was only in the twentieth century, especially in the thirties and sixties, when the government, besieged by protests and fearful of the stability of the system, passed social legislation for the poor that political leaders and business executives complained about "big government."

President Clinton reappointed Alan Greenspan as head of the Federal Reserve System, which regulated interest rates. Greenspan's chief concern was to avoid "inflation," which bondholders did not want because it would reduce their profits. His financial constituency saw higher wages for workers as producing inflation and worried that if there was not enough unemployment, wages might rise.

Reduction of the annual deficit in order to achieve a "balanced budget" became an obsession of the Clinton administration. But since Clinton did not want to raise taxes on the wealthy, or to cut funds for the military, the only alternative was to sacrifice the poor, the children, the aged—to spend less for health care, for food stamps, for education, for single mothers.

Two examples of this appeared early in Clinton's second administration, in the spring of 1997:

• From the *New York Times*, May 8, 1997: "A major element of President Clinton's education plan—a proposal to spend $5 billion to repair the nation's crumbling schools—was among the items quietly killed in last week's agreement to balance the federal budget. . . ."
• From the *Boston Globe*, May 22, 1997: "After White House intervention, the Senate yesterday . . . rejected a proposal . . . to extend health insurance to the nation's 10.5 million uninsured children . . . Seven lawmakers switched their votes . . . after senior White House officials . . . called and said the amendment would imperil the delicate budget agreement."

Meanwhile, the government was continuing to spend at least $250 billion a year to maintain the military machine. The assumption was that the nation must be ready to fight "two regional wars" simultaneously. However, after the Soviet Union collapsed in 1989, Bush's Secretary of Defense, Dick Cheney (hardly a dove), said, "The threats have become remote, so remote that they are difficult to discern."

The government, Republicans and Democrats agreeing, was going ahead with a program to build F-22 fighter planes that would cost at least $70 billion. The Associated Press reported estimates by the General Accounting Office that the entire Joint Strike Fighter Program would eventually cost a trillion dollars.

The use of force was still central to U.S. foreign policy. Clinton had been in office barely six months when he sent the Air Force to drop bombs on Baghdad, presumably in retaliation for an assassination plot against George Bush on the occasion of the former president's visit to Kuwait. The evidence for such a plot was very weak, coming as it did from the notoriously corrupt Kuwaiti police. Nevertheless, U.S. planes, claiming to target "Intelligence Headquarters" in the Iraqi capital, bombed a suburban neighborhood, killing at least six people, including a prominent artist and her husband.

Columnist Molly Ivins suggested that the asserted purpose of the bombing of Baghdad—"sending a powerful message"—fit the definition of terrorism. "The maddening thing about terrorists is that they are indiscriminate in their acts of vengeance, or cries for attention, or whatever. . . . What is true for individuals . . . must also be true of nations."

The United States continued to supply lethal arms to some of the most vicious regimes in the world. Indonesia had a record of mass murder, having killed perhaps 200,000 out of a population of 700,000 in its invasion and occupation of East Timor. Yet the Clinton administration approved the sale of F-16 fighter planes and other assault equipment to Indonesia. The *Boston Globe* wrote (July 11, 1994):

The arguments presented by senators solicitous of Suharto's regime—and of defense contractors, oil companies and mining concerns doing business with Jakarta—made Americans seem a people willing to overlook genocide for the sake of commerce.

In 1996 the Nobel Peace Prize was awarded to Jose Ramos-Horta of East Timor. Speaking at a church in Brooklyn shortly before he won the prize, Ramos-Horta said:

> In the summer of 1977, I was here in New York when I received a message telling me that one of my sisters, Maria, 21 years old, had been killed in an aircraft bombing. The aircraft, named Bronco, was supplied by the United States. . . . Within months, another report about a brother, Guy, 17 years old, killed along with many other people in his village by Bell helicopters, supplied by the United States. Same year, another brother, Nunu, captured and executed with an [American-made] M-16. . . .

Similarly, American-made Sikorski helicopters were used by Turkey to destroy the villages of rebellious Kurds, in what writer John Tirman (*Spoils of War: The Human Cost of the Arms Trade*) called "a campaign of terror against the Kurdish people." By early 1997 the United States was selling more arms abroad than all other nations combined. Lawrence Korb, a Department of Defense official under Reagan but later a critic of arms sales, wrote: "It has become a money game: an absurd spiral in which we export arms only to have to develop more sophisticated ones to counter those spread out all over the world."

Human rights clearly came second to business profit in U.S. foreign policy. When the international group Human Rights Watch issued its 1996 annual report, the *New York Times* (December 5, 1996) summarized its findings:

> The organization strongly criticized many powerful nations, particularly the United States, accusing them of failing to press govern-

ments in China, Indonesia, Mexico, Nigeria and Saudi Arabia to improve human rights for fear of losing access to lucrative markets.

A similar concern for profit over human rights was evident in policy toward the new Russia that emerged from the exploded Soviet Union. Anxious to steer Russia toward capitalism, and in the process to open it up as a market for American goods, the U.S. government simply overlooked the bullying policies of Russian president Boris Yeltsin. The Clinton administration firmly supported Yeltsin, even after Russia initiated a brutal invasion and bombardment of the outlying region of Chechnya, which wanted independence.

The historic use of economic aid to gain political influence was underlined when in November 1993, an Associated Press dispatch reported the phasing out of economic aid to thirty-five countries, most of them very poor. The administrator for the Agency for International Development, J. Brian Atwood, explained: "We no longer need an A.I.D. program to purchase influence."

The World Bank and the International Monetary Fund, both dominated by the United States, adopted a hard-nosed banker's approach to debt-ridden Third World countries. They insisted that these poor nations allocate a good part of their meager resources to repaying loans to the rich countries, at the cost of cutting social services to their already desperate populations.

Foreign economic policy was presumably based on "free trade" agreements, most notably those signed with Canada and Mexico. Democrats and Republicans, enthusiastically supported by corporate interests, joined to pass the North American Free Trade Agreement (NAFTA), which Clinton signed. Labor unions opposed it, because it meant businesses would be free to move across borders to find workers who would work at lower wages, under poor conditions. The claim of "free trade" was hardly to be believed, since U.S. policy was to interfere with trade when it served certain political or economic ends (although the phrase always used was "national interest"). Thus, the United States went to lengths to prevent tomato growers in Mexico from entering the U.S. market and put pressure on Thailand to open its markets to American tobacco companies, even while at home mounting public protest led to restrictions on the sale of tobacco.

In an even more flagrant violation of the principle of free trade, the United States would not allow shipments of food or medicine to Iraq or to Cuba, the result being the deaths of tens of thousands of children. In 1996, on the television program *60 Minutes*, U.S. Ambassador to the United Nations Madeleine Albright was asked about the report that "a half million children have died as a result of sanctions against Iraq. . . . That is more children than died in Hiroshima. . . . Is the price worth it?" Albright replied: "I think this is a very hard choice, but the price, we think the price is worth it."

The United States, with 5 percent of the earth's population, consumed 30 percent of what was produced worldwide. But only a tiny portion of the American population benefited; this richest 1 percent of the population saw its wealth increase enormously starting in the late 1970s. As a result of changes in the tax structure, by 1995 that richest 1 percent had gained over a trillion dollars and now owned over 40 percent of the nation's wealth.

According to the business magazine *Forbes*, the 400 richest families owned $92 billion in 1982. Thirteen years later, this had jumped to $480 billion. The Dow Jones average of stock prices had gone up 400 percent between 1980 and 1995, while the average wage of workers had declined in purchasing power by 15 percent.

It was therefore possible to say that the U.S. economy was "healthy"—but only if you considered the richest part of the population. Meanwhile, 40 million people were without health insurance, and infants died of sickness and malnutrition at a rate higher than that of any other industrialized country. For people of color, the statistics were worse: Infants died at twice the rate of white children, and the life expectancy of a black man in Harlem, according to a United Nations report, was 46 years, less than that in Cambodia or the Sudan.

The United States (forgetting, or choosing to forget, the disastrous consequence of such a policy in the twenties) was consigning its people to the mercy of the "free market." The "market" did not care about the environment or the arts. And it left many Americans without jobs, or health care, without a decent education for their children, or adequate housing. Under Reagan, the government had reduced the number of housing units getting subsidies from 400,000 to 40,000; in the Clinton administration the program ended altogether.

Despite Clinton's 1997 Inaugural Day promise of a "new government," there was no bold program to take care of these needs. Such a program would require huge expenditures of money. There were two ways of raising this money, but the Clinton administration (like its predecessors) was not inclined to turn to them, given the powerful influence of corporate wealth.

One of those sources was the wealth of the superrich. Taxing very high incomes at post–World War II levels—that is, at 70–90 percent instead of at 37 percent—could make available several hundred billion dollars a year. In addition, a "wealth tax"—something not yet done as national policy, but perfectly feasible—could retrieve the trillion dollars gained by the superrich over the years in tax breaks.

The other major source of funds was the military budget. During the 1992 presidential campaign, Randall Forsberg, an expert on military expenditures, had suggested, "A military budget of $60 billion, to be achieved over a number of years, would support a demilitarized U.S. foreign policy, appropriate to the needs and opportunities of the post–Cold War world."

Instead, in 1996, the United States was spending more money on the military than the rest of the world combined—four times as much as Russia, eight times as much as China, forty times as much as North Korea, eighty times as much as Iraq. It was a bizarre waste of the nation's wealth.

A radical reduction of the military budget would require a renunciation of war, a refusal to use military solutions for international disputes. It would speak to the fundamental human desire (overwhelmed too often by barrages of superpatriotic slogans) to live at peace with others.

The public appeal for such a dramatic policy change would be based in a simple but powerful moral argument: that given the nature of modern warfare, the victims, by a ratio of 10:1, have been civilians. To put it another way, war in our time is always a war against children. And if the children of other countries are to be granted an equal right to life with our own children, then we must use our extraordinary human ingenuity to find nonmilitary solutions for world problems.

With the four or five hundred billion dollars gained by progressive taxation and demilitarization, there would be funds available to pay for health care for everyone, to guarantee jobs to anyone willing and able to work. Instead of giving out contracts for jet bombers and nuclear submarines, contracts could be offered to nonprofit corporations to hire people to build homes, construct public transport systems, clean up the rivers and lakes, turn our cities into decent places to live. (One of Marge Piercy's poems ends with: "The pitcher cries for water to carry/And a person for work that is real.")

The alternative to such a bold program was to continue as before, allowing the cities to fester, forcing rural people to face debt and foreclosures, offering no useful work for the young, creating a larger and larger marginal population of desperate people. Many of these people would turn to drugs and crime, some of them to a religious fanaticism ending in violence against others or themselves (in 1996, one such group committed mass suicide), some to a hysterical hatred of government (as in the bombing of the federal building in Oklahoma City in 1995, killing at least 168 people). The response of the authorities to such signs of desperation, anger, alienation has been, historically, quite predictable: Build more jails, lock up more people, execute more prisoners. And continue with the same policies that produced the desperation.

But another scenario remained possible, one that envisioned a time, somewhere around the beginning of the new millennium, when citizens would organize to demand what the Declaration of Independence promised: a government that protected the equal right of everyone to life, liberty and the pursuit of happiness. This meant economic arrangements that distributed the national wealth rationally and humanely. This meant a culture where the young no longer were taught to strive for "success" as a mask for greed.

By the midnineties, the elements for such a scenario were there. Public opinion surveys showed the public much more inclined than either major party to curtail the military budget, tax the rich, clean up the environment, have universal health care, end poverty. And in the nineties there were thousands of groups in cities and towns all over the country already working for such goals. But they had not yet united into a national movement.

Still, there were signs of such a possibility. In 1995 a million black men gathered in the nation's capital to express their solidarity around common frustrations. The following year half a million adults and children of all colors arrived in Washington to "Stand for Children." The country was becoming more diverse—more Latino people, more Asians, more interracial marriages. There was at least a chance for a true "Rainbow Coalition," one that would fulfill the promise proclaimed by black leader Jesse Jackson. In the late eighties, speaking for the poor and dispossessed of all colors, Jackson gave the nation a brief, rare surge of political excitement.

The culture had been affected by the movements of the sixties in a way that could not be obliterated. There was a distinctly new consciousness—manifested in the cinema, on television, in the world of music—an awareness that women deserved equal rights, that the sexual preferences of men and women were their own affair, that the growing gap between rich and poor gave the lie to the word "democracy."

The labor movement was showing signs of a new energy, moving to organize white-collar workers, farm workers, immigrant workers, and to tap the idealism of young people by inviting them to help in this organizing. Employees were "blowing the whistle" on corporate crimes.

Religious leaders, who had been quiet since their involvement in the movements for civil rights and against the Vietnam war, began to speak out on economic inequality. In the summer of 1996, the *New York Times* reported:

> More than at any other time in decades, religious leaders are making common cause with trade unions, lending their moral authority to denounce sweatshops, back a higher minimum wage and help organize janitors and poultry workers. The clergy has not lined up with labor to such an extent since the heyday of Cesar Chavez, the charismatic farm workers' leader, in the 1970's and perhaps the Depression. . . .

There was at least the beginning of a rebellion against the domination of the mass media by corporate wealth (financial mergers had created supermonopolies in television, the press, publishing). In 1994, a television station in San Francisco initially refused to air *Deadly Deception*, an Academy Award–winning documentary that exposed the General Electric Corporation's involvement in the nuclear weapons industry. Activists projected the entire film on the side of the television station's building and invited the community to watch. The station yielded, and agreed to show the film.

Disillusionment with both Democratic and Republican Parties led in the mid-nineties to a number of attempts to create independent political movements. In Texas, there was a founding convention of the Alliance for Democracy, which hoped to initiate a new anticorporate populist movement in the country. In the Midwest, the New Party sprang up, to give voters an alternative to conservative candidates. Rank-and-file trade unionists from across the nation met in 1996 to set up a Labor Party.

Would these elements come together in the next century, the next millennium, to fulfill their promise? No one could predict. All one could do was to act on the possibility, knowing that inaction would make any prediction a gloomy one.

If democracy was to be given any meaning, if it was to go beyond the limits of capitalism and nationalism, this would not come—if history was any guide—from the top. It would come through citizens' movements, organizing, agitating, striking, boycotting, demonstrating, threatening those in power with disruption of the stability they needed.

Sometime in 1992, the Republican Party held a dinner to raise funds, for which individuals and corporations paid up to $400,000 to attend. (The fee for Democratic dinners was slightly less.) A White House spokesman told questioning reporters: "It's buying access to the system, yes." When asked about people who didn't have so much money, he replied: "They have to demand access in other ways."

That may have been a clue to Americans wanting real change. They would have to demand access in their own way.

THE COMING REVOLT
OF THE GUARDS

The title of this chapter is not a prediction, but a hope, which I will soon explain.

As for the subtitle of this book, it is not quite accurate; a "people's history" promises more than any one person can fulfill, and it is the most difficult kind of history to recapture. I call it that anyway because, with all its limitations, it is a history disrespectful of governments and respectful of people's movements of resistance.

That makes it a biased account, one that leans in a certain direction. I am not troubled by that, because the mountain of history books under which we all stand leans so heavily in the other direction—so tremblingly respectful of states and statesmen and so disrespectful, by inattention, to people's movements—that we need some counterforce to avoid being crushed into submission.

All those histories of this country centered on the Founding Fathers and the Presidents weigh oppressively on the capacity of the ordinary citizen to act. They suggest that in times of crisis we must look to someone to save us: in the Revolutionary crisis, the Founding Fathers; in the slavery crisis, Lincoln; in the Depression, Roosevelt; in the Vietnam-Watergate crisis, Carter. And

that between occasional crises everything is all right, and it is sufficient for us to be restored to that normal state. They teach us
that the supreme act of citizenship is to choose among saviors, by
going into a voting booth every four years to choose between two
white and well-off Anglo-Saxon males of inoffensive personality
and orthodox opinions.

The idea of saviors has been built into the entire culture,
beyond politics. We have learned to look to stars, leaders, experts
in every field, thus surrendering our own strength, demeaning
our own ability, obliterating our own selves. But from time to
time, Americans reject that idea and rebel.

These rebellions, so far, have been contained. The American
system is the most ingenious system of control in world history.
With a country so rich in natural resources, talent, and labor
power the system can afford to distribute just enough wealth to
just enough people to limit discontent to a troublesome minority.
It is a country so powerful, so big, so pleasing to so many of its
citizens that it can afford to give freedom of dissent to the small
number who are not pleased.

There is no system of control with more openings, apertures,
leeways, flexibilities, rewards for the chosen, winning tickets in
lotteries. There is none that disperses its controls more com-
plexly through the voting system, the work situation, the church,
the family, the school, the mass media—none more successful in
mollifying opposition with reforms, isolating people from one
another, creating patriotic loyalty.

One percent of the nation owns a third of the wealth. The rest
of the wealth is distributed in such a way as to turn those in the
99 percent against one another: small property owners against the
propertyless, black against white, native-born against foreign-
born, intellectuals and professionals against the uneducated and
unskilled. These groups have resented one another and warred
against one another with such vehemence and violence as to
obscure their common position as sharers of leftovers in a very
wealthy country.

Against the reality of that desperate, bitter battle for resources made scarce by elite control, I am taking the liberty of uniting those 99 percent as "the people." I have been writing a history that attempts to represent their submerged, deflected, common interest. To emphasize the commonality of the 99 percent, to declare deep enmity of interest with the 1 percent, is to do exactly what the governments of the United States, and the wealthy elite allied to them—from the Founding Fathers to now—have tried their best to prevent. Madison feared a "majority faction" and hoped the new Constitution would control it. He and his colleagues began the Preamble to the Constitution with the words "We the people . . . ," pretending that the new government stood for everyone, and hoping that this myth, accepted as fact, would ensure "domestic tranquillity."

The pretense continued over the generations, helped by all-embracing symbols, physical or verbal: the flag, patriotism, democracy, national interest, national defense, national security. The slogans were dug into the earth of American culture like a circle of covered wagons on the western plain, from inside of which the white, slightly privileged American could shoot to kill the enemy outside—Indians or blacks or foreigners or other whites too wretched to be allowed inside the circle. The managers of the caravan watched at a safe distance, and when the battle was over and the field strewn with dead on both sides, they would take over the land, and prepare another expedition, for another territory.

The scheme never worked perfectly. The Revolution and the Constitution, trying to bring stability by containing the class angers of the colonial period—while enslaving blacks, annihilating or displacing Indians—did not quite succeed, judging by the tenant uprisings, the slave revolts, the abolitionist agitation, the feminist upsurge, the Indian guerrilla warfare of the pre–Civil War years. After the Civil War, a new coalition of southern and northern elites developed, with southern whites and blacks of the lower classes occupied in racial conflict, native workers and immigrant workers clashing in the North, and the farmers dispersed over a big country, while the system of capitalism consolidated itself in industry and government. But there came rebellion among industrial workers and a great opposition movement among farmers.

At the turn of the century, the violent pacification of blacks and Indians and the use of elections and war to absorb and divert white rebels were not enough, in the conditions of modern industry, to prevent the great upsurge of socialism, the massive labor struggles, before the First World War. Neither that war nor the partial prosperity of the twenties, nor the apparent destruction of the socialist movement, could prevent, in the situation of economic crisis, another radical awakening, another labor upsurge in the thirties.

World War II created a new unity, followed by an apparently successful attempt, in the atmosphere of the cold war, to extinguish the strong radical temper of the war years. But then, surprisingly, came the surge of the sixties, from people thought long subdued or put out of sight—blacks, women, Native Americans, prisoners, soldiers—and a new radicalism, which threatened to spread widely in a population disillusioned by the Vietnam war and the politics of Watergate.

The exile of Nixon, the celebration of the Bicentennial, the presidency of Carter, all aimed at restoration. But restoration to the old order was no solution to the uncertainty, the alienation, which was intensified in the Reagan-Bush years. The election of Clinton in 1992, carrying with it a vague promise of change, did not fulfill the expectations of the hopeful.

With such continuing malaise, it is very important for the Establishment—that uneasy club of business executives, generals, and politicos—to maintain the historic pretension of national unity, in which the government represents all the people, and the common enemy is overseas, not at home, where disasters of economics or war are unfortunate errors or tragic accidents, to be corrected by the members of the same club that brought the disasters. It is important for them also to make sure this artificial unity of highly privileged and slightly privileged is the only unity—that the 99 percent remain split in countless ways, and turn against one another to vent their angers.

How skillful to tax the middle class to pay for the relief of the poor, building resentment on top of humiliation! How adroit to bus poor black youngsters into poor white neighborhoods, in a violent exchange of impoverished schools, while the schools of the rich remain untouched and the wealth of the nation, doled out carefully where children need free milk, is drained for billion-dollar aircraft carriers. How ingenious to meet the demands of blacks and women for equality by giving them small special benefits, and setting them in competition with everyone else for jobs made scarce by an irrational, wasteful system. How wise to turn the fear and anger of the majority toward a class of criminals bred—by economic inequity—faster than they can be put away, deflecting attention from the huge thefts of national resources carried out within the law by men in executive offices.

But with all the controls of power and punishment, enticements and concessions, diversions and decoys, operating throughout the history of the country, the Establishment has been unable to keep itself secure from revolt. Every time it looked as if it had succeeded, the very people it thought seduced or subdued, stirred and rose. Blacks, cajoled by Supreme Court decisions and congressional statutes, rebelled. Women, wooed and ignored, romanticized and mistreated, rebelled. Indians, thought dead, reappeared, defiant. Young people, despite lures of career and comfort, defected. Working people, thought soothed by reforms, regulated by law, kept within bounds by their own unions, went on strike. Government intellectuals, pledged to secrecy, began giving away secrets. Priests turned from piety to protest.

To recall this is to remind people of what the Establishment would like them to forget—the enormous capacity of apparently helpless people to resist, of apparently contented people to demand change. To uncover such history is to find a powerful human impulse to assert one's humanity. It is to hold out, even in times of deep pessimism, the possibility of surprise.

True, to overestimate class consciousness, to exaggerate rebellion and its successes, would be misleading. It would not account for the fact that the world—not just the United States, but everywhere else—is still in the hands of the elites, that people's movements, although they show an infinite capacity for recurrence, have so far been either defeated or absorbed or perverted, that "socialist" revolutionists have betrayed socialism, that nationalist revolutions have led to new dictatorships.

But most histories understate revolt, overemphasize statesmanship, and thus encourage impotency among citizens. When we look closely at resistance movements, or even at isolated forms of rebellion, we discover that class consciousness, or any other awareness of injustice, has multiple levels. It has many ways of expression, many ways of revealing itself—open, subtle, direct, distorted. In a system of intimidation and control, people do not show how much they know, how deeply they feel, until their practical sense informs them they can do so without being destroyed.

History which keeps alive the memory of people's resistance suggests new definitions of power. By traditional definitions, whoever possesses military strength, wealth, command of official ideology, cultural control, has power. Measured by these standards, popular rebellion never looks strong enough to survive.

However, the unexpected victories—even temporary ones—of insurgents show the vulnerability of the supposedly powerful. In a highly developed society, the Establishment cannot survive without the obedience and loyalty of millions of people who are given small rewards to keep the system going: the soldiers and police, teachers and ministers, administrators and social workers, technicians and production workers, doctors, lawyers, nurses, transport and communications workers, garbagemen and firemen. These people—the employed, the somewhat privileged—are drawn into alliance with the elite. They become the guards of the system, buffers between the upper and lower classes. If they stop obeying, the system falls.

That will happen, I think, only when all of us who are slightly privileged and slightly uneasy begin to see that we are like the guards in the prison uprising at Attica—expendable; that the Establishment, whatever rewards it gives us, will also, if necessary to maintain its control, kill us.

Certain new facts may, in our time, emerge so clearly as to lead to general withdrawal of loyalty from the system. The new conditions of technology, economics, and war, in the atomic age, make it less and less possible for the guards of the system—the intellectuals, the home owners, the taxpayers, the skilled workers, the professionals, the servants of government—to remain immune from the violence (physical and psychic) inflicted on the black, the poor, the criminal, the enemy overseas. The internationalization of the economy, the movement of refugees and illegal immigrants across borders, both make it more difficult for the people of the industrial countries to be oblivious to hunger and disease in the poor countries of the world.

All of us have become hostages in the new conditions of doomsday technology, runaway economics, global poisoning, uncontainable war. The atomic weapons, the invisible radiations, the economic anarchy, do not distinguish prisoners from guards, and those in charge will not be scrupulous in making distinctions. There is the unforgettable response of the U.S. high command to the news that American prisoners of war might be near Nagasaki: "Targets previously assigned for Centerboard remain unchanged."

There is evidence of growing dissatisfaction among the guards. We have known for some time that the poor and ignored were the nonvoters, alienated from a political system they felt didn't care about them, and about which they could do little. Now alienation has spread upward into families above the poverty line. These are white workers, neither rich nor poor, but angry over economic insecurity, unhappy with their work, worried about their neighborhoods, hostile to government—combining elements of racism with elements of class consciousness, contempt for the lower classes along with distrust for the elite, and thus open to solutions from any direction, right or left.

In the twenties there was a similar estrangement in the middle classes, which could have gone in various directions—the Ku Klux Klan had millions of members at that time—but in the thirties the work of an organized left wing mobilized much of this feeling into trade unions, farmers' unions, socialist movements.

We may, in the coming years, be in a race for the mobilization of middle-class discontent.

The fact of that discontent is clear. The surveys since the early seventies show 70 to 80 percent of Americans distrustful of government, business, the military. This means the distrust goes beyond blacks, the poor, the radicals. It has spread among skilled workers, white-collar workers, professionals; for the first time in the nation's history, perhaps, both the lower classes and the middle classes, the prisoners and the guards, were disillusioned with the system.

There are other signs: the high rate of alcoholism, the high rate of divorce (from one of three marriages ending in divorce, the figure was climbing to one of two), of drug use and abuse, of nervous breakdowns and mental illness. Millions of people have been looking desperately for solutions to their sense of impotency, their loneliness, their frustration, their estrangement from other people, from the world, from their work, from themselves. They have been adopting new religions, joining self-help groups of all kinds. It is as if a whole nation were going through a critical point in its middle age, a life crisis of self-doubt, self-examination.

All this, at a time when the middle class is increasingly insecure economically. The system, in its irrationality, has been driven by profit to build steel skyscrapers for insurance companies while the cities decay, to spend billions for weapons of destruction and virtually nothing for children's playgrounds, to give huge incomes to men who make dangerous or useless things, and very little to artists, musicians, writers, actors. Capitalism has always been a failure for the lower classes. It is now beginning to fail for the middle classes.

The threat of unemployment, always inside the homes of the poor, has spread to white-collar workers, professionals. A college education is no longer a guarantee against joblessness, and a system that cannot offer a future to the young coming out of school is in deep trouble. If it happens only to the children of the poor, the problem is manageable; there are the jails. If it happens to the children of the middle class, things may get out of hand. The poor are accustomed to being squeezed and always short of money, but in recent years the middle classes, too, have begun to feel the press of high prices, high taxes.

In the seventies, eighties, and early nineties there was a dramatic, frightening increase in the number of crimes. It was not hard to understand, when one walked through any big city. There were the contrasts of wealth and poverty, the culture of possession, the frantic advertising. There was the fierce economic competition, in which the legal violence of the state and the legal robbery by the corporations were accompanied by the illegal crimes of the poor. Most crimes by far involved theft. A disproportionate number of prisoners in American jails were poor and non-white, with little education. Half were unemployed in the month prior to their arrest.

The most common and most publicized crimes have been the violent crimes of the young, the poor—a virtual terrorization in the big cities—in which the desperate or drug-addicted attack and rob the middle class, or even their fellow poor. A society so stratified by wealth and education lends itself naturally to envy and class anger.

The critical question in our time is whether the middle classes, so long led to believe that the solution for such crimes is more jails and more jail terms, may begin to see, by the sheer uncontrollability of crime, that the only prospect is an endless cycle of crime and punishment. They might then conclude that physical security for a working person in the city can come only when everyone in the city is working. And that would require a transformation of national priorities, a change in the system.

In recent decades, the fear of criminal assault has been joined by an even greater fear. Deaths from cancer began to multiply, and medical researchers seemed helpless to find the cause. It began to be evident that more and more of these deaths were coming from an environment poisoned by military experimentation and industrial greed. The water people drank, the air they breathed, the particles of dust from the buildings in which they worked, had been quietly contaminated over the years by a system so frantic for growth and profit that the safety and health of human beings had been ignored. A new and deadly scourge appeared, the AIDS virus, which spread with special rapidity among homosexuals and drug addicts.

In the early nineties, the false socialism of the Soviet system had failed. And the American system seemed out of control—a runaway capitalism, a runaway technology, a runaway militarism, a running away of government from the people it claimed to represent. Crime was out of control, cancer and AIDS were out of control. Prices and taxes and unemployment were out of control. The decay of cities and the breakdown of families were out of control. And people seemed to sense all this.

Perhaps much of the general distrust of government reported in recent years comes from a growing recognition of the truth of what the U.S. Air Force bombardier Yossarian said in the novel *Catch-22* to a friend who had just accused him of giving aid and comfort to the enemy: "The enemy is anybody who's going to get you killed, no matter which side he's on. And don't you forget that, because the longer you remember it the longer you might live." The next line in the novel is: "But Clevinger did forget, and now he was dead."

Let us imagine the prospect—for the first time in the nation's history—of a population united for fundamental change. Would the elite turn as so often before, to its ultimate weapon—foreign intervention—to unite the people with the Establishment, in war? It tried to do that in 1991, with the war against Iraq. But, as June Jordan said, it was "a hit the same way that crack is, and it doesn't last long."

With the Establishment's inability either to solve severe economic problems at home or to manufacture abroad a safety valve for domestic discontent, Americans might be ready to demand not just more tinkering, more reform laws, another reshuffling of the same deck, another New Deal, but radical change. Let us be utopian for a moment so that when we get realistic again it is not that "realism" so useful to the Establishment in its discouragement of action, that "realism" anchored to a certain kind of history empty of surprise. Let us imagine what radical change would require of us all.

The society's levers of powers would have to be taken away from those whose drives have led to the present state—the giant corporations, the military, and their politician collaborators. We would need—by a coordinated effort of local groups all over the country—to reconstruct the economy for both efficiency and justice, producing in a cooperative way what people need most. We would start on our neighborhoods, our cities, our workplaces. Work of some kind would be needed by everyone, including people now kept out of the work force—children, old people, "handicapped" people. Society could use the enormous energy now idle, the skills and talents now unused. Everyone could share the routine but necessary jobs for a few hours a day, and leave most of the time free for enjoyment, creativity, labors of love, and yet produce enough for an equal and ample distribution of goods. Certain basic things would be abundant enough to be taken out of the money system and be available—free—to everyone: food, housing, health care, education, transportation.

The great problem would be to work out a way of accomplishing this without a centralized bureaucracy, using not the incentives of prison and punishment, but those incentives of cooperation which spring from natural human desires, which in the past have been used by the state in times of war, but also by social movements that gave hints of how people might behave in different conditions. Decisions would be made by small groups of people in their workplaces, their neighborhoods—a network of cooperatives, in communication with one another, a neighborly socialism avoiding the class hierarchies of capitalism and the harsh dictatorships that have taken the name "socialist."

People in time, in friendly communities, might create a new, diversified, nonviolent culture, in which all forms of personal and group expression would be possible. Men and women, black and white, old and young, could then cherish their differences as positive attributes, not as reasons for domination. New values of cooperation and freedom might then show up in the relations of people, the upbringing of children.

To do all that, in the complex conditions of control in the United States, would require combining the energy of all previous movements in American history—of labor insurgents, black rebels, Native Americans, women, young people—along with the new energy of an angry middle class. People would need to begin to transform their immediate environments—the workplace, the family, the school, the community—by a series of struggles against absentee authority, to give control of these places to the people who live and work there.

These struggles would involve all the tactics used at various times in the past by people's movements: demonstrations, marches, civil disobedience; strikes and boycotts and general strikes; direct action to redistribute wealth, to reconstruct institutions, to revamp relationships; creating—in music, literature, drama, all the arts, and all the areas of work and play in everyday life—a new culture of sharing, of respect, a new joy in the collaboration of people to help themselves and one another.

There would be many defeats. But when such a movement took hold in hundreds of thousands of places all over the country it would be impossible to suppress, because the very guards the system depends on to crush such a movement would be among the rebels. It would be a new kind of revolution, the only kind that could happen, I believe, in a country like the United States. It would take enormous energy, sacrifice, commitment, patience. But because it would be a process over time, starting without delay, there would be the immediate satisfactions that people have always found in the affectionate ties of groups striving together for a common goal.

All this takes us far from American history, into the realm of imagination. But not totally removed from history. There are at least glimpses in the past of such a possibility. In the sixties and seventies, for the first time, the Establishment failed to produce national unity and patriotic fervor in a war. There was a flood of cultural changes such as the country had never seen—in sex, family, personal relations—exactly those situations most difficult to control from the ordinary centers of power. And never before was there such a general withdrawal of confidence from so many elements of the political and economic system. In every period of history, people have found ways to help one another—even in the midst of a culture of competition and violence—if only for brief periods, to find joy in work, struggle, companionship, nature.

The prospect is for times of turmoil, struggle, but also inspiration. There is a chance that such a movement could succeed in doing what the system itself has never done—bring about great change with little violence. This is possible because the more of the 99 percent that begin to see themselves as sharing needs, the more the guards and the prisoners see their common interest, the more the Establishment becomes isolated, ineffectual. The elite's weapons, money, control of information would be useless in the face of a determined population. The servants of the system would refuse to work to continue the old, deadly order, and would begin using their time, their space—the very things given them by the system to keep them quiet—to dismantle that system while creating a new one.

The prisoners of the system will continue to rebel, as before, in ways that cannot be foreseen, at times that cannot be predicted. The new fact of our era is the chance that they may be joined by the guards. We readers and writers of books have been, for the most part, among the guards. If we understand that, and act on it, not only will life be more satisfying, right off, but our grandchildren, or our great grandchildren, might possibly see a different and marvelous world.

BIBLIOGRAPHY

This book, written in a few years, is based on twenty years of teaching and research in American history, and as many years of involvement in social movements. But it could not have been written without the work of several generations of scholars, and especially the current generation of historians who have done immense work in the history of blacks, Indians, women, and working people of all kinds. It also could not have been written without the work of many people, not professional historians, who were stimulated by the social struggles around them to put together material about the lives and activities of ordinary people trying to make a better world, or just trying to survive.

To indicate every source of information in the text would have meant a book impossibly cluttered with footnotes, and yet I know the curiosity of the reader about where a startling fact or pungent quote comes from. Therefore, as often as I can, I mention in the text authors and titles of books for which the full information is in this bibliography. Where you cannot tell the source of a quotation right from the text, you can probably figure it out by looking at the asterisked books for that chapter. The asterisked books are those I found especially useful and often indispensable.

I have gone through the following standard scholarly periodicals: *American Historical Review, Mississippi Valley Historical Review, Journal of American History, Journal of Southern History, Journal of Negro History, Labor History, William and Mary Quarterly, Phylon, The Crisis, American Political Science Review, Journal of Social History.*

Also, some less orthodox but important periodicals for a work like this: *Monthly Review, Science and Society, Radical America, Akwesasne Notes, Signs: Journal of Women in Culture and Society, The Black Scholar, Bulletin of Concerned Asian Scholars, The Review of Radical Political Economics, Socialist Revolution, Radical History Review.*

1. THE EMPIRE AND THE PEOPLE

Aptheker, Herbert, ed. *A Documentary History of the Negro People in the United States.* New York: Citadel, 1973.

Beale, Howard K. *Theodore Roosevelt and the Rise of America to World Power.* New York: Macmillan, 1962.

Beisner, Robert. *Twelve Against Empire: The Anti-Imperialists, 1898–1902.* New York: McGraw-Hill, 1968.

*Foner, Philip. *A History of the Labor Movement in the United States.* 4 vols. New York: International Publishers, 1947–1964.

*———. *The Spanish-Cuban-American War and the Birth of American Imperialism.* 2 vols. New York: Monthly Review Press, 1972.

Francisco, Luzviminda. "The First Vietnam: The Philippine-American War, 1899–1902," *Bulletin of Concerned Asian Scholars,* 1973.

*Gatewood, Willard B. *"Smoked Yankees" and the Struggle for Empire: Letters from Negro Soldiers, 1898–1902.* Urbana: University of Illinois Press, 1971.

Lafeber, Walter. *The New Empire: An Interpretation of American Expansion.* Ithaca, N.Y.: Cornell University Press, 1963.

Pratt, Julius. "American Business and the Spanish-American War," *Hispanic-American Historical Review,* 1934.

Schirmer, Daniel Boone. *Republic or Empire: American Resistance to the Philippine War.* Cambridge, Mass.: Schenkman, 1972.

Williams, William Appleman. *The Roots of the Modern American Empire.* New York: Random House, 1969.

———. *The Tragedy of American Diplomacy.* New York: Dell, 1972.

Wolff, Leon. *Little Brown Brother.* Garden City, N.Y.: Doubleday, 1961.

Young, Marilyn. *The Rhetoric of Empire.* Cambridge, Mass.: Harvard University Press, 1968.

2. THE SOCIALIST CHALLENGE

*Aptheker, Herbert. *A Documentary History of the Negro People in the United States.* New York: Citadel, 1974.

*Baxandall, Rosalyn, Gordon, Linda, and Reverby, Susan, eds. *America's Working Women.* New York: Random House, 1976.

Braverman, Harry. *Labor and Monopoly Capital: The Degradation of Work in the Twentieth Century.* New York: Monthly Review, 1975.

Brody, David. *Steelworkers in America: The Non-Union Era.* Cambridge, Mass.: Harvard University Press, 1960.

Chafe, William. *Women and Equality: Changing Patterns in American Culture.* New York: Oxford University Press, 1977.

Cochran, Thomas, and Miller, William. *The Age of Enterprise.* New York: Macmillan, 1942.

Dancis, Bruce. "Socialism and Women," *Socialist Revolution,* January–March 1976.

Dubofsky, Melvyn. *We Shall Be All: A History of the Industrial Workers of the World.* New York: Quadrangle, 1974.

Du Bois, W. E. B. *The Souls of Black Folk.* New York: Fawcett, 1961.

Faulkner, Harold. *The Decline of Laissez Faire 1897–1917.* White Plains, N.Y.: M. E. Sharpe, 1977.

*Flexner, Eleanor. *A Century of Struggle.* Cambridge, Mass.: Harvard University Press, 1975.

Flynn, Elizabeth Gurley. *The Rebel Girl.* New York: International Publishers, 1973.

Foner, Philip, ed. *Helen Keller: Her Socialist Years.* New York: International Publishers, 1967.

*———. *A History of the Labor Movement in the United States.* 4 vols. New York: International Publishers, 1947–1964.

Gilman, Charlotte Perkins. *Women and Economics.* New York: Harper & Row, 1966.

*Ginger, Ray. *The Bending Cross: A Biography of Eugene Victor Debs.* New Brunswick: Rutgers University Press, 1969.

Goldman, Emma. *Anarchism and Other Essays.* New York: Dover, 1970.

Green, James. *Grass-Roots Socialism: Radical Movements in the Southwest, 1895–1943.* Baton Rouge: Louisiana State University Press, 1978.

Hays, Samuel. "The Politics of Reform in Municipal Government in the Progressive Era," *Pacific Northwest Quarterly,* October 1964. (Reprinted by New England Free Press.)

Haywood, Bill. *The Autobiography of Big Bill Haywood.* New York: International Publishers, 1929.

Hofstadter, Richard. *The American Political Tradition.* New York: Random House, 1954.

James, Henry. *The American Scene.* Bloomington: Indiana University Press, 1968.

Jones, Mary. *The Autobiography of Mother Jones.* Chicago: Charles Kerr, 1925.

Kaplan, Justin. *Mr. Clemens and Mark Twain: A Biography.* New York: Simon & Schuster, 1966.

*Kolko, Gabriel. *The Triumph of Conservatism.* New York: Free Press, 1977.

*Kornbluh, Joyce, ed. *Rebel Voices: An I.W.W. Anthology.* Ann Arbor: University of Michigan Press, 1964.

*Lerner, Gerda, ed. *Black Women in White America.* New York: Random House, 1973.

*———. *The Female Experience: An American Documentary.* Indianapolis: Bobbs-Merrill, 1977.

London, Jack. *The Iron Heel.* New York: Bantam, 1971.

Naden, Corinne J. *The Triangle Shirtwaist Fire, March 25, 1911.* New York: Franklin Watts, 1971.

Sanger, Margaret. *Woman and the New Race.* New York: Brentano's, 1920.

Schoener, Allon, ed. *Portal to America: The Lower East Side, 1870–1925.* New York: Holt, Rinehart and Winston, 1967.

Sinclair, Upton. *The Jungle.* New York: Harper & Row, 1951.

Sochen, June. *Movers and Shakers: American Women Thinkers and Activists, 1900–1970.* New York: Quadrangle, 1974.

Stein, Leon. *The Triangle Fire.* Philadelphia: Lippincott, 1965.

Wasserman, Harvey. *Harvey Wasserman's History of the United States.* New York: Harper & Row, 1972.

*Weinstein, James. *The Corporate Ideal in the Liberal State, 1900–1918.* Boston: Beacon Press, 1968.

*Wertheimer, Barbara. *We Were There: The Story of Working Women in America.* New York: Pantheon, 1977.

Wiebe, Robert H. *The Search for Order, 1877–1920.* New York: Hill & Wang, 1966.

*Yellen, Samuel. *American Labor Struggles.* New York: Pathfinder, 1974.

Zinn, Howard. *The Politics of History.* Boston: Beacon Press, 1970.

3. WAR IS THE HEALTH OF THE STATE

Baritz, Loren, ed. *The American Left.* New York: Basic Books, 1971.

*Chafee, Zechariah, Jr. *Free Speech in the United States.* New York: Atheneum, 1969.

Dos Passos, John. *1919.* New York: Signet, 1969.

Du Bois, W. E. B. "The African Roots of War," *Atlantic Monthly,* May 1915.

Fleming, D. F. *The Origins and Legacies of World War I.* Garden City, N.Y.: Doubleday, 1968.

*Fussell, Paul. *The Great War and Modern Memory.* New York: Oxford University Press, 1975.

*Ginger, Ray. *The Bending Cross: A Biography of Eugene Victor Debs.* New Brunswick: Rutgers University Press, 1969.

Goldman, Eric. *Rendezvous with Destiny.* New York: Random House, 1956.

Gruber, Carol S. *Mars and Minerva: World War I and the Uses of Higher*

Learning in America. Baton Rouge: Louisiana State University Press, 1975.

Joughin, Louis, and Morgan, Edmund. *The Legacy of Sacco and Vanzetti.* New York: Quadrangle, 1964.

Knightley, Philip. *The First Casualty: The War Correspondent as Hero, Propagandist, and Myth Maker.* New York: Harcourt Brace Jovanovich, 1975.

Kornbluh, Joyce, ed. *Rebel Voices: An I.W.W. Anthology.* Ann Arbor: University of Michigan Press, 1964.

Levin, Murray. *Political Hysteria in America.* New York: Basic Books, 1971.

Mayer, Arno J. *The Politics and Diplomacy of Peace-Making 1918–1919.* New York: Knopf, 1967.

*Peterson, H. C., and Fite, Gilbert C. *Opponents of War, 1917–1918.* Seattle: University of Washington Press, 1968.

Simpson, Colin. *Lusitania.* Boston: Little, Brown, 1973.

Sinclair, Upton. *Boston.* Cambridge, Mass.: Robert Bentley, 1978.

Weinstein, James. *The Corporate Ideal in the United States 1900–1918.* Boston: Beacon Press, 1969.

4. SELF-HELP IN HARD TIMES

Adamic, Louis. *My America, 1928–1938.* New York: Harper & Row, 1938.

*Baxandall, Rosalyn, Gordon, Linda, and Reverby, Susan, eds. *America's Working Women.* New York: Random House, 1976.

Bellush, Bernard. *The Failure of the N.R.A.* New York: W. W. Norton, 1976.

Bernstein, Barton, J., ed. *Towards a New Past: Dissenting Essays in American History.* New York: Pantheon, 1968.

Bernstein, Irving. *The Lean Years: A History of the American Worker, 1920–1933.* Boston: Houghton Mifflin, 1960.

———. *The Turbulent Years: A History of the American Worker, 1933–1941.* Boston: Houghton Mifflin, 1969.

Borden, Morton, ed. *Voices of the American Past: Readings in American History.* Lexington, Mass.: D. C. Heath, 1972.

Boyer, Richard, and Morais, Herbert. *Labor's Untold Story.* United Front, 1955.

*Brecher, Jeremy. *Strike!* Boston, Mass.: South End Press, 1979.

Buhle, Paul. "An Interview with Luigi Nardella," *Radical History Review,* Spring 1978.

*Cloward, Richard A., and Piven, Frances F. *Poor People's Movements.* New York: Pantheon, 1977.

Conkin, Paul. *F.D.R. and the Origins of the Welfare State.* New York: Crowell, 1967.

Curti, Merle. *The Growth of American Thought.* New York: Harper & Row, 1943.

*Fine, Sidney. *Sit-Down: The General Motors Strike of 1936–1937.* Ann Arbor: University of Michigan Press, 1969.

Galbraith, John Kenneth. *The Great Crash: 1929.* Boston: Houghton Mifflin, 1972.

General Strike Committee. *The Seattle General Strike.* Charlestown, Mass.: gum press, 1972.

*Hallgren, Mauritz. *Seeds of Revolt.* New York: Knopf, 1934.

*Lerner, Gerda, ed. *Black Women in White America: A Documentary History.* New York: Random House, 1977.

Lewis, Sinclair. *Babbitt.* New York: Harcourt Brace Jovanovich, 1949.

Lynd, Alice and Staughton, eds. *Rank and File: Personal Histories by Working-Class Organizers.* Boston: Beacon Press, 1974.

Lynd, Robert and Helen. *Middletown.* New York: Harcourt Brace Jovanovich, 1959.

Mangione. Jerre. *The Dream and the Deal: The Federal Writers Project, 1935–1943.* Boston: Little, Brown, 1972.

Mills, Frederick C. *Economic Tendencies in the United States: Aspects of Pre-War and Post-War Changes.* New York: National Bureau of Economic Research, 1932.

Ottley, Roi, and Weatherby, William J. "The Negro in New York: An Informal History," *Justice Denied: The Black Man in White America,* ed. William Chace and Peter Collier. New York: Harcourt Brace Jovanovich, 1970.

Painter, Nell, and Hudson, Hosea. "A Negro Communist in the Deep South," *Radical America.* July-August 1977.

Renshaw, Patrick. *The Wobblies.* New York: Anchor, 1968.

*Rosengarten, Theodore. *All God's Dangers: The Life of Nate Shaw.* New York: Knopf, 1974.

Steinbeck, John. *The Grapes of Wrath.* New York: Viking, 1939.

Swados, Harvey, ed. *The American Writer and the Great Depression.* Indianapolis: Bobbs-Merrill, 1966.

*Terkel, Studs. *Hard Times: An Oral History of the Great Depression in America.* New York: Pantheon, 1970.

Wright, Richard. *Black Boy.* New York: Harper & Row, 1937.

Zinn, Howard. *La Guardia in Congress.* Ithaca, N.Y.: Cornell University Press, 1959.

5. A PEOPLE'S WAR?

Alperovitz, Gar. *Atomic Diplomacy.* New York: Vintage, 1967.

Aronson, James. *The Press and the Cold War.* Indianapolis: Bobbs-Merrill, 1970.

Barnet, Richard J. *Intervention and Revolution: The U.S. and the Third World.* New York: New American Library, 1969.

Blackett, P. M. S. *Fear, War and the Bomb: Military and Political Consequences of Atomic Energy.* New York: McGraw-Hill, 1948.

Bottome, Edgar. *The Balance of Terror: A Guide to the Arms Race.* Boston: Beacon Press, 1972.

Butow, Robert. *Japan's Decision to Surrender.* Stanford: Stanford University Press, 1954.

Catton, Bruce. *The War Lords of Washington.* New York: Harcourt Brace, 1948.

Chomsky, Noam. *American Power and the New Mandarins.* New York: Pantheon, 1969.

Davidson, Basil. *Let Freedom Come: Africa in Modern History.* Boston: Little, Brown, 1978.

Feingold, Henry L. *The Politics of Rescue: The Roosevelt Administration and the Holocaust.* New Brunswick, N.J.: Rutgers University Press, 1970.

Freeland, Richard M. *The Truman Doctrine and the Origins of McCarthyism.* New York: Knopf, 1971.

Gardner, Lloyd. *Economic Aspects of New Deal Diplomacy.* Madison: University of Wisconsin Press, 1964.

Griffith, Robert W. *The Politics of Fear: Joseph R. McCarthy and the Senate.* Rochelle Park, N.J.: Hayden, 1971.

Hamby, Alonzo L. *Beyond the New Deal: Harry S. Truman and American Liberalism.* New York: Columbia University Press, 1953.

Irving, David. *The Destruction of Dresden.* New York: Ballantine, 1965.

Kahn, Herman. *On Thermonuclear War.* New York: Free Press, 1969.

*Kolko, Gabriel. *The Politics of War: The World and United States Foreign Policy, 1943–1945.* New York: Random House, 1968.

Lemisch, Jesse. *On Active Service in War and Peace: Politics and Ideology in the American Historical Profession.* Toronto: New Hogtown Press, 1975.

Mailer, Norman. *The Naked and the Dead.* New York: Holt, Rinehart and Winston, 1948.

Miller, Douglas, and Nowak, Marion. *The Fifties: The Way We Really Were*. New York: Doubleday, 1977.

Miller, Marc. "The Irony of Victory: Lowell During World War II." Unpublished doctoral dissertation. Boston University, 1977.

Mills, C. Wright. *The Power Elite*. New York: Oxford University Press, 1970.

Minear, Richard H. *Victor's Justice: The Tokyo War Crimes Trial*. Princeton, N.J.: Princeton University Press, 1973.

Offner, Arnold. *American Appeasement: U.S. Foreign Policy and Germany, 1933–1938*. New York: W. W. Norton, 1976.

Rostow, Eugene V. "Our Worst Wartime Mistake," *Harper's*, September 1945.

Russett, Bruce. *No Clear and Present Danger*. New York: Harper & Row, 1972.

Sampson, Anthony. *The Seven Sisters: The Great Oil Companies and the World They Shaped*. New York: Viking, 1975.

Schneir, Walter and Miriam. *Invitation to an Inquest*. New York: Doubleday, 1965.

*Sherwin, Martin. *A World Destroyed: The Atom Bomb and the Grand Alliance*. New York: Knopf, 1975.

Stone, I. F. *The Hidden History of the Korean War*. New York: Monthly Review Press, 1969.

United States Strategic Bombing Survey. *Japan's Struggle to End the War*. Washington: Government Printing Office, 1946.

Weglyn, Michi. *Years of Infamy: The Untold Story of America's Concentration Camps*. New York: William Morrow, 1976.

Wittner, Lawrence S. *Rebels Against War: The American Peace Movement, 1941–1960*. New York: Columbia University Press, 1969.

*Zinn, Howard. *Postwar America: 1945–1971*. Indianapolis: Bobbs-Merrill, 1973.

6. "OR DOES IT EXPLODE?"

Allen, Robert. *Black Awakening in Capitalist America*. Garden City, N.Y.: Doubleday, 1969.

Bontemps, Arna, ed. *American Negro Poetry*. New York: Hill & Wang, 1974.

Broderick, Francis, and Meier, August. *Black Protest Thought in the Twentieth Century*. Indianapolis: Bobbs-Merrill, 1971.

Cloward, Richard A., and Piven, Frances F. *Poor People's Movements*. New York: Pantheon, 1977.

Conot, Robert. *Rivers of Blood, Years of Darkness*. New York: Morrow, 1968.

Cullen, Countee. *On These I Stand*. New York: Harper & Row, 1947.

Herndon, Angelo. "You Cannot Kill the Working Class," *Black Protest*, ed. Joanne Grant. New York: Fawcett, 1975.

Huggins, Nathan I. *Harlem Renaissance*. New York: Oxford University Press, 1971.

Hughes, Langston. *Selected Poems of Langston Hughes*. New York: Knopf, 1959.

Lerner, Gerda, ed. *Black Women in White America: A Documentary History*. New York: Random House, 1977.

Malcolm X. *Malcolm X Speaks*. New York: Meret, 1965.

Navasky, Victor. *Kennedy Justice*. New York: Atheneum, 1977.

Perkus, Cathy, ed. *Cointelpro: The FBI's Secret War on Political Freedom*. New York: Monad Press, 1976.

Wright, Richard. *Black Boy*. New York: Harper & Row, 1937.

Zinn, Howard. *Postwar America: 1945–1971*. Indianapolis: Bobbs-Merrill, 1973.

———. *SNCC: The New Abolitionists*. Boston: Beacon Press, 1964.

7. THE IMPOSSIBLE VICTORY: VIETNAM

*Branfman, Fred. *Voices from the Plain of Jars*. New York: Harper & Row, 1972.

Green, Philip, and Levinson, Sanford. *Power and Community: Dissenting Essays in Political Science*. New York: Pantheon, 1970.

Hersch, Seymour. *My Lai 4: A Report on the Massacre and Its Aftermath*. New York: Random House, 1970.

Kovic, Ron. *Born on the Fourth of July*. New York: McGraw-Hill, 1976.

Lipsitz, Lewis. "On Political Belief: The Grievances of the Poor," *Power and Community: Dissenting Essays in Political Science*, ed. Philip Green and Sanford Levinson. New York: Pantheon, 1970.

Modigliani, Andrew. "Hawks and Doves, Isolationism and Political Distrust: An Analysis of Public Opinion on Military Policy," *American Political Science Review*, September 1972.

Pentagon Papers. 4 vols. Boston: Beacon Press, 1971.

Pike, Douglas. *Viet Cong*. Cambridge, Mass.: MIT Press, 1966.

Schell, Jonathan. *The Village of Ben Suc*. New York: Knopf, 1967.

Zinn, Howard. *Vietnam: The Logic of Withdrawal*. Boston: Beacon Press, 1967.

8. Surprises

Akwesasne Notes. *Voices from Wounded Knee, 1973.* Mohawk Nation, Rooseveltown, N.Y.: Akwesasne Notes, 1974.

Baxandall, Rosalyn, Gordon, Linda, and Reverby, Susan, eds. *America's Working Women.* New York: Random House, 1976.

Benston, Margaret. "The Political Economy of Women's Liberation," *Monthly Review,* Fall 1969.

Boston Women's Health Book Collective. *Our Bodies, Ourselves.* New York: Simon & Schuster, 1976.

Brandon, William. *The Last Americans.* McGraw-Hill, 1974.

*Brown, Dee. *Bury My Heart at Wounded Knee.* New York: Holt, Rinehart and Winston, 1971.

Brownmiller, Susan. *Against Our Will: Men, Women and Rape.* New York: Simon & Schuster, 1975.

Coles, Robert. *Children of Crisis.* Boston: Little, Brown, 1967.

Cottle, Thomas J. *Children in Jail.* Boston: Beacon Press, 1977.

The Council on Interracial Books for Children, ed. *Chronicles of American Indian Protest.* New York: Fawcett, 1971.

Deloria, Vine, Jr. *Custer Died for Your Sins.* New York: Macmillan, 1969.

———. *We Talk, You Listen.* New York: Macmillan, 1970.

Firestone, Shulamith. *The Dialectics of Sex.* New York: Bantam, 1970.

9. The Seventies: Under Control?

Blair, John M. *The Control of Oil.* New York: Pantheon, 1977.

Dommergues, Pierre. "L'Essor Du conservatisme Americain," *Le Monde Diplomatique,* May 1978.

*Evans, Les, and Myers, Allen. *Watergate and the Myth of American Democracy.* New York: Pathfinder Press, 1974.

Frieden, Jess. "The Trilateral Commission," *Monthly Review,* December 1977.

Gardner, Richard. *Alternative America: A Directory of 5000 Alternative Lifestyle Groups and Organizations.* Cambridge: Richard Gardner, 1976.

Glazer, Nathan, and Kristol, Irving. *The American Commonwealth 1976.* New York: Basic Books, 1976.

New York Times. *The Watergate Hearings.* Bantam, 1973.

*U.S., Congress, Senate Committee to Study Governmental Operations with Respect to Intelligence Activities. *Hearings.* 94th Congress. 1976.

10. CARTER-REAGAN-BUSH:
THE BIPARTISAN CONSENSUS

Barlett, Donald, and Steele, James. *America: What Went Wrong?* Kansas City: Andrews & McMeel, 1992.

Barlett, Donald, and Steele, James. *America: Who Really Pays the Taxes?* New York: Simon & Schuster, 1994.

Chomsky, Noam. *World Orders Old and New.* New York: Columbia University Press, 1994.

Croteau, David, and Hoynes, William. *By Invitation Only: How the Media Limit the Political Debate.* Monroe, Maine: Common Courage Press, 1994.

Danaher, Kevin, ed. *50 Years Is Enough: The Case Against the World Bank.* Boston: South End Press, 1994.

Derber, Charles. *Money, Murder and the American Dream.* Boston: Faber & Faber, 1992.

Edsall, Thomas and Mary. *Chain Reaction.* New York: W. W. Norton, 1992.

Ehrenreich, Barbara. *The Worst Years of Our Lives.* New York: Harper-Collins, 1990.

Greider, William. *Who Will Tell the People?* New York: Simon & Schuster, 1992.

Grover, William F. *The President as Prisoner.* Albany: State University of New York, 1989.

Hellinger, Daniel, and Judd, Dennis. *The Democratic Facade.* Pacific Grove, California: Brooks/Cole Publishing Company, 1991.

Hofstadter, Richard. *The American Political Tradition.* New York: Vintage, 1974.

Kozol, Jonathan. *Savage Inequalities: Children in America's Schools.* New York: Crown Publishers, 1991.

Piven, Frances Fox, and Cloward, Richard. *Regulating the Poor.* New York: Vintage Books, 1993.

Rosenberg, Gerald N. *The Hollow Hope.* Chicago: University of Chicago Press, 1992.

Savage, David. *Turning Right: The Making of the Rehnquist Supreme Court.* New York: John Wiley & Sons, 1992.

Sexton, Patricia Cayo. *The War on Labor and the Left.* Boulder: Westview Press, 1991.

Shalom, Stephen. *Imperial Alibis.* Boston: South End Press, 1993.

11. THE UNREPORTED RESISTANCE

Ewen, Alexander, ed. *Voice of Indigenous Peoples*. Santa Fe, New Mexico: Clear Light Publishers, 1994.

Grover, William, and Peschek, Joseph, ed. *Voices of Dissent*. New York: HarperCollins, 1993.

Loeb, Paul. *Generations at the Crossroads*. New Brunswick: Rutgers University Press, 1994.

Lofland, John. *Polite Protesters: The American Peace Movement of the 1980s*. Syracuse: Syracuse University Press, 1993.

Lynd, Staughton and Alice. *Nonviolence in America: A Documentary History*. Maryknoll, New York: Orbis Books, 1995.

Martinez, Elizabeth, ed. *500 Years of Chicano History*. Albuquerque: Southwest Organizing Project, 1991.

Piven, Frances, and Cloward, Richard. *Why Americans Don't Vote*. New York: Pantheon Books, 1988.

Vanneman, Reeve, and Cannon, Lynn. *The American Perception of Class*. Philadelphia: Temple University Press, 1987.

NOTE: Much of the material in this chapter comes from my own files of social action by organizations around the country, from my collection of news clippings, and from publications outside the mainstream, including: *The Nation, In These Times, The Nuclear Resister, Peacework, The Resist Newsletter, Rethinking Schools, Indigenous Thought*.

12. THE CLINTON PRESIDENCY AND THE CRISIS OF DEMOCRACY

Bagdikian, Ben. *The Media Monopoly*. Boston: Beacon Press, 1992.

Chomsky, Noam. *World Orders, Old and New*. New York: Columbia University Press, 1994.

Dowd, Doug. *Blues for America*. New York: Monthly Review Press, 1997.

Garrow, David. *Bearing the Cross*. New York: Morrow, 1986.

Greider, William. *One World or Not*. New York: Simon & Schuster, 1997.

Kuttner, Robert. *Everything for Sale*. New York: Knopf, 1997.

Smith, Sam. *Shadows of Hope: A Freethinker's Guide to Politics in the Time of Clinton*. Bloomington: Indiana University Press, 1994.

Solomon, Norman. *False Hope: The Politics of Illusion in the Clinton Era*. Monroe, Maine: Common Courage Press, 1994.

The State of America's Children. Washington, D.C.: Children's Defense Fund, 1994.

Tirman, John. *Spoils of War: The Human Cost of the Arms Trade*. New York: Free Press, 1997.

13. THE COMING REVOLT OF THE GUARDS

Bryan, C. D. B. *Friendly Fire*. New York: Putnam, 1976.

Levin, Murray B. *The Alienated Voter*. New York: Irvington, 1971.

Warren, Donald I. *The Radical Center: Middle America and the Politics of Alienation*. Notre Dame, Ind.: University of Notre Dame Press, 1976.

Weizenbaum, Joseph. *Computer Power and Human Reason*. San Francisco: Freeman, 1976.

INDEX